the urban generation

the urban generation

Chinese Cinema and Society at the

Turn of the Twenty-first Century

ZHANG ZHEN, EDITOR

DUKE UNIVERSITY PRESS • DURHAM AND LONDON 2007

© 2007 Duke University Press

All rights reserved

Printed in the United States

of America on acid-free paper ∞

Designed by Katy Clove

Typeset in Minion by Keystone Typesetting, Inc.

Frontispiece: *Lunar Eclipse:* The problem of vision

and telepathic pain. Courtesy of Wang Quan'an.

Library of Congress Cataloging-in-Publication Data

appear on the last printed page of this book.

For Loke and his generation

contents

III • THE PRODUCTION OF DESIRE AND IDENTITIES

Acknowledgments

The initial work for this volume began in the spring of 2001, with a touring film program I co-organized with Zhijie Jia, as well as an accompanying symposium at New York University. I am grateful to the four filmmakers, in particular Ning Ying and Wang Quan'an, who actively took part in the symposium. Robert Sklar and Rebecca Karl, both of NYU, and Richard Peña of Columbia University, graciously served as panel moderators. Richard was also instrumental, in his capacity as the program director of the Film Society at Lincoln Center, in helping us get the "Urban Generation" on the calendar of the Walter Reade Theater. Tom Bender, Director of the International Center for Advanced Studies at NYU, provided crucial support for the symposium, recognizing the relevance of the symposium to the center's comparative project on Cities and Urban Knowledges. Mary Schmidt Campbell, Dean of the Tisch School of the Arts, and Chris Straayer, Chair of the Department of Cinema Studies, gave me much needed moral and financial support. Thanks are also due to NYU's programs in Asia Pacific Studies and East Asian Studies and its Humanities Council, as well as the Asian Cultural Council, the China Institute and New York Women and Film, for their support. Among many other individuals at NYU whose contributions were indispensable for the project as a whole, Shi-yan Chao, Xiangyang Chen, Lucas Hilderbrand, Mai Kiang, Charles Leary, Jeryl Martin-Hannibal, and Augusta Palmer deserve special mention. I am also grateful to Chris Berry, Adam Chau, Yoshikuni Igarashi, Tom Gunning, Miriam Hansen, and Wu Hung for providing me with additional venues for discussing the project and constructive comments, and to Harry Harootunian for bringing the volume to Duke University Press. I appreciate much the editorial assistance from Reynolds Smith and Sharon Torian at Duke, who cheered me on along the way. With unwavering enthusiasm, Charles Leary assisted me with the project throughout and especially with the final preparation of the manuscript. Above all, I thank the contributors to the volume, for their intellectual contributions as well as for their solidarity and patience, putting up with the seemingly endless process of bringing this book to the readers. Last but not least, I owe my family large and small a great deal for their unfailing love and support.

Introduction

bearing witness

Chinese Urban Cinema in the Era of

"Transformation" (*Zhuanxing*)

ZHANG ZHEN

Since the early 1990s the landscape of film culture in Mainland China has been radically reshaped. While the state-owned studios have been faced with the dire reality of financial and ideological constraints exacerbated by the top-down institutional reforms of the mid-decade, there has emerged both within and outside of the studio walls an alternative or "minor cinema."[1] This cinema is largely represented by what my colleagues and I call the "Urban Generation" filmmakers and their supporters, followers, and fans.

The term "Urban Generation" was coined for a film program presented in spring 2001 at the Walter Reade Theater at New York's Lincoln Center for the Performing Arts. The program showcased an array of works centered on the experience of urbanization by young filmmakers who emerged in the shadow both of the international fame of the Fifth Generation directors and of the suppressed democracy movement in 1989.[2] The term also refers to a film practice caught in the dynamic tension between "deterritorialization" by the state or commercial mainstream (both domestic and transnational) and the constant "reterritorialization" by the same forces that have alienated or marginalized it. The "minor" status of this new urban cinema is marked on one hand by its youth, by virtue of its overlap with the "coming of age" of the so-called Sixth Generation and the appearance of other newcomers in the 1990s. On the other hand, the term signals its position as a "minority" in relation to but also in dialogue with the officially sanctioned mainstream cinema. The latter includes the state-sponsored "leitmotif" (*zhuxuanlü*) films, which by and large are aimed at repackaging (or fetishizing) the founding myth of the Communist Party and the socialist legacy in an age riddled with ideological and moral uncertainty. The Urban Generation also includes both domestic- and foreign-produced commercial cinema. The Sixth Generation started as a small maverick group consisting of mainly disaffected graduates of the Beijing Film Academy (notably Zhang Yuan, Wang Xiaoshuai, He Yi, and Lou Ye), who emerged immediately after the events at Tiananmen Square in 1989.[3] Over the past decade, this group has transformed itself and converged with a broadly defined and increasingly influential movement of young urban cinema that is breaking new ground on many levels. The multifarious institutional, social, and artistic identities of this emergent cinema and its relation to contemporary Chinese film culture and society in the era of the so-called *zhuanxing* (transformation), or the "post–New Era" (*hou xinshiqi*),[4] constitutes the central focus of the collective project of this book.

The actual far from "minor" significance of this urban cinema stems not so much from its recent arrival as from its singular preoccupation with the destruction and reconstruction of the social fabric and urban identities of post-1989 China. Harry Harootunian, in his theorization of modernity and everydayness across the uneven but coeval global arena, recasts Benjamin's critical thinking on the fragmented yet ceaseless "new" as the "unavoidable 'actuality' of everyday life." In so doing Harootunian reaffirms that the city "make[s] up the contemporary scene, the now of the present."[5] The historicity of this particular "new" or contemporary urban cinema is precisely anchored in the unprecedented large-scale urbanization and globalization of China on the threshold of a new century. The intensity of these changes in China, along with the socioeconomic unevenness, psychological anxiety, and moral confusion caused by the upheaval can perhaps only be compared to the first wave of modernization of major treaty ports such as the rise of the Chinese metropolis of Shanghai around the beginning of the twentieth century. To be sure, over the past century the Chinese city has not stood still in terms of urban development. But such development has been largely contained or hampered alternately or concomitantly by war, natural disasters, or ideological imperatives. It was not until the 1990s when the post-Mao reform programs (first adopted in 1978 but primarily applied in the 1980s to the agricultural sector and, to some extent, the service sector) began to exert a visible impact on the cities where the majority of the state sectors—industrial, political, as well as cultural—are located, and where an exuberant consumer culture and mass culture began to take root.

If the swath of yellow earth—economically and culturally impoverished but cinematically enriched and eternalized by Chen Kaige and Zhang Yimou's ground-breaking film *Yellow Earth* (1984)—has been etched in our mind's eye as the quintessential symbolic image of the Fifth Generation cinema that took the world by storm in the mid-1980s, I would offer as the trademark of Urban Generation cinema the ubiquity of the bulldozer, the building crane, and the debris of urban ruins as carrying a poignant social indexicality. While the mythic, larger-than-life icons of the repressed peasant woman (embodied by Gong Li) dominate the Fifth Generation's glossy canvas in the era of reform, the subjects that populate the new urban cinema are a motley crew of plebeian but nonetheless troubled people on the margins of the age of transformation —ranging from aimless bohemians, petty thieves, KTV bar hostesses, prostitutes, and postmen to neighborhood police officers, taxi drivers, alcoholics, homosexuals, the disabled, migrant workers, and others. More importantly, these characters, often played by nonprofessional actors, share the same contemporary social space as the filmmakers as well as of the viewers. This cinema thus constructs a specific temporality that is constantly unfolding in the present, as both a symbiotic partner and a form of critique of the social to which it tries to give shape and meaning.

In the 1990s Chinese cities both large and small have seen tremendous changes in both infrastructural and social dimensions. Vernacular housing compounds (the *hutong* in Beijing and the *longtang* in Shanghai, for example), neighborhoods, and old communities of commerce and culture have been torn down to give way to expressways, subway stations, corporate buildings, and shopping malls—all in the wake of a ruthlessly advancing market economy and the incursion of global capitalism. The reforms in the 1980s are best described as an ideological reorientation that effected an ambivalent embrace of a postsocialist ethos and the adoption of a "march into the world" (*zouxiang shijie*) attitude in intellectual discourse, cultural production, and popular

A residential area in central
Shanghai in the process of being
demolished. (Photo by Zhang Zhen)

"A major change in
Shanghai in three years"
(Chinese characters on the wall).
(Photo by Zhang Zhen)

consciousness.[6] All the while, the concrete mantles of the socialist economy and social order stayed mostly intact. The relentless urban demolition and transformation in the 1990s has forever altered the spiritual as well as the material topography of socialist China and has ushered the reforms to points of no return. The mantra of the new decade, following Deng Xiaoping's "southern trip" in 1992, is the notion of *zhuanxing*, or transformation and system shift. In a speech reflecting on the success of the Special Economic Zone in Shenzhen and other coastal cities following his tour there, and in an effort to jump-start the "modernization" program that had encountered a serious challenge in 1989, Deng resolutely pronounced that "socialism can also practice market economy." The fourteenth Communist Party Congress officially ratified Deng's new formula, which then propelled the large-scale "transformation" of state-owned enterprises.[7] This transformation is no longer about gradualist reforms and a half-hearted embrace of the market but about a kind of structural overhaul in mentality and ideology as well as infrastructure. While the central government and the ruling party still uphold socialism (and essentially one-party rule) as a window-dressing ideology affirming its legitimacy in the name of continuity and stability, the tides of commercialization and globalization which it helped to bring in and now to accelerate have resulted in widespread privatization and a blatant form of capitalism that voraciously mixes the rawness of industrial capitalism and the slickness of the computer-age postindustrial capitalism thriving alongside the residues of socialism.

The cities are the most visible and concentrated sites of this drastic and at times violent economic, social, and cultural transformation.[8] On the one hand, urbanization has spurred an energetic mass-consumer culture, including the establishment of a real estate market that effectively has turned housing units and office and retail space into consumer goods. The relative stasis in the 1980s of the boundary between the city and countryside has been replaced by a far-flung nationwide movement, with millions of migrant workers, men as well as women, swarming into urban centers to partake in the demolition of old cities and the construction or expansion of globalizing enclaves such as Shenzhen, Zhuhai, Guangzhou, Shanghai, and Beijing.[9] While a large contingent of working men from the country are engaged in demolition and construction, countless young rural women have entered the booming service and entertainment industry. It is hardly surprising that the portrayal of this group of floating new urban subjects was to become one of the defining features of the new urban cinema, as illustrated in films such as *So Close to Paradise* (1997), *Beijing Bicycle* (2001) (both by Wang Xiaoshuai), *On the Beat* (Ning Ying, 1995), *Call Me* (Ah Nian, 2000), *Xiao Wu* (Jia Zhangke, 1997), *City Paradise* (Tang Danian, 1999), and *A Beautiful New World* (Shi Runjiu, 2000) and in documentaries like Li Hong's *Back to Phoenix Bridge* (1997) and Wu Wenguang's *Jiang Hu: On the Road* (1999) and *Dance with Farm Workers* (2001). The salience of the floating urban subjects, particularly the figure of the migrant worker or *mingong* (literally, "peasant worker"), registers the scale and intensity of the urbanizing process and acknowledges the labor of migrant workers in the building of the new Chinese city. The centrality of the floating urban subjects foregrounds the radical unevenness of this process, which has created new class divisions and social inequity and hence some of the most glaring contradictions in China's latest drive toward modernization. The figure of the migrant worker, unlike the timeless cipher of Gong Li, is hardly an icon for a "national cinema." Migrant labor problematizes China's image as a "third world" country by exposing the internal rift between the city and the countryside, or the affluent eastern seaboard and the impoverished "vast west" (*da xibu*), within one of the most rapidly developing economies in the world. The new urban cinema, especially its independent segment, articulates with this figure its radical contemporaneity and its localized critique of globalization.

The effort to make visible the migrant workers and other marginal urban subjects, which is often done through the conscious exploration of a combination of humanist and modernist concerns and in an aesthetic both documentary and hyperreal, has endowed this cinema with a distinctive social urgency as well as a formal rigor. The strength of that urgency to document the rapidly changing urban physiognomy and to expose through the cinematic lens the accompanying social contradictions is, in view of Chinese film history, comparable only to the socially engaged urban cinema produced in Shanghai in the 1930s. While selecting films for the "Urban Generation" series I was also working on a separate project on the topic of early Shanghai film culture.[10] During this period I was struck by the glaring similarity between the two urban cinemas separated almost by a life span. The exponential change in urban infrastructure, demography, and class formation in major Chinese cities, particularly in Shanghai in the late 1920s and early 1930s, was famously captured and made into a historical archive in a body of classic silent and early sound films, such as *Daybreak* (Tianming, 1933), *Morning in the Metropolis* (Duhui de zaocheng, 1933), *Boatmen's Song* (Yuguang qü, 1934), *Little Toys* (Xiao wanyi, 1933), *Spring Silkworms* (Chuncan, 1933), and *Sister Flowers* (Zimeihua, 1934). In modern Chinese history, the 1930s and 1990s stand out as strikingly parallel in terms of accelerated modernization and urban transformation, aggressive industrial or postindustrial capitalism, and an explosion of mass culture with the accompanying issues of social fragmentation and dislocation. Shanghai in the 1930s and the vibrant urban cinema it yielded has become an object of nostalgia in both popular culture and academic scholarship inside and outside of China.[11] The analogy I am drawing here, however, comes with an emphasis on the irreducible social experience of both eras and the lessons we have yet to learn from each epoch's struggle over the meaning of "modernization" and its human cost.

Although in terms of film form there are many differences between the two eras, I choose to concentrate on their shared features such as the prevalent use of documentary footage of the actual city and the use of a combination of melodrama and a form of critical realism. This approach allows the filmmakers to explore the dialectic relationship between the cinematic and the social, both in form and content. When asked about the influence on him of the cinema of the 1930s, Zhang Yuan characterized it as the "most stylish and moving" and the "most lively period" in Chinese film history.[12] The phenomenological excess of the social and the anarchy of the market during these two periods, coupled with media explosion, provided ample material for cinematic representation while also challenging the filmmakers to seek an innovative film language that comments and critiques social reality instead of simply mirroring it. While the filmmakers of the 1930s tried to create a collage of Hollywood narration and Soviet montage in order to appeal to and educate the masses, many of the young filmmakers of the 1990s draw on both the Chinese legacy of critical realism and more recent international art cinema. They favor in particular the long take and the hyperrealist aesthetic for foregrounding the rawness and emotional charge of social experience while also revealing its often absurd or unjust causes or consequences. In this regard the contemporary filmmakers depart consciously from the more didactic tradition of Chinese cinema as a whole, be it critical realism or socialist realism, by taking up instead a more humble position of the witness who produces testimonials rather than epistles. Yet this form of witness is one mediated through the visual technologies used for making the films or embedded in the films as metacommentaries, which are deployed as resources for social critique, collective recovery, memory production, and reflections on the nature of cinematic representation itself.[13]

This volume as a whole seeks not to construct a parallax film historiography, although a few of the authors do suggest connections between these two cinemas. Suffice it here to state that a critical juxtaposition and differentiation will indeed facilitate a nuanced reinterpretation of Chinese film history in view of the question of modernity, and to a certain extent postmodernity, in the past century as a whole. This volume is instead directly concerned with the radical contemporaneity and formal innovation of this emergent cinema, for which our first aim is to identify and define the Urban Generation in relation to the restructuring of the film system and the urban and social experience in the wake of intensified globalization. Second, by engaging in the intertextual and textual interpretations of a number of representative works we attempt to outline some of the formal and aesthetic features that characterize this stylistically innovative cinema. In moving away from a central focus on the Beijing Film Academy and a chronological ordering of "generations" of Chinese filmmakers, we focus instead on the substantive temporal-spatial configuration of this new film practice. Though we refer primarily to the generation that emerged in the 1990s, we conjoin this group by overlapping generations and practices, including the new documentary movement and commercial cinema along with other cultural practices such as photography and avant-garde art. Thus, rather than designating a cohesive movement, the rubric of Urban Generation provides a shared platform for a number of allied or competing filmmakers and their creative engagement with the shared historical moment. The term also allows us to move away from the auteur-centered discourse that has contributed to elevating the elite status of a few directors from the Fourth Generation and the Fifth. Instead we use it to include a wide range of urban, quasi-urban, and cosmopolitan subjects who populate the representational space as well as the social and spectatorial space of this cinema. In this sense, then, the Urban Generation is as much a term for periodizing contemporary film history as it is a critical category that places film practice right in the middle of a living, if often agitated, social, cultural, and political experience.

While the 2001 film program in New York consisted of works by the young filmmakers of the 1990s, the symposium from which this volume evolved addressed issues and films beyond the 2001 program per se. Taken together, all of these films, despite their diverse styles and approaches, document with care, originality, and a sense of urgency both the demolition of old cities, lifestyles, and identities and the construction of new ones. Though by no means a self-declared cinematic movement, this new wave of independent and semi-independent Chinese filmmaking has come of age—ironically, but also rather hopefully—in a time when the existing Chinese film industry is faced with a deep crisis. What used to be a small-scale underground phenomenon (named variously the "Sixth Generation" or "Newborn Generation" cinema) has, following on all the changes in China and the world in the past decade, increasingly transformed itself into a vibrant and diverse form of film practice that is not only going international but also going public inside China. In this volume we do not offer definitive conclusions on this formation but rather aim to understand the historical and social conditions that gave rise to the new cinema and its aesthetic uniqueness and complexity, including its ambivalent relationship to the mainstream film industry at home as well as to the international film market.

THE IDENTITY OF AN "INDEPENDENT" CINEMA

The badge of independence, with its troubled baggage, is perhaps the single most important attribute of the Urban Generation, one that is shared both by experimental filmmakers (Zhang Yuan, Zhang Ming, Lou Ye, Jia Zhangke, Wang Quan'an, and documentarians like Wu Wenguang and Jiang Yue) and by more commercially oriented directors (Zhang Yang and Shi Runjiu, for example). The Fifth Generation directors, despite their reputation for avant-garde art cinema as well as the political controversy surrounding some of their productions, worked by and large within the state-sponsored studio system. Many younger filmmakers, however, have identified themselves at the outset as institutionally and financially independent. They have resigned from assigned jobs in state-owned studios, engaged in underground low-budget productions, and participated in international film festivals without official sanction. In this sense, the key difference between the Urban Generation and the earlier generations of filmmakers, who were trained and employed by the state is defined by their different social and professional identities as well as by their aesthetic outlooks.

The thorny crown of "independent cinema" (*duli dianying*), however, did not descend upon the heads of the Sixth Generation filmmakers gratuitously. Just how "independent" the Sixth Generation cinema was in its formative years, or remains today, has been the focus of critical debates both inside and outside of China—an issue that is also addressed in this volume by several contributors. The early international recognition of the independently produced works by Zhang Yuan, Wang Xiaoshuai, He Yi, and Wu Wenguang gained at several less commercially oriented or second- or third-tier film festivals (notably Rotterdam, Tokyo, Nantes, and Cairo) was regarded with suspicion by various interest groups. The friction between the status quo and the independents was exacerbated by the events in Tokyo in 1993 and then in Rotterdam in 1994, when several of these filmmakers submitted their works for competition and screening without the official approval from home. As a result, they were promptly punished by the authorities for "illegally" shipping their films abroad, which resulted in the confiscation of their passports and a ban on further filmmaking. On the other hand, the Chinese critics and established directors, though patronizingly sympathetic to some extent, also regarded the victims as artistically immature and engaging in too much political savvy. Zhang Yimou, once a maverick himself, frowned upon the newcomers as opportunists who he described as "so well-informed about the outside world and so familiar with the path to success" and eagerly catering to Western critics.[14] By 1993 the Fifth Generation as a whole (except for Tian Zhuangzhuang) had been finally and decisively embraced and even given crowning awards by the Chinese official film apparatus, as well as skillfully transitioned into the market through big-budget hits (Zhang Yimou again shows his mastery in this league), and thus it is ironic that the younger generation would take over wearing the hat of "sinner" that used to be worn by their own precursors in the Fifth Generation.

The takeoff of the Fifth Generation built on the advantage of the relatively stable studio system and the transnational coproduction trend that attracted large amounts of Hong Kong and Taiwan funds—an advantage that reached its apex in the early 1990s. The young directors were excluded at the outset from such institutional support. After embarking upon the independent path, it is much more difficult to avail oneself of "official" resources (even overseas funds for coproduction managed by the studios). The ban issued by China's Film Bureau on Zhang Yuan and six other filmmakers in 1993 was sent to sixteen state-owned studios, processing labs, and equipment rental services nationwide so as to effectively forestall any further independent moves on the part of these filmmakers. Even for those with formal affiliations at state-owned studios, their junior status leaves them at the bottom of a hierarchy based on seniority and loyalty (to the system). In response, many of the young filmmakers take long leaves of absence (paying meanwhile a maintenance fee to the studios to retain their job titles and health or pension benefits) in order to engage in MTV and TV productions. Meanwhile they try to muster non-official or nonstate (i.e., *minjian* or *shehui*, meaning "popular" in the sense of nongovernment) resources to prepare for their feature projects.

Significantly, the erratic trajectory of independent cinema paralleled that of the structural changes in the film industry in the 1990s. The ban on the seven filmmakers in 1993 coincided with a series of "deepened" (*shenhua*) reforms, or more thorough marketization, in the (socialist) film system as it began its tortuous metamorphosis into a (quasi-capitalist or state-capitalist) industry. The restrictions placed on so-called "underground" film are part of an effort to ensure that there is minimal disruption in the enforcement of the new policies, which overtly facilitate the often imposed or organized populariza-tion of the leitmotif films.[15] These policies also privilege covertly commercial, "harmless" genres such as the "New Year celebration" comedies (*hesuipian*). A decisive move in this reform is the official endorsement of the share-based distribution (*fengzhan*) policy that applies to both domestic and imported products, promulgated to stimulate the exhibition sectors and draw the au-dience back to movie theaters. The independent young filmmakers were thus pushed further to the margins, alienated both by the authorities and by a market dominated by the so-called big pictures (*dapian*), domestic or for-eign. These daunting circumstances, however, hardly deterred the determined young filmmakers from exploring the narrow space created by the shifts in the studios and the market economy. In the most difficult years of 1994 to 1996, some of the most daring films by the new generation were made almost simultaneously by Zhang Yuan (*The Square, East Palace, West Palace*), Wang Xiaoshuai (*Frozen, So Close to Paradise*), Hu Xueyang (*Morning Glory*), Guan Hu (*Dirt*), Lou Ye (*Weekend Lovers*), He Jianjun (*Postman*), Ning Ying (*On the Beat*), Zhang Ming (*Rainclouds over Wushan*, a.k.a. *In Expectation*). Most of these films won critical acclaim and awards at various international film festivals, even though many of them remain inaccessible to the Chinese audience at home due either to stringent censorship or to disinterest on the part of profit-driven distributors and exhibitors.

While many explicitly "independent" films are still censored and banned for release in China, a new kind of flexible "independent" has begun to emerge in the context of a new wave of policy changes and institutional restructuring. The 1996–1997 reforms—riding on the momentum created by the celebration of the centenary of cinema, the ninetieth anniversary of Chinese cinema, and the imminent fiftieth anniversary of the PRC—were aimed primarily at reasserting the top-down "support" for, or rather control of, film and TV production to ensure their proper contributions to the "construction of socialist spiritual civilization" (*shehui zhuyi jinshen wenming jianshe*). A number of new regulations on censorship, coproduction, taxation (on box office receipts), and the protection of the ratio of domestic films were promulgated,[16] along with the installation of a set of official awards (for example, the Xia Yan Award for film literature and Huabiao Government Award for best feature film, which carries a hefty monetary prize) to stimulate the aesthetic improvement and popularization of leitmotif films.

The institutional change that shocked film circles most is the complete shift of administrative power over film, with all of the ensuing financial, cultural, and political consequences, from the Ministry of Culture to the newly established Ministry of Broadcasting, Television and Film as the central organ overseeing all government-sponsored media production. (The ban on the seven filmmakers mentioned above was issued by this new authority, which obviously tried to show its iron fist upon taking over the film sector.) Needless to say, this change created a serious identity crisis in the film industry as a whole. Mainstream cinema welcomed the crackdown on the maverick filmmakers because such action would free up space at the international festivals (official entries are not allowed to compete with independent ones). The film branch as a whole, however, found itself confronting a reality in which film began to lose its elite status in the cultural arena and ceased to be the standard-bearer in the business of moving-image production, while ideologically it would still be more closely monitored. In financial terms the studios, already deprived of the protection of prepaid blanket sales following the reform of

1993–1994, have been forced to solicit more resources on their own while competing with other entities for limited government funds under the jurisdiction of the Ministry of Broadcasting, Television and Film. This set of straitjackets, often tailored according to conflicting principles, resulted in further rigidifying and weakening the studios. The output of studio feature products reached a forlorn total of 88 in 1997, and in 1998 reached a low of only 82—a sharp drop from the earlier years when the output amounted to around 150.[17]

The simultaneous dispersal of the entitlement and locations to make films, coupled with the tightening of ideological controls, has created a cultural space fraught with tension and contradictions. As the most firmly entrenched state-owned sector, the film system—because of its paramount ideological function as the arbiter of the regime's authoritarian discourse and because of potential financial value for the state—stands as the emblematic force field where convoluted and competing claims for "transformation" collide. This is where the ambiguity of the postsocialist ethos and its attendant modes of production are made most visible. If, above all, *zhuanxing* means the dissolution of a planned economy—or the giving way of state control to privatization and capitalist modes of management, which affects the national economy and social experience on a large scale—the state is reluctant to completely let loose of the film system while "unleashing" it, albeit with many strings attached, into the market.

Paradoxically, the withering of the state-owned studios stimulated film production by different groups of independents or semi-independents outside of, or partially overlapping with, the "system." One particular regulation promulgated in December 1997 further legitimized alternative channels of feature production, thereby allowing other institutions such as television stations and licensed production entities to submit scripts to the Film Bureau for approval and to obtain a permit for a "single feature production." This act spurred the establishment of a host of production entities, often under the umbrella of an official institution or commercial enterprise. The trend of financially independent and successful MTV, advertisement, and other media-related enterprises also inspired independent filmmakers, who often are entangled with the more free-spirited producers of popular or mass culture, to set up creative workshops or form media companies, mostly in a cottage-

industry fashion. The majority of this new crop of independent films continues to seek cooperation with official studios in some capacity in order
either to access the facilities or acquire a release label, or both.

The popular and commercial turn of independent film practice was marked
by the domestic and international success of Jiang Wen's independently produced *In the Heat of the Sun* (Yangguang canlan de rizi, 1994), which came
about in part as a result of the celebrity status of the producer and director
(who is widely regarded as a top actor) and the popularity of Wang Shuo's
original novel. This event was followed by Zhang Yang's *Spice Love Soap*
(Aiqing malatang, 1998), which, along with *A Beautiful New World* (Meili xin
shijie) and *Shower* (Xizao), was produced by the Beijing-based Imar Film Co.
Ltd. Founded in 1996 by the American Peter Loehr (Chinese name Luo Yi),[18]
the Imar phenomenon, which involves foreign investors and producers but
also collaborates with the Xi'an Studio, clearly testifies to the advantage of
marketization and multimedia approaches (Imar made and marketed music
and TV products and also ran a Web site) for sustaining an alternative cinema
that is neither "mainstream" nor confrontational toward the political status
quo. Meanwhile, Lu Xuechang's *The Making of Steel*, less confrontational than
other recent independent work in both subject matter (about a young man's
painful journey through the 1970s to the 1990s and his nostalgia for revolution) and film form (told in a mostly realist manner), was affirmed as the
milestone work for the Sixth Generation's "coming of age" (a pun on its
alternate Chinese title, *Zhangda chengren*).[19] Its release and box office success
in 1998 signaled the beginning of an uneasy cooperation between a changing
film system and the young filmmakers who regard themselves as more or less
"independent."

In 1998, both the Beijing Studio and the Shanghai Studio launched a Young
Directors' Hope Project (Qingnian daoyan xiwang gongcheng)—a variation
on the theme of the Hope Project in supporting rural education—which
invested an average of two million Chinese yuan (US$250,000) in each film-
maker's individual project (subject to censor's approval). In some instances
the support is given in the form of equipment, service, and a release label.
Both veteran Sixth Generation directors, such as Zhang Yuan, Wang Xiaoshuai, and He Jianjun, and new talents, including Wang Quan'an, Jin Shen,
Wang Rui, Li Hong and Mao Xiaorui, were in various capacities recruited to
this project. The studios even made efforts to publicize it, such as organizing a

high-caliber critics' forum (also attended by studio officials and directors) and even securing the public release of some of the films. This overt move to co-optation, while diluting the avant-garde edge of the Sixth Generation,[20] unwittingly acknowledged the emergence of the Urban Generation as a broad and consequential trend.

AMATEURS ON LOCATION

The independent spirit that characterizes the early Sixth Generation, however, has not dissipated altogether but rather has taken on a new visage charged with new energy. In my view, the appearance in the late 1990s of Jia Zhangke and his films *Xiao Shan Going Home* (1995), *Xiao Wu* (1997), and *Platform* (2000) inaugurated a different phase in the independent movement that effectively ended the era of the Sixth Generation. Most of them were born in the 1960s and share the memory of the intense tail-end of the Cultural Revolution and its aftermath (as exemplified in *How Steel Is Made*). Jia, born 1970, is emphatically a product of the reform era of the 1980s and represents a different mode of filmmaking. Rather than engaging in the anxious takeover of its precursors, the "amateur cinema" (*yeyu dianying*), or "unofficial cinema" (*minjian dianying*), advocated and practiced by Jia and his group (Beijing Film Academy Young Experimental Film Workshop),[21] has found a following among emerging filmmakers mostly outside of the elite academy in particular and the professional branch in general. Despite its genesis in the Beijing Film Academy (BFA), this trend takes leave of BFA-centered genealogy and its elitism and joins forces with an incipient DV (digital video) movement. Jia and his friends took up the work of filming while studying in the Film Literature/ Criticism Department. Their burning desire to make their own films and their distaste for the entrenched nepotism as well as for the kind of academic style of filmmaking perpetuated at the BFA plunged Jia and his group (including Wang Hongwei, who plays the lead role in all of Jia's three features to date) headlong into their extracurricular and extremely low-budget film projects.[22]

   Although here I am not able to offer a detailed account of the early amateur exploits of Jia's group and the social and aesthetic valence of Jia's acclaimed films (which is the exclusive focus of Jason McGrath's chapter in this volume), I would like to underscore the key shift in the transformation of the Urban Generation relating to questioning the issues of the nature and "ownership" of cinema by the rise of a new wave of independent filmmaking that is less embroiled in a symbiotic relation with the state. Jia has described himself as an "ordinary director who comes from the lower ranks of the Chinese society."²³ The term's *minjian daoyan* (literally "unofficial director," or one who works outside the state system) and *jiceng* (grassroots) are in direct opposition to conventional perceptions, both within and outside of the "system," about the elite status of directors as a "high" class of artist and intellectual. Most of the Sixth Generation directors came from privileged backgrounds in big cities and studied in the elite departments of directing or cinematography. In contrast, Jia came from an ordinary lower-middle-class family in a small town in Shanxi, one of the poorest provinces. As an adolescent, he worked as a breakdance dancer in a local traveling troupe. Yearning for the big city, Jia spent much of his years after high school writing fiction, doing odd jobs, and living as a migrant "artisan" by painting advertisement billboards and putting up shop signs in Taiyuan, the provincial capital. While not a fully matriculated student at the BFA, he paid the tuition and supported himself in part by taking on "ghost writing" jobs piecing together TV drama episodes. Jia's firsthand experience (as opposed to ethnographic "fieldwork") as a migrant urban subject and his desire to reclaim cinema as a communicative tool for the ordinary Chinese citizen caught up in the tides of urbanization and socioeconomic transformation have compelled him to place the "migrant-artisan" at the center stage of his cinema. As a result Jia has been called, admiringly, the "migrant-worker director" (*mingong daoyan*).²⁴

The distinction between the disaffected but nonetheless haughty urban bohemians found in early Sixth Generation films (e.g., *Beijing Bastards, Days,* and *Frozen*) and the "artisans" (petty thieves or migrant amateur performers) in small towns may be a visible marker for a paradigmatic shift within the Urban Generation in the late 1990s. From *Beijing Bastards* to *Platform,* from the angry yet fashionable artist with disheveled hair to the ordinary or even awkward-looking artisan with nerdy eyeglasses in the backwaters of urban modernity, the 1990s witnessed not only the emergence of the Urban Generation but also its diversification, quotidianization, and transformation. The bespectacled Xiao Wu is an incarnation of Robert Bresson's poor bookworm thief in *Pickpocket* (1959). In a deadpan manner, he claims himself to be an "artisan" rather than a criminal, especially in contrast to his former cohort who reinvented himself as a "model entrepreneur" by dealing in imported cigarettes on the black market.[25] The pickpocket "artisan" finds his craft out of fashion in a town in the process of being torn down and rebuilt in the race toward a market-governed economy and social order. While Xiao Wu's figure stands as a feeble, passive protest as a lone outsider, the group of amateur performers in *Platform*, who transformed their collective identity from a Peasant Culture Troupe to a Breakdance Electronic Band, anticipates the emergence of the "amateur cinema" as a grassroots movement that has taken on a more salient shape at the beginning of the twenty-first century.

The advent of the "amateur cinema" as a significant ramification of the Urban Generation cannot be separated from a decade-long struggle of the new documentary movement, which has run a parallel, at times intersecting, course alongside the experimental narrative film.[26] In terms of technology and method, instead of the bulky film camera it is the video camera and, more recently, digital video and editing software that have served as the critical catalyst for the conception and dissemination of "amateur cinema" as a democratic form of film practice. Many of the filmmakers mentioned above have made documentaries or docudramatic works, particularly Zhang Yuan. The documentary impulse found in many films of the Urban Generation, alternately passionate or clinical, resonates more with the contemporary documentary movement heralded by figures like Wu Wenguang and Jiang Yue than with the "documentary aesthetic" programmatically conceptualized and practiced by several Fourth Generation directors in the early 1980s (e.g., the works of Zhang Nuanxin and Lin Dongtian). A reading of Zhang Yuan's *Beijing Bastards* and Wang Xiaoshuai's *Days* (1993), for instance, is not complete without a consideration of their intertextual links to Wu's *Bumming in Beijing* (Liulang Beijing, 1990), which documents the lives of four migrant aspiring artists in that city. Similarly, Jiang Yue's *The Other Bank* (Bi'an, 1994), which addresses a group of trainee/amateur actors' disenchanted life after leaving the BFA,[27] and Wu's recent *Jianghu—Life on the Road*, which happens to be about a traveling amateur troupe in the same area where Jia's film is set, can greatly aid our understanding of *Platform* as an epic of the lived experience of an entire generation. The ensemble characters, played by nonprofessionals (including the poet Xi Chuan, who plays the leader of the troupe) and framed in Jia's master-shot tableaux, perform the historical process of a momentous change through the interweaving of everyday life (including the changing fashion in dress and hairstyle) and the history of popular culture (including film). The time and space traversed by these amateur actors is also traversed by the Urban Generation as a collective, which takes as its primary task to bear witness to the rupture and transformation of history. More urgently, this cinema attempts to record and interpret the collective's relationship to the ordinary people around them—friends, family members, neighbors, colleagues, as well as strangers, who inhabit or come to inhabit the ever-expanding social and material space of the cities, be they large or small, metropolitan centers or provincial capitals, Special Economic Zones or inland county seats—a space that is at once enchanting and oppressive, liberating and violent.

The documentary form is inspiring because it speaks to an aesthetic interest that seeks to connect André Bazin's photographic realism and Sigfried Kracauer's materialist phenomenology with postmodern hyperrealism to find the shape and meaning of a multifaceted social experience in the era of transformation. In representing a new episteme, the spread of the documentary method—which has quickly seeped into mainstream TV programs—attests to the proliferation and visibility of everyday life in the wake of a burgeoning mass culture,[28] and in the popular desire to reclaim reality with the aid of more accessible visual technologies. Deployed with an experimental lens, the documentary method is instrumental in laying bare the oscillation between representation and actuality and in foregrounding the subject-object relation between the filmmaker and his or her subject matter so as to create a more intersubjective or democratic cinema. The quasi-documentary and hyper-realist aesthetic reveals that cinematic representation is hardly a transparent window onto reality but rather a form of interrogation of the "truth" value of both its referent and its image and their indexical rapport.

Contemporaneous with the popularization and advancement of video technology, the Urban Generation is decidedly a video-film amphibious generation. Many films deliberately incorporate footage shot with a video camera (interviews, street scenes, etc.), which gives the film surface an added documentary look and feel of actuality and liveness. This tangible sense of being "on the scene" (*xianchang*) allows both the filmmaker and the viewer to witness the film as raw life and as a history of the present. For those filmmakers drawn to documenting the everyday and the immediacy of happenings, video enhances the cinema verité style and the power of long takes that respect the "unity of the event."[29] For those who have dabbled in MTV and commercials, supple video editing can crystallize the montage of a fragmented urban space and its psychic undercurrents. Because of its portability, directness, and economy, video is often used in both preproduction research and on location shooting. In an interview by Wu Wenguang, Jia mentions that because he had no means of projection on location, in order to view the rushes shot on 16mm he had to have the person who transported the takes to Beijing for developing shoot the rushes in the screening room with a M9000 home video camera and then bring the tape back to Fenyang. This procedure was repeated at a three-day interval until shooting was completed, which altogether took only fifteen days.[30]

The experience and conception of *xianchang*, or "on the scene," indeed captures the contemporary spirit (*dangxiaxing*) of the Urban Generation in general and the "amateur cinema" in particular. It is also the space in which the conventional boundaries that separate documentary and fiction, video and celluloid film, and professional and amateur practice are challenged and transgressed. By insisting on blurring these boundaries, filmmakers subject such genre distinctions as well as the cinematic medium itself to critical scrutiny. Marginalized by the studios, and thus the exclusion from or limited access to expensive indoor shooting, the low-budget independent or semi-independent filmmakers take their cameras and crews to the street, the marketplace, the residential areas—in short, the vast "location" outside the walls of the system. For a filmmaker like Jia Zhangke, the documentary method is not only necessary when the film is set in his hometown, which supplied all the "locations" for *Xiao Wu*, but also critical for the particular kind of story he wanted to tell about people *in* their social milieu. It is an aesthetic grounded in social space and experience—contingent, immanent, improvisational and open-ended. In Jia's own words, it is an "adventure on the scene of shooting, which will yield unexpected situations but also possibilities."[31] One such situation and its possibility created the unforgettable ending of *Xiao Wu*, where the gawking crowd during the shooting, refusing to be dispersed, came to "play" the diegetic witnesses "on the scene" of the crime, as it were, of a pickpocket's utter humiliation and exposed marginality when he has been caught and chained to a telephone pole on the sidewalk of a booming town street.[32] This is but one of many instances when the penchant for the palpability of xianchang evident in many Urban Generation films echoes Trinh T. Minh-ha's astute observation that "reality is more fabulous, more maddening, more strangely manipulative than fiction." By throwing into relief the "unnaturalness" of a familiar reality—as Jia amply shows in his most recent film *The World* (2004), which is set in a "global" theme park—both the filmmaker and the viewer can "recognize the naivety of a development of a cinematic technology that promotes increasing unmediated 'access' to reality."[33] While conveying a rawer sense of authenticity or believability by plumbing the depth of the real beyond the "frame," this edgy realism also confronts the limits or adequacy of cinematic representation. As Lou Ye aptly puts it, "I wanted to touch that edge, the edge of film, to see how far it could go; or rather, to touch the edge of myself to see where it leads to."[34]

The poetics of xianchang goes hand in hand with a new politics represented by "amateur cinema," which attempts returning to ordinary people the right to participate in the production of filmic images about themselves. Small wonder, then, that so many of the Urban Generation films, fictional or documentary or docudramatic, often engage nonprofessional actors to play themselves. Ning Ying, the only prominent woman director of the Urban Generation, admits that the stories that she likes to tell are particularly suitable for casting nonprofessional actors.[35] In fact, her work *For Fun* (1993), about the struggles of a group of retirees to keep an activity center open for practicing Beijing Opera, presages Jia's *Platform* about amateur performers. Ning Ying's third feature, *On the Beat*, a deadpan look at everyday life in a police precinct of Beijing, has a group of real policemen playing themselves. The use of dialects or local inflections, as opposed to the standard Mandarin Chinese (*putonghua*) that was uniformly adopted in Chinese cinema (except for a few local opera-films) in the entire socialist era, thus becomes the aural signature of the new urban cinema. Even in films set in Beijing, the characters speak heavily inflected Beijing vernacular rather than *putonghua.*

Suddenly, the vivacity of the texture of quotidian life, with multiple voices in multiple inflections emanating from multiple concrete localities, enters cinematic space as never before. Xianchang thus constitutes a particular social and epistemic space in which orality, performativity, and an irreducible specificity of personal and social experience are acknowledged, recorded, and given aesthetic expression. The operation of xianchang hence also stands for a particular temporality, which Wu Wenguang (its major practitioner and theorist) incisively interprets as of the "present tense" by virtue of "being present on the scene."[36] The urgency of this temporality of the here and the now is fueled by the relentless pace of urbanization but also the urge to intervene in a process that is rapidly erasing urban memory and producing a collective amnesia.

The documentary concreteness of xianchang is more often than not articulated through the meticulous use of locations that often bear concrete geographical identities. These could be as large as real cities (Beijing, Fenyang, Shanghai, Wuhan, and so on) or as microscopic as streets or rivers (for instance, the two important intersections in Beijing named Jiaodaokou and Xisi, or the Suzhou River in Shanghai). The scenes in a large number of Urban Generation films are not artificial sets but material entities in contemporary urban geography. Ning Ying and Jia Zhangke are particularly keen on retaining the bleak and even dusty tone of their locations rather than glossing over them with lighting or decor. As the Chinese film critic Ni Zhen observes, the "police station, the empty lot in the midst of houses being demolished, alleyways in the old city, an abandoned temple—in these seemingly taken-for-granted environments which lack the effects of a visual spectacle, Ning Ying's camera stubbornly reveals to us the spots branded with social and historical traces."[37] The insistence on spatial indexicality and linguistic particularity in these films about and by "amateurs" may be an influence of the documentary movement (and, to some extent, the avant-garde performance art) that flourished in the 1990s.[38] More likely, however, is that fact that the narrative filmmakers share with their contemporaries who work with a more direct and accessible video medium a similar conviction in the power of moving images for grasping a transforming society as well as in the power of these images to bring about change in the perception and use of both old and new representational technologies. Their production methods, aesthetic orientations, and social engagement have propelled them to create not simply a new cinema anchored in the social and the now but also, in aesthetic terms, an alternative cinematic space that is haptic rather than optic, sensuous and open rather than abstract and closed.

THE TRANSLOCATION OF AN ALTERNATIVE SPECTATORSHIP

As discussed above, the emergence and diversification of the Urban Generation cinema in the 1990s is intertwined with a series of imposed and market-driven reforms, primarily in the distribution and exhibition sectors. These fitful structural changes have seriously shaken the studios and forced them to yield, albeit involuntarily, the exclusive power as the sole state-sanctioned producers of celluloid culture that they had held since the early 1950s, after the completion of the nationalization of the film industry. The withering of the Chinese Film Distribution, Exhibition and Import and Export Corporation, the mammoth despot ruling every realm apart from production itself, further opened up space for a range of possibilities. This change has, however, posed new challenges to those who want to seize the opportunity to build an active and diverse local film culture before the avalanche of Hollywood blockbusters becomes an everyday reality in China. The attempt to create an open film market following the 1993 reforms proved stillborn due to the sudden severance of the link between production and distribution,[39] the lack of adequate policies regulating the now locally controlled, profit-driven market, and the continued harsh censorship of domestic and, in particular, innovative films. In the second half of the decade, while the output of domestic films and total box office receipts continued to decline, a more competitive domestic film market emerged, though with mixed repercussions. At the same time, an alternative space and practice of exhibition devoted to independent film and video—a Chinese cineclub culture of sorts—has also stubbornly appeared, against all odds.

The ascendance to the global stage of Chinese-language film in general and mainland cinema in particular in the last two decades of the twentieth century is inexorably linked to international festival culture, which itself experienced an expansion in this period. While Hong Kong cinema has enjoyed a booming local market, where the popularity of domestic cinema often surpassed Hollywood and other imports, the critical successes of the Taiwan and Mainland new wave cinemas in the 1980s have trod the path of glory paved by the festivals.[40] The Golden Lion Award for Zhang Yimou's *Story of Qiu Ju* (1992) at the forty-ninth Venice International Film Festival and the Palm d'Or award for Chen Kaige's *Farewell, My Concubine* (1993) at Cannes, and their subsequent releases both overseas and at home, marked the culminating success, both critical and popular, of the Fifth Generation cinema. This success then contributed to the consolidation of the international status of Chinese cinema as a whole. The success saga of the Fifth Generation was studied and repeated in varying degrees by its peers and latecomers. Chinese filmmakers realized that the festivals were not only a venue for obtaining critical acclaim and financial reward abroad, but for many such a venue seemed also to be a stepping stone toward gaining recognition and a potential audience at home—even though it might be a long shot. And, indeed, the Urban Generation, both popular and experimental strands alike, has done just that. In his interview with Wu Wenguang, Jia Zhangke confessed that part of his "education" at the BFA included reading a book in Chinese called *A Survey of International Film Festivals*.[41]

As China has became deeply implicated in the global arena of the post–cold war era, the young filmmakers, who came of age in a time saturated with personal computers and the Internet, and in a China made smaller by the ease and expansion of transcontinental travels, are readily cosmopolitan in their outlook and professional conduct. More than any generation of filmmakers before them since 1949, who benefited from both the "iron rice bowl" and the prestige of a cultural elite, members of the Urban Generation have found themselves obliged to manage and promote their own projects, especially the independently financed ones. Like their contemporaries from other countries, they are at home at international festivals, large or small. Various documentary and short-film festivals, notably Yamagata, Rotterdam, and the Margaret Mead Festival in New York, present new arenas with which the big-feature-exclusive Fourth and Fifth Generations did not concern themselves. The major international awards garnered by the Fifth Generation in the late 1980s and early 1990s for their lavish historical melodramas or cultural allegories helped establish Chinese cinema as a "national" (and mostly *fictional*) cinema in the film studies curriculum in the West. The participation of the young independent filmmakers in the festivals in the 1990s have challenged that uniform perception of contemporary Chinese cinema by precisely opening up the time and space of the "contemporaneity" of Chinese society and its coeval relation, and tension, with global currents.

The festivals are, however, not necessarily final destinations where the fate of such films is sealed. A cosmopolitan audience does not have to consist of sympathetic foreign connoisseurs of Chinese cinema with an eye for the exotic or the dissenting. While most independent Chinese films that file through the festivals do not find a foreign distributor, they often travel further to local or small-scale "festivals" at universities, archives, museums, diaspora communities, and other art house programs. The "Urban Generation" series through which we participated in this international subculture is a case in point.

Enthusiastic reception of the Urban Generation at the Walter Reade Theater, February 2001. (Photo by Liu Xiaojin)

During several weeks in February and March 2001, about twelve films, including both award-winning films and new premiers, were shown to enthusiastic crowds at the Harvard Film Archive, the Walter Reade Theater at Lincoln Center, and the National Gallery of Art in Washington, D.C., in addition to audiences at several universities.

These "second-tier festivals" create audience responses that go beyond conventional expectations. Several months after the "Urban Generation" series event I learned of the existence of an online discussion among a group of young Chinese architects and architecture students (and their friends) who live in the New York metropolitan area and who had religiously attended the series and followed it by engaging in a heated discussion among themselves. When I logged onto the Web site maintained by these "archicomrades," I found a special link created for the "Urban Generation."[42] Most of the online discussion revolved around Jia Zhangke's *Xiao Wu*, with some members offering lengthy and incisive readings of the artistic and social significance of the film. Some members also tried to contrast the different approaches to the notion of urban made by the Fifth Generation directors such as Zhang Yimou

(*Keep Cool*) and Huang Jianxin (*Stand Up, Don't Stoop*) relative to the Urban Generation filmmakers. One member addressed the question by astutely pointing out that the earlier urban films are mostly about the "urban" as a given condition, whereas the new Urban Generation distinguishes itself by dealing directly with urbanization as a "process." Another member made an attempt to compare, with palpable urgency, the social responsibility of his or her own group of aspiring architects with the filmmakers: "Today's new Urban Generation—actually the same generation as us—is starting a new cycle of ideological struggle, by looking through the contemporary Chinese urbanization with their subversive aesthetics and producing strategy. . . . [For] Chinese architects, it may take at least five more years to fully conceptualize and then start their own critical work from their own discipline."

Reading this online discussion by these future Chinese and Chinese-American architects, I was struck by how they wholeheartedly embraced the term "Urban Generation" as a "natural" designation for the cinema as well as for themselves. I was thrilled and encouraged by how organizing such an event could inadvertently create new, albeit "minor" and contingent, publics such as this Internet group.[43] By introducing this online cinephile community here, I intend to stress the permeability of different media as well as national boundaries in the formation of an alternative public sphere for Chinese cinema "against" the backdrop of globalization as both a homogenizing as well as differentiating process. Just as the young filmmakers are savvy about the festival industry, their fans are equally adept in finding films they like and ways of sharing their enthusiasm and insight. Long after the "festival" is over, the event seems to have gained an afterlife thanks to new communicative technologies.

Does a similar kind of audience or group of "filmmaniacs" (as the "archicomrades" call themselves) exist in China? Does Urban Generation cinema, especially the independent productions, have a chance to be seen there? Since the mid-1990s the distribution system in China has, ahead of the production sector, marched by leaps and bounds into the market under internal as well as external pressure. After the retreat of the central power represented by the former Chinese Film Distribution, Exhibition and Export and Import Corporation (in 1995 changed to China Film Co.), a plural configuration began to emerge in the film industry. After 1997 in Shanghai and Beijing, where control had been most stringent but where film culture has always been most vital (due to the high concentration of film resources there and the metropolitan culture), semiautonomous companies were established.[44] The leading players are the Zijincheng Company in Beijing and the Yongle Company in Shanghai, respectively. These companies engage in both production and distribution, promoting in particular the popular comedies of Feng Xiaogang (Zijincheng) and the "new mainstream" films by Feng Xiaoning (Yongle).[45] In the two cities there are now at least two competing distribution lines (*yuanxian*) in conjunction with separate chains of theaters that showcase different sets of films simultaneously. Occasionally, less commercially promising but innovative films by young directors have the luck to be picked up. I saw, for instance, Ning Ying's *I Love Beijing* in a full room with an enthusiastic audience at a newly opened multiplex in Shanghai; as a result I was compelled to rethink the incursion of global-style multiplexes financed by transnational capital. While new distribution practices obviously pave the way for the influx of more Hollywood films (now twenty per year, with an increase expected in coming years) which poses a real threat to domestic cinema, it inadvertently also provided the arena for a new spectatorship with sophisticated, sometimes unpredictable "window-shopping" ability.[46] Popular films produced by the independent Imar company, such as *Shower*, are also favorites at these venues, generating formidable box office returns for such low-budget domestic products. In November 2004 *The Last Level* (Shengdian)—a small-budget (2 million yuan, or about US$240,900) film directed by Wang Jing about a young computer-game addict's adventures in cyberspace—had a successful premiere at the Huaxing International Multiplex following sold-out screenings at Beijing University.[47]

What about other independent films that do not ostensibly cater to a mass audience, as well as those films that are explicitly banned? With the loosening of official control in the distribution and exhibition sectors and the boom in alternative venues other than state-owned cinemas, a whole cluster of new screen practices have been shaping a different kind of public sphere for moving images. Venues such as KTV bars, projecting videos and VCDs (often pirated versions featuring a mixture of soft-porn and action materials) have become ubiquitous in cities large and small, and in rural towns all over China. With their cheap price and other "services" (ranging from drinking to massage and more) they predominately attract the migrant and lower social classes. More recently, a number of movie bars, in part modeled on their

The Yellow Pavilion, the base for a cineclub near the Beijing Film Academy.
(Photo by Zhang Zhen)

lowbrow KTV and karaoke cousins, have appeared in big cities catering to students, intellectuals, foreign expatriate communities, and other film buffs who are eager to see, and talk about, both the foreign and Chinese art cinema that the mainstream cinemas rarely offer.

As Beijing is the center for Chinese independent cinema and for avant-garde culture as a whole, it is not surprising that several movie bars there are actively involved in the formation of a new cineclub culture. The popularization of the VCD and DVD has made it possible for the movie bars to screen a wide range of European, American, and Japanese art cinema. It is significant that the revival of a cinephile culture in China is in large part made possible by the "primitive" or "pirated" form of postmodern technology of the VCD. The development of this culture also benefited from the proliferation of urban venues with screen practices that hark back, in their heterotopic and communal character at least, to the teahouse form of spectatorship associated with early Chinese film culture.[48] I visited three such venues during a research trip in summer 2001: the Yellow Pavilion Bar near the BFA (which is probably the first of its kind), the Butterfly Swallow Movie Bar in the bar-congested Sanlitun area in the eastern part of the city, and the Box Café near Qinghua

University in the northeast corner of the city where colleges and research institutions concentrate. The Box Café has a separate movie room that in the program pamphlets is called "space for imagination." The movie bars have varied formats of video or laser projection capacities and often hold informal discussions after screenings. Registered as commercial establishments, they take advantage of the loose regulations applied to the service industry. Such a space, which shares the same spirit with the numerous avant-garde gallery bars (such as the Top Gallery in Shanghai and the Courtyard in Beijing), combines leisure and education, consumption and cultural production, and provides a much-needed home for an alternative film culture.

At the time of my visit, the programs at the movie bars in Beijing were mostly coordinated by an association called Practice Society (Shijianshe), which was established in April 2000 by several BFA graduates and other cinephiles. A centerpiece of the Practice Society's agenda has been its effort to promote independent and amateur cinema. True to its name, the Practice Society has also been committed to the filmmaking practice, in particular digital video making. Its DV documentary group met regularly to screen and discuss members' works-in-progress. The influence of the Practice Society extended to traditional media (such as literary and arts journals like *Furong* and *Vision 21*, through a special "Practice" column or forum) as well as to the Internet. It also collaborated with culturally oriented Web sites (e.g., www.sina.com) by conducting online discussion groups with cinephiles interested in their activities. The fourth issue of the Practice Society's *semizdat* journal, *Touch Film*,[49] published a set of online responses to the question: "If you had a [video] camera, on what subject would you focus your lens?" Cinephiles with aliases as varied as "witch's mirror," "cinekino," and "Godard" sent in their intimate, imaginative, and sometimes outlandish film plans. The subjects seemed infinite, and a community of aspiring "amateur" filmmakers was created through participating in the "practice" of a collective dream factory online, part of which was realized in actual practice. This online association of amateurs, in a virtual yet instantly connected space, exemplifies the "tactile" perception of cinema (i.e., "touch film," or *jiechu dianying*, where the members are only a mouse-click away from one another) and the "hands-on" approach of the Practice Society. Amateur cinema is not simply about an optically centered spectatorship derived from a passive love for watching films

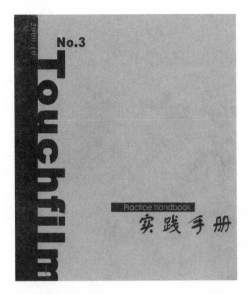

Touch Film, the publication
of the Practice Society.

but also constitutes a productive spectatorial experience that includes using
one's own hands to construct and share moving images that restore sensuality
to everyday life. Such a tactile practice, through either the experience or
production of an alternative cinema, and in its emphasis on directness, proximity, and involvement, embodies the spirit of xianchang. It is hardly surprising, then, that the DV group attached to the Practice Society is devoted primarily to the making of documentaries.

The kind of cineclub culture led by the Practice Society in Beijing has, in
fact, precursors with a less ostensible avant-garde posture in Shanghai and
Shenzhen. In October 1996 a number of cinephiles in Shanghai formed the 101
Workshop—named after the day, October 1, when it was formed. The organization consisted mostly of members of the "Readers' Club" of the journal *Film
Story*, published by the aforementioned Yongle Company. According to one
report, in 2001 the club had 160 members and 300 new applicants. Although
the majority of its members are young urban professionals in Shanghai, and
most of its activities take place in the metropolis, its membership extends to
about thirty cities. During the 1999 Shanghai International Film Festival,
which is sponsored by the Shanghai Municipal Government, members of the
101 Workshop, concerned by the absence of a film guide and criticism in past

festival editions, created a pamphlet titled "10-Day Talk on the Festival," which they distributed in the participating theaters. The pamphlet turned out to be very popular, selling out more quickly than tickets to the festival.[50]

The devotion or, rather, obsession of this generation of cinephiles has been compared to that of the "feverish friends" (*fashaoyou*) of music and video who spend large amounts of money and time acquiring and enjoying top-notch audiovisual equipment, and who form a loose network of exchange among themselves. The crucial difference between "feverish friends" and the cineclub members lies in the latter's active participation in the formation of an alternative public sphere by organizing discussions and programs, publishing reviews, and more importantly, exchanging and networking with other similar cinephile groups in cities nationwide. The founding of the Yuanyinghui Club (Film Connection) in Shenzhen, which bridges the two phenomena, is a case in point. An editor at the Guangzhou-based film magazine *Dianying zuoping* (Film works) shared his idea about a viewing club with the general manager of an audiovisual equipment company who was himself a fashaoyou and had set up a special demo space for the company's products. In 1999 they turned the demo space into the club's headquarters, where they printed a newsletter; organized regular screenings of foreign and Chinese art films both old and new as well as award-winning commercials and shorts; and held discussions with filmmakers including the Hong Kong director Ann Hui. Within the walls of their exquisitely designed screening room with its high-caliber equipment, the "feverish friends" of sound and images spend countless hours "sharing film and sharing life" (*fenxiang dianying, fenxiang rensheng*).[51]

The examples of the 101 Workshop, Film Connection, and Practice Society have among cinephiles in Shenyang, Nanjing, and Wuhan spurred great interest and desire for this type of fellowship, and similar clubs, though on a smaller scale, have been formed in all three provincial capitals. The Rear Window Film Appreciation Club was initiated by a lone Internet surfer who is also an avid vcd consumer. After going online to search for likeminded people, he realized that obsessed cinephiles existed not only in his hometown of Nanjing but all over the world. Using the pseudonym Weixidi (a homophone for vcd in Chinese), he started the Rear Window club along with friends like "Godard" in Nanjing. A cineclub in Wuhan was founded in spring 2000 by several vcd fashaoyou who, after a visit to Beijing to learn from their comrades there, began screenings at a university and then moved to the Provincial Capital Library. The same year, the northeastern city of Shenyang (where the Changchun Film Studio is based) also saw the birth of a club, boldly named Ziyou dianying, or Free Cinema, accentuating the independent spirit of this grassroots-level cultural movement.[52]

Indeed, independence is the common characteristic of this new breed of not-for-profit cinephile community, which has extended into a large number of university campuses. Neither commercially oriented nor socially pretentious, cinephile groups are dedicated to the enjoyment of alternative cinema as an antidote to the isolation of the individual in the age of the Internet, VCD, and DVD and to the contrived film culture dominated by the deluge of Hollywood blockbusters and the continued hegemony of state-sponsored "correct" cinema. At a time when using every possible minute for profit making is the trend in China, these amateurs willingly "kill time" by immersing in and sharing celluloid dreams. But their leisure-time hobby also has important social and even political implications. As Yangzi, one of the core members of the Practice Society, notes, the congregation of concerned critics, filmmakers, students, and other "feverish friends" of cinema is part of an effort to create an "open platform" for cinema. As a forum for alternative moving images that often have no chance of being shown at regular theaters, the movie bars and other venues engaged by the cineclubs thus become a kind of quasi-public outlet for the display of "nonofficial images" (*minjian yingxiang*) that articulate, in Yangzi's words, "private discourse and personal expressions."[53] These scattered spots are "like the oases in the desert, which signifies possibility."[54]

This possibility of forming a "minor" and "nomadic" film culture that engages both the margins and the center was tested and realized with considerable success during the first Unrestricted New Image Festival held in Beijing and in a number of other cities in fall 2001. The previously dispersed cells of a cultural phenomenon, linked together as "virtual neighborhoods" in cyberspace,[55] are through this festival coalesced, if momentarily, into an embodied movement in real time and physical location. Initiated collectively by the Practice Society, 101 Workshop, Yuanyinghui, and Free Cinema, and sponsored by a number of journals and Web sites, the festival showcased a wide selection of independent short features, experimental video works, and documentaries made since 1996. Works by foreign students were also admitted, and an official committee presided over the competition. The festival was held at the BFA, to a full house of enthusiasts. In addition to the general programs, a workshop on digital video was conducted and two special series were offered dedicated to the works of Wang Xiaoshuai and Jia Zhangke in conjunction with seminar discussions.[56] During the festival, Web sites carried ongoing reports and reviews. In November, the festival arrived in Shanghai. For three days the screening room inside the new state-of-the art Shanghai Library repeated the sensation that premiered in Beijing. To give the Shanghai edition a local accent, the program there highlighted works by several Shanghai-based filmmakers who met and talked with the audience.[57]

I offer this sketch of a fast-emerging cineclub community and alternative film spectatorship around the turn of the century in part to underscore the broad empirical range as well as conceptual possibility of the Urban Generation cinema as both a descriptive and analytical category. The coming into being of this vivacious amateur film culture exemplifies in more tangible and meaningful ways the "amateur cinema" theory and practice advocated by independent filmmakers like Jia Zhangke and Wu Wenguang. As forces that are dispersed yet increasingly joining together through the Internet and touring programs, these localized small groups are coalescing into an informal grassroots movement. The intimate movie bars, the nomadic style of the cineclub operations, and the diversity of the chosen film forms and formats (especially the shorts and DV film) encapsulate this grassroots movement as a "minor cinema" that potentially can reshape the structure of film knowledge and practice. Consciously going against the rampant commercializing trends in all sectors in China today, these cinephile associations are nevertheless not shy about strategically using resources from the official public sphere, such as the print media, TV, the BFA, and a host of semiofficial enterprises. Indeed, they cannot truly be described as "underground" because they also make forays into various public institutions such as universities and libraries. This form of cultural production that is amateur rather than activist (which can hardly be allowed in China) does not avowedly represent the disenfranchised social groups as the kind of "grassroots globalization" efforts described by, among others, Arjun Appadurai. In its attempt to challenge the existing power apparatus of image making and dissemination, represented by both the official mainstream and the Hollywood encroachment (and the complicity between the two), the goals of the amateur cinema movement are nothing short of striving, in Appadurai's words, "for a democratic and autonomous standing in respect to the various forms by which global power further seeks to extend its dominion."⁵⁸ The success of the first Unrestricted New Image Festival represents the first concrete fruit of globalization from below in the realm of cinema, one of the most visible and consequential grounds where the war of globalization is waged and where the reclaiming of an alternative public sphere is being attempted by an army of Chinese amateur filmmakers and their "feverish friends." Together they are coming forward to embody a new century of image making and social, cultural, and political imagination.

The twelve essays in this volume are divided into three sections. Together they provide a framework for conceptualizing the Urban Generation and the attendant social transformation in contemporary China as well as detailed analysis of specific cinematic articulations of the recent urbanizing experience and the formation of new urban identities. The different approaches taken by each author, with some canvassing larger concerns and others concentrating on individual films or filmmakers, present both long views and close-ups of a rich yet varied cinematic and social landscape. In sharing the focus on urbanization and the method of contextual and intertexual analysis of films and other related audio-visual or literary material, our aim is to make broader, though by no means facile, connections between cultural production and its referents. For too long cinema studies has concentrated on self-contained textual analysis that tends to isolate films from their rich intertextual and contextual relations. This volume does not simply present an artistic movement per se, but rather attempts both to identify its unique contribution and to anchor it in the process of a widespread and complex transformation taking place in Chinese society and culture as a whole. While the issues and themes covered in the three sections of this book are not mutually exclusive, there is a sense of progression and deepening of the inquiry that begins by outlining the contours of the sociocultural ecology of the new urban cinema and moves to specific topoi in its imaginative terrain.

The first part, "Ideology, Film Practice, and the Market," offers not so much an overarching definition of the Urban Generation as a nuanced analysis of the complex historical conditions involved in the rise of the new urban cinema, including the documentary movement. The authors in this section evaluate the applicability of "postsocialism" as at once a periodizing, analytic, and aesthetic category. In so doing, they outline the connections between the emergence of the Urban Generation and the rise of the new market economy and mass culture within China, on one hand, and the impact of the transnational film practice, on the other. Yingjin Zhang attempts to map out the changing topography of the Urban Generation in the postsocialist landscape and the complex configuration of the underlying political economy involving four "players": politics, art, capital, and marginality. He takes Guan Hu's *Dirt* (1993) as a starting point for examining post-1989 Chinese filmmaking in general and the transformation of the Sixth Generation in particular. Zhang identifies the figure of the rock musician as the quintessential "rebel" in early Sixth Generation works and the rock music, along with the MTV that made it popular, as having left discernible aesthetic marks on these films. Challenging the prevalent notion of "underground" used by Western critics in describing the Sixth Generation, Zhang argues that the Newborn Generation as a whole is in fact defined by its ambivalent and at times symbiotic relationship with the official apparatus, the commercial mainstream, and the international art film market, especially toward the late 1990s.

Jason McGrath's chapter, through close readings of Jia Zhangke's works, extends and deepens the discussion on postsocialism by locating it squarely in film production methods and the resulting aesthetics, in particular the issues of realism. McGrath traces Jia's career in terms of both his changing visual style and its local and global context—from the influence of a rough-hewn postsocialist critical realism inaugurated by independent documentary and fiction filmmakers in the early 1990s to the retooling of the more stylized long-take realism in the tradition of international art cinema. The power of postsocialist realist films lies in their direct "confrontation with reality through the rhetoric of their narratives and their cinematic style." In Jia's early works, this stylistic boldness is emblematized by cinema verité–style shooting and the frequent "look to the camera" by pedestrian "extras," which foregrounds the unevenness of "extradiegetic" reality and limits of representation. McGrath argues that Jia's works in fact oscillate between two kinds of realism while suggesting a discernible trajectory of stylistic shift as the director marches further into the international scene. The oscillation ultimately also speaks to the aesthetic flexibility or anxiety of Jia and other filmmakers whose social and artistic aspirations are caught not only between the contradictory temporalities of an unruly Chinese reality but also the competing cinematic discourses and practices in the transnational arena.

The importance of the documentary approach in the new urban cinema is more directly tackled in Chris Berry's contribution on the innovative and socially engaged documentary film and video practice since 1989. Quite separate from Sixth Generation or Urban Generation narrative filmmaking, this new documentary movement, institutionally speaking, has emerged for the most part from the world of television. Yet both forms share an acute desire to "get real," which Berry sees as the primary condition of contemporary post-socialist cinema in China. What makes the new documentary uniquely different from the official documentary is the method of spontaneous shooting (or "on-the-spot" realism) and the absence of the lecture format. These features give voice to ordinary people and their everyday concerns. The documentary trend (including its extensions such as the talk show) has helped create an emerging public sphere on television, taking advantage of its more rapid expansion and thorough commercialization than that seen in the film system in the 1990s.

Moving toward the more specific phenomenon of the intensified urbanization of the last fifteen years, the chapters in part 2 trace the engagement by cinematic and other media (including avant-garde art and literature) with a new politics and poetics of the urban. The contributions by Sheldon Lu and by Yomi Braester focus on the transforming cityscape, specifically the widespread phenomenon of demolition and relocation (*chaiqian*), and the concomitant fragmentation of the social fabric in 1990s urban China. Lu and Braester both survey a wide range of filmic and nonfilmic material while observing important distinctions between the variations in aesthetic appeal and social function.

Sheldon Lu approaches the phenomenon of demolition and its impact through a multimedia exploration of the changed sensory economy and competing temporalities in popular cinema (specifically the Imar productions *Shower* and *Beautiful New World* and Feng Xiaogang's *A Sigh*) and avant-garde photography and video. While the popular films portray in a direct and sentimental manner the destructive impact on family structure and old neighborhoods, in them and in certain avant-garde art Lu discovers different attempts to "project new zones of hopes, desires, and dreams" in metropolitan public spaces such as hotels, bars, and galleries. If popular cinema tends to be more descriptive and cathartic, the avant-garde works make more explicit interventions into the social process—albeit with limited impact on the public at large. These cultural practices, be they popular or avant-garde in approaches and manners of exhibition, negotiate with or even challenge the prevalent discourse of modernization and globalization.

Yomi Braester, on the other hand, is concerned with the tropes of nostalgia and self-reflexivity in selected popular urban films. He finds in the ubiquitous presence of the camera within film narratives evidence of a "documentary impulse" and a self-conscious attempt to preserve a "record of the vanishing cityscape" while collectively working through the trauma of dislocation. Braester traces the emergence of this impulse and demolition as a "symbolic economy" to works by the Fifth Generation directors Huang Jianxin (*Stand Up, Don't Stoop*, 1992) and Zhou Xiaowen (*No Regret about Youth*, 1992) in order to provide a larger historical context for recent urban cinema. Moving on to younger directors' popular urban films, such as *A Tree in the House* (1999), Braester finds in them a disconcerting nostalgic tendency of "legitimizing a filmic erasure of history" even in their apparent attempt to register the experience of dislocation.

In her essay Augusta Palmer addresses the question of urban nostalgia from a different angle—notably the architectural images of a more distant past, specifically old Shanghai. She offers a comparative reading of *A Beautiful New World* (1998) and *Street Angel* (1937), particularly the similar yet historically varied use of the skyscraper as the marker of cosmopolitan consumption. She regards the former as an instance of "a totalizing nostalgic relinkage to the mythical past of the city of Shanghai" in the advent of a "consumer revolution." The images of urban nostalgia in films such as *A Beautiful New World* are "totalizing" rather than "fragmentary" (which foregrounds displacement and discontinuity of history) because they are geared toward the rebuilding of a cosmopolitan "home," an imagined paradise, as it were, through an uncritical celebration of the "new freedom to consume" (in this case, the skyscraper and its attendant lifestyle).

By comparing Huang Jianxin's "urban attitude" films and several independent works that feature the figure of the "drifter" (as different from Huang's film lens as *flâneur*), Linda Lai astutely argues that the differing spatial practices and aesthetic strategies evidenced in two groups of films stem not so much from the generation divide as from their disparate "speaking positions within the creative community." She finds that Huang's realist films, while concerned with the everyday experience in a changing urban milieu, crystallize a "unified vision and single perspective" of a prophetic intellectual, whereas the other experimental films about drifting (*Xiao Wu, Suzhou River,* and *In Expectation*) display the city as a "heterotopia" or a kind of "psychogeography" that allows the coexistence of diverse experience and alternative modes of social ordering. The serious art films by the independent directors cultivate a "negative poetics" that combines modernist intentions and postmodern tactics, deviating from mainstream cinema's demand for dramatic actions, motivations, and resolutions while still trapped in existing Chinese intellectual trends. In the final analysis, "drifting" is not only an empirical content captured cinematically but also constructs a distinctive film form and a subjective position of the filmmaker.

Rapid marketization and privatization have introduced a wide range of new urban subjects (including large marginal and migrant populations) and has effected changes in existing ones. The essays in the third section of the book explicitly approach the questions of desire, gender, and urban identities in the wake of the rise of a mass-consumer culture as seen both on and off the screen. Part 3 opens with a chapter on the female director Ning Ying's works in the form of a Beijing Trilogy. Shuqing Cui's investigation of the disappearance of the socialist or communal urban space leads her to concentrate on Ning Ying's status as a female director, the point of view she chooses, and the cinematic space that her films construct. Cui discusses Ning's vision in the film *For Fun* of urban space on the social margins as occupied by the elderly; issues of class and gender in *On the Beat,* about policemen's uneasy place in a rapidly changing city; and the question of sexuality in a fast-changing urban environment in *I Love Beijing,* which addresses a taxi-driver's frenzied but futile search for love after divorce. Taken together her films show, through both critical and humorous lenses, how urbanization and globalization transform social and gender relations while also raising the urgent issues of family, marriage, and divorce as the ancient capital rushes toward its capitalist future.

In a similar manner Bérénice Reynaud investigates the cinematic representation of the new hybrid urban identities in Zhang Yuan's works and provides an overview of Zhang's career and stylistic development. In concentrating on the mise-en-scène in Zhang's films, Reynaud argues that Zhang's cinematic vision, a "sidelong glance" from the margins, is fueled by a dynamic tension between realism, hyperrealism, and surrealism. The urban spaces inventoried and reconstituted range from the prosaic everyday living space in *Sons* to the fluid, evolving spaces in *Seventeen Years* and finally to the imaginary or even operatic spaces in a film like *East Palace, West Palace*. All of these elements, however, coexist in varying combinations in his provocative cinematic vision as a whole, giving uncompromising expression to the "bastardized" Chinese urban landscape and social experience. Noting the predominant male perspective in Zhang's oeuvre, Reynaud points to the increasing presence of a female perspective in his most recent works, which interestingly coincide with his (re)turn to the domestic market.

Picking up the theme of sexuality in a male filmmaker's work, Xueping Zhong's contribution focuses exclusively on the problem of male desire and masculinity. Zhong analyzes the problem of "male discontent" manifested in Lü Yue's *Mr. Zhao* (1998) in particular and the widespread phenomenon of extramarital affairs in Chinese society today in general. The story of the college professor Mr. Zhao's troubled love and family life, which ultimately paralyzes him, is according to Zhong told from a male-centered perspective despite the fact the film is an independent production. The film articulates with other films and numerous TV dramas the confused subject position of the male intellectual, the impoverishment of collective social and moral standards, as well as a problematic gender and sexual politics in a postrevolution and promarket China. The film's position on the issue retains a degree of ambiguity due to Lu Yue's innovative film language, including the use of the Shanghai dialect.

After decades of absence on the Chinese screen, the sudden reemergence of the people's police in several recent "cop films" by the Urban Generation directors (in particular *On the Beat, In Expectation,* and *East Palace, West Palace*) is the focus of Yaohua Shi's essay. Shi argues that the chief difference between the representation of police officers in this group of films and their scarce predecessors in Chinese film history lies in the move away from socialist realism to a hyperrealism. This shift is encapsulated in the diametrically different characterization of the pig farmer figure in *My Day Off* (1959) and *On the Beat* (1995), respectively. On a more fundamental level, Shi also at-

tempts to shed light on the changing dynamics in the triad relationship between city, police, and cinema.

Fascinated by the figure of the female double, or what I call the "phantom
sisters" in Wang Quan'an's *Lunar Eclipse* (1999) and Lou Ye's *Suzhou River*
(2000), my own essay, also the last chapter of the book, offers an intertextual reading of these two noir-inflected art films set in fin-de-siècle Beijing
and Shanghai, respectively. I probe the social and epistemological uncertainty embodied by the figure of the female doppelganger as well as the male
photographer/videographer who serves as the narrative linchpin in these
contemporary tales of the strange. I identify the creative fusion of avant-garde
elements, pop idioms, and classical allusions (to the ghost story, for example)
found in these films. By examining the manner of their production and
reception, these two films, along with other experimental films by the Urban
Generation, signal in my view the beginning of an independent art cinema
with both local and cosmopolitan aspirations.

This anthology, in representing some of the most recent and original research on a significant cinematic phenomenon, contributes to the growing
body of work on the ongoing urban and social transformation in Mainland
China from, but not limited to, the cinematic perspective. In this collective
project we aim to open up a new field of inquiry into contemporary Chinese
culture and engage with current discussions on postsocialism and transnational cultural production. We try to trace the origins and outline the
defining features and complex structure of a broad trend in cinema and
culture that emerged in China in the 1990s and continues to expand and
ramify in the new century. As Chinese cinema is rapidly changing and diversi-
fying in the wake of the entry of China into the World Trade Organization and
the recent changes in film and cultural policy—and as the stakes remain high
for China's social, cultural, and political change—filmmakers, spectators, and
critics alike are charged with the responsibility to bear witness to a historical
process with enormous implications for the new century.

NOTES
1. The idea of a "minor" cinema draws on Deleuze and Guattari's discussion of
Kafka. See Gilles Deleuze and Felix Guattari, *Kafka: Toward a Minor Literature*,
trans. Dana Polan (Minneapolis: University of Minnesota Press, 1986). See also
Gilles Deleuze, *Cinema 2: The Time-Image* (London: Athlone, 1989). For an eluci-

dation of the philosophical as well as political implications of Deleuze's idea of a "minor cinema," see D. N. Rodowick, *Gilles Deleuze's Time Machine* (Durham: Duke University Press, 1997), especially chapter 5, "Series and Fabulation: Minor Cinema."

2. "The Urban Generation: Chinese Cinema in Transformation" was the title of a touring film program I co-organized with Jia Zhijie for a number of venues on the East Coast in February and March 2001. In May 2000, Jia Zhijie and Shi Yaohua drove to New York from Massachusetts to meet with me about the series. During an intense day-long meeting we discussed titles such as "New Urban Realism" and "The Independent Generation," but finally arrived at the "Urban Generation." We felt the term would provide a historical reference to the generation discourse while also moving away from it by anchoring the new generation in the current vast process of urbanization and social transformation.

3. For several majors, including directing, the Beijing Film Academy does not admit students every year. After Zhang Yimou and Chen Kaige's class graduated in 1982, the BFA admitted a new class in 1985 that included Zhang Yuan and others. Another class was admitted in 1987. The two classes make up the so-called "Sixth Generation." He Jianjun was not a formal undergraduate student but studied in a special short-term training program at about the same time.

4. Zhang Yiwu was among the first of the Chinese critics to coin the term "Post New Era" to describe the radical break between the reforms of the 1980s and the rapid turn to a market economy, consumption, and mass culture governing a new (depoliticized) pragmatism. See his essay "Hou xinshiqi: Xinde wenhua kongjian" [Post–New Era: A new cultural space], *Wenyi zhengmin*, no. 6 (1992): 9–12; as well as his essay on cinema, "Hou xinshiqi Zhongguo dianying: Fenglie de tiaozhan" [Chinese cinema of the Post–New Era: The challenge of fragmentation], *Dangdai dianying*, no. 5 (1994): 4–11.

5. Harry Harootunian, "Introduction: The Unavoidable 'Actuality' of Everyday Life," in *History's Disquiet: Modernity, Cultural Practice, and the Question of the Everyday Life* (New York: Columbia University Press, 2000), 18.

6. On this subject see, among others, Geremie Barmé, *In the Red: On Contemporary Chinese Culture* (New York: Columbia University Press, 1999); Xudong Zhang, *Chinese Modernism in the Era of Reform* (Durham, N.C.: Duke University Press, 1997); and Jing Wang, *Culture Fever: Politics, Aesthetics, and Ideology in Deng's China* (Berkeley: University of California Press, 1996).

7. Meng Xianli, "Lun houxiandai yujingxia Zhongguo dianyingde xiezuo" [On Chinese cinematic inscription in the postmodern discursive context], in *Dangdai dianying lilun wenxuan* [An anthology of contemporary film theory], ed. Hu Ke, Zhang Wei, and Hu Zhifeng (Beijing: Beijing guangbo xueyuan chubanshe, 2000), 173.

8. For recent studies on social and cultural changes in contemporary urban China see, among others, Deborah Davis et al., eds., *Urban Spaces in Contemporary*

China: The Potential for Autonomy and Community in Post-Mao China (New York: Cambridge University Press, 1995); and Nancy N. Chen et al., eds., *China Urban: Ethnographies of Contemporary Culture* (Durham, N.C.: Duke University Press, 2001).

9. Rapid globalization and the concentration of large number of migrant laborers in these Chinese coastal cities, SEZs, and metropolitan centers have turned them, too, into "global cities" as described by Saskia Sassen. See her *The Global City: New York, London, Tokyo* (Princeton, N.J.: Princeton University Press, 1996), and *Globalization and Its Discontents* (New York: New Press, 1998).

10. See my *An Amorous History of the Silver Screen: Shanghai Cinema, 1896–1937* (Chicago: University of Chicago Press, 2005).

11. See Dai Jinghua, "Imagined Nostalgia," in *Postmodernism and China*, ed. Arif Dirlik and Xudong Zhang (Durham, N.C.: Duke University Press, 2000), 205–21. See also the chapter by Augusta Palmer in this anthology.

12. Cheng Qingsong and Huang He, *Wode sheyingji bu sahuang* [My camera doesn't lie] (Beijing: Zhongguo youyi chuban gongsi, 2002), 126.

13. The concept of the witness derives in part from the growing field of trauma studies. For some key texts, see Dominick La Capra, *Representing the Holocaust: History, Theory, Trauma* (Ithaca, N.Y.: Cornell University Press, 1996); Michael Rothberg, *Traumatic Realism: The Demands of Holocaust Representation* (Minneapolis: University of Minnesota Press, 2000); and Dora Apel, *Memory Effects: The Holocaust and the Art of Secondary Witnessing* (New Brunswick, N.J.: Rutgers University Press, 2002).

14. Tang Ye, "From the Fifth to the Sixth Generation: An Interview with Zhang Yimou," *Film Quarterly* 53, no. 2 (winter 1999): 12. This interview is also included in Frances Gateward, ed., *Zhang Yimou: Interviews* (Jackson: University of Mississippi Press, 2001).

15. The term "organized" is used because the large number of box office receipts is often the result of the distribution of tickets by state sectors—including factories, administrative entities, schools, cultural institutions, and organizations. This practice is similar to the organized mass viewing of the "model opera" films during the Cultural Revolution period.

16. The entire text of the new regulations, "Dianying guanli tiaoli" (Regulations on the supervision of cinema), was published through the Xinhua News Agency on June 25, 1996, and in the party mouthpiece paper, *Renmin ribao* [People's daily] on June 26, 2001. The Office of State Affairs issued it as the "no. 200 official document," and it was signed by the then prime minister Li Peng.

17. Huang Shixian, "Wenhua zhuanxing: Quanqiuhua qushi yu dianying tizhi gaige (1996–1999)" [Cultural transformation: Globalization and the reform of the film institution (1996–1999)], published in the bilingual illustrated catalogue *Spectrums of the Century: Chinese Cinemas 1896–1999* (Taipei: Council for Cultural Affairs and the Chinese Taipei Film Archive, 2000), 419.

18. After five films, Peter Loehr moved on to found an independent company called Ming Productions in Beijing in 2004, in which his aim was to make more ambitious films with larger budgets. The company's first product was Zhang Yang's *Sunflowers*.

19. The film was completed in 1996, but due to Tian Zhuangzhuang's involvement as the film's coproducer and one of its leading actors (as the "father" or mentor figure), the film was, after six edits, finally released in 1998. (Tian had been under attack after his *Blue Kite* was spirited out of the country and won major awards at international festivals.)

20. The consciously formulated tactic of co-optation is as follows: "There will be one 'underground' film less if there is one more person making film within the 'system.'" See Fu Cheng, "Bei Ying 2000" [Beijing Film Studio in 2000], in *Dianying tongxun*, no. 6 (2000), cited in Rao Shuoguang, "Shehui/wenhua zhuanxing yu dianyingde fenghua jiqi zhenghe" [Socio-cultural transformation and the fragmentation and reintegration of cinema], *Dangdai dianying*, no. 1 (2000): 16.

21. The term "amateur cinema" was first coined by Jia Zhangke. The choice of the term initially was a replacement for "independent cinema" (*duli dianying*) in order to avoid potential political problems. The term, which resonates with Wu Wenguang's views, suggests a change in the conception of independent cinema in the wake of the quick spread of DV in the late 1990s.

22. They spent allegedly only 20,000 yuan (US$2,500) to make *Xiao Shan Going Home*. *Xiao Wu*, however, was more "ambitious" and had a budget of US$30,000.

23. Lin Xudong, interview with Jia Zhangke, "Yige laizi Zhongguo jicengde minjian daoyan" [A people's director who comes from the grassroots level of China], *Today*, no. 3 (1999): 19.

24. Jia accepts this label gladly, admitting that he felt that he shared the same "substance" (*tong xi xing*) with the migrant worker. He recalls that he was compelled to portray someone like Xiao Wu precisely because he was dissatisfied with the mainstream cinema, which overlooks the experience and existence of such ordinary people: "If we were to find out years later how people lived in this period through this kind of cinema, we would only find falsehood and lies. In this regard, I realize that cinema is really a means of memory" (quoted in Cheng and Huang, *Wode sheyingji bu sahuang*, 362).

25. In my June 2001 interview with Jia Zhangke at his Beijing workshop, he told me that he conceived the character Xiao Wu, the "most intellectual looking person in town," based on several people he knew in his hometown Fenyang, where the film is set and shot.

26. For a detailed genealogy of the new documentary movement (a term that Wu Wenguang disputes), see Wu Wenguang, "Just on the Road: A Description of the Individual Way of Recording Images in the 1990s," in *Reinterpretation: A Decade of Experimental Chinese Art 1900–2000*, ed. Wu Hung et al. (Guangzhou: Guangdong

Museum of Art, 2002), 132–38. For a historical and conceptual account of the movement, see Chris Berry's chapter in this volume.

27. On the "performative impulse" in the new documentary movement, in particular in the film *The Other Bank*, see Charles Leary, "Performing the Documentary; or Making It to the Other Bank," online at http://www.sensesofcinema.com/contents/03/27/performing documentary.html.

28. On the "documentary" turn in Chinese television culture in the 1990s, see Zhu Yujun, *Xiandai dianshi jishi* [Contemporary television documentaries] (Beijing: Beijing Guangbo xueyuan chubanshe, 2000).

29. Roy Armes, *On Video* (London: Routledge, 1995 [1985]), 130.

30. Wu Wenguang, "Fangwen *Xiao Wu* daoyan Jia Zhangke" [An interview with Jia Zhangke, director of *Xiao Wu*], in *Xianchang* [Document], ed. Wu Wenguang (Tianjing: Tianjing shehui kexueyuan chubanshe, 2000), 200.

31. Lin Xudong, interview with Jia Zhangke, 10.

32. Ibid., 15.

33. Trinh T. Minh-ha, *When the Moon Waxes Red: Representation, Gender and Cultural Politics* (New York: Routledge, 1991), 39–40.

34. Quoted in Cheng and Huang, *Wode sheyingji bu sahuang*, 254.

35. Shen Yun, "Guanyu *Zhaole* he *Minjing gushi*—Yu Ning Ying de Fangtan" [On *For Fun* and *On the Beat*—An interview with Ning Ying], *Dangdai dianying*, no. 3 (1996): 33–38.

36. Wu Wenguang, "He jilu fangshi youguande shu" [A book that has something to do with documenting], in *Xianchang*, 274–75.

37. Ni Zhen, "Jishixing dianying he geren fenggede wanshan—ping *Minjing gushi*" [The perfection of documentary aesthetic and personal style—on *On the Beat*], in *Jiushi niandai de "Di wudai"* [The "Fifth Generation" in the 90s], ed. Yang Yuanying, Pan Hua and Zhang Zhuan (Beijing: Beijing Guangbo xueyuan chubanshe, 2000), 428.

38. Dai Jinghua has linked the genesis of *xianchang* in the new documentary movement with the experimental (often improvisational) theater and performance art that also emerged in the early 1990s. She argues that "xianchang is not a constructed category, but a kind of truth, a naked materiality; it means witness or testimony, but also an intervention in the real, a kind of overhaul or deconstruction of culture" (*Yingxing shuxie: Jiushi niandai Zhongguo wenhua yanjiu* [Invisible writing: Cultural studies of the China of the 90's] [Nanjing: Jiangsu renmin chubanshe, 1999], 226).

39. For examples of the agitated reaction to the 1993 change, see, for instance, "Dianying shichang kaifang zhihou—Shoudu dianyingjie renshi geshu jijian" [After the opening of the film market—The film professionals in the Capital express their different views], *Beijing ribao* [Beijing Daily], December 11, 1992, 5. For a report on the confusion in the process of reform in 1993, see Ding Renren, "1993

Zhongguo dianying 'mozhe shitou guohe'" [Chinese cinema in 1993: "Crossing the river by feeling the stones"], *Beijing ribao*, January 26 and 31, 1994. According to the statistics cited by Ding, the exhibition sector suffered a huge loss in 1993 compared to 1992—declining 50 percent in the number of screenings, 60 percent in the total number of audience visits, 35 percent in total box office receipts and 40 percent in revenues from distribution. While big cities like Beijing and Shanghai actually saw increases in theater attendance, the smaller cities, in particular those in the rural areas, became a casualty of the transition. For a more systematic evaluation of the film reform of 1993, especially the case of Jiangsu Province, see Guo Changmao, "Dianying tizhi gaige yinian deshi tan" [On the gains and losses during a year of reform in the film system], *Dianying yishu*, no. 5 (1994): 66–68.

40. For a meticulous account of the number and nature of mainland films that won awards at international festivals between 1978 and 1996, see Li Xingfa, "Ruhe kan Zhongguopian zai guowai huojiang?" [How to view the winning of international awards of Chinese films?], *Dangdai dianying*, no. 4 (1997): 33–37. According to the article, the total number of awards during this period was 250, which were garnered by 119 films at 187 festivals. Tellingly, these figures do not include the awards won by banned or independent films.

41. Wu, *Xianchang*, 188.

42. The address for this site is http://www.hyzonet.com/.

43. During and after the event I also received numerous e-mails from film buffs and students in many countries who had found out about the series on the Internet. It is interesting to think how many viewers could be reached if these films could be put online using streaming technology.

44. Such semi-independent enterprises are often formed according to the model of *guanshang heying*, or "official-commercial joint management," as is commonly practiced in other sectors in the national economy and cultural industry.

45. Huang, "Wenhua zhuanxing," 420.

46. This term is from Ann Friedberg, *Window Shopping: Cinema and the Post-modern* (Berkeley: University of California Press, 1993).

47. "Low-Budget Films Go Up Against Hollywood Big Boys," online at http://english1.people.com.cn:80/200411/11/eng20041111_163566.html.

48. For a discussion on the teahouse mode of spectatorship and early Chinese cinema, see my "Teahouse, Shadowplay, Bricolage: *Laborer's Love* and the Question of Early Chinese Cinema," in *Cinema and Urban Culture in Shanghai, 1922–1943*, ed. Yingjin Zhang (Stanford: Stanford University Press, 1999).

49. The literal translation would be *Cahiers de practice*, as modeled on the French *Cahiers de cinema* (or *Dianying shouce* in Chinese).

50. Mei Bing, "Chengshi dianying gaoshaozu" [Urban film buffs], online at http://www.Beida-online.com (accessed in November 2001; no original publication data available). I rely on this article for most of my discussion on cineclubs outside Beijing.

51. Ibid. The club headquarters allegedly was forced by the authorities to shut down. But it is doubtful that its members would cease their activities, which could likely take more mobile and informal forms.

52. Mei Bing, "Chengshi dianying gaoshaozu."

53. Yangzi, "Fengge yizhong, huo qita" [A style, or something else], *Shijian shouce*, no. 4 (2001): 49.

54. Cited in Mei, "Chengshi dianying gaoshaozu."

55. Arjun Appadurai, *Modernity at Large: Cultural Dimensions of Globalization* (Minneapolis: University of Minnesota Press, 1996), 195.

56. Publicity material, the first Unrestricted New Image Festival, 2001. Because they were prohibited from screening Jia's *Platform* at the BFA's auditorium, the organizers used a drive-in space on the outskirts of the city, where the film was shown to an enthusiastic crowd (telephone conversation with Yang Zi, January 2002).

57. Yaolingyao, "Minjian yingxiang Shanghai zhang diandi" [Tidbits on independent film images in Shanghai], posted on www.Beida-online.com.

58. Arjun Appadurai, "Grassroots Globalization and the Research Imagination," *Public Culture* 12, no. 1 (winter 2000): 3.

I

IDEOLOGY, FILM PRACTICE, AND THE MARKET

rebel without a cause?

China's New Urban Generation

and Postsocialist Filmmaking

YINGJIN ZHANG

I n this chapter I seek to remap the varied landscape of postsocialist Chinese filmmaking since the early 1990s by focusing on the new Urban Generation. In particular I undertake a close reading of Guan Hu's (b. 1967) debut feature *Dirt* (Toufa luanle, 1994), a little-known film that is symptomatic of this generation's existential crisis. In addressing issues such as alienation, nostalgia, and rebellion, *Dirt* provides an entry point to explore this new generation's formative years in the mid-1990s, which coincided with a phase of sea change in China's recent history of postsocialism.

At the beginning of the 1990s, Chinese film production fell into three major categories. First, the state-subsidized and propagandist leitmotif films (*zhuxuanlü dianying*) were to become an increasingly visible presence. Second, the art films (*yishu dianying*)—less avant-garde than a few years before—were reduced to a shrinking minority in quantity more than in quality. And third, the entertainment (*yulepian*) or commercial films (*shangye dianying*), of numerous genres and varied production values, constituted a dominant majority. By the end of the decade, as exemplified by the 1999 season celebrating the fiftieth anniversary of the People's Republic of China, both art films and entertainment films moved closer to official ideology, while leitmotif films gradually acquired commercial features and successfully recruited several leading art film directors. The result is a new alliance of art, politics, and capital—a powerful new force that has redirected much of the creative energy to the market and at least temporarily compelled "underground" or "independent" directors to try filmmaking inside the studio system.[1] As I elaborate in the conclusion to this essay, co-optation and complicity prevailed in the postsocialist filmmaking of the late 1990s, and the events of 2000–2002 have presented alternatives to an even newer group of filmmakers.

POSTSOCIALISM (AND POST-TIANANMEN): THE VARIED LANDSCAPE OF FILMMAKING

Schematically, in the current scholarship in English the following four concepts of postsocialism can be differentiated: postsocialism as a label of historical periodization; postsocialism as a structure of feelings; postsocialism as a set of aesthetic practices; and postsocialism as a regime of political economy. Paul Pickowicz, the first scholar to connect postsocialism with Chinese cinema, takes for his work hints from Fredric Jameson's theory of postmodernism and constructs a parallel system in modern China. If the "modern" refers to "postfeudal, bourgeois culture that developed in capitalist societies in eighteenth- and nineteenth-century Europe," and the "modernist" refers to "avant-garde . . . culture that arose in the West in the late nineteenth and early twentieth centuries,"[2] then the modernist framework for a study of post-Mao China is neither useful nor productive but simply misleading, especially in light of the long history of delegitimizing modernism in socialist China. For the same reason, Pickowicz strongly resists the postmodernist framework on a historicist ground: "The postmodern framework refers primarily to postindustrial contexts. Postmodernism, that is, presupposes advanced capitalism."[3] In lieu of postmodernism, Pickowicz endorses the use of postsocialism as "the ideological counterpart of postmodernism."[4] For him, since "postsocialism presupposes socialism," this new framework illuminates Chinese culture in the 1980s, which "contained the vestiges of late imperial culture, the remnants of the modern or bourgeois culture of the Republican era, the residue of traditional socialist culture, and elements of both modernism and postmodernism."[5]

After proposing postsocialism as a periodizing label referring "in large part to a negative, dystopian cultural condition that prevails in late socialist societies," Pickowicz further defines postsocialism in China as a "popular perception" and "an alienated . . . mode of thought and behavior" that certainly predate the death of Mao.[6] Postsocialism, in this definition, appears to be a structure of feelings that remained repressed in the Mao years but has found vocal articulation in the post-Mao era, with alienation and disillusion as its two thematic foci. In a study of Huang Jianxin's first urban trilogy, Pickowicz regards *Black Cannon Incident* (Heipao shijian, 1985) as a postsocialist critique of the Leninist political system, *Dislocation* (Cuowei, 1986) as a parody that links postsocialism to a theater of the absurd, and *Transmigration* (Lunhui, 1988) as a story of individual resignation and anomie in the postsocialist society. Elsewhere, Pickowicz uses *The Troubleshooters* (Wanzhu, 1988; dir. Mi Jiashan) and *The Price of Frenzy* (Fengkuang de daijia, 1988; dir. Zhou Xiaowen) as further examples of postsocialist urban cinema. From the perspective of the political economy of filmmaking in the reform era, Pickowicz concludes that the post-Tiananmen scene was a jumble of contradictions, where quasi-dissident filmmakers like Zhang Yimou and Chen Kaige specialized in reverse orientalism; the "Sixth Generation" (*diliudai*) directors like Zhang Yuan (b. 1961) and He Yi (He Jianjun, b. 1960) produced films outside the studio system; and even crude propaganda works sometimes would undermine state power.[7]

Pickowicz's study illustrates that, as a structure of feelings, postsocialism could be articulated in a wide spectrum of cinematic works. Even the earlier post-Mao films by the renowned Third Generation director Xie Jin would qualify as postsocialism to the extent that they express an alienated mode of thought and behavior. For this reason, postsocialism may be further conceived of as a set of alternative aesthetic practices adopted by directors of various generations—alternative, that is, to the dominant mode of socialist realism in the Mao years. In the category of urban cinema, *Black Snow* (Benming nian, 1989; dir. Xie Fei) thus predates the Sixth Generation in its treatment of disillusion and pessimism by way of following a marginalized ex-prisoner in his fatal struggle in a new urban society generated by the emerging market economy. In expanding Pickowicz's notions of postsocialism to include cinematic styles, Chris Berry and Mary Ann Farquhar raise the following pressing questions: "Can postsocialism be seen as a complement to postmodernism? Is its pastiche of other styles, its ambiguity and play, part of an aesthetic parallel to postmodernism?"[8] In other words, can we ever adequately address the question of postsocialism without confronting its haunting other—postmodernism?

For Arif Dirlik and Xudong Zhang, the answer to the latter question is definitely negative. "What we need to keep in mind," they argue, is "that the postmodern is also the postrevolutionary and the postsocialist."[9] The ensuing conception of postsocialism is that of a new regime of political economy, which includes all conceivable aspects of a changing socioeconomic condition responsible for the formation of the postmodern in contemporary China. This explains why Xudong Zhang proceeds to analyze a vast array of issues in his double mapping of postmodernism and postsocialism in contemporary China. These issues range from the ambiguity of reforms, overproduction crises, the utopian impulse of Sino-Marxism (especially Maoism), the shared space between the state and civil society, market madness and plebeian excess, as well as political anxieties of intellectuals now divided into several contending ideological camps. Chinese postmodernism, he concludes, "emerges with the anxiety-causing intensification and articulation of economic-social-class-political-ideological differentiations, contradictions, polarization, and fragmentation of Chinese society"—a society that is unequivocally characterized as "postsocialist."[10]

My brief summary here of the recent scholarship on postsocialism is meant to delineate it *not* as a singular concept governing the entire post-Mao era (i.e., from 1977 onward); rather, I envision postsocialism as a varied landscape of culture in post-Mao China against which filmmakers of different generations, aesthetic aspirations, and ideological persuasions struggle to readjust or redefine their different strategic positions in different social, political, and economic situations. My emphasis on *difference* derives from my conviction that the period in which the Sixth Generation came into being marks a new regime of political economy and therefore constitutes a new chapter of cultural history in contemporary China. Sometimes labeled "post–New Era" (*hou xinshiqi*), this post-Tiananmen period—namely, the period subsequent to the government's crackdown on the prodemocratic student demonstration on June 4, 1989—differs significantly from the New Era studied by Pickowicz and others.[11] Consequently, filmmaking in the post-Tiananmen period demands paying attention to different configurations of cultural production, artistic pursuit, political control, ideological positioning, and institutional restructuring.

Difference, indeed, has been frequently used as a marker to distinguish the Sixth Generation as a unique group in postsocialist China.[12] Critics have established a list of binary oppositions to highlight the differences between the Fifth and the Sixth generations. Whereas the former is associated with rural landscape, traditional culture, ethnic spectacle, grand epic, historical reflection, allegorical framework, communal focus, and depth of emotion, the latter is sided with the urban milieu, modern sensitivity, narcissistic tendency, initiation tales, documentary effects, contingent situation, individualistic perception, and precarious moods.[13] Ostensibly, markers of difference like these, together with their unofficial or semiofficial production, do not favor the Sixth Generation as the standard-bearer of postsocialism in terms of aesthetic practices. But these distinctions nonetheless characterize these young directors as among the most experimental in the 1990s when the Fifth Generation —many of whom were avant-garde auteurs themselves in the mid- and late 1980s—had reverted to more traditional genres and styles such as the tearjerker melodrama and the spectacular historical epic.

What makes the works of the Sixth Generation more symptomatic of postsocialism than their predecessors is their institutionally imposed but selfglorified status of marginality in a crucial turning point in postsocialism as a regime of political economy. After the government had launched the program of wholesale market economy and had instituted a series of reforms in the post-Tiananmen era, the Sixth Generation entered the film market in confrontation (not yet quite in competition) with several major forces in film production. The mainstream or leitmotif film was given substantial state subsidies in the wake of Tiananmen. The art film as practiced by the leading figures of the earlier generations continued to attract transnational capital (from Hong Kong, Taiwan, and Japan, for instance). In the meantime, cheap commercial films (especially comedies and martial arts movies) flooded the market, and by the mid-1990s some leading studios had teamed up with private investors and coproduced films of high artistic values and box office appeal, such as *Red Cherry* (Hong yingtao, 1995; dir. Ye Daying).

Yet underground operation constitutes but only one set of the strategies deployed by the young directors. What is less known—or intentionally ignored

—in the Western media is that many new graduates from the Beijing Film Academy and other institutions have retained nominal affiliations with their assigned units. In addition to Guan Hu, the Beijing Film Studio listed on its staff other active young directors such as Lu Xuechang (b. 1964) and Zhang Yang (b. 1967). By the mid-1990s, several of their films were approved for public release in China. Guan's *Dirt* was joined by Lou Ye's (b. 1965) *Weekend Lovers* (Zhoumo qingren, 1994), Lu Xuechang's *The Making of Steel* (Zhangda chengren, 1995), Wang Rui's (b. 1962) *No Visit after the Divorce* (Lihun le, jiu bie zailai zhaowo, 1995), Wu Di's (b. 1970) *Yellow Goldfish* (Huang jinyu, 1995), and Zhang Ming's (b. 1961) *Rainclouds over Wushan* (Wushan yunyu, 1995).

Situated in this brand-new political-economic regime, the Sixth Generation is itself a cultural phenomenon made possible by the postsocialist market economy, which developed rapidly in the 1990s in full complicity with transnational capitalism and which values the ideology of entrepreneurship.[14] Somewhat ironically, underground filmmaking may be treated as a byproduct —even if unintentional—of postsocialism in the 1990s because, as entrepreneurs themselves, "independent" filmmakers turned their financial disadvantages into ideological advantages and negotiated their ways through the cracks and fissures opened up by the market economy. Relaxed state regulations enabled them to become independent in the first place, notably by being able to rent film equipment and facilities and deal directly—albeit unofficially— with overseas distribution agents. Nonetheless, given their initial dependence on state equipment for production and their reliance on international film festival circles for exhibition, the status of the Sixth Generation's as "independent" filmmakers is rather dubious.[15]

The qualified existence of the Sixth Generation as "independent" filmmakers leads back to postsocialism as a periodizing concept. Even in an attempt to set a starting date or a high point for postsocialism (as Pickowicz did in his work of the mid-1990s), it is evident that postsocialism as delineated in this chapter is a reality evolving along an unexplored path and toward an uncertain future. As such postsocialism has remained a source of anxiety that continues to generate feelings of deprivation, disillusion, despair, disdain, and sometimes even indignation and outrage. To explore feelings like these, I now turn to *Dirt* as a text symptomatic of the Sixth Generation in their formative years.

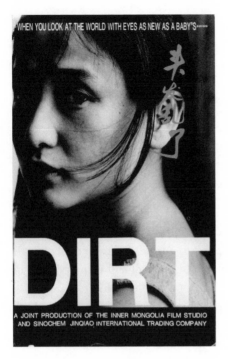

WHEN YOU LOOK AT THE WORLD WITH EYES AS NEW AS A BABY'S······

DIRT

A JOINT PRODUCTION OF THE INNER MONGOLIA FILM STUDIO
AND SINOCHEM JINQIAO INTERNATIONAL TRADING COMPANY

Poster for *Dirt*.
(Courtesy of Guan Hu)

DIRT: HISTORY AND MEMORY IN RUINS

Guan Hu started his career by making the second choice for independently minded filmmakers mentioned above: by pursuing a major studio
label. In 1991, he managed to obtain an investment of 800,000 yuan (roughly
US$100,000) from the Golden Bridge International Trading Company, a sub-
sidiary of Sino-Chemicals (Zhonghua), through the connections of the actress Kong Lin. With her prominent roles in the films *Bloody Morning* (Xuese
qingchen, 1990; dir. Li Shaohong) and *Raise the Red Lantern* (Da hong denglong gaogao gua, 1991; dir. Zhang Yimou), both internationally released and
acclaimed, Kong had acquired enough star power for fund-raising purposes.
After paying the Inner Mongolian Studio 150,000 yuan for the studio label fees
(an amount that although 18.75 percent of their budget was cheaper than
other big-name studios), Guan Hu assembled a crew and a cast (whose average age was twenty-four) and started in May 1992 to work on what he envisioned to be the first Chinese MTV-style rock feature.[16]

Dirt opens with a full screen of Mao Zedong's celebrated quotation during the Cultural Revolution: "The world belongs to you as well as to us; but it is eventually yours. You youngsters . . . are like the rising sun. Hope is rested on your shoulders." A group of children gather at a neighbor's house and play a record of the Beatles song "Hey Jude":

> Hey Jude, don't make it bad.
> Take a sad song and make it better.
> Remember to let her into your heart,
> Then you can start to make it better.

Against the soundtrack Ye Tong (Kong Lin) walks along a set of railroad tracks, carrying a guitar on her back.[17] She has just arrived from Guangzhou to revisit her childhood friends and to pursue medical training in Beijing. In an MTV-like fashion, fragments of her childhood memory crosscut with glimpses of the modern cityscape, and the Beatles soundtrack intensifies her melancholy. As Ye meets her friends one by one in the *hutong* (back alleys), the viewer gradually realizes the social values attached to each of them. In the positive realm, Weidong, whose name means "defending the East," is a policeman in charge of the neighborhood. In the middle, Chi Xuan, a former weakling, now makes a small fortune as a private entrepreneur, and Peng Wei, a longhaired rock musician, appears to defy all social norms. In the negative realm, Big Head (the nickname of Lei Bing) is an escaped prisoner who hides in a deserted house that used to belong to Ye's family before their relocation to Guangzhou at the beginning of the Cultural Revolution. "We were five kids living in the same hutong," Ye reminisces, "and we never imagined we would grow up like this."

With Ye's voice-over commenting throughout the film, *Dirt* foregrounds the female consciousness and thus distances itself from the type of male narcissism—sometimes even misogyny—typical of the all-male Sixth Generation.[18] Nevertheless, like his classmates, Guan Hu cannot but depict his female lead as the "other" against whom male characters negotiate their social, sexual, and "aesthetic" identities. Even Big Head is attracted to Ye, and this eventually leads to an incident in which he stabs Weidong and, confronted by the police, dies accidentally by falling down a road bridge.

One of the central tensions in the film is the romantic rivalry between Weidong and Peng Wei, whose physical appearances codify them as the opposing

Ye Tong and her friends. (Courtesy of Guan Hu)

forces of law and rebellion.[19] As a childhood musical talent, Ye is attracted to Peng and his rock group—played by Beijing's heavy-metal band Pressure Points (Chaozai), who helped compose the film's score. Ye experiences in their rehearsals a kind of newfound freedom, or at least a much-needed release from her tedious medical training. Donning a Chicago Bulls cap, which marks her desire for a more stimulating life, she sings of revisiting her childhood dreams. In spite of her romantic involvement, however, Ye soon realizes the futility of Peng's rebellion and is repulsed by his irresponsible sex life.

If Ye's involvement with Peng has much to do with the desperation of two alienated souls, her relationship with Weidong seems to originate from a collective childhood dream of home and community. The Zheng's house used to be the favorite hangout for the five childhood friends. Now, the same hutong still exists, but each of its members has drifted in a different direction. Four of them (Big Head is not present) briefly reunite at Ye's birthday party in Zheng's house, but Zheng's father, an aging music teacher long paralyzed by a stroke, soon thereafter passes away, thereby signifying the end of the socialist era. After the incident in which Weidong is stabbed, Ye visits him in the hospital, and later they roam the streets hand in hand and end up in Ye's deserted house. "I often dreamed of us five playing in this house," says Ye, and their intimacy is unraveled in ambivalent images in the following sequences.

In one sequence, Chi Xuan sets up a film projector in Zheng's house to entertain Weiping, Weidong's sister who works for a foreign venture and who is nearly ready to give birth to her ex-husband's baby. A fast tracking shot then reveals people wearing white mourning flowers lining up along the streets. A

Rebel without a Cause? • 57

Peng Wei (center) and his rock band. (Courtesy of Guan Hu)

medium shot of a funeral car passing the mourners in front of Tiananmen is followed by an extreme long shot of a sea of people in Tiananmen Square. A woman in tears appears in a close-up, holding a child who wears a black armband. Then the camera pans to other weeping mourners.

Another close-up presents Weidong and Ye embracing each other in the deserted house. As the camera tracks behind the film projector and pans through Chi's indifferent face to Weiping's puzzled look, a group of cheerful men and women are seen on-screen dancing in *yangge* (traditional dance accompanied by drums) style in front of Tiananmen, while others parade with a billboard sign that reads "Smashing the Gang of Four. Celebrating the Victory." A frontal shot of the defiant look of Peng Wei in Zheng's house is followed by a close-up of the back of Ye's lovely hair and Weidong gazing at her. An old portrait of Mao Zedong is barely visible on the wall behind Weidong's naked shoulders. As Ye lies down on the bed, her head tipping over the edge and her long hair streaming down, the sex scene cuts to a tracking shot of mourners lining the street and a panoramic shot of tens of thousands of people in Tiananmen Square.

A mixture of unsettling feelings of contradiction, bewilderment, and irony is generated in these sequences. For Guan Hu, *Dirt* is intended as a "rebellious film" (*fanpan de dianying*) that articulates a kind of "nostalgia for the past and indulgence in the future" and "a lingering sense of idealism and sentimentality" unique to his generation of filmmakers who experienced "moments of

Weidong and Ye Tong: an old relationship on the rocks.
(Courtesy of Guan Hu)

crisis" in the postsocialist China of the 1990s.[20] Indeed, back in the early 1990s, the images of public mourning in Tiananmen Square could not help but to evoke the publicly unspeakable moments of idealism and crisis of the 1989 Tiananmen.[21] The juxtaposition of the private (a sex scene) with the public (the documentary footage of Mao Zedong's 1976 funeral) in the film raises the issues of history and memory, as the cross-cutting simultaneously suggests the fragmentation of private memory and the seeming irrelevance of public history in postsocialist China.

Sure enough, the fragments of private memory are everywhere found in the typical visual presentation in *Dirt*: that is, the MTV-style collage of images connected to a soundtrack of rock music. The kind of sentimentality and nostalgia envisioned by Guan Hu finds the best expression in the song "A Night without Dreams" (Yiye wumeng) that Ye Tong sings at her school's anniversary party near the end of the film. In a rapid succession of fragments of private and collective memories, the song sequence alternatively features Ye and Peng (who are identical in their body movements and their long hair) and the events that may or may not have taken place in the film. These images include the marching red guards and the reading of *Cankao xiaoxi* (an internally circulated newspaper) in the era of the Cultural Revolution, as well as bulldozers and the hutongs in ruins as a result of the contemporary demolition of old Beijing.

The end of the film resembles its beginning, with a sentimental scene of Ye's departure on a Beijing street. What emerges as extremely ironic, however, is that the convalescent Weidong, who cannot speak, is pushed by Chi Xuan in a wheelchair—an exact replica of the image of his father earlier in the film. This is a decidedly symbolic gesture through which *Dirt* pays lip service to the sanctity of the law while exposing its fundamental vulnerability and its utter inability to fully justify itself in human terms (and hence is another implicit critique of 1989 Tiananmen). In the rest of the scene the traffic lights turn red and a team of elementary school students singing "Song of the Young Pioneers" passes in front of Ye and separates her from her childhood friends. Suppressing tears, Ye waves to Chi and Weidong, bidding farewell to a city where her childhood dreams are twice lost. As the ending credits roll on, the Beatles song "Hey Jude" fills the soundtrack again, but this time the following lyrics are subtitled in Chinese:

Hey Jude, don't be afraid.
. . . .
And anytime you feel the pain, hey Jude, refrain,
Don't carry the world upon your shoulders.[22]

This rebellious film thus ends with a vision of history and memory in ruins, leaving only fragments of images and songs to evoke a lingering sense of nostalgia, emptiness, and irony. In spite of its heightened nostalgia, it should be kept in mind that *Dirt* was a product of collective work. The film's original Chinese title was *Zang ren* (Dirty guys), an unmistakable reference to the longhaired defiant artist that the Sixth Generation fashioned as a self-image or ego ideal in their formative years. Even though the title of the Chinese release was changed to *Toufa luanle* (Disheveled hair) due to censorship pressure, a small seal bearing the mark 87 (the year the class of 1991 entered the Beijing Film Academy) significantly accompanies the title in the initial credit sequence. From the outset, therefore, Guan Hu had anticipated *Dirt* to be a collective expression of the group's rebellious spirit and their particular type of aesthetic aspirations—both embodied in the rock music popular among young Chinese urban audiences since the late 1980s.

Rock music arose in China around the mid-1980s from the "subcultural margins" where its participants—musicians, college students, and private entrepreneurs—share, in the words of Andrew Jones, "a coherent ideology of cultural opposition."[23] Almost synonymous with Chinese rock, Cui Jian has for over a decade been typecast internationally as a "rebel rocker" and has been variously hailed as "China's Bob Dylan" or "China's John Lennon."[24] The rebellious nature of his work is captured in his metaphoric use of rock music "like a knife" (also the title of one of his famous songs) to "cut away at social and political problems."[25] The common perception of rock music as an effective means for the articulation of dissent and resistance thus united in the early 1990s the rock musicians and the emergent Sixth Generation directors. Their united stance vis-à-vis the mainstream political and commercial cultures further engendered several significant parallels between these two groups of rebel artists.

First, in terms of its ideological function, the rock musicians' pursuit of "authentic self-expression (*ziwo biaoxian*) and emotional release (*xuanxie*) in the face of oppression (*yayi*)" is not only shared by but also physically embodied in many Sixth Generation works.[26] By featuring Cui Jian as both a star in and a producer of *Beijing Bastards*, Zhang Yuan was quick to forge an alliance between rock music and cinematic rebellion in China. Other young directors quickly followed in their own explorations of this thematic link of rock music as an expression of alienation from and opposition to the mainstream. Lu Xuechang, for instance, admits that he added the rock scenes in *The Making of Steel* precisely because a few previous titles by his classmates, including *Dirt* and *Weekend Lovers*, had done so.[27]

Second, in terms of its aesthetic practice, both the early rock musicians and the Sixth Generation directors emphasize collective performance not simply as a common ritual of release and resistance, but more as a process of "self-discovery and moral self-redefinition."[28] In *Beijing Bastards* and *Weekend Lovers*, the process of looking for one rehearsal site after another functions as an allegorical process of looking for a rebellious identity and a marginal place in a hostile, or at least unsympathetic, society. In *Dirt*, the recurring image of an uncomprehending crowd of neighbors outside the band's rehearsal site (an abandoned warehouse) constantly reminds the rock band of their alienation and isolation as a result of public disapproval.

Third, in terms of its institutional operation, the lack of state support for rock musicians and their subsequent reliance on private and foreign venues for performance are mirrored in the early practice of the Sixth Generation. Just as rock musicians have depended almost exclusively on the patronage of friends and foreign venues, so too have the young filmmakers sought private money to finance—and sometimes to distribute overseas—their early features. The unofficial or semiofficial channel of such operations serves to heighten the public perception of their avowed resistance to the establishment. Ironically, for these rebel artists in the 1990s, cultural marginalization and political censorship at home might quickly translate into financial support from abroad. A rock singer like Cui Jian could expect the financial support of multinational recording companies (often via Hong Kong and Taiwan) and proceed to convey his "authentic feelings" through rebellious rock.[29] Similarly, as an indispensable component of his "formulas for success," a young director like Zhang Yuan could use the government's latest ban on his film to generate more overseas investment money and more international fame for himself.[30] Since the late 1990s, this kind of transnational investment in "authentic" Chinese voices and images has constituted a notable trend of cultural production in postsocialist China.

In Jones's view, given the tightened censorship of the post-Tiananmen period, "the Chinese rock subculture has not reached the level of articulated *political* opposition, [but] the rock sensibility does hinge upon a clearly articulated, self-consciously held ideology of *cultural* opposition."[31] As demonstrated above, many early Sixth Generation films share such an ideology of cultural opposition. Although the nature of film production and distribution in China prohibited any direct treatment of the 1989 pro-democratic movement, which the young filmmakers' rock counterparts were able to allude to from time to time, the filmmakers turned to the Cultural Revolution as an allegorical reference. In one of its MTV images, *Dirt* shows the young Ye being paraded as a spy by her close friends. Similarly, in *Urban Love Affair* (Chengshi aiqing, 1997), Ah Nian (Xu Hongyu, b. 1965) includes dreamlike sequences of the Cultural Revolution in which the male lead remembers his parents' humiliation at the hands of the Red Guards. In another little-known film, *Yellow Goldfish*, the male lead is infatuated with the revolutionary ballet *The*

Red Detachment of Women that was restaged for nostalgic public consumption in the 1990s.

The Sixth Generation's revisiting of the chaotic decade in cryptic, fragmented, and surreal images forms a sharp contrast to the Fifth Generation's lavish, full-scale dramatization of the Cultural Revolution. *Farewell, My Concubine* (Bawang bieji, 1993; dir. Chen Kaige), *The Blue Kite* (Lan fengzheng, 1993; dir. Tian Zhuangzhuang), and *To Live* (Huozhe, 1994; dir. Zhang Yimou) were released when many early Sixth Generation filmmakers were struggling with their debut features. What is interesting here is how the younger generation explains their perceived differences. Just as their rock counterparts claim for their music a kind of truthfulness missing in other forms of popular music,[32] the young directors tend to insist on the "authenticity" of their cinematic vision as a distinctive marker. Zhang Yuan, for example, distances himself from the Fifth Generation as follows: "Our thinking is completely different . . . They are intellectual youths . . . [who] went through the Cultural Revolution . . . We don't . . . I don't like being subjective, and I want my films to be objective. It's objectivity that'll empower me."[33]

However, considering the possibility that the Fifth Generation's rebellious attitude may prove to be more symbolic posturing than ideological opposition,[34] the extensive use of rock as a subversive form of resistance must not obscure the other dimensions of the artistic pursuits of the Sixth Generation. The framing soundtrack of the Beatles song in *Dirt*, for instance, functions as much as an intensification of nostalgia for lost youth as an evocation of a rebellious spirit through a European rock musical tradition. In this context, it is worth remembering that even Cui Jian's songs like "A Piece of Red Cloth" contain a large measure of nostalgia and self-confession.[35]

In addition to rebellion (in terms of an explosive outcry) and nostalgia (a sentimental retrospection), the concept of monologue (an implosive introspection) appears to be a third form of aesthetic expression preferred by several Sixth Generation directors. The male artist in *The Days*, after losing his wife and his own creative energy, confines himself in his studio and is reduced almost to lunacy in which he repeats and imitates his own gestures in a mechanical manner. *Postman* (Youchai, 1995; dir. He Yi) continues this representation of monologue and solitude, this time featuring a taciturn postman who takes pleasure—which borders on autoeroticism—in opening the letters in his charge and prying into others' secrets. In *Rainclouds over Wushan* another reticent character, a socially and professionally secluded signalman, acts out the meaninglessness of life in a mountain town. As these films elaborate the theme of oppression—a target of the rock musicians' outcry—in its various social, political, and psychological manifestations, the atmosphere of silence and suffocation can sometimes reach the point of implosion—an emotional discharge that aims to expose the truth behind disguise, hypocrisy, and pretension.

As Jones observes in his discussion of Chinese rock music in comparison with Euro-American subcultures: "This rebellion is invariably met with outrage, stiff resistance, and eventually, co-optation from the dominant culture."[36] In choosing to work within the studio system, many young directors were even more restricted than their rock counterparts and were under pressure not only to tone down their antisocial sentiments but also to disguise their oppositional stance by adding a token "repentance" of their rebellious adolescent years. To clear censorship, *Weekend Lovers* adds a final disclaimer announcing that all of the transgressive acts in the film took place years before and that the characters have changed since then. A different kind of disclaimer is conveyed by the female voice-over in *Dirt*, through which Ye passes judgment on the characters' "childish" behavior and pays lip service to law and order: "Weidong was correct . . . all of us acted just like kids back then." On the one hand, disclaimers like these might also be seen as a sure sign of co-optation, an index to what went on behind the scene that might have eventually helped such films pass strict censorship, albeit not without years of waiting and numerous cuts and revisions.[37] On the other hand, however, as material witness to the historical existence of a rebellious spirit that the Sixth Generation held in high regard, disclaimers like these symbolically serve as a tactical indictment of political oppression.

In light of this we might reassess the seeming irrelevance of Mao's quotation at the beginning of *Dirt*. By emphasizing the eventual triumph of time—"Hope is rested on your shoulders"—the film in effect has staged a subversion of superimposed disclaimers that the main characters have outgrown their adolescent rebellion. In short, their disclaimers work best as a tactic of survival in the repressive sociopolitical environment, for they could anticipate that their young age itself would guarantee their future success in accordance with the logic of Mao's quotation—that is, in the final analysis the world belongs to the young.

Unlike Jones's choice of the term "subculture," Geremie Barmé prefers to use the term "nonofficial culture" to cover a wide range of urban youth culture, counterculture, and dissident culture, to which rock music and some early Sixth Generation films certainly belong. Since "nonofficial culture can also be spoken of as a parallel or even *parasite* culture . . . it is neither nonofficial nor necessarily antiofficial," and for China's cultural scene of the 1990s "the term *nonmainstream* or *underculture* was more appropriate."[38] As Barmé contends, an "underculture" in postsocialist China cannot be simply oppositional to the "overculture" sponsored by the state, because this is a state "whose gravitational pull is often all too irresistible and that has itself undergone an extraordinary transformation."[39] The result of combined efforts of censorship and co-optation is the mutual interdependence of the mainstream and the marginal in a distinctively new phase of postsocialism in China: "Both have matured together and used each other, feeding each other's needs and developing ever new coalitions, understandings, and compromises."[40]

By 1999, the government was ready to promote a newly "reformed" Sixth Generation. In November 1999, the editorial office of *Film Art* (Dianying yishu) organized a critical forum on "young directors," a term judiciously chosen to distance if not dissolve the rebellious connotation of the "Sixth Generation." Among the official sponsors of the forum were the China Film Association (Zhongguo dianyingjia xiehui), the Beijing-based China Film Group (Zhongguo dianying jituan), and the Beijing Film Studio. Several of the directors mentioned above and a few first-timers sent films to the forum. Ah Nian sent *Call Me* (Huwo, 1999), Huo Jianqi sent *Postmen in the Mountains* (Nashan naren nagou, 1998; winner of the Best Film at the 1999 Golden Rooster Awards), Li Hong (b. 1974) sent *Tutor* (Banni gaofei, 1998), Lu Xuechang sent *A Lingering Face* (Feichang xiari, 1999), Wang Quan'an (b. 1965) sent *Lunar Eclipse* (Yueshi, 1999), Wang Rui sent *Sky Leopards* (Chongtian feibao, 1999), Wang Xiaoshuai sent *A Dream House* (Menghuan tianyuan, 1999), and Zhang Yang sent *Shower* (Xizao, 1999).[41] Zhang Yuan's *Seventeen Years* (Guonian huijia, 1999) was originally included on the invitation list, but the film's earlier entry in an international film festival without due procedure probably cost him a last-minute cancellation. Nevertheless, *Seventeen Years* opened in Beijing in January 2000 as scheduled, and the public showing of his films for the first time in China created some anxiety in the Western press.[42]

Technically, several of the films invited to the Beijing forum belong to a group that emerged in the late 1990s—some of whom, like Zhang Yang, Jin Chen (b. 1970), and Shi Runjiu (b. 1969), graduated from the Central Drama Academy.[43] These newcomers do not have the Fifth Generation's heavy burden of historical consciousness, nor do they share their immediate predecessors' taste in alienation and narcissism. Ni Zhen has examined the work of the directors on the new commercial films such as *Spicy Love Soup* (Aiqing malatang, 1998; dir. Zhang Yang) and *A Beautiful New World* (Meili xin shijie, 1999; dir. Shi Runjiu), and he sums up their distinctive features as follows: First, they discard tragic sentiments and embrace an optimistic outlook. Second, they emphasize narrative and plot and provide a visual therapy for the troubled life. Third, they prefer conventional camera work, bright colors, and a smooth flow of images typical of TV commercials.[44] Produced by Imar Film Co. Ltd., a joint venture managed by the American producer Peter Loehr (Luo Yi as known in China, b. 1967), and funded in part by Taiwan's Tower Records, Zhang's and Shi's works adopt new strategies in film production, distribution, and exhibition. Their market success is due as much to their creativity as to the new producer-centered model of management.

Lacking a better designation, some young directors favor the general terms "city" or "urban" (*chengshi*) as more appropriate for themselves. In an interview in 2000, Lu Xuechang makes it clear that although the so-called Sixth Generation directors did not have a coherent program, there is a commonality of their work in its urban character—they were born and grew up in the city, and they naturally tell urban stories.[45] Similarly, Guan Hu believes that their generation has an advantage over the Fifth Generation because their urban sensibilities are more "authentic" and their films are more "urbanized."[46] While their repeated claims to authenticity, truthfulness, and objectivity must be subject to further scrutiny, the urban focus surely stands out as a rallying point for most Sixth Generation directors.

Differences, however, persist between the earlier directors and the newcomers. On the one hand, as represented by Zhang Yang, the newcomers seem to prefer bright colors, glossy images, famous stars, bittersweet sentiments, and mostly happy endings in the increasingly affluent city. On the other hand, as suggested by Wang Xiaoshuai in *So Close to Paradise* (Biandan, guniang,

Poster for *A Beautiful New World:*
"A visual therapy for the
troubled life."

1998), the old-timers retain individual styles and seek to expose the sinister sides of urban life (e.g., kidnap, rape, murder, prostitution, and the illegal blood market). In their confrontation with social problems, films like *So Close to Paradise* subtly convey a lingering sense of pessimism reminiscent of the directors' earlier, more rebellious works.

As noted above, there is no uniform program in this generation as far as their strategies are concerned. In their early phase, the rebellious spirit—embodied in rock music—seemed to rule the scene. Alternatively, they have chosen a more subdued version of protest—as exemplified in *The Days* and *Postman*—to express their alienation from and disillusionment with the new political-economic regime and their adolescent male subjectivity in crisis. Or more recently, as in *Shower*, they use nostalgia as an engaging method to communicate their visions to a larger audience. By the late 1990s, the development of the new market economy had compelled almost all of these marginal or self-marginalized directors to reenter or at least to reconnect with the mainstream. Like Wang Xiaoshuai and Zhang Yuan, He Yi was willing to make his *Butterfly Smile* (Hudie de meng, 2001) within the system.

But again we see noticeable differences among members of the group. Whereas the younger filmmakers like Zhang Yang and Shi Runjiu embrace commercial filmmaking by producing new social fantasies, the directors associated with the Beijing Film Studio have sought a compromised route whereby their artistic visions and box office concerns can coexist. Yet nothing is fixed at a time of rapid transformation, and the auteur status is so attractive that Zhang Yang has changed his style in *Quitting* (Zuotian, 2001), which explores a drug addict's rehabilitation and in so doing harks back to the underground-marginal tradition in the first half of the 1990s. What is more, the experimental art film is not yet passé—as was the contention of many leading critics in China leading up to the release of *Lunar Eclipse*, a surprise debut feature that challenges critics' ability to decode cinematic doublings in a postsocialist urban milieu.[47] The doubling as an effective means of exploring the ever-changing urban milieus is also successfully implemented in *Suzhou River* (Suzhou he, 2000; dir. Lou Ye), an internationally acclaimed film that focuses on Shanghai.[48] What is encouraging is that the members of the new Urban Generation have extended their cameras far beyond Beijing and Shanghai as the two dominant tropes in urban imagination.

At this point I would like to offer two reminders. First, the quest of the new Urban Generation as delineated above does not mean that the search for ever-changing urban images in postsocialist China is exclusive to this generation. Directors from other groups or generations have since the early 1990s continued to project their own urban visions. Ning Ying's first two Beijing tales, *For Fun* (Zhaole, 1992) and *On the Beat* (Minjing gushi, 1995), for example, exhibit an entirely different aesthetic dimension of urban cinema in China, one that is at once upbeat, humorous, and humane (see Shuqin Cui's essay in this volume). As a latecomer in the Fifth Generation, Xia Gang has directed melodramatic tales set in the city such as *Yesterday's Wine* (Yu wangshi ganbei, 1995) and *Life on a Tune* (Shengming ruge, 1997). Meanwhile, even Zhang Yimou has directed lively urban tales like *Keep Cool* (Youhua haohao shuo, 1997), in which he appears in a cameo as a migrant rural worker in the city. Huang Jianxin, another veteran urban director, has released the much-acclaimed *Tell Your Secret* (Shuochu ni de mimi, 2000) and *Marriage Certificate* (Jiehun zheng, aka Shuishuo wo bu zaihu, 2001), two dramas of contemporary bourgeois life marked by sentimentality. Indeed, the era of postsocialism—especially in the decade since Tiananmen—has provided enormous possibilities for the new

Urban Generation as much as for older directors, and their visions of new cityscapes and new urban desires call for our continued investigation.

My second reminder concerns the emergence in the new millennium of an even newer group of talents. Just as the 1999 *Film Art* forum announced the official acceptance of the new Urban Generation, in 2002 *Contemporary Cinema* (Dangdai dianying), another Beijing-based academic journal, extended the parameters of the new directors to include twenty-one debut features released in 2001 and in the first half of 2002. Supported by articles from the new directors (not all of whom are young),[49] as well as from leading critics and industry leaders, the editors of *Contemporary Cinema* declare that the new millennium is witness to a phenomenon unprecedented in Chinese film history with the exception of 1979 when three generations of directors embarked on filmmaking after a decade of delay during the Cultural Revolution. Like previous works from the urban generation, the new films are mostly low-budget productions (averaging two million yuan per title). But, unlike their predecessors, the majority of the new films are produced by private companies (in part because the Film Bureau now permits private companies to finance production without necessarily using state-run studio labels), and many new directors themselves have been involved in the processes of screen-writing, financing, production, promotion, and distribution.[50]

A willingness to participate in mainstream filmmaking is similarly reflected in the new directors' preference for contemporary urban life as their subject matter. Contrary to the tales of personal frustration and symbolic rebellion told by the early Sixth Generation, the new directors address social issues without always compromising their artistic visions, and in some cases they also demonstrate a high level of sophistication in making genre films. The film *Roots and Branches* (Wode xiongdi jiemei, 2001; dir. Yu Zhong)—a tear-jerker melodrama similar to the Xie Jin model, featuring the Hong Kong star Gigi Leung (Liang Yongqi) and the erstwhile rock star Cui Jian as the soon-to-die father—became number three in the 2001 domestic top-ten box office list.[51] At the 2002 Beijing College Students Film Festival, Lu Chuan's (b. 1971) *The Missing Gun* (Xunqiang, 2002), a Sichuan-dialect detective film mixing humor and suspense, won the award for best debut film. In addition, *Spring Subway* (Kaiwang chuntian de ditie, 2002; dir. Zhang Yibai), a relationship film set against rapidly changing urban configurations dominated by the subway trains, was voted as the audience's favorite.

What happened in the first three years of the new millennium is that the members of the new Urban Generation, including those "young" and "new" directors promoted by *Film Art* and *Contemporary Cinema,* have chosen to focus their cameras in a noncondescending way on the everyday as the primary experiential or emotional realm of ordinary people. Following the success of *A Love of Blueness* (Lanse aiqing, 2000), a romantic story mixing suspense with avant-garde elements, Huo Jianqi directed *Life Show* (Shenghuo xiu, 2002), a sympathetic portrayal of a divorcèe restaurant owner in a city night market who is caught between the ruins of her traditional family and the uncertainty of her emotional and financial future.[52] Likewise concentrated on ordinary urbanites, *Cala, My Dog* (Kala shi tiao gou, 2002; dir. Lu Xuechang) features the actor Ge You as an otherwise good-for-nothing factory worker who acts as an antihero in his pathetic efforts to save his pet dog in Beijing. Consistent with a recent trend toward sentimentality, as illustrated by Huang Jianxin's newest urban films as well as the film *Together with You* (He ni zai yiqi, 2001; dir. Chen Kaige), the new Urban Generation seeks truth or what is "real" (*zhenshi*) in the ever-changing life of postsocialism. Zhang Yibai, despite his experimental visual images, claims that his *Spring Subway* aims to capture the truths in life as well as in emotions: "Fashion (*shishang*) is not the worshipping of the city nor the fetishistic exhibition of skyscrapers, neon lights, pretty dresses, and luxury cars . . . Rather, fashion must rest on the basis of truth."[53]

CONCLUSION: CO-OPTATION AND COMPLICITY
IN THE NEW MILLENNIUM

In the preceding text I establish that the notion of truth has been appropriated as a strategic position by the new Urban Generation; in light of this I wish to refer back to the tripartite division of Chinese filmmaking described at the beginning of this essay as well as reconfigure the political economics of postsocialism in the age of the World Trade Organization (WTO), which approved China's membership as of December 2001. To the tripartite division I would add "marginality" as exemplified in underground films, with its explicit claims to truth and reality, as an emergent player. In a schematic way, as shown in the accompanying diagram, we can now rearrange art, politics, capital, and marginality as four competing players and speculate on their modes of engagement and combination.

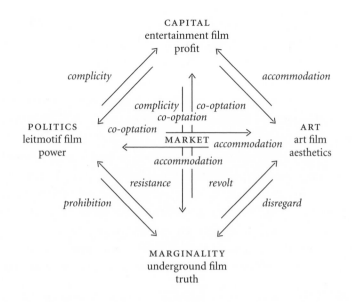

CAPITAL
entertainment film
profit

complicity

complicity | | co-optation

co-optation

accommodation

POLITICS
leitmotif film
power

co-optation

MARKET accommodation

ART
art film
aesthetics

accommodation

resistance | | revolt

prohibition

disregard

MARGINALITY
underground film
truth

First, characterized by imagination and generated by creativity, *art* pursues aesthetics and prestige and draws sufficient funding from private and overseas sources to produce art films targeted at relatively small (*xiaozhong*), educated audiences at home and abroad. Second, characterized by power and sustained by censorship, *politics* pursues propaganda and domination and draws on state subsidies to produce leitmotif films at a huge financial loss and impose them on the masses (*qunzhong*) nationwide. Third, characterized by money and motivated by the market, *capital* pursues profits and domination and draws considerable funding from private and sometimes state sources to produce entertainment films targeted at mass audiences (*dazhong*). Finally, characterized by "truth" and inspired by dissent, *marginality* pursues reality and prestige and draws low-budget funding from private and overseas sources to produce "underground" films circulated abroad and, occasionally, at home through irregular channels.

What happened after the mid-1990s is that all four players now revolve around the *market*—domestic as well as overseas—as their center stage and, except for the nexus of politics and marginality, there have been increasing accommodations and compromises between various players. While politics readjusts its strategic relations to art from all-out domination to sugarcoated co-optation, art may have willingly accommodated politics to such an extent as to be at times entirely complicit with official ideology, as in *My 1919* (Wode 1919, 1999; dir. Huang Jianzhong) and *The National Anthem* (Guoge, 1999; dir. Wu Ziniu). Similarly, capital also changes its strategic position on art from domination to co-optation, and in some cases the lure of prestige and profit sharing has compelled art to accommodate capital, as in *Beijing Bicycle* (Shiqi sui de danche, 2001; dir. Wang Xiaoshuai), or become complicit with—if not dependent on—capital, as in *Hero* (Yingxiong, 2002; dir. Zhang Yimou).[54] The nexus of art and marginality is the least stable element of all. Whereas from the establishment's standpoint, art tends to disregard marginality's claim to truth, marginality pretends to revolt against art by exposing offensive pictures of postsocialist reality.[55] Sometimes a playful combination of or compromise between art and marginality may surface, as in *Lunar Eclipse* and *Suzhou River*, both of which verge on underground filmmaking but also are acclaimed as artistic successes (see Zhang Zhen's essay in this volume). Indeed, although by definition marginality must show contempt for capital, in actual operation it can accommodate capital when capital has co-opted it through investment in production of a special type of "Chinese" reality deemed more truthful than that represented by art and politics, as in *Postman* and *Platform* (Zhantai, 2000; dir. Jia Zhangke).[56]

The most striking change since the mid-1990s occurred in the nexus of politics and capital. Under the pretext of sharing profits and resources, politics and capital have entered a complicit partnership, as with the "private" company named Forbidden City (Zijincheng), which at once seeks to achieve political correctness and maximum market effects.[57] Two commercial pictures from Forbidden City, *A Time to Remember* (Hongse lianren, 1998; dir. Ye Daying) and *Be There or Be Square* (Bujian busan, 1999; dir. Feng Xiaogang), are early products of such politics-capital partnership. As an exception to the rules of engagement and compromise, the nexus of politics and marginality is the only site where dissent and resistance are possible. But as a result of prohibition by politics and dismissal by art, the impact of marginality and its pictures of reality have been largely felt overseas at international film festivals, as, for example, with *Devils on the Doorstep* (Guizi laile, 2000; dir. Jiang Wen). Now that private capital can easily lure potential players of marginality to art, the future of marginality as a site (or "parasite" as Barmé puts it) of dissent and resistance remains uncertain. The lack of engagement with the domestic market also renders marginality an ineffective player in the political economy of Chinese filmmaking in the new millennium, which is once again dominated by a tripartite division of—or, more precisely, a new alliance of—art, politics, and capital.

Deng Guanghui, in his overview of 1990s Chinese filmmaking, locates a pattern of confluence whereby "new mainstream films" (*xinzhuliu dianying*) command art films, entertainment films, and Newborn Generation films. Deng notices the Newborn Generation's movement toward the new mainstream in terms of narrative, narration, and visual styles; entertainment films' preference for the pleasure principle over sensitive subjects like sex and violence; and art films' descent from the ivory tower of cultural critique to the backstage of personal fantasies.[58] To rephrase Deng's position, we may argue that co-optation and complicity are now integral to the dominant pattern of postsocialist filmmaking.

While I have reservations about the term "new mainstream film,"[59] I concur with Deng that those new changes since the mid-1990s have reconfigured the political economy of Chinese filmmaking. "In other words," as Dai Jinhua contends, "*marginal* cultural forces banished during the social turmoil of the eighties and nineties now gathered strength along with other exiles and began the *march toward the center.*"[60] Dai's contrastive questions regarding the future are unsettling, to say the least: "Is the margin undertaking a successful march to occupy the center? Or has the omnipresent cultural industry and its market engineered a takeover? Is a new generation of filmmakers injecting vigor into the shaky Chinese cinema or is the system overwhelming the feeble individual artist?"[61] Even though Dai hopes that neither of her scenarios is the case, I believe that signs from the new millennium indicate the speedy consolidation of the postsocialist system of filmmaking and the increased dependency or complicity on the part of film artists, who have been largely institutionalized or professionalized within the system and who are being swept into rather than "marching" toward the center—the center of the market.

Ostensibly, the necessity of survival for Chinese cinema in the WTO age has been a driving force behind recent cases of the strategic alliance of art, politics, and capital. The state has implemented further reform measures of horizontal and vertical integration in media industries, launching new film groups based on the existing regional studios on the one hand, and forming media conglomerates by merging film studios, theater chains, TV and radio stations, and advising companies on the other.[62] Institutionally, the current industry restructuring has created urgent needs for more accommodation and compromise on the part of all players involved, and enterprising directors have gladly seized opportunities to assert their presence—if not yet their own voice—in the market. The press has also devoted much attention to the new Urban Generation and has envisioned its members as vanguards in China's confrontation with the projected double or triple increase from 2002 onward in the annual import of Hollywood blockbusters.

Many directors from the Sixth Generation or the new Urban Generation have remained optimistic with regard to the future of Chinese cinema in the age of the WTO. In response to questions from the magazine *Popular Cinema* (Dazhong dianying) in 2000, Wang Xiaoshuai reasons that Hollywood will not impact Chinese art directors too much and that Chinese cinema should develop more "Eastern flavors." Zhang Yuan perceives Hollywood imports as "cultural invasion" and posits that young directors, with their talent and styles, will become the most promising group of Chinese filmmakers in the decade to come. Guan Hu, who since *Dirt* has directed *Tales of the Ancient City* (Gucheng tonghua, 1999) and *The Beauty's Eyes* (Xishi yan, 2002), admits that a consensus has been formed that a film must first and foremost offer "a pleasing look" (*haokan*) and that a director will be deserted if he or she refuses to consider market factors. With two recent box office successes to his credit, Zhang Yang puts it more bluntly: a "good film" (*hao dianying*) by definition carries commercial values.[63] However, just as is the case with terms such as authenticity, objectivity, reality, and truth, these directors have refrained from defining what they mean by a good film or a pleasing look. In this sense, Zhang Yimou may be right when he considers the Sixth Generation's aesthetics to be too expanded—"as if there were a lot of different standards and contrasts"—and hence responsible for its conspicuous lack of groundbreaking works.[64] Several critics have likewise noticed such lack in the debut films of the new millennium.

Arguably, the postsocialist market in the WTO age might account for the inconsistency of artistic styles (from avant-garde to melodramatic), ideological positions (from radical to conservative), genre experiments (from comedy to crime thriller), and thematic choices (from misplaced love to social criticism) in the new Urban Generation. In spite of their apparent shortcomings, however, the sheer numbers of new directors who have emerged in the new millennium, along with the eye-catching quality of some of their debut films, provide enough reason for optimism. To rephrase Mao's Cultural Revolution quotation, "The world belongs to the young"—although this time around the world is no longer either an isolated red kingdom awash in political idealism or a self-exiled marginal space imploded with youthful rage but rather one subject to the force fields of power—the power of capital, politics, art, and hopefully marginality—in postsocialist filmmaking.

NOTES

1. For a survey of the 1990s, see Yingjin Zhang, *Chinese National Cinema* (London: Routledge, 2004), 281–96.

2. Paul Pickowicz, "Huang Jianxin and the Notion of Postsocialism," in *New Chinese Cinemas: Forms, Identities, Politics*, ed. Nick Browne, Paul Pickowicz, Vivian Sobchack, and Esther Yau (New York: Cambridge University Press, 1994), 58–59.

3. Ibid., 60.

4. Ibid., 80.

5. Ibid., 83, 60.

6. Ibid., 61–62.

7. Paul Pickowicz, "Velvet Prisons and the Political Economy of Chinese Film-making," in *Urban Spaces in Contemporary China: The Potential for Autonomy and Community in Post-Mao China*, ed. Deborah Davis, Richard Kraus, Barry Naughton, and Elizabeth Perry (New York: Cambridge University Press, 1995), 193–220.

8. Chris Berry and Mary Ann Farquhar, "Post-Socialist Strategies: An Analysis of *Yellow Earth* and *Black Cannon Incident*," in *Cinematic Landscapes: Observations on the Visual Arts and Cinema of China and Japan*, ed. Linda Ehrlich and David Desser (Austin: University of Texas Press, 1994), 84.

9. Arif Dirlik and Xudong Zhang, "Introduction: Postmodernism and China," *boundary 2* 24, no. 3 (1997): 4.

10. Xudong Zhang, "Epilogue: Postmodernism and Post-Socialist Society—Historicizing the Present," in *Postmodernism and China*, ed. Arif Dirlik and Xudong Zhang (Durham, N.C.: Duke University Press, 2000), 437–38.

11. See Xudong Zhang, *Chinese Modernism in the Era of Reforms: Cultural Fever, Avant-Garde Fiction, and the New Chinese Cinema* (Durham, N.C.: Duke University Press, 1997); Xudong Zhang, ed., *Whither China? Intellectual Politics in Contemporary China* (Durham, N.C.: Duke University Press, 2001); and Sheldon H. Lu, *China, Transnational Visuality, Global Postmodernity* (Stanford, Calif.: Stanford University Press, 2001).

12. It is worth noting Dai Jinhua's caution: "But being different does not in itself say anything about the Sixth Generation. This is precisely the cultural absurdity of the 'Sixth Generation'" (quoted in *Cinema and Desire: Feminist Marxism and*

Cultural Politics in the Work of Dai Jinhua, ed. Jing Wang and Tani Barlow [London: Verso, 2002], 78). In other words, Dai suspects that the artists may have generated differences so as to meet expectations from the West.

13. Han Xiaolei, "Dui diwudai de wenhua tuwei: Houwudai de geren dianying xianxiang" [A cultural breakaway from the Fifth Generation: The phenomenon of individualist film in the post–Fifth Generation], *Dianying yishu*, no. 2 (1995): 58–56; and Yin Hong, "Zai jiafeng zhong zhangda: Zhongguo dalu xinsheng dai de dianying shijie" [Growing up between the fissures: The film world of the Newborn Generation], *Ershiyi shiji* 49 (October 1998): 88–93.

14. See Lydia H. Liu, "*Beijing Sojourners in New York:* Postsocialism and the Question of Ideology in Global Media Culture," *positions* 7, no. 3 (winter 1999): 763–97.

15. For obvious political reasons, Zhang Yuan, like many other members of his generation, prefers the term "independent filmmaker" to the labels "underground" or "dissident" films; see Wang and Barlow, *Cinema and Desire*, 90; and Jenny Lau, "Globalization and Youthful Subculture: The Chinese Sixth-Generation Films at the Dawn of the New Century," in *Multiple Modernities: Cinemas and Popular Media in Transcultural East Asia*, ed. Jenny Lau (Philadelphia: Temple University Press, 2003), 13–27. See also Shuqin Cui, "Working from the Margins: Urban Cinema and Independent Directors in Contemporary China," *Post Script* 20, nos. 2–3 (2000): 77–91.

16. Yu Yunke, "Toufa luanle? Mei luan!" [Disheveled hair? No], *Dazhong dianying*, no. 1 (1995): 32–33. It is worth noting that many Sixth Generation directors had experience in shooting MTV pieces before their film debuts. Zhang Yuan, for instance, directed music videos for artists like Ai Jing and Cui Jian. See Geremie R. Barmé, *In the Red: On Contemporary Chinese Culture* (New York: Columbia University Press, 1999), 195; and Bérénice Reynaud, "New Visions/New Chinas: Video-Art, Documentation, and the Chinese Modernity in Question," in *Resolutions: Contemporary Video Practices*, ed. Michael Renov and Erika Suderburg (Minneapolis: University of Minnesota Press, 1996), 238. Many other directors are also involved in shooting TV commercials.

17. Railroad tracks, along with crossing junctions and signal lights, simultaneously suggest an otherwise definitively charted direction of travel and the paths not taken or abandoned, and have thus become a recurring motif among members of this generation. In addition to *Dirt*, where Kong Lin walks along railroad tracks, two of Lu Xuechang's films depict protagonists working near the railroad tracks in Beijing: a young apprentice in *The Making of Steel* and an ordinary petlover in *Cala, My Dog*.

18. Stephanie Hemelryk Donald argues that the Sixth Generation directors tend to displace male anxiety onto the female body and that abortion not only functions as a metaphor for disguising the empty anarchy of male subjectivity but also reduces the woman to her reproductive capacity alone (see Stephanie Hemelryk Donald, *Public Secrets, Public Spaces: Cinema and Civility in China* [Lanham, Md.:

Rowman and Littlefield, 2000], 106–19). Surely, male anxiety over the notion of the pregnant woman—a body out of male control—runs consistently from *Beijing Bastards* and *The Days* through *No Visit after the Divorce* and *Urban Love Affair* and then all the way to *Mr. Zhao* (Zhao xiansheng, 1998; dir. Lü Yue) and *Platform*.

19. Drawing the sartorial lexicon from their Western counterparts, the Chinese male rock musicians typically wear long hair, torn jeans, T-shirts, studded leather jewelry, and sunglasses. See Andrew F. Jones, *Like a Knife: Ideology and Genre in Contemporary Chinese Popular Music* (Ithaca, N.Y.: East Asia Program, Cornell University, 1992), 118.

20. Han, "Dui diwudai de wenhua tuwei," 61.

21. Lü Xiaoming observes the relevance of the Tiananmen event of 1989, when many of these young directors experienced for the first time in their life something close to a mass revolution movement. If their acute sense of alienation and disillusion originated in part from this experience, then their screen rebellion might be seen as a belated revisit to this hidden trauma. See Lü Xiaoming, "90 niandai Zhongguo dianying jingguan zhiyi 'diliu dai' jiqi zhiyi" [An inquiry into "the Sixth Generation" as a Chinese film spectacle in the 1990s], *Dianying yishu*, no. 3 (1999): 23–28.

22. The released DVD version has changed all of the original uses of the "Hey Jude" song to an Italian opera soundtrack, presumably to avoid the potential subversion symbolized by the Beatles song. Ironically, in the final credit sequence, the Chinese subtitles of the Beatles lyrics remain to mock (or even to protest, in light of the case) the irrationality of film censorship. The government's suspicion of rock music was obvious in this case, as I elaborate later in this essay.

23. Jones, *Like a Knife*, 4.

24. See Barmé, *In the Red*, 360–61; Jones, *Like a Knife*, 127.

25. Jones, *Like a Knife*, 2. As the song's lyric goes: "This guitar in my hands is like a knife . . . I want to cut at your hypocrisy till I see some truth" (97).

26. Ibid., 91.

27. Wu Guanping, "Fang qingnian daoyan Lu Xuechang" [An interview with the young director Lu Xuechang], *Dianying yishu*, no. 4 (2000): 64.

28. Jones, *Like a Knife*, 102.

29. Ibid., pp. 100–101.

30. Barmé, *In the Red*, 194–96.

31. Jones, *Like a Knife*, 117.

32. Ibid., 89.

33. Quoted in Reynaud, "New Visions/New Chinas," 236.

34. Hence, Barmé characterizes Zhang Yuan as an example of "bankable dissent" or "packaged dissent" in postsocialist China (*In the Red*, 188).

35. Jones, *Like a Knife*, 138–42.

36. Ibid., 117.

37. It took three years for *The Making of Steel* to clear censorship. Another case of an extensive wait for censorship clearance is Wang Xiaoshuai's *So Close to Paradise*, previously known as *Vietnam Girl* (Yuenan guniang).

38. Barmé, *In the Red*, xiv (emphasis added).

39. Barmé himself does not seem to endorse the term "postsocialism," but at least he once refers to "the post–Sino-socialist cultural palette" (*In the Red*, xx).

40. Ibid., xv.

41. For a complete list of the invited films, see Yingjin Zhang, *Screening China: Critical Interventions, Cinematic Reconfigurations, and the Transnational Imaginary in Contemporary Chinese Cinema* (Ann Arbor: Center for Chinese Studies, University of Michigan, 2001), 327–28.

42. Partly because Zhang Yuan was willing to shoot *Seventeen Years* with government endorsement, his other films like *Mama* (Mama, 1991) and *Crazy English* (Fengkuang Yingyu, 1999) were also approved for public release. This unexpected turn for an "outlawed" filmmaker prompted Western journalists like Eric Eckholm to ask: "Will he always be able to find topics that excite him and are acceptable to the censors?" (Eckholm, "Feted Abroad, and No Longer Banned in Beijing," *New York Times*, December 16, 1999.

43. Jin Chen directed *Love in the Internet Generation* (Wangluo shidai de aiqing, 1999).

44. Ni Zhen, "Shouwang xinsheng dai" [Expectations for the Newborn Generation], *Dianying yishu*, no. 4 (1999): 72. For more discussion on the newcomers, see Han Xiaolei, "Tuwei hou de wenhua piaoyi" [Cultural drifting after the breakaway], *Dianying yishu*, no. 5 (1999): 58–65.

45. Wu Guanping, "Fang qingnian daoyan Lu Xuechang," 65.

46. Quoted in Li Yan, "wTo laile women zenme ban?" [What should we do when the wTo comes?], *Dazhong dianying*, no. 6 (2000): 53.

47. See *Dazhong dianying*, ed., "Xinren xinzuo *Yueshi*" [A new work from a newcomer: *Lunar Eclipse*], *Dazhong dianying*, no. 4 (2000): 12–13.

48. See Jerome Silbergeld, *Hitchcock with a Chinese Face: Cinematic Doubles, Oedipal Triangles, and China's Moral Voice* (Seattle: University of Washington Press, 2004), 11–46; and Zhang Zhen's essay in this volume.

49. The age difference among these new directors is estimated at as much as twenty years. One of the oldest is Meng Jinghui, a renowned drama director whose experimentalist debut film is *Chicken Poet* (Xiang jimao yiyang fei, 2002). Like many earlier members of the urban generation, several new directors have formal ties with the Beijing Film Academy and the Central Drama Academy. Those from the Beijing Film Academy include Li Honghe (b. 1969), Lu Chuan, Luo Jian (b. 1967), and Yu Zhong (all four from graduate classes in directing); Li Jixian (b. 1962), Shi Jiandu, and Zhang Fanfan (b. 1973) (all three from art design); Chen Daming, Xu Jinglei, and Zhao-Yan Guozhang (b. 1966) (all three from acting); Teng Huatao (literature); Wu Bing (management); and Li Chunbo and Li Hong (training class). Those from Central Drama include Ma Xiaoying (directing), Yu Zhong (acting), and Zhang Yibai (literature).

50. *Dandai dianying,* ed., "Xin shiji xin dao yan zongtan" [A forum on new directors in the new century], *Dangdai dianying,* no. 5 (2003): 8–33. The China Film Group, which now owns the Beijing Film Studio as a subsidiary, was behind the production or coproduction of ten out of twenty-one debut titles in 2001–2002.

51. With its estimated nationwide box office value at fifteen million yuan, *Roots and Branches* has been credited as 2001's top grosser because the year's first place, *The Big Shot's Funeral* (Dawan, 2000; dir. Feng Xiaogang), coproduced by Columbia Asia, had actually opened in December 2000 and the second place was a science and education (*kejiao*) documentary about the universe and humans.

52. *A Love of Blueness* won the prize for best director at the Huabiao Awards and at the Golden Rooster Awards as well as for best picture at the Beijing College Students Film Festival in 2000. *Life Show* won the best actress prize (for the role by Tao Hong) at the Golden Rooster, as well as best actress and best picture at the Shanghai International Film Festival in 2002.

53. Zhang Yibai, "Tongwang chuntian de wuge zhantai" [Five platforms in the subway to spring], *Dianying yishu* 2002, no. 6: 77.

54. *Beijing Bicycle* is a sentimental art film coproduced by Taiwan and France, whereas *Hero,* the highest-grossing work in Chinese film history, involved Beijing, Hong Kong, and Columbia's studio in Asia.

55. Zhang Yimou's words illustrate this tension between art and marginality: "The same youthful defiance exists in other walks of life too. This is also true with the Sixth Generation's rebellion. It is not clear whether the rebellion is against politics, or art forms, or art content, or older generations, or traditional aesthetics" (quoted in Frances Gateward, ed., *Zhang Yimou: Interviews* [Jackson: University Press of Mississippi, 2001], 153).

56. For the production of *Platform* Jia Zhangke received funding from Hu Tong Communications of Hong Kong, Bandai Entertainment of Japan, and Artcam of France. Somewhat ironically, Zhang Yimou, who had benefited tremendously from overseas funding in the early 1990s, complained about the young directors' complicity with capital in 1999: "The Sixth Generation was subject to practical considerations. It cannot be resisted: the need for money, the dilemma caused by censorship, and the awards at international film festivals" (quoted in Gateward, *Zhang Yimou,* 162).

57. I put "private" in quotation marks because Forbidden City was founded in 1996 exclusively with state money. Its total funding of 5.18 million yuan came from the following government units: Beijing TV Station (25.5 percent), Beijing TV Art Center (25.5 percent), Beijing Film Company (24.5 percent), and Beijing Culture and Arts Audio-Visual Press (24.5 percent). See Zhongguo dianying nianjian she, ed., *1997 Zhongguo dianying nianjian* [1997 China film book] (Beijing: Zhongguo dianying nianjian she, 1998), 342. After launching the ever-popular "new year's picture" (*hesui pian*), a comedy genre masterminded by Feng Xiaogang, Forbidden City has prospered in the postsocialist market economy.

58. Deng Guanghui, "Lun 90 niandai Zhongguo dianying de yiyi shengchan" [Production of meaning in 1990s Chinese cinema], *Dangdai dianying*, no. 1 (2001): 39.

59. For a critique of the Shanghai-based proposal for the "new mainstream film," see Zhang, *Screening China*, 324–31.

60. Wang and Barlow, *Cinema and Desire*, 85 (emphasis added).

61. Ibid., 97.

62. In addition to the large film corporation based in Beijing (the China Film Group), in Shanghai (the Shanghai Film Group), and in Changchun (the North China Film Group), the new millennium saw the establishment of the Northwest Film Group in Xi'an, the South China Film Group in Guangzhou, and the Southwest Film Group in Chengdu.

63. Li, "WTO laile women zenme ban?" 50–53.

64. Gateward, *Zhang Yimou*, 162.

the independent cinema of jia zhangke

From Postsocialist Realism

to a Transnational Aesthetic

JASON MCGRATH

I n a scene in Jia Zhangke's third major film, *Unknown Pleasures* (Ren xiaoyao, 2002), one of the characters browses through a selection of pirated video disks sold by a street vendor. He then asks for copies of *Xiao Wu* (1997), *Platform* (Zhantai, 2000), and *Love Will Tear Us Apart* (Tianshang renjian, 1999)—the former two of which are in fact the earlier feature films of Jia himself, while the latter was directed by his cinematographer, Yu Lik Wai. Consequently, when the vendor rebuffs the request and is then criticized for not stocking such films, the act constitutes an in-joke as well as a self-reflexive comment on the Chinese film market and the situation of filmmakers who work outside of the state-regulated studio system.

The scene in *Unknown Pleasures* relies on the viewer's knowledge of the director's previous films, with a further wink provided by the fact that the DVD shopper is none other than the character Xiao Wu, the eponymous protagonist of the movie that he is now attempting to buy. Although a foreign viewer may appreciate the joke and also perhaps sigh (with a hint of condescension) over the fact that the domestic Chinese audience is largely cut off from the very Chinese art cinema enjoyed by the international audience, viewers in China are likely to be implicated by the joke because most will see this scene only after the film has appeared in pirated DVD bins in Chinese cities. The irony here is not only that the viewers have succeeded where the character in *Unknown Pleasures* has failed, but also that they are tacitly congratulated for buying a pirated disk from which the filmmakers will gain no profit.[1] With this minor scenario, then, the director makes a metatextual reference to the conditions of production and distribution of his own films. By the time *Unknown Pleasures* was released, Jia had become one of the most prominent young directors from China recently to emerge and attract global attention. His films had obtained funding from elite production companies and government ministries in Japan and Europe, and major Western critics had pronounced him to be among the finest of the new directors and his films landmarks of Chinese cinema.[2] Within China, however, the same films could for the most part be seen only on pirated video disks, with viewings in their original formats limited to a handful of locally organized screenings in major cities.

In this chapter I will explore the rich thematics and aesthetics of Jia's films and place them in the context of both the domestic "underground" or independent film movement and the global art-cinema market. Jia's films offer a penetrating view into Chinese society in the postsocialist or reform era and make implicit claims regarding the nature of Chinese urban reality today and the ethics and aesthetics of its documentation and memory. It is generally agreed that Jia's films embody a bold new style of urban realism in contemporary Chinese cinema. However, I will argue that the realism of Jia's works must be understood as drawing upon two distinct sources. The first source is the broader indigenous movement of postsocialist realism that arose in both documentary and fiction filmmaking in China in the early 1990s. In many ways Jia's films continue, and even epitomize, the concerns and accomplishments of this movement. Nevertheless, the realism of his films must also be understood in the context of a second source, namely the tradition of international art cinema—in particular a type of aestheticized long-take realism that became prominent in the global film festival and art house circuit by the late 1990s. Of these two foundations of Jia's realism, the former is most evident in his early projects and short films, while the latter is exemplified by his epic *Platform*—which, not surprisingly, was the work that garnered the rave reviews from Western critics noted above. Consequently, while the director's career resists a narrative of a clear-cut successive progression from one form of realism to another, his films can nonetheless be understood as comprising, each to varying degrees, both an intervention into a specifically Chinese cultural discourse and a cultural commodity that appeals to contemporary global art film aesthetics.

INDEPENDENT CINEMA AND POSTSOCIALIST REALISM

Independent film production did not exist in the People's Republic of China until 1990, when Zhang Yuan's *Mama* pioneered the practice of producing films outside the official studio system and then entering them in international film festivals, which potentially generated the attention necessary to find funding for later projects.[3] Zhang Yuan himself was able to make a series of independent films that received partial funding and considerable attention from abroad despite being largely unseen in China as well as occasionally drawing the ire of the authorities. Other young directors who followed this path in the 1990s included Wang Xiaoshuai, He Jianjun, and, shortly later, Jia himself. However, the careers of these directors demonstrate not just the emergence of "independent" filmmaking but also the way such a practice, almost as a requirement of reaching any audience, will necessarily be drawn into cooperation with either the state studio system or the international production companies that supply the global art-cinema market.[4]

Jia's early career follows the model of Zhang Yuan not only in its independent mode of production but also in its filmmaking style, which can be described as postsocialist critical realism.[5] This aesthetic is postsocialist both in the sense of being the successor and a contrast to the previously dominant aesthetic of socialist realism and in the sense that it is a realism of the post-socialist condition. In the first respect, this style of realism directly contradicts the tenets of socialist realism, the remnants of which could still be seen in state media representations and officially sponsored, patriotic "main melody" (*zhuxuanlü*) films even well into the reform era. Socialist realism, as borrowed from the Soviet Union and later elaborated into a Maoist brand of "revolutionary realism," claims to depict not merely the raw, visible surface of reality but, more importantly, an underlying ideological truth composed of class struggle and the inexorable historical movement toward a Communist utopia. In contrast, the postsocialist realism of independent cinema of the 1990s essentially flips the relationship between the two levels: rather than professing to show an ideological truth that underlies apparent reality, it seeks to reveal a raw, underlying reality by stripping away the ideological representations that distort it. Thus, in describing the style of Jia and others of his generation, Chinese critics hailed a "return to original life conditions," which is contrasted with the "prolonged political passions of the last century."[6] Such descriptions are reminiscent of some literary critics' praise for a "new realism" (*xin xieshizhuyi*) in Chinese fiction said to forsake both the "politicized appeal" of previous socialist realism and the modernist experiments of the avant-garde in favor of "a return to the original condition of real life in its primary form."[7]

We need not belabor the point that the "real" ostensibly unearthed by a postsocialist realist filmmaker must be understood as a historically situated representation of the world rather than as some nondiscursive thing in itself that actually appears before the audience. However, to admit as much is not to deny the particular strengths of the realist aesthetic. André Bazin, the most celebrated champion of cinematic realism, attributed its power to a "need for illusion" that is "purely psychological,"[8] and he further maintained that even the Italian neorealists "demonstrated that every realism in art was first profoundly aesthetic."[9] Indeed, Jia himself has acknowledged the impossibility of true objectivity for even the most realist style, calling it simply an "attitude" and an unattainable "ideal" of the filmmaker.[10] Thus the question raised by Jia's realism is not whether it divulges an elemental real so much as *how* it constructs the powerful impression of a confrontation with reality through the rhetoric of the films' narratives and their cinematic style.

The realist impulse in contemporary Chinese cinema had in fact manifested itself from the very beginning of the reform era, as imported theories of realism in film were linked to the "modernization of cinematic language" and many new realist elements appeared in the major films of the 1980s.[11] With the turn of the decade, however, a more radical wave of cinematic realism appeared, taking at least three forms: the documentary video movement rising out of Beijing's marginal artist colonies; the related phenomenon of low-budget independent cinema exemplified by Zhang Yuan's early directorial career; and finally even a turn toward a new sort of realism among established Fifth Generation directors by the early 1990s. The new documentary movement was launched in 1990 by Wu Wenguang's *Bumming in Beijing* (Liulang Beijing), which depicted the struggles of marginal artists and other young intellectuals at a time of uncertainty and political turmoil.[12] Zhang Yuan traveled in the same artistic circles in Beijing and pursued a similar raw realism in his early films. The groundbreaking *Mama*, for example (which appeared in the same year as *Bumming in Beijing*), intercuts a fictional narrative with documentary interview footage. Finally, *The Story of Qiu Ju* (Qiu Ju da guansi, 1992; dir. Zhang Yimou) involves a leading Fifth Generation director shooting a major film in an unprecedented quasi-documentary style, using many nonprofessional actors, radio microphones, and hidden cameras to elicit naturalistic performances in actual contemporary settings. While the Urban Generation directors in the 1990s hoped to distance themselves from their Fifth Generation predecessors in general, *The Story of Qiu Ju* nevertheless helped to set a new standard for realist techniques in Chinese fiction film.

Aside from its realist devices, *The Story of Qiu Ju* is also significant as a work of critical realism, insofar as it depicts the struggles of the marginal and powerless. Similarly, the independent cinema movement of the 1990s was concerned with laying bare the contradictions of the contemporary postsocialist condition of China. In this sense the cinematic realism of the 1990s carried on the modern Chinese legacy of critical realism, an aesthetic that was especially dominant in film and other arts of the 1930s. Marston Anderson has described the critical realist style of that time as seeking not necessarily "to promulgate a new ideological vision of the world" but rather "to explore . . . the gap between a discredited worldview and the actual functioning of society."[13] Similarly, postsocialist realist cinema does not directly promulgate an oppositional ideology but rather indirectly critiques mainstream ideology by foregrounding the suffering of ordinary people that is repressed both by officially sanctioned media representations and by mainstream entertainment cinema. This tactic of exposing rather than opposing rests upon the belief that social contradictions are apparent in everyday life but elided in representation. The postsocialist realist films of the 1990s are thus imbued with the faith that just going out into public with a camera and capturing the unvarnished street life found there serves to unmask ideology while documenting the realities of contemporary China.

Exemplifying this documentary impulse is Jia's first work, a fifteen-minute Betacam video titled *One Day, in Beijing* (You yitian, zai Beijing, 1994). Produced by a small group of students calling themselves the Beijing Film Academy Youth Experimental Film Group, the video documented passing crowds in Tiananmen Square on a random day in May 1994.[14] The project's main goal was simply to record the movement of ordinary people in China's perhaps most quintessential public space. The layers of symbolism accumulated by the official representations of Tiananmen are thus belied by the quotidian activities of the people passing through, and the work as a whole demonstrates the capacity of the videographer to directly capture "real" life even in the most ideologically encumbered of settings.

Jia also directed the group's next project, *Xiao Shan Going Home* (Xiao Shan huijia, 1995), the beginning of which recalls *One Day, in Beijing* with a still shot of a woodcut depicting a person holding a camera in profile against the background of Tiananmen—an image that served as the emblem of the Youth Experimental Film Group.[15]

This vision of the filmmaker's empowerment is further reinforced during the opening credits montage, one shot of which shows a military policeman walking directly toward the camera and gesturing for it to stop filming. Instead, the camera stubbornly documents his approach right up to the moment his hand is about to block out the lens. Such images establish a basic rhetoric of opposition between the officially sanctioned point of view and the view revealed by the independent filmmaker's camera, or quite simply between ideological narratives and the reality they ostensibly mask.

Xiao Shan Going Home is a fifty-eight minute narrative video also shot on Betacam, with a budget of less than US$2,500. The film is about a restaurant worker in Beijing who wants to return to his home in the provincial city of Anyang for the Spring Festival. In a series of encounters, Xiao Shan drinks with friends, has a brief fling with a young woman, and repeatedly tries and fails to find a ticket to go home for the holiday during the busiest travel season of the year. The fact that Xiao Shan never in fact goes home, despite the title of the video, indicates that the main interest is not in tracing a narrative arc but in documenting the lives of a few of Beijing's "outsiders" (*waidi ren*), or migrant workers (*mingong*), and in the process recording some of the sights

Logo of the Beijing Film Academy Youth Experimental Film Group, used as the opening image of *Xiao Shan Going Home.*

and sounds of Beijing as the Spring Festival approaches. To this end, the video frequently follows its small, nonprofessional cast out into the streets, subways, and train stations, trailing them with a jerky handheld camera amid hundreds of unwitting extras. As was the case with the documentary project in Tiananmen Square, much of the work's energy and interest come directly from the exhilaration of taking a camera into an uncontrolled public space and documenting its random events and objects—an old man playing harmonica, a subway station newsstand, and an angry, unexplained confrontation between people on a crowded sidewalk.

This documentary tone is set early in the video when Xiao Shan and a hometown acquaintance, now a prostitute in Beijing, walk together through the streets. The segment begins with a shot facing a crowded stream of foot traffic out of which the two characters appear. The shot thus recalls the celebrated opening shot of *The Story of Qiu Ju*, in which a stationary camera records the flow of a similar street crowd for nearly two minutes, only at the end of which does the movie star Gong Li herself emerge from the unstaged real-world crowd to enter the film as its heroine. However, as the street sequence in *Xiao Shan Going Home* progresses, a major difference becomes apparent. In *The Story of Qiu Ju* the camera, though documenting real people, is itself camouflaged so that it does not draw the attention of those it records passing by. As a result, the random "extras" remain unaware of and thus unengaged with the camera, while part of the spectacle is the very fact that the famous and glamorous Gong Li is so well disguised as a pregnant peasant that she can walk through the crowd unnoticed, thereby preserving the film's *fictional* realism. In *Xiao Shan Going Home*, in contrast, the protagonists are played by unknown nonprofessional actors, and rather than being hidden the camera is clearly right out in the streets with the crowd it documents—as is obvious by the repeated looks directed at the lens by random people in the crowd, thus breaking the "fourth wall" between the diegetic events and the camera that records them or the audience that views them.

Such looks to the camera in fact occur a total of more than eighty times during the public scenes in *Xiao Shan Going Home*. The effect of the "real" people looking at the camera while the actors do not indicates the priorities of this type of filmmaking, which implicitly values a cinema verité[16] or "on-the-spot"[17] documentary realism, with its emphasis on immediacy, over a seamless fictional realism. That is, with each scene in which bystanders look to the camera while the protagonists ignore it, the world depicted suffers from a noticeable rupture between the diegetic characters and the "extras," who in fact now are revealed as extradiegetic. As was indicated by the camera shown prominently in the woodcut of the film's opening shot, the presence of the camera in the fictional video is not concealed but rather flaunted. In one shot, while exiting a clothing store the camera operator's hand even becomes visible as it parts the hanging plastic flaps of a door covering. In short, the sacrifice of fictional realism due to the obvious presence of the camera is trumped by the effect of documentary realism gained by the clear evidence that the camera was taken into an uncontrolled public space, where it documented in part the spontaneous reactions of real people to the camera itself.

Xiao Shan Going Home remained an obscure student work until a reporter from Hong Kong suggested that the filmmakers enter it in the Hong Kong Independent Short Film and Video Awards competition. This effort eventually earned a prize for the video as well as entry into the 1997 Hong Kong International Film Festival. The resulting exposure put Jia in contact with the Hong Kong-based collaborators: producer Li Kit Ming (Li Jieming) and cinematographer Yu Lik Wai (Yu Liwei), himself a graduate of the Belgium Film Academy who had worked on films in Europe as well as in China.[18] Consequently, even at this early stage of his career Jia's work started to draw on both financial and artistic resources outside of Mainland China at the same time that it began its shift from limited exposure to a small circle in Beijing to participation in the international art cinema scene.

Nevertheless, the work that followed, *Xiao Wu* (aka *Pickpocket*), showed several similarities to *Xiao Shan Going Home*. Despite a higher budget, better production values, more careful framing, and a switch from Betacam video to 16mm film, *Xiao Wu* retains much of the on-the-scene immediacy and documentary directness of its predecessor. The episodic plot about a drifting pickpocket, Xiao Wu, in the minor county-seat city of Fenyang in Shanxi province (Jia's hometown) is played entirely by nonprofessional actors.[19] Further, as with *Xiao Shan Going Home*, the exterior scenes are filmed amid the actual street crowds in Fenyang, and thus without the control afforded by shooting permits, a large crew, and a compliant group of extras. The raw, realist style is thus partially attributable to issues of funding and official sanction, but it is also a matter of the ongoing priorities of the filmmakers. As Jia has said, they wished to maintain a certain "crude" appearance "because we wanted to shoot something with a very strong on-location feeling."[20] The effort to document immediate reality and eschew obvious aesthetic or ideological manipulation contrasts with accounts promulgated by the official media, themselves represented within *Xiao Wu* by television news reports and announcements over ubiquitous public loudspeakers.

Despite the continuity in approach between *Xiao Shan Going Home* and *Xiao Wu*, some stylistic differences are apparent. In particular, while both films tend toward shots of long duration by Hollywood standards, in *Xiao Wu* the long take becomes an especially pronounced technique with shots up to six minutes long in certain key scenes, whereas the previous work had only once exceeded a two-minute take (and then only slightly). Chris Berry discusses the organization of time in *Xiao Wu* as a "narrative distension" that presents a radical vision of postsocialist realist time countering any master narrative of teleological progress, whether that of the march toward a communist utopia or that of official reform-era modernization. This distended postsocialist time is the time of the reform era's "losers" rather than its more oft-represented "winners."[21] My view of the rhetorical effect of *Xiao Wu*'s realism is very much in keeping with Berry's theoretical reading of the time of the film. *Xiao Wu* presents an intractable Chinese "reality" that is explicitly juxtaposed against both the official media representations and the promises of global capitalist ideology. A closer look at three of the film's exceptionally long takes will illustrate how stylistic choices structure the bleak urban "reality" uncovered.

In the first instance, Xiao Wu has gone to visit his estranged friend Xiaoyong on the day before Xiaoyong's wedding. Although Xiaoyong once was Xiao Wu's sworn brother and fellow delinquent, he is now a successful businessman who enjoys the high social standing of the nouveaux rich in reform-era China, and his wedding is a major community event reported by the local news media. To protect his reputation, Xiaoyong has distanced himself from his former friend, who remains a petty thief. Nevertheless, a determined Xiao Wu goes on a crime spree in order to accumulate cash for a wedding gift, which he then takes to Xiaoyong's house to confront his old friend. The meeting between the two men consists mainly of a single shot lasting three and three-quarters minutes. The men sit half facing each other at a desk in a long-shot composition, both nervously chain-smoking. Xiao Wu berates Xiaoyong for failing to invite him to the wedding, repeatedly muttering, "You've fucking changed." Xiaoyong then tries to refuse Xiao Wu's wedding gift. Ultimately they have little to say to each other, and the tension is accentuated by the continuous take filled with awkward silences and anxious cigarette puffing. The shot ends after Xiao Wu rises to leave, throwing his gift packet onto the desk in front of Xiaoyong and challenging the latter to look at the tattoo on his forearm that once symbolized their friendship.

This single long take dramatizes the central relationship of Xiao Wu and Xiaoyong and by extension interrogates the relationship between the new classes they represent. Having been not long ago virtually identical in social standing, the two friends now belong to quite distinct social spheres. Indeed, their relationship, as represented in the film, forces us to contemplate the generally suppressed issue of class in reform-era China. When Xiao Wu makes forays from his nearby village to the county seat, he becomes in effect a minor provincial version of the "floating population" (*liudong renkou*) in the Chinese urban environment—that is, peasants who lack official residence status and legitimate social standing, and who instead are widely viewed as the principal sources of problems such as rising crime rates and prostitution. Xiao Wu is thus at the bottom of the new class structure of urban China in the reform era, while Xiaoyong, an admired businessman and community leader, is at the top.

Xiao Wu, however, problematizes the class distinction between Xiao Wu and Xiaoyong by making countervailing ethical distinctions. During the confrontation, Xiao Wu appears not as a petty thief but rather as a loyal friend who fulfills his promises, and Xiaoyong seems less an admirable businessman than an evasive deceiver who has forgotten the bonds of sworn brotherhood. *Xiao Wu* thus presents two contrasting perspectives on the character Xiaoyong, one given by the media reports bracketed within the diegesis, the other the apparently objective view of the story as a whole, filmed in a realist style and aligned with Xiao Wu's point of view. These contrasting takes on Xiaoyong dramatize Wang Xiaoming's distinction between *xin furen*, the nouveaux rich, and *chenggong renshi*, literally "successful personage." *Xin furen* names an emergent social class that has seized an inordinate share of China's new material wealth largely through questionable business practices and collaboration with corrupt officials. The term *chenggong renshi*, on the other hand, identifies a mainstream cultural symbol, a new model for admiration and emulation widely promulgated through images in commercial advertising as well as the official news media. According to Wang, *chenggong renshi* should thus be viewed as a "portrait" of *xin furen*, but a deceptive one that is only a "half-faced portrait" (*banzhanglian de xiaoxiang*) presenting an image of a life of comfort and leisure without revealing the actual material practices behind such an imagined lifestyle.[22] Xiaoyong, then, is a provincial version of the nouveaux rich, celebrated by local media as their own local "successful personage" worthy of praise and emulation; his new social standing and the local media's lionization of him replicate the national discourse on how success and the good life should be envisioned in the reform era.

In *Xiao Wu*, the contrast between the formulaic and superficial media reports on the wedding of Xiaoyong and the realist aesthetic of the film that frames them effectively points to the unseen half of the *chenggong renshi* portrait, the underlying material reality of class inequality that puts the nouveaux rich and the floating population at opposite extremes of the social spectrum. While exposing the ideological falsehood of the "successful person-age" portrait, the film undercuts any presumed ethical justification for the class division between the two former friends. For example, when Xiaoyong has one of his underlings return Xiao Wu's wedding gift on the grounds that the money's origins are dubious, Xiao Wu angrily retorts that Xiaoyong's own money is equally unclean, having been made from trafficking in black-market cigarettes and exploiting bargirls. Xiaoyong soon replies that his so-called cigarette "smuggling" (*zousi*) is really simply "trade" (*maoyi*) and that he does not exploit his bargirls but merely engages in the "entertainment business" (*yule ye*). Hence, by correcting the blunt language of Xiao Wu's accusations with an insistence on the legitimate-sounding labels of the reform-era econ-omy, Xiaoyong attempts to reassert the distinction between his calling and that of Xiao Wu and thereby justify his social position as *chenggong renshi*. However, his efforts are controverted by the film as a whole, which effectively calls into question the boundary between legitimate business and outright stealing in the age of free-market reforms.

A second key long take in *Xiao Wu* occurs nearly one hour into the film, when Xiao Wu goes to visit his romantic interest, Meimei, in the dormitory of the karaoke bar where she works. Like Xiao Wu, Meimei is a marginal figure in the urban landscape, an outsider who has come to the city looking for opportunity but finding only exploitation. While working as a karaoke bargirl paid to accompany male customers in private karaoke rooms—a role that leads easily to prostitution—Meimei calls home and lies to her parents by telling them that she is actually in Beijing pursuing her dream of becoming a movie star. She meets Xiao Wu when he patronizes the karaoke bar, but their relationship only becomes romantic when one day he goes to see her after she has stayed home sick. In a remarkable shot lasting just over six minutes, the two are seen visiting in Meimei's room in a distancing long-shot composition. Although at first they appear awkward and listless, as the shot proceeds their yearning becomes more palpable, and a hint of hope, if not sentimentality, makes a rare appearance in the film. As the ambient exterior noises of traffic fill the silences in their conversation, Xiao Wu and Meimei struggle to pene-trate each other's loneliness. When Xiao Wu asks Meimei to sing for him, her choice of song—Faye Wong's "Tiankong" [Sky]—vocalizes the feelings of soli-tude and desire they cannot otherwise express. The shot length and the per-sistence of the noise pollution coming seemingly from just outside the room serve to accentuate both the couple's determination to carve out a space of togetherness amid their despair and the ultimate futility of that effort as the outside world relentlessly enters to disperse the dreams of their marginal lives.

The temporary hint of hopefulness is nevertheless carried over into the next scene, in which Xiao Wu goes by himself to an empty bathhouse. His desires awakened and his usual deadpan guardedness discarded, he strips naked and sings loudly to himself as he wades in the bath pools. As he sings, the camera pans up to a window high on the wall of the bathhouse that lets in a wash of light illuminating the interior mist—a surprisingly utopian image that is in keeping with Xiao Wu's good mood as well as the song sung by Meimei in the previous scene. In a later meeting, Xiao Wu and Meimei cement a new romantic relationship, and Xiao Wu buys a pager so that Meimei can get in touch with him anytime. Before long, however, Meimei in her desperation runs off with a wealthy out-of-town client, and for much of the remainder of the film Xiao Wu waits in vain for her call to appear on his pager. Instead of realizing the hopes raised by their early courtship, he eventually has lost her as well as fallen out with his former best friend and his family back in his home village.

Xiao Wu's downward spiral is inevitably concluded by his arrest for picking pockets during a government crackdown on theft. This crackdown is revealed during the opening minutes of *Xiao Wu*, and references to it are scattered throughout the film in the form of public loudspeaker announcements, television reports, and news media interviews taking place in the streets of Fenyang. As was the case with the media accounts of the wedding of the "model entrepreneur" Xiaoyong, the reports on crime—the last of which is on the arrest of Xiao Wu himself—serve as an internal counterpoint to the film as a whole, with its sympathetic portrayal of the "real" life of one of the public enemies targeted by the police crackdown. In other words, the truth claim or effect of realism of the film as a whole is again rhetorically bolstered by its depiction of the very layer of official ideology it ostensibly cuts through to expose the obscured underlying reality. Just as the media's "half-faced portrait" of Xiaoyong as a model of success is stripped away, the depersonalized criminals vilified in the media are fleshed out into the "real" Xiao Wu, a marginalized dreamer with a stronger moral compass than the successful businessman lionized by the same media.

The television street-reporting depicted in *Xiao Wu* also puts an interesting twist on the problem of the bystanders' looks to the camera of the kind that was so prevalent in *Xiao Shan Going Home*. Dozens of such looks occur in *Xiao Wu* as well, but the majority of them happen during depictions of media street interviews. As a result, gawking spectators can be interpreted as attracted by the street interviews and the accompanying cameras within the story rather than calling attention to the filmmaker's camera and thus the constructedness of the fiction as a whole. That is, fictional realism is here less threatened by the extras' gazes at the lens than was the case with the previous video project. With the spontaneity of people's reactions to the camera seeming now to have narrative motivation, the cinema verité immediacy of on-location shooting within street crowds is maintained and yet integrated into the diegetic world.

The most notable case of bystanders staring directly at the camera, however, occurs in the film's final shot in which the tendency of random passersby to stop and gape at a movie camera is manipulated in a different and particularly inventive way. In a shot lasting over two and a half minutes, Xiao Wu, while being led after his arrest to another location by a police station chief, is temporarily handcuffed to a cable next to the street and left there alone. The handheld camera stays with Xiao Wu squatting helplessly tethered to the cable in the foreground as a few people on the sidewalk behind him are gradually drawn to the spectacle. Finally the camera suddenly pans to a view of the previously hidden street, which turns out to be rapidly filling with other gawkers. From a low-angle position approximating the perspective of Xiao Wu, who is now out of the frame, the camera simply returns the gaze of the gathering bystanders for a full one and one-quarter minutes until the film ends.

With this camera movement, then, despite the lack of cutting, the shot seems to change from an objective shot of Xiao Wu to a virtual point-of-view shot from his perspective. This impression is achieved by the combination of the pivotal pan, the very length of the shot (which in effect allows us to forget how it began), and the subsequent pans that seem to mimic Xiao Wu's head suddenly turning. This highly effective final shot thus stages a direct confrontation between the perspective of the film's isolated protagonist and the gaze of the anonymous public for whom he is objectified and estranged by the mass media. In addition, like the scenes of street interviews by the news media, this shot very cunningly turns the problem of looks to the camera

The final shot of *Xiao Wu* begins as a seemingly objective view of Xiao Wu . . .

The camera pans to reveal the view of gathering crowd from Xiao Wu's perspective.

during on-site shooting into a storytelling device in itself. The crowd of onlookers in reality was of course attracted by both the actor handcuffed to the cable and the movie camera shooting him,[23] but by having the camera face the crowds from approximately the character's point of view, the stares at the lens appear to be at Xiao Wu and are thus integrated into the diegesis. In short, the fissure opened up by looks to the camera in *Xiao Shan Going Home*—the divergence between the priorities of "on-the-spot" cinema verité realism and those of fictional realism—is largely sutured in *Xiao Wu*, with somewhat more preference now given to the latter.

Despite this shift to solve the problem of looks to the camera during on-location shooting in unrestricted public spaces, the style of *Xiao Wu* continues the previous work's strong presence of the camera by the use of mostly hand-held camerawork and frequent close shooting in small interior spaces, where the maneuverings of the camera become more apparent. In many ways, *Xiao Wu* epitomizes a gritty, low-budget realist style that has since been echoed in other notable Chinese films such as Wang Chao's *Orphan of Anyang* (Anyang de gu'er, 2001) and Li Yang's *Blind Shaft* (Mang jing, 2003). For the purposes of my argument, here I will distinguish this type of "on-the-spot" realism from a related yet distinct style that also begins to emerge more strongly in *Xiao Wu*—namely an aesthetic characterized by long shots, exceptionally long takes, and a relatively immobile camera. This style is exemplified in *Xiao Wu* by such scenes as the meeting between Xiao Wu and Xiaoyong and the visit to Meimei's dormitory; scenes that more closely typify a Bazinian-style realism in which the continuity of real time is preserved and the viewer is allowed in long-shot compositions to choose the details on which to focus rather than being more obviously manipulated by camera movements and close-ups. However, it was only with his next film, *Platform*, that Jia's shift toward this more measured and aestheticized realist style became apparent in the work as a whole rather than just in certain scenes. In *Platform*, camera movements are limited for the most part to slow and steady pans; looks to the camera in crowd scenes are eliminated altogether; and shot duration expands dramatically to an average of seventy-six seconds, compared with thirty-three seconds for *Xiao Wu* and just eighteen seconds for *Xiao Shan Going Home*. Indeed, sequence shots are the rule, and thus there is little continuity editing. Close-up shots are virtually eliminated, while long-shot and extreme-long-shot compositions are used frequently, so that the feeling of the physical immanence of the camera is lost in favor of an evocative distance from the historical subject.

A production on the scale of *Platform* was made possible by the impact that *Xiao Wu* had in the international film festival circuit, where it won a total of seven prizes at six film festivals on three continents, most notably two awards at the Berlin International Film Festival. In the wake of this success, Jia moved decisively from being simply a recent Film Academy graduate pursuing low-budget independent productions of marginal films in China to being a significant presence in the international art cinema scene. As a result, *Platform* was made with a professionalism and an aesthetic that fit comfortably with the prevailing industry standards. As a truly globalized production, *Platform* was financed through the combined resources of production companies and/or government agencies in Japan, France, Switzerland, Hong Kong, and mainland China. After *Xiao Wu*, Jia had many willing new investors, and he chose Takeshi Kitano's T-Mark Inc. as his main production company, partly in order to work with a certain producer who had collaborated successfully with Hou Hsiao-hsien, a favorite inspiration.[24] The result (after a much more involved production process than had been the case with *Xiao Wu*) was Jia's first 35mm film—a beautifully executed, sprawling work. *Platform*'s story spans the entire decade of the 1980s, and its playing time was reduced from the originally screened cut of 193 minutes to a still-lengthy 155 minute final cut. The film traces the evolution of a performing arts or "cultural troupe" (*wengongtuan*) from Fenyang as it negotiates the rapidly changing conditions of the early post-Mao reform era, during which its young members face the various disappointments and excitement of lives that always seem to be on the verge of, without ever quite reaching, some sort of promised fulfillment. By these means the film simultaneously represents and interrogates the reform era itself, in which the call for "modernization" continually invokes the goal of achieving modernity in all its plenitude, which nonetheless always seems to be just out of reach for the majority of the Chinese population.

As the performing arts troupe evolves from a state-run enterprise in 1979 performing revolutionary songs for the masses to, by the end of the 1980s, a privatized operation selling disco dance routines and punk rock imitations to any audience the troupe can attract, both the promise and the elusiveness of a new vision of modernity are exemplified for its young members by popular music. As the 1980s begin, although the troupe members sing political songs in their public performances, in private they listen to illegal shortwave broadcasts of the Taiwan pop singer Deng Lijun (Teresa Teng).[25] Later their troupe is allowed to perform nonpolitical "light music" (*qing yinyue*), but its members become more excited by the cassette tapes of pop-rock songs that one of them brings back from a trip to Guangzhou—the cutting-edge site of "opening and reform" in China of the early 1980s. The contemporary pop-rock song from which *Platform* draws its title encapsulates the feelings in the film of both anticipation and disappointment:

Long long platform, long slow waiting
Long long train, carrying my love everlasting
Long long platform, lonely waiting
There's only my love departing, never my love returning

In the image of waiting on a long, desolate train station platform for a train that never arrives, the song captures both the promise of an approaching modernity and the frustration of waiting endlessly for it in an inconsequential (yet therefore representative) small city in China's hinterland. Indeed, at the time depicted in the film no railroad even ran through Fenyang, and thus during their travels in one key scene the performance troupe members dash across a dry riverbed and up to a bridge just to get a glimpse of a passing train. The train is thus both a literal industrial emblem of modernization and a more abstract symbol of a modernity actually experienced largely as an absence and a longing. While the train has already rushed by before the performers have even made it up to the train track, their own old truck lies broken and idle in the dry riverbed.

The thematic tension in *Platform* between anticipation and disappointment also finds expression in the way the film manages to depict epochal historical change largely through scenes of trivial events and even boredom. The use of filmic ellipses is a major part of its realist style. Jia has described how he made the conscious choice to minimize obvious cause-effect narrative progressions so as to allow the viewer gradually to observe the results of historical and personal change without necessarily knowing how they came about. This preference is justified as being more true to life: as we observe the changes in the lives around us, we are rarely aware of the details of how they happened but we see the results nonetheless.[26] Such an approach recalls Bazin's praise of ellipses in the films of De Sica and Rossellini: "The empty gaps, the white spaces, the parts of the event that we are not given, are themselves of a concrete nature: stones which are missing from the building. It is the same in life: we do not know everything that happens to others."[27] What we do see of the lives of the characters in *Platform* often approaches Bazin's "cinema of time" or (as he quotes Bergson) "cinema of 'duration,'" in which the priority is to organize time not according to dramatic needs but rather in accordance with "life time"—the experience of time as simple duration in a life that is more full of quotidian moments, inactivity, and boredom than spectacular events even in an era of dramatic historical change.[28] Thus the importance of ellipses in *Platform* goes hand in hand with the favored use of extremely long takes that depict temporal intervals rather than just narrative events. Such stylistic decisions produce a particular vision of the historical and geographical setting, bringing out the tension between sweeping historical change as the master narrative of reform-era China and actual inertia as lived experience in a small, remote provincial city—an inertia all the more apparent because of its contrast with the official account of the "Four Modernizations."[29]

The temporal organization of *Platform*, then, continues and even intensifies the "narrative distension" that Chris Berry discusses in the case of *Xiao Wu*. This narrative distension amounts to a radical representation of postsocialist time, but in this case it is a remembered time of the 1980s rather than an obdurate motionlessness of the present as perceived by those whose lives in the 1990s are going nowhere. *Platform* as a whole (which Jia has often stated is based largely on personal memories of the times and places depicted) is a looking back to a bygone age and a now-transformed geography. However, the era depicted is on the contrary filled with a continuous anticipation of a coming fulfillment, as discussed above. Thus, while the time of the film is subjectively experienced by the characters as melancholy over a *future* that remains forever out of reach, the film as a whole is imbued with melancholy over a lost *past*—specifically Fenyang in the 1980s but also the lost hopefulness of youth in general. The film is, then, a document not of an immediate reality but of a complex network of personally experienced temporal displacements shot through with distance and duration. The distances that the film explores include not only the spatial distance of a marginal geographical location far from the centers of reform-era cultural change in the 1980s, but also the temporal distances of, on one hand, the characters from their hoped-for futures and, on the other, the filmmaker (and perhaps audience) from the past that must now be recalled. These distances are not overcome but literally are *endured*, as both the characters within the film and the viewer watching it experience the empty duration of the present moment largely as the absence of some future or past fulfillment, lending the film as a whole a gradually increasing sense of melancholy.

Platform is thus easily read as a product of nostalgia, but such a reading must take care not simply to dismiss it as a nostalgia that is complacent, transparent, or reassuring. To borrow the distinction made by Svetlana Boym in her study of nostalgia in postsocialist Europe and Russia, the nostalgia of *Platform* is of the "reflective" rather than the "restorative" type; that is, instead of being generated by a national imaginary of smooth progress and recoverable essences, it arises from ambivalent personal and cultural memories and embraces ambiguity, distance, irony, and fragmentation as inseparable aspects of its object of meditation.[30] It neither longs for the lost society that preexisted the reform era nor embraces the ideology of the "Four Modernizations" that underlay the transformations of the decade depicted. It is a nostalgia of the past as duration rather than as a simple, quickly recognized snapshot.[31] For example, the film eschews easily identified, monolithic changes in the characters' dress and hairstyles as the narrative (and decade) progresses; rather than all characters transparently signifying the transition, say, from 1979 to the early 1980s, some characters suddenly appear with permed hair or in track suits, while others retain the earlier styles of the Mao era, reflecting the multiple temporal frames of reference that actually coexist at any particular historical moment. The predominant use of long-shot compositions and long-take cinematography is, of course, an integral part of the reflective nostalgia of the film. The almost exclusive use of long shots and extreme long shots maintains a distance between the viewer and the object of nostalgia that mitigates against easy sentimentality even in the most dramatic scenes.[32] Long takes, meanwhile, convey the sense of time as endured, demanding reflection by the viewer rather than the simple consumption of nostalgic images or narrative information.[33]

The differences in style between *Platform* and *Xiao Wu* are thus largely attributable to the divergences in historical period depicted and the changed priorities that result from trying to convey a decade of fictional time through a reflective poetics of nostalgia. The significant increase in both the filmmaker's budget and human resources undoubtedly also allowed for a more thoroughgoing realization of an aesthetic vision. In any case, *Platform* arguably pursues a very different sort of realist aesthetic than that of Jia's earlier works. Due to the choice of shooting locations, for example, Fenyang has an entirely different presence than it had in *Xiao Wu*. Instead of the ramshackle modern urban architecture and dirty, chaotic streets of the earlier film, *Platform* makes frequent use of beautiful old walls as a backdrop for its lengthy shots. In fact, these scenes were filmed in Fenyang's neighboring, much more picturesque, city of Pingyao, where the city wall dates to the Ming dynasty and where enough traditional architecture survives to have made the town a major domestic tourist destination starting in the late 1990s. In addition to this change of actual shooting location, the fictional Fenyang of *Platform* appears relatively deserted, as the use of extras is vastly reduced relative to Jia's previous two works (for the obvious reason of historical fidelity). In short, due to the combination of a more controlled environment, changed shooting locations, much longer takes, more careful framing, slower camera movement, and an extreme reliance on long-shot compositions, not only the city itself but the very experience of both space and time reaches a new level of aestheticization in *Platform*.

One sequence shot will suffice to illustrate this changed filmmaking style in *Platform*. The film's main protagonist, Cui Mingliang, is atop the old city wall with his love interest, Yin Ruijuan. In a shot lasting three and a half minutes, beginning in extreme long shot, the pair approaches the camera, which slowly pans to follow them until they pause to talk by the wall next to it. Eventually Mingliang asks Ruijuan whether they can be considered a couple. In response Mingliang receives an ambiguous answer (and in fact is later rejected, adding to the mood of anticipation and disappointment in the film), and subsequently the pair continue walking along the wall, now away from the camera. During the bulk of the shot, while they have paused to talk, the stationary camera frames them in a bold composition in which exactly half of the screen is filled by a large brick wall in the foreground. Behind it, the two characters take turns walking back and forth, with one of them hidden behind the looming wall in the foreground while the other leans against a perpendicular wall on the still-unobscured right side of the frame.

In carefully choreographed succession, the two characters change places four times, with each leaning, always in the same position, on the right while the other is hidden by the wall on the left. Occasionally, when changing positions, both disappear behind the wall for a few seconds, so that the entire frame resembles an almost abstract still photograph. When they both finally leave the space, the camera again slowly pans and records their retreat without following until they are again in extreme long shot. With shots such as this one (along with several others of the same type) the combination of shot duration, composition, and a careful manipulation of mise-en-scène results in a filmic style so aestheticized as to become striking in its own right, without

A typical aestheticized composition during a long take in *Platform*.

regard to the "reality" it allegedly depicts. In this sense, to understand the formal characteristics of *Platform* we must at least partly shift our framework away from the documentary or on-the-spot realism movement in China and instead consider the context of current trends in international art cinema. In fact, a large number of contemporary art films have displayed formal preferences quite similar to those of *Platform*. Such films become so exclusively reliant on the long take, so concerned with showing in detail the real-time intervals between narrative actions, that the Bazinian long-take realism is pushed nearly to, and sometimes past, the point that it becomes its ostensible opposite—an intriguing kind of formalism. This aesthetic was a favorite of the international art cinema and film festival circuit during the 1990s and is exemplified by directors such as Hou Hsiao-hsien, Abbas Kiarostami, and Tsai Ming-liang.[34] It overlaps at least in part with the neo-Bazinian elements of the Dogma 95 movement that arose in Denmark,[35] and it is pushed to its almost minimalist limit in such works as Hou's *Flowers of Shanghai* (Haishang hua, 1998), Tsai's *The River* (Heliu, 1997), and Béla Tarr's *Werckmeister Harmonies* (Werckmeister harmóniák, 2000).[36] To the extent that this new international style had theoretical or academic support, it was not only the Bazinian notion of cinematic realism (which had been widely critiqued in the Western academy during the very years it held sway in China in the post-Mao period), but also, by the turn of the century, the rising influence of Gilles Deleuze's two-volume philosophy of cinema.[37] In Deleuze's terminology, a film composed largely of long takes and minimal cause-and-effect narrative movement will tend to approximate the "time-image"—an image of time itself rather than of rational or plot-driven movements in time.[38] In the Deleuzian formulation, the usual contrast between national art cinemas and the classical Hollywood style is rewritten as a binary opposition between the time-image and the "movement-image," the latter of which is at least in part yet another way of conceptualizing the classical method of plot-driven narration and "invisible" editing.

Thus, an art film such as *Platform* can perhaps best be understood not as an extension of the radical cinema verité realism of Jia's earlier works, which drew more directly on the Chinese postsocialist realism of the 1990s, but rather in this broader context of art cinema as an aesthetic and theoretical antipode to entertainment cinema. In the local Chinese context, whereas the postsocialist realist aesthetic arose in opposition to the Fifth Generation's allegorical cinema as well as the residual socialist realism of "main melody" patriotic films, the foil of *Platform*'s Bazinian long-take art cinema can be thought of both as Hollywood and as the emerging Chinese entertainment cinema of directors such as Feng Xiaogang.[39] The international style of aestheticized realism, with its durations and ellipses, presents an alternative to Hollywood-style storytelling, which in fact is equally operative in the popular films of Feng Xiaogang and the state-supported ideological drills of the "main melody" films. In any case, however, the aestheticized realism of the transnational aesthetic exemplified by *Platform* is unavoidably itself a commodity within the specialized market that supports it, and as such it competes with alternative trends and aesthetics on the art film circuit. Given its excellent critical reception and its strong showing at the box office, particularly in Europe, *Platform* can be said to have been a success in its particular niche market.

With the 2002 feature *Unknown Pleasures*, Jia and the cinematographer Yu Lik Wai departed somewhat from the extremes of the slow and distanced international style of *Platform*, and perhaps not surprisingly the film received somewhat less ecstatic reviews from foreign film critics. In terms of subject matter, *Unknown Pleasures* returns to a contemporary setting in the northern Shanxi mining town of Datong. The immediacy of the period depicted is accompanied by the return of a mobile, often handheld camera that feels immanent to the environments it shoots and even occasionally indulges in devices such as whip pans (which would have been unthinkable in *Platform*). A switch to digital video (a remarkable fourth different format among the four main films discussed here) facilitates this return of a cinema vérité style of realism in many scenes, as does the reappearance of random crowds from the actual city streets, along with the occasional looks to the camera by these bystanders. In other ways, however, *Unknown Pleasures* continues the trend from *Xiao Shan Going Home* to *Xiao Wu* to *Platform*, with the average shot length, for example, further expanding to nearly a minute and a half and with some shots including almost painfully slow and deliberate pans along the lines of Hou Hsiao-hsien's *Flowers of Shanghai*. In still other respects—the use of a pair of stylish and attractive lead characters, for example—the film seems to have a younger and hipper appeal bordering on the commercial. The director himself has said that he tried to make *Unknown Pleasures* somewhat more mainstream, with a more dramatic and tightly knit plot.[40] However, in the end the picture is as oblique and uncompromising as its predecessors, depicting young lives that seem already to have reached a dead end amid a wrecked urban landscape filled with the rubble of demolished buildings and construction sites, and with nuclear reactor cooling towers looming in the background. Indeed, while *Platform* shifted shooting locations from Fenyang to Pingyao in an effort to find a more nostalgic backdrop, in its use of Datong *Unknown Pleasures* seems to have found a contemporary urban setting even more ruined and bleak than the Fenyang of *Xiao Wu*—a bombed-out looking backdrop that silently repudiates the colorful fashions of its youthful protagonists.

Indeed, as was the case in *Xiao Wu* and *Platform*, a key theme of *Unknown Pleasures* is the gap between the imaginary of popular culture and the intractable reality that the characters actually inhabit. The film's Chinese title, meaning "allowed to wander free and easy," is borrowed from a contemporary popular song that appears twice in the film. The song title itself echoes the Daoist philosopher Zhuangzi, who used *xiaoyao*, or "carefree wandering" to describe the ideal state of spiritual freedom. One of the film's protagonists, nineteen-year-old Bin Bin, is enamored of a cartoon version of the Monkey King from the classic Chinese novel *Journey to the West* (Xiyou ji)—an embodiment of a similar ideal combination of empowerment, freedom, and enjoyment, which are the very qualities Bin Bin most lacks in his own life. In another ironic depiction of mass-mediated identification, a group of poor

Youth on the town in *Unknown Pleasures.*

mill workers are shown wildly cheering a televised announcement that far-away Beijing has won the competition to host the 2008 Summer Olympics. The accessibility of popular media also allows the young protagonists of the film to immerse themselves in global youth culture. There is an extended scene of rapturous dancing (a motif that also appears in *Xiao Shan Going Home* and in *Platform*) in a techno club throbbing to the strains of a dance mix of the mid-1990s Chinese rock song "My Love Is Stark Naked" (Wo di ai chiluoluo). Wry references are made to touchstones of recent global popular culture such as Quentin Tarantino's *Pulp Fiction* (1994), which is invoked by one of the lead male characters, Xiao Ji, for the daring of its restaurant robbery scene. However, when Xiao Ji and his friend Bin Bin later attempt to bridge the gap between fantasy and reality by carrying out their own heroic robbery of a bank using fake explosives, the ploy is easily countered by a security guard in what must be one of the most morose and anticlimactic bank heist scenes in cinema history. As Bin Bin is taken into custody by the guard, Xiao Ji tries to flee on his motorbike down the new highway to Beijing, but, characteristically, his motorbike breaks down in the middle of the highway outside of town. Thus, while early on in the film the Chinese title may seem to refer to the carefree lifestyle of its protagonists, by the time Xiao Ji is stranded on the highway and Bin Bin pathetically delivers on command an a cappella version of the pop song "Ren xiaoyao" while in police custody, the

The Cinema of Jia Zhangke • 105

ironic undertones of the film's Chinese title have come fully to the surface. The poses of hipness that the young protagonists strike are eventually betrayed by their own powerlessness and vulnerability to disappointment, and thus the film's attractive and trendy-looking characters again become objects of melancholy reflection rather than idealized identification. To draw a parallel between the careers of Jia and one of his inspirations, Hou Hsiao-hsien, if *Platform* recalled such films as *Dust in the Wind* (Lianlian fengchen, 1986) and *A Time to Live, A Time to Die* (Tongnian wangshi, 1985), then *Unknown Pleasures* takes its place beside *Goodbye South, Goodbye* (Nanguo zaijian, nanguo, 1996) and *Millennium Mambo* (Qianxi manbo, 2001)—films that subject the sexy rebellion of the young lead characters to such a prolonged and penetrating gaze as to reveal its underlying despair.

CAVING IN OR SELLING OUT

After the tentative gestures toward a more mainstream sensibility in *Unknown Pleasures*, and in the context of the state's relaxation in official censorship of independent directors, Jia's next film was coproduced by the official Shanghai Film Studio and approved by the authorities for domestic commercial release. While space constraints do not permit a thorough discussion of *The World* (Shijie, 2004), the director's switch from "underground" to legitimate status further illustrates the predicament of China's "independent" directors: in order to have any significant audience, they must successfully move either toward the international art cinema market, in which case they may be accused of pandering to foreigners, or toward the Chinese studio system, in which case they risk accusations of caving in to the authorities or to the mainstream audience.[41] In either case the autonomous, home-grown spirit of the original independent film movement can appear to be compromised.

When Chinese filmmakers are successful abroad, they are often accused of kowtowing to Western tastes. In terms of aesthetic style, however, there is no reason to assume that the sort of aestheticized neo-Bazinian realism of a film like *Platform* is essentially Western; its contemporary masters hail from East Asia and the Middle East, and its important progenitors certainly include Ozu and Mizoguchi, to which one might add the brilliant but less globally known Fei Mu, China's art film pioneer. A more substantial charge is that Chinese films aimed at international film festivals tend to present exotic, self-

Youth at the World Park in *The World*.

orientalizing images of China and/or cater to Westerners' stereotypes of total-itarian oppression under communism. In this view, the embrace of a Chinese director by foreign audiences is primarily political; as Yu Aiyuan notes, "Polit-ical factors are generally greater than artistic factors in the reasons these 'underground films' win awards."[42]

Interestingly, the official domestic approval of *The World* quickly aroused fears of an opposite sort of compromise—that of caving in to domestic cen-sors. In anticipation of the film's release, some questioned whether going mainstream would compromise, as stated by Chen Pingshu, "the valuable ability to think independently and the courage to be challenging."[43] In fact, the thematic consistency between *The World* and Jia's "independent" works has largely exonerated the director of the charge of compromising his vision. The film—about migrant laborers who staff a Beijing theme park featuring scale models of world landmarks—follows the critical realist impulse that has re-mained constant in the works of Jia, all of which attempt to document the problems of the postsocialist condition. In *The World* as in the earlier films, the intractable problems depicted include the hardships of the migrant labor force, the turn to theft and prostitution among some of those left behind by the postsocialist economy, and in general the loneliness and longing of ordi-nary young Chinese, whose new autonomy and access to an emerging mass-mediated youth culture are counterbalanced by the dangers of economic marginalization and social alienation. However, despite its continuation of the documentary impulse of the earlier postsocialist realist films, *The World* also is perhaps the most stylistically aestheticized of Jia's films to date—notably in its use of techniques such as titles and animation sequences to insert formalist commentary on the otherwise realist narrative action.

With its paradoxical mixtures of stylistic devices (realist and formalist), sponsors (foreign production companies and a domestic, government-owned studio), and audiences (the global film festival circuit as well as domestic distribution, however limited), *The World* provides ample evidence that trends launched in Chinese cinema in the 1990s would eventually lead to entirely new conditions and possibilities. While Jia and others have been critiqued for dependence upon international capital and foreign critical approval, they clearly have a sizable potential audience in China, where the proliferation of film clubs, informal viewing spaces, and Internet discussion forums demonstrates that at least a significant subset of educated urban youth have a lively interest in Chinese art cinema.[44] Thus, while the sensationalized marketing in the West of independent Chinese cinema as "banned in China!" is an undeniable phenomenon symptomatic of a lingering cold war cultural discourse, the hope remains that some of China's most accomplished directors are finally gaining access to the domestic market that they have been condemned for ignoring. Indeed, in his career to date, having journeyed from remote Fenyang to Beijing and on to film festivals across the world, Jia himself has been facing the dilemma of his characters: negotiating the often incommensurable distances between a provincial small-town past, a global cultural imaginary, and a difficult but always changing Chinese reality.

NOTES

1. This contrasts sharply, for example, with the message regarding video piracy inserted into the mainstream blockbuster *Big Shot's Funeral* (Dawan, 2001; dir. Feng Xiaogang). While selling advertising for a public spectacle, the protagonist, played by the popular star Ge You, refuses to sell billboard space to a manufacturer of video disk players reputed to excel at reading flawed, pirated disks, and he instead replaces it with a billboard promoting the crushing of video piracy and the protection of intellectual property rights. (In contrast to *Unknown Pleasures*, *Big Shot's Funeral* itself was distributed throughout China and set a new box office record for domestically produced films despite the feared competition from pirated disks.)

2. For example, Ulrich Gregor, the German critic and a major force in the Berlin and Cannes Film Festivals, has called Jia "the dazzling light of hope flashing like lightning in Asian cinema." In the wake of the release of *Platform*, in particular, J. Hoberman of the *Village Voice* called the film "a major work by a striking new talent" and "one of the richest films of the past decade," while Jonathan Rosenbaum of the *Chicago Reader* proclaimed it "one of the most impressive Chinese films I've ever seen" and even said it "might be the greatest film ever to come out of mainland China." See Chen Pingshu, "Jia Zhangke, Wang Xiaoshuai huigui zhuliu: Dianying 'diliudai' jiedong" [Jia Zhangke and Wang Xiaoshuai return to the mainstream: The thaw of cinema's "sixth generation"?], *Zhongguo qingnian bao* [China youth daily], January 17, 2004; J. Hoberman, "Conflict Management," *Village Voice*, March 2, 2001; J. Hoberman, "Cults of Personality," *Village Voice*, March 12, 2003; Jonathan Rosenbaum, "Critic's Choice: *Platform*," *Chicago Reader*, May 17, 2002; and Jonathan Rosenbaum, *Essential Cinema: On the Necessity of Film Canons* (Baltimore: Johns Hopkins University Press, 2004), 191.

3. For much more on the emergence of independent cinema in the 1990s, see Zhang Zhen's introduction to this volume as well as Bèrènice Reynaud's essay on Zhang Yuan.

4. For example, after a string of independent works, Zhang Yuan began making films through the official studios with *Seventeen Years* (Guonian huijia, 1999) and *I Love You* (Wo ai ni, 2002). He Jianjun and Wang Xiaoshuai also have vacillated between independent and/or internationally financed productions such as *Postman* (Youchai, 1995) and *Frozen* (Jidu hanleng, 1995), respectively, and state studio works such as He Jianjun's *Butterfly Smile* (Hudie de weixiao, 2002) and Wang Xiaoshuai's *So Close to Paradise* (Biandang guniang, 1998).

5. For a more thorough discussion of the various forms of postsocialist realism in Chinese cinema, see Chris Berry's essay in this volume. I am also grateful to him for sharing his essay "Watching Time Go By: Narrative Distension, Realism, and Postsocialism in Jia Zhangke's *Xiao Wu*" (forthcoming in the *South Atlantic Quarterly*) and the text of his presentation "Postsocialist Realism: Towards a Genealogy of *Jishizhuyi* in the Chinese Cinema," given at the Annual Meeting of the Association for Asian Studies, New York City, March 28, 2003. As these references indicate, my ideas regarding postsocialist realism have evolved in dialogue with Chris Berry.

6. Yin Hong, "Shiji zhi jiao: Jiushi niandai zhongguo dianying beiwang" [The turn of the century: Memo on Chinese cinema in the nineties], in *Bainian Zhongguo dianying lilun wenxuan* [Selected works of one hundred years of Chinese film theory], ed. Ding Yaping (Beijing: Wenhua yishu chubanshe, 2002), 2: 678. The critic Lü Xiaoming also described "Sixth Generation" films in general as conveying "primary life conditions." See his "90 niandai Zhongguo dianying jingguan zhi yi: 'Diliu dai' ji qi zhiyi" [One of the landscapes of 1990s Chinese film: The "Sixth Generation" and doubts thereof], *Dianying yishu* [Film art] (May 10, 1999): 24.

7. "'Xin xieshi xiaoshuo da lianzhan' juanshou yu" ["Grand exposition of new realist fiction"], preface to *Zhong Shan* [Zhong mountain], no. 3 (1989): 4.

8. André Bazin, "The Ontology of the Photographic Image," in *What Is Cinema?* vol. 1 (Berkeley: University of California Press, 1967), 11.

9. André Bazin, "An Aesthetic of Reality: Neorealism," in *What Is Cinema?* vol. 2 (Berkeley: University of California Press, 1971), 25.

10. See Stephen Teo, "Cinema with an Accent: Interview with Jia Zhangke, Director of *Platform*," *Senses of Cinema*, no. 15 (July/August 2001), http://www.sensesof cinema.com/contents/01/15/zhangke_interview.html. In another interview, Jia summed up his realism in the following way: "For me, all the realist [*jishi*] methods are there to express the real world of my inner experience. It is almost impossible for us to approach reality in itself, and the meaning of cinema is not simply to reach the level of reality. I pursue the feeling of the real in cinema more than I pursue reality, because I think the feeling of the real is on the level of aesthetics whereas reality just stays in the realm of sociology" (quoted in Sun Jianmin, "Jingyan shijiezhong de yingxiang xuanze: Jia Zhangke fangtan lu" [Selecting images in the experiential world: An interview with Jia Zhangke], *Jinri xianfeng* [Avant-garde today] 12 (March 2002): 31.

11. See Zhang Nuanxin and Li Tuo, "Tan dianying yuyan de xiandaihua" [On the modernization of cinematic language], *Bainian Zhongguo dianying lilun wenxuan* 2 (2003): 10–36; originally published in *Dianying yishu* [Film art], no. 3 (1979). In the 1980s, many films by both Fourth and Fifth Generation directors showed tendencies toward the Bazinian-style realism praised in this groundbreaking essay. These characteristics included on-location shooting, natural lighting and sound, long shots and long takes, and enough narrative ambiguity to require active audience interpretation.

12. For a comprehensive discussion of the new documentary movement, see Chris Berry's essay in this volume; see also Zhang Zhen's discussion in the introduction. In addition, see Dai Jinhua, "A Scene in the Fog: Reading the Sixth Generation Films," in *Cinema and Desire: Feminist Marxism and Cultural Politics in the Work of Dai Jinhua*, ed. Jing Wang and Tani E. Barlow (London: Verso, 2002), especially 85–88.

13. Marsten Anderson, *The Limits of Realism: Chinese Fiction in the Revolutionary Period* (Berkeley: University of California Press, 1990), 202.

14. This documentary short was the latest in a series of documentaries on Tiananmen Square made by young directors in the early 1990s. Wu Wenguang's *Tiananmen* (1991) had featured interviews with people in the vicinity of the square, while the feature-length *The Square* (Guangchang, 1994), directed by Zhang Yuan and Duan Jinchuan, like Jia's shorter project, focused on everyday activities on the site.

15. For a detailed firsthand account of the Beijing Film Academy Youth Experimental Film Group, see Gu Zheng, "Women yiqi lai pai dianying ba: Hui wang 'qingnian shiyan dianying xiaozu'" [Let's make a movie together: A look back at

the "Youth Experimental Film Group"], in *Xianchang* (Document), vol. 1, ed. Wu Wenguang (Tianjin: Tianjin shehui kexueyuan chubanshe, 2000), 213–22. The group also made a VHS short video, *Dudu* (1996), after *Xiaoshan Going Home.*

16. Cinema verité originally referred to the French version of a broader film movement of the 1960s (known elsewhere as "direct cinema," "free cinema," or "candid eye"). It indicates a style of documentary filmmaking that places the highest priority on directly recording unscripted events as they unfold in the uniqueness of the moment. While its roots go back to the age of silent cinema, the style flourished as a series of technological innovations in mobile cameras and synchronized sound from the late 1950s to the digital age that allowed filmmakers much greater freedom in following and responding to spontaneous events.

17. I borrow this term from Chris Berry's translation of *jishizhuyi*; see his essay "Getting Real" in this volume for a discussion of "on-the-spot" realism and its importance to the style of both the new documentary movement and the postsocialist realist fiction filmmakers.

18. As Jia has often made clear in interviews, Yu Lik Wai would play a key role in realizing the stylistic vision of Jia's feature films, and Jia has paid tribute by inserting in-jokes about him in the scripts. Besides the one in *Unknown Pleasures* mentioned at the beginning of this essay, in *Platform* there is a background loud-speaker announcement at a bus station telling people to be on the lookout for criminals including one Yu Liwei, who is said to "speak with a heavy Cantonese accent" and be "proficient in French"; the name as written in the Chinese subtitles is an exact homophone for the cinematographer's name, while the English-subtitled version uses the Cantonese spelling "Yu Lik Wai."

19. This fact is prominently noted, as a kind of neorealist badge of honor, in the first title following the final shot of the film. For details about how the cast members of *Xiao Wu* were recruited and directed during the shooting of the film, see Wu Wenguang, "Fangwen 'Xiao Wu' daoyan Jia Zhangke" [Interview with *Xiao Wu* director Jia Zhangke], *Document*, vol. 1, 184–212.

20. Jia Zhangke, "Zhongguo de duli dianying ren" [China's independent film-maker (interview)], *Dianying chufang: Dianying zai Zhongguo* [Film kitchen: Film in China], ed. Wang Shuo (Shanghai: Shanghai wenyi chubanshe, 2001), 152.

21. See Berry, "Watching Time Go By."

22. Wang Xiaoming, *Banzhanglian de shenhua* [Myth of the half-faced portrait] (Guangdong: Nanfang ribao chubanshe, 2000), 11–19.

23. The director has verified that the crowd was composed entirely of random passersby attracted not simply by a handcuffed man but by a handcuffed man being filmed (Jia Zhangke, taped interview by the author, Beijing, April 26, 2003).

24. This T-Mark producer, Shozo Ichiyama, had worked on Hou's *Good Men, Good Women* (Hao nan hao nü, 1995), *Goodbye South Goodbye* (Nanguo, zaijian nanguo, 1996), and *Flowers of Shanghai* (Haishang hua, 1998). As Jia Zhangke later said of the producer, "I deeply love Hou Hsiao-hsien's movies, and thought if he could work with Hou Hsiao-hsien over a long period, he must be a trustworthy person, or at the very least be someone who likes this kind of film." Quoted in "Jia Zhangke: Zai 'zhantai' shang dengdai" [Jia Zhangke: Waiting on the "Platform"], interviewed by Cheng Qingsong and Huang Ou, in *Wo de sheyingji bu sahuang: Liushi niandai Zhongguo dianying daoyan dang'an* [My camera doesn't lie: Files on the '60s generation of Chinese film directors], ed. Cheng Qingsong and Huang Ou (Beijing: Zhongguo youyi chuban gongsi, 2002), 344. Aside from Hou Hsiao-hsien, other influences that Jia Zhangke has acknowledged are *Nanook of the North* (1922; dir. Robert J. Flaherty), *Street Angels* (Malu tianshi, 1937; dir. Yuan Muzhi), *Spring in a Small Town* (Xiaocheng zhi chun, 1948; dir. Fei Mu), and the films of Yasujiro Ozu. See Jia Zhangke, "Zhongguo de duli dianying ren," 154, 162; and Stephen Teo, "Cinema with an Accent." In interviews, Jia frequently cites a 1991 initial viewing of Chen Kaige's *Yellow Earth* (Huang tudi, 1984) as first inspiring him to pursue filmmaking, though he usually adds that he likes few other Fifth Generation films.

25. The effect of exposure to Deng Lijun's songs so soon after the end of the Cultural Revolution is summarized by Sheldon H. Lu as follows: "The soft, sentimental, private, and humane melodies found in popular culture struck a note that contrasted with the official language of revolution and class struggle" (Lu, *China, Transnational Visuality, Global Postmodernity* [Stanford, Calif.: Stanford University Press, 2001], 198). On the arrival of pirated Deng Lijun pop tapes in Fenyang, Jia Zhangke has said that "you then felt a kind of new life had begun" ("Jia Zhangke: Zai 'zhantai' shang dengdai," 343).

26. See "Jia Zhangke: Zai 'zhantai' shang dengdai," 346; and "Jia Zhangke fangtan —You yigu qi zhengzai ningju" [Jia Zhangke interview—There's a puff of vapor that's now condensing], *Nanfang dushi bao* (Nanfang metropolitan news), March 4, 2003.

27. André Bazin, "De Sica: Metteur en scène," in *What Is Cinema?* vol. 2, 66.

28. Ibid., 76. Speaking here of Vittorio De Sica's *Umberto D* (1952), Bazin defines "life time" as "the simple continuing to be of a person to whom nothing in particular happens."

29. The Four Modernizations—industry, agriculture, national defense, and science and technology—were the ideological mantra of the Deng Xiaoping era. At one point in *Platform* the main protagonist dutifully recites them at the demand of his troupe leader. Jia Zhangke has noted that the preference for the combination of ellipses and quotidian duration in shot selection is related to geographical location: "When I started shooting this film, it was as if I had two alternatives. One was to film the very strong changes of the era, and the other was to show more deeply the experience of this in the hinterlands, so that it seems as if nothing has happened, and yet everything is happening" (Jia Zhangke, "Zhongguo de duli dianying ren," 159).

30. Svetlana Boym, *The Future of Nostalgia* (New York: Basic Books, 2001), esp. 49–55.

31. Ibid., 49.

32. When one of the main characters tearfully revolts against getting an abortion, for example, the entire scene is shot from the other end of a hospital corridor, so that the viewer lacks even clear access to the facial expressions of the characters as they speak.

33. In an aside about Hollywood editing, Boym asserts that the avoidance of real time is the "one inviolable code in Hollywood cinema," in which "it is no longer the content of the images but the pace of editing itself that has a visceral impact on the viewer and puts an invisible taboo on any form of reflective longing" (Boym, *The Future of Nostalgia*, 38).

34. Despite their stylistic similarities, I do not mean to imply that these filmmakers share identical concerns. For example, many of the films of Kiarostami and some of his contemporaries in Iran contain a self-critique of their own realist impulses and are at least partially about the invasiveness of the very attempt to capture the real on film and the impossibility of its success. Examples include Jafar Panahi's *The Mirror* (1997) and Kiarostami's *Close-Up* (1990), *The Taste of Cherry* (1997), and *The Wind Will Carry Us* (1999).

35. Dogma 95 aimed to counter the conception of cinema as illusion with a manifesto-like "vow of chastity," drafted by Lars von Trier and Thomas Vinterberg, in which the filmmakers swear to uphold such restrictions as natural lighting and sound, on-location shooting, realistic subjects, and contemporary settings. Representative films include Vinterberg's *The Celebration* (1998) and von Trier's *The Idiots* (1998).

36. Andrew Grossman blasts this aesthetic as an "alleged minimalist solution to Hollywood bombast" and mocks "the fallaciously 'transcendental' promise of uneventfulness," and in particular the critical reception of *The Wind Will Carry Us*: "We must endure tired formalist arguments from Kiarostami cultists who insist that the film's meditative uneventfulness is in fact an intellectually demanding existential challenge—as if this were the cinematic equivalent of Kierkegaard— and that the film's organic structure transcends the mundanity of its content by paradoxically presenting something more real than reality through a monastically ascetic style. (So, then, is style reality?) The mere recognition of conspicuously realistic time in a medium known for its temporal trickery becomes a *de facto* false ideology of naturalist realism" (Grossman, "The Wind Will Carry Us," *Scope: An On-Line Journal of Film Studies*, May 2001, http://www.nottingham.ac.uk/ film/journal/filmrev/the-wind-will-carry-us.htm). While I do not share Grossman's evaluation of *The Wind Will Carry Us*, his broadside effectively points to the fine line between naturalist realism and minimalist formalism in some art cinema.

37. Gilles Deleuze, *Cinema 1: The Movement—Image*, trans. Hugh Tomlinson

(Minneapolis: University of Minnesota Press, 1986). As different as their concerns are—Deleuze the poststructuralist philosopher and Bazin the humanist critic—both share a direct debt to Bergson in their theories of cinematic time.

38. See Berry, "Watching Time Go By," for an application of Deleuze's notion of the time-image to *Xiao Wu.*

39. In the course of the 1990s, Hollywood went from having no presence in the Mainland China film market to being the dominant force at the box office. For details, see Stanley Rosen, "The Wolf at the Door: Hollywood and the Film Market in China," in *Southern California and the World,* ed. Eric J. Heikkila and Rafael Pizarro (Westport, Conn.: Praeger, 2002), 49–77. As mentioned earlier, despite their lack of official distribution even Jia's early films constitute an alternative viewing experience in mainland China if such a category includes video watching in private homes, cafés, and bars, which is dominated by pirated video compact disks (vcds) and dvds. *Xiao Shan Going Home* and *Xiao Wu* have long been available in a small number of video shops on poor-quality home-burned vcds, and the latter could also be downloaded to computers with broadband Internet connections (now common in Internet cafés if not private homes). Moreover, high-quality pirated dvds of *Platform* and *Unknown Pleasures* began to turn up in many urban neighborhood video stores after their release in the West (leading to the speculative scenario described in the first paragraph of this essay) and *The World* was released in China on dvd.

40. "Jia Zhangke: Keyi shuo shi yi zhong tuoxie" [Jia Zhangke: You can say it's a kind of compromise], *Qingnian bao* (Youth daily), April 15, 2003.

41. In the invaluable documentary *My Camera Doesn't Lie* (2003; dir. Solveig Klassen and Katharina Schneider-Roos), for example, some independent Chinese directors express their disappointment with Zhang Yuan for working in the mainstream studio system. Jia is a notable exception in this group; he states that Zhang Yuan had built up enough credibility to be trusted to maintain his integrity in any system within which he chose to work.

42. Yu Aiyuan, "Tuwei, taoli, luowang" (Breakthrough, escape, ensnarement), *Jinri xianfeng* (Avant-garde today) 12 (March 2002): 39. Note that recently a more thorough discussion of the issue of Jia Zhangke's "banned" status has appeared: see Valerie Jaffee, "Bringing the World to the Nation: Jia Zhangke and the Legitimation of Chinese Underground Film," *Senses of Cinema,* no. 32 (July-September 2004), http://www.sensesofcinema.com/contents/04/32/chinese_underground_film.html.

43. Chen Pingshu, "Jia Zhangke, Wang Xiaoshuai huigui zhuliu: dianying 'diliudai' jiedong."

44. The sizable minority who seek out independent cinema in China are by no means unaware of filmmakers such as Jia Zhangke. Essays about Jia as well as interviews with him abound on Chinese Web sites, and cinephiles avidly discuss his films (likely seen on video) on fan sites such as http://www.fanhall.com.

getting real

Chinese Documentary, Chinese Postsocialism

CHRIS BERRY

Since 1989 innovative documentary has been one of the hallmarks of Chinese film and video. Most of the documentary makers associated with this new direction have professional backgrounds completely separate from the Urban or Sixth Generation of young feature filmmakers. They usually shoot on video and come from the world of television, which has its own training institutions and regulations that are apart from those of film. However, there are also notable similarities between their works and those of the Urban or Sixth Generation. In this essay I examine the new documentaries within a comparative framework, arguing that the new documentary and feature filmmakers both operate under the imperative to "get real."

"Getting real" has two meanings here. On the one hand, it indicates the drive to represent the "real" behind both the new documentaries and the feature films. On the other hand, it also refers to the slang phrase "get real," meaning "wise up" or "stop dreaming." In the People's Republic since 1989, this has meant developing a new understanding of the limits of the emergent public sphere and the possibilities of social transformation after, on the one hand, the Tiananmen Square massacre (or "incident," as the regime prefers to call it) and, on the other, the negative example of the former Soviet Union's fragmentation and decline following the transition to democracy and capital-ism in the 1990s. In a nutshell, "getting real" is the condition of contemporary postsocialist cinema in China. There is no doubt that these two senses of "getting real" work together as a productive tension, or overdetermining contradiction, that conditions the new Chinese documentary. A more diffi-cult question is whether the new documentary participates in the mainte-nance of Chinese postsocialism or disturbs it.

I specify "Chinese postsocialism" here for two reasons. First, I wrote this essay out of the conviction that the new documentary in China can only be understood in this locally specific context. By way of comparison, Bérénice Reynaud has introduced some of the work considered here in a survey essay that bristles with wonderful insights and provocations by placing the work along with a range of other critical and independent Chinese videos from the period before 1989, from Hong Kong, from Taiwan, and from the diaspora, including the United States. Reynaud links this material with the framework of response to the experience of colonialism and a general progressive politics of critical intervention.[1] While I do not challenge broad (and detailed) takes such as Reynaud's, in this essay I supplement them with an emphasis on the local specificity that makes independent documentary distinctive in post-1989 China. For example, many of the new documentary makers have drawn upon the cinema verité of Fred Wiseman and Ogawa Shinsuke's socially engaged documentary modes. But beyond the formal similarities, both the appeal and the significance of these modes in post-1989 China is quite different from that in 1960s United States and Japan, as well as that in Taiwan and South Korea, where Ogawa's mode has also been appropriated.

The second reason stems from the fact that postsocialism is at once a condition shared across many different countries and experienced in locally specific ways. The term "postsocialism" has been used colloquially to mean simply "after the end of socialism." This makes sense in the countries that have appeared after the break-up of the Soviet Union, for instance. In the People's Republic of China, however, postsocialism has more parallels with Lyotard's postmodernism, where the forms and structures of the modern (in this case socialism) persist long after faith in the grand narrative that authorizes it has been lost.[2] Furthermore, the general postsocialist condition has also been felt among the forces in the West of what was the Left, where the fall of the Berlin Wall in 1989 has forced the remaining diehards to confront not only a declining faith in liberal capitalist democracy but also the absence of any "actually existing" alternative. In other words, I write this essay not with a neo–cold war hope that China may one day join the "free world," but out of a shared interest in the question of tactical responses to having to work in the globalizing territory of what de Certeau calls "the space of the Other" at a time when the absence of visible and viable outside space threatens the meaningfulness of the very phrase.[3]

Who, then, are the new documentary makers in the People's Republic? What characterizes their work, and when did it begin? Probably the best-known Chinese documentary internationally and the one many would assume initiated the new documentary form is *River Elegy* (Heshang, a.k.a. *Death Song of the River*, 1988; dir. Xia Jun). This polemic on cultural isolationism and the persistence of feudalism aired on the national state television network China Central Television (CCTV) in the months prior to the 1989 Tiananmen Square massacre, and in its wake placed the show's producers among China's most-wanted fugitives.[4] However, although its message was challenging, in other ways it followed existing paradigms. All Chinese documentaries made prior to 1989 took the form of the pre-scripted illustrated lecture. For the most part they were known as *zhuanti pian* (literally, "special topic films") as opposed to newsreels (*xinwen pian*), which cover a range of topics in short reports. With the benefit of hindsight, the criticism is often made that the "cultural fever" and "democracy spring" of the late eighties were events isolated from ordinary people. And indeed, the continued use of the illustrated lecture format in *River Elegy* implies that its arguments are part of disputations among the governing elite. It belies both the Maoist rhetoric of going down among the people to learn from them and the newer participatory rhetoric of democracy, suggesting that the ordinary people (*laobaixing*) are not involved in the process of determining the future of their society but are waiting to be educated about the decisions made above and about them through documentaries such as *River Elegy* and other pedagogical materials.[5] Therefore, *River Elegy* cannot be considered the beginning of new documentary in China; the defining feature of the new documentary is a more spontaneous format.

Furthermore, the first Chinese documentary to move away from the illustrated lecture format and toward spontaneity was made outside the state-run system. Wu Wenguang's *Bumming in Beijing: The Last Dreamers* (Liulang

Beijing, 1990; dir. Wu Wenguang) was first shown outside China at the Hong Kong Film Festival in 1991, after which it traveled the world. It has, of course, never been broadcast in China. *Bumming In Beijing* provoked the same excited response that the feature film *Yellow Earth* (Huang tudi, 1984, dir. Chen Kaige) did when it screened in Hong Kong in 1985.[6] Bérénice Reynaud speaks of "the feeling that a new chapter of the history of representation was being written in front of my eyes."[7] Lu Xinyu, author of *The New Documentary Film Movement in China,* also traces to *Yellow Earth* the first manifestations of that "movement."[8]

Four main characteristics, all shared with the other new documentaries that began to appear in China at this time, made *Bumming in Beijing* so striking. These characteristics also provide a framework for comparing the film to the new feature filmmaking and for situating both forms within contemporary Chinese postsocialism. First, the experience and memory of June 4th (*liusi*) 1989 is a crucial structuring absence. Second, the focus is directly on contemporary city life in China among educated people like the documentary makers and the filmmakers themselves. Third, as mentioned above, the illustrated lecture format is abandoned for more spontaneous shooting. And fourth, production within the state-owned system is eschewed for independent production. All of these characteristics change over time. The first fades as the immediate possibility of redress and political change also fades. The second increasingly comes to mean a focus on ordinary people in China today rather than on the educated elite. The third undergoes a shift from more experimental to more mainstream modes of spontaneous documentary shot on more lightweight technology, including digital video. And the fourth is increasingly imbricated with television, making it more difficult to draw lines between independence, government direction, and determination by the market in a manner following the broader social and economic direction of postsocialist China, where it is harder and harder to draw a clear line between the state and private enterprise.

To start with the issue of June 4th, *Bumming in Beijing* consists of four vignettes about four artists living in Beijing and working, like Wu Wenguang himself, outside the state-run system. Shooting began in mid-1988 and ended in late 1990.[9] In the film we observe the independent artists' difficult living conditions along with their depression. With one exception, by the end of the documentary all but one of the artists have married foreigners and are preparing to leave or have left China.[10] Although the documentary does not directly address the 1989 Tiananmen Square massacre and the associated dashing of ideals, it resonates with its absent presence; without any other reason offered for the overwhelming atmosphere of hopelessness and the desire to leave the country the Tiananmen event is most likely understood as accounting for both. Indeed, the lack of discussion of the event may imply that it is too dangerous to mention and thus effectively communicates the conditions producing the mood of the interviewees and the documentary itself.

The June 4th issue is also the structuring absence at the heart of other relatively early new documentaries. Shi Jian, who together with his colleagues ran a documentary-making team known as Structure, Wave, Youth and Cinema (aka the SWYC Group), is another pioneer of the new Chinese documentary. The film *I Graduated!* (Wo biyele, 1992; dir. SWYC Group) was screened at the Hong Kong International Film Festival in 1993. Also based on interviews, it focuses on members of the graduating class of Beijing University. There is much handheld camera work, possibly because, as we see in the film itself, the equipment has to be smuggled onto campus in sports bags. Also, these soon-to-graduate students are not at all ebullient. Instead, they worry about their job assignments and mention other students that they miss.[11] Eventually, viewers may recall that this campus and this class of students were very active in the 1989 democracy movement. That is why the campus is so strictly guarded, why they miss friends (shot? arrested? executed?) and why their futures are so uncertain. As the documentary develops, the interviewees allude more and more to the events that haunt them. In the years before and after 1989, SWYC also made an eight-part series called *Tiananmen Square* (Tiananmen, 1991; dir. SWYC Group), which also was marked by an absence of the events of 1989 themselves. An important later documentary film that also seems overdetermined by the taboo on June 4th is the feature-length documentary *The Square* (Guangchang, 1994; dir. Zhang Yuan and Duan Jinchuan). As a cinema verité portrait of the various daily activities and power plays that occur on the stagelike square, no one in the film addresses the event, precisely because it is taboo.

This structuring absence of June 4th also lies at the heart of two of the earlier examples of the new feature filmmaking of the 1990s, *Red Beads* (Xuanlian, 1993; dir. He Jianjun), and *The Days* (Dongchun de rizi, 1993; dir. Wang Xiaoshuai). The title of the first film refers to bloodshed, and the narrative centers on post-traumatic mental illness. The second film, like *Bumming in Beijing*, focuses on alienated artists and the question of whether or not to go overseas. Here it seems important to note that whereas documentary filmmaking played little or no role in the wave of new Chinese cinema associated with the Fifth Generation directors in the 1980s, it seems to have been central to post-1989 cinema, as well as possibly to set the tone for feature filmmaking.

Both the new documentaries and feature films allude to politically sensitive topics indirectly, as the Fifth Generation also did. But where Fifth Generation films like *Raise the Red Lantern* (Da hong denglong gao gao gua, 1991; dir. Zhang Yimou), *Yellow Earth*, and *Horse Thief* (Daoma zei, 1986; Tian Zhuang-zhuang) use historical and/or geographically remote settings as allegories for the present, the new documentaries and feature films focus squarely on contemporary life. This second characteristic has continued, even after the triggering event of 1989 receded into the background with the passing of time, new economic growth, and the negative example of democratic change accompanied by social chaos in the former Soviet Union. But where the new features have the reputation for focusing on urban youth—earned through features ranging from *Beijing Bastards* (Beijing zazhong, 1991; dir. Zhang Yuan) to *Beijing Bicycle* (Shiqi sui de danche, 2001; dir. Wang Xiaoshuai)—the documentaries have diversified more within the common focus on contemporary life.

Initially, documentaries like *Bumming in Beijing* and *I Graduated!* examined the lives of young, urban, educated people who are similar to the filmmakers themselves. Wu Wenguang continued this trend in, for example, his follow-up to *Bumming in Beijing, At Home in the World* (Sihai rujia, 1995), where he interviews the same subjects in their new homes around the world, as well as in *1966, My Time in the Red Guards* (1966, Wo de hongweibing shidai, 1993), where he interviews former Red Guards, including the Fifth Generation filmmaker Tian Zhuangzhuang. But other filmmakers have moved out to cover everyday life outside of the major cities and as experienced by more ordinary people, with such notable examples as Duan Jinchuan's trilogy of films about Tibet (discussed further below); Lu Wangping's video about a traveling rural opera troupe, *The Story of Wang Laobai* (Wang Laobai de gushi, 1996; dir. Lu Wangping); and Wen Pulin's various videos about his own involvement in contemporary Tibetan Buddhism, such as *The Living Buddha of Kangba* (Kangba huofu, 1991), *The Nuns of Minqiong* (Minqiongan de ninü, 1992), *The*

Secret Site of Asceticism (Qingpu, 1992; codirected with Duan Jinchuan), and *Pa-dga' Living Buddha* (Bajia huofu, 1993).

The interest of many documentary filmmakers in "minority nationalities" and the far-flung border regions of China is a feature shared more with the Fifth Generation of feature filmmakers than with the Sixth or Urban Generation that forms the primary framework in which the documentaries are considered here. This link can be traced to the mid-1980s fascination with these regions and peoples as some kind of "others" within China. By virtue of that paradoxical status, they could express the sense of alienation and distance from their own culture felt by many educated Chinese amid the disillusion of the post-Mao era.[12] At this time, feature filmmakers went to shoot in these areas, and many who in the future would become independent documentary makers went to visit, live, or work in these areas. For Wen Pulin, Tibet is clearly an appealing place of refuge from the failure of modern materialist culture, whereas Duan Jinchuan seems to approach life in contemporary Tibet as one aspect of life in the People's Republic as a whole.

In the process of recording scenes of contemporary Chinese life, many documentaries have inevitably also touched on contemporary Chinese post-socialism's turn to the market economy for economic growth under the overall umbrella of the state-run system. In some cases, this effort is clearly deliberate. For example, *Diary of Tai Fu Xiang* (Taifuxiang riji, 1998; dir. Lin Xudong) details the efforts to put ownership of a bankrupt state-owned department store in Shijiazhuang into the hands of its employees, including the difficulties that many of those employees have in finding the funds to invest in this dubious venture. *Out of Phoenix Bridge* (Huidao fenghuangqiao, 1997; dir. Li Hong) follows a group of young women who as undocumented workers from the village of Phoenix Bridge in Anhui province have come to Beijing to seek employment as maids, a phenomenon that could not have occurred before the new mixed economic and social structure. And the DV (digital video) documentary *Jiang Hu: Life on the Road* (Jianghu, 1999; dir. Wu Wenguang), follows the efforts of an entertainment troupe to find forms that will appeal to the market. This diversification in subject matter means the new documentary is no longer a phenomenon among the educated elite.

But even more significant in this broadening of the new documentary is how the films and videos are made, both stylistically and institutionally, as well as their wide appeal. For not only do these new documentaries regularly "go down among the people" but they also give (or appear to give) the ordinary people a direct voice, which enables (or appears to enable) them to speak directly to other ordinary people and resonates with the economic agency that the development of a market sector gives (or appears to give) them.

Stylistically, this giving of a voice is centered in unscripted spontaneity. This was also one of the most immediately striking features of *Bumming in Beijing*, and of all the other new documentaries that have followed it. In Chinese, the most frequently used term in publications to describe this filmmaking mode is "on-the-spot realism" (*jishizhuyi*). In practice, in terms of documentary it refers to a spontaneous and unscripted quality that is a fundamental and defining characteristic distinguishing them from the old scripted realism of the "special topic" documentaries. It is frequently accentuated by handheld camera work and technical lapses and flaws characteristic of uncontrolled situations. The documentaries often also highlight events that conspicuously signify spontaneity and a lack of script. The most obvious example in *Bumming in Beijing* would be the nervous breakdown suffered on camera by the painter Zhang Xiaping. In *I Graduated!* the cracked voices and tears of the interviewees function in the same way.

This drive to produce a new vision of the real is one aspect of the "getting real" referred to above. The political significance of this change should not be sidestepped by invoking the rhetoric of emerging Chinese pluralism (*duoyuanhua*), but at the same time it must be acknowledged that its precise political significance is difficult to determine in an environment where economic liberalization has been accompanied by tighter political and ideological control. At a minimum it suggests the old realism is out of touch with China today and needs to be updated. But it may also be read as suggesting implicit contestation and challenge to the authority and legitimacy of those associated with the older pedagogical mode, appropriate to a structure where agency and leadership is concentrated in the state apparatus and its functionaries.

The same term used to describe the new documentary, *jishizhuyi* or "on-the-spot realism," is often also used to describe the contemporary urban films made by the younger generation of feature filmmakers. However, whereas for documentary makers "on-the-spot realism" is distinguished from the scripted quality of the old "special topic" or *zhuanti* films, "on-the-spot realism" distinguishes the new features from two older stylistic traditions. One is the

Girls from Phoenix
Bridge Village have their
picture taken in Tiananmen Square.

realism associated with "socialist realism," which is expressed in Chinese using a different term, *xianshizhuyi*, which means representational realism. With the decline of faith in socialism, *xianshizhuyi* has come into disrepute. Where once it simply meant "realism," these days it seems to carry a connotation of fakery or at best reality as the authorities wish it were. This disrepute has prevailed for twenty years now, and indeed the Fifth Generation directors also saw many of the key characteristics of their work as reclaiming the real from *xianshizhuyi*. The use of locations as opposed to sets; of natural light or darkness rather than artificial lights and blue filters; and of unknown actors rather than stars are all examples that can be readily observed in foundational Fifth Generation works like *One and Eight* (Yige he bage, 1984; dir. Zhang Junzhao) and *Yellow Earth*. However, the use of "on-the-spot realism" or *jishizhuyi* to describe the new trend of the nineties in feature films also distinguishes it from the art film stylizations and historical allegory of much Fifth Generation work, where it pursues instead an unadorned contemporary look that is the fictional counterpart of the new documentary's spontaneous style.[13]

Deleuze's ideas on the "movement-image" versus the "time-image" present perhaps one framework in which to consider the shift from the more conventional structures of the illustrated lecture format documentaries, socialist realist feature films, and even some of the more dramatic Fifth Generation films, on the one hand, and the new documentaries and Sixth or Urban Generation films on the other. For Deleuze, the movement-image refers to the regime most commonly associated with Hollywood studio filmmaking. Here, time appears indirectly as a regime of movement, where framing, cutting, and the like follow movement as a marker of change and therefore of time. The rational, step-by-step logic of the documentary lecture also fits this logic.[14] By contrast, when the rational cause-and-effect subtending these linear structures disappears and it becomes less possible to predict when the cut will come, how the next shot will be linked to the last, or how long the shot will last, Deleuze believes that a more direct access to time as duration opens up.[15]

On occasion, this seems like a quest for some sort of transcendent truth. But the prime examples of the cinema of the time-image are for Deleuze more historically and socially grounded. They are drawn from European art films, and he links them to the collapse of faith in the grand narratives of modernity following Nazism and World War II; the same environment that laid the groundwork for the kind of postmodernity discussed by Lyotard. I have already indicated that the Chinese postsocialist environment and culture bear comparison to this phenomenon. Some of the independent documentaries and Urban or Sixth Generation features also break away from the logic of the "movement-image" toward a distended form in which shots continue beyond any movement logic either in the literal sense or in the sense of narrative development. Both Jia Zhangke's feature films and Wu Wenguang's documentaries seem to follow this pattern, dwelling on time passing in a seemingly uncontrolled manner. (Perhaps it is not a pure coincidence that Jia's second feature, *Platform* (Zhantai, 1999), followed an entertainment troupe, as does Wu's *Jiang Hu: Life on the Road*. Although this sense of time passing is not the philosophical sense of "duration" invoked by Deleuze in reference to the time-image, this distended form does loosen the structure of the films. The relation between shots never becomes completely unpredictable, and although chronology is followed (in not quite the condition of what Deleuze calls "any-space-whatever") it becomes hard to have a sense of teleology or progress as interviewees ramble verbally in Wu's films and characters ramble literally in Jia's. One loses any sense of knowing when a shot will end or exactly what it will cut to, and this is quite different from the certain sense of progress invoked by the ideologies of modernity, be it driven by the socialist command economy or the alleged socialist market economy of the new era. Instead, the certainty of progress is replaced by a contingent life in which characters react and respond rather than initiate, looking for ways to get by rather than having a clear sense of purpose.

Both Duan Jinchuan and Wu Wenguang have told me that their preference for unscripted work, handheld cameras, and events that signal spontaneity can be traced back to their encounters with the foreign television crews that started coming to shoot in China at the stations where they worked in the eighties. This preference for spontaneity also helps to explain why they and other new documentary makers were drawn to cinema verité, be it in the French interview style associated with Jean Rouch and his classic film *Chronicle of a Summer* (Chronique d'un eté, 1961) that is echoed in the interview films of Wu, or the American observational style associated with filmmakers such as Fred Wiseman that is evoked in some of the films of Duan. After some of the early independent works were screened in Hong Kong and elsewhere, documentary makers such as Wu and Duan were invited to attend Asia's leading documentary film festival at Yamagata. There, in 1993, a special retrospective of Wiseman's work was held. The most direct evidence of the impact of this event can be seen in two films that Duan directed after the Yamagata festival: *The Square* (codirected with Zhang Yuan) and *No. 16 Barkhor Street South* (Bakuonanjie shiliuhao, 1996), part of his trilogy of Tibetan works. Both of these films scrupulously follow Wiseman's formula of pure observational work with no interviews or arranged scenes, no extra-diegetic music, and complete dependence on editing to bring the material together into a coherent whole through "mosaic structures."[16] *Barkhor Street* also followed Wiseman's well-known interest in social institutions, for the address that gives the film its title is that of the neighborhood office on Barkhor Street in central Lhasa where pilgrims circumambulate and protestors sometimes gather. Duan's own residence of eight years in Lhasa in the 1980s, and his links with local Tibetan audio-visual and cultural groups, put him in a unique position to carry out this project. The result is also unique in that it comprises an unscripted record of the workings of the Chinese government at the grassroots level and a picture of daily life in Tibet not written according to the ideological requirements of either Beijing or Dharamsala. For this film, Duan won the 1996 Prix du Réel in France, the first major international prize awarded to a Chinese documentary film.[17]

The appeal of cinema verité and other more spontaneous documentary techniques because of their ability to reclaim the authority of realism from the increasingly devalued "special topic" films can be understood as an example of cultural translation. Most theorists of cultural translation emphasize incommensurability and the idea that everything is somewhat changed in the process of translation. Lydia Liu, in her essay "Translingual Practice," recognizes not only how the direction and impact of translation may be conditioned by power but also the idea that whatever may enter a culture or society from overseas can only be made sense of in terms of the existing local cultural conditions and conventions. She therefore emphasizes the role of local agency in this process.[18] Given this, some additional local factors should be borne in mind in accounting for the appeal and significance of spontaneous documentary techniques in the nineties.

First, in an environment saturated by institutional and self-censorship, spontaneous documentary techniques have a distinct advantage. For example, it is impossible for the authorities to require that a script be submitted. Also, it is difficult to blame the documentary makers for what subjects say or do if they are not being told what to say or do by the documentary maker. Furthermore, if the subjects are the ordinary people revered by socialism, it is difficult for the censors to complain if the people say things that they do not want to hear.

Second, these spontaneous documentary techniques seem like an extension of the well-established and very popular local genre of reportage literature (*baogao wenxue*, also known more recently as *jishi wenxue*). Reportage also derives a certain authority and ability to withstand censorship from its claim to veracity. Although this fact has not always exempted reportage writers from trouble with the authorities after publishing accounts of events the authorities wish had not happened, it has made reportage a powerful site of resistance within China.[19]

Third, by giving voice to ordinary people, spontaneous documentary also taps into the longstanding practice of seeking out a public space for airing otherwise unresolved grievances. Most famously, this practice was co-opted by the communists in the tradition of "speaking bitterness" (*suku*), where public meetings were held after a community was liberated and the local poor were encouraged to speak out about their sufferings at the hands of the local rich and powerful as a prelude to punishment. This pattern is less relevant regarding the spontaneous documentaries made by individual filmmakers and given little circulation within China, but the spontaneous techniques of the new documentary have spread like wildfire. In addition to all manner of home movie documentaries produced by complete amateurs with access to digital video cameras and no training or idea of broadcast standards— but often with an eye for remarkable materials—the spontaneous documentary has become a television staple. It appears most famously in magazine shows such as *Oriental Moment* (Dongfang shikong) and *Life Space* (Shenghuo kongjian), both aired by the national state-run station China Central Television, and the successors to these shows, but it has also been taken up by all manner of local stations and programs. The resulting shows have been extremely popular, most likely at least in part because of the refreshing nature of seeing ordinary people speaking relatively openly and without rehearsal.[20] However, although there may be no kindly Party Secretary "uncle" (*shushu*) on-screen to guide what happens, television broadcasting does raise issues relating to commercial sponsorship, television station "gatekeepers" who self-censor, and government censorship itself.

That brings us finally to the original distinguishing characteristic of the new documentary: independence. As indicated by the increasing appearance of television programs that take on many of the characteristics of the early new documentary films, independent production may no longer be such a hallmark. But at the beginning of both the new documentary and the new feature films of the nineties, this was a very notable characteristic. In a country where any form of production of anything outside the state-owned system was for many years frowned upon as "capitalist roading," such independence was very striking indeed. Furthermore, it seems that after the many difficult negotiations with the government censors experienced by feature filmmakers in the late eighties, and the specter of much tighter control in the wake of the events of 1989, the decision to pioneer independent production was a common and distinguishing feature of both new documentary and new feature filmmaking. All the early films that won attention as new documentaries, such as *Bumming in Beijing* and *I Graduated!*, as well as many of the early feature films of the younger Urban Generation of directors, such as *The Days, Beijing Bastards*, and *Red Beads*, were made independently.

However, what does "independence" mean for documentary makers in postsocialist China? There are two aspects that need to be addressed to answer this question. First, there is the difference between independence for feature filmmakers and for documentary makers that is the result of their different places in the administrative structures of the state and the different regulations and laws applying to them. Second, there is the issue of what independence means under contemporary Chinese postsocialist conditions. In many ways, independent production is the film- and video-making equivalent of the broader appearance of a market sector of the economy within the overall state-planned socialist framework, which is one of the defining hallmarks of Chinese postsocialism. The market sector is not only licensed by the state but also as a smaller sector of the overall socioeconomic structure. It is thus dependent upon and has to work with the state-owned sector regardless of tension, frictions, and disjunctures.

The implications of independent status for the documentary makers and for the feature filmmakers are quite different. Both China's independent documentary and feature filmmakers resist the label "underground" and insist that independence does not necessarily equate opposition to the state, the Party or the government. However, film and television historically have been two separate worlds in China, where until the mid-nineties each was administered by separate offices and thus governed by very different regulations. Filmmakers and television program makers train in different institutes and there are few connections between them. While many connections can be seen among the documentary makers—in codirection, for example, none of them have made feature films. There is, however, one notable exception to this pattern. Zhang Yuan is a member of the so-called Sixth Generation of feature filmmakers who graduated from Beijing Film Academy in 1989. But he has also shown a strong interest in documentary since his first feature, *Mama* (Mama, 1990)—a film about the mother of a disabled child, which includes documentary sequences of interviews with real-life mothers of disabled children. Although since then Zhang has continued to make both features and documentaries, he is the only one to do so,[21] and despite similar aesthetic strategies and thematic interests, feature film and documentary makers are two separate groups operating in separate worlds.

The most serious consequence of this concerns the possibility of independent production in the sense of production outside the state system. When the separate regulations designed to monitor and control television and film production were drawn up many years ago, they could not and did not envisage the physical and organizational possibility of independent production. The equipment was too expensive and there was no independent sector.

Within the state-run film system, various proactive and reactive local and national censorship regulations have been in place at different times, insisting on script approval prior to production as well as approval of completed films prior to release. Throughout the nineties, the government has actively intervened to close any loopholes enabling filmmakers to avoid scrutiny— loopholes such as investment from overseas, editing overseas, sending films to film festivals prior to submitting them for approval for release, and so forth. Finally, in July 1996 the government passed a new film law that explicitly made illegal any film production other than that done within the state-owned studio system.[22] This means that although would-be independent feature filmmakers might not think of themselves as underground or subversive, they have been defined as such by the government.

Within the state-run television system, however, the situation is significantly different. The regulation is of television stations and what they air, not the production of materials on video. Furthermore, unlike film, the production of video materials can be achieved with ever cheaper and more accessible equipment, so it is not viable to attempt to gain proactive control over video production. In these circumstances, although many new documentaries have not been aired and may never be aired, so far there have not been any regulatory or legal interventions against the makers of these independent documentaries. In other words, unlike their film colleagues, video makers can be independent without being forced into a position of seeming underground or subversive.

However, this does not mean that the new documentary makers feel free to make whatever kinds of films they might like. An example of this issue is how the highly influential mode of production associated with the late Japanese documentary maker Ogawa Shinsuke has been taken up in China. The Yamagata International Documentary Film Festival was initiated by Ogawa and his associates, and thus it is perhaps not surprising that Ogawa's impact has been felt among the independent Chinese documentary makers who have attended the festival.[23] Ogawa's filmmaking has two main features. First, Ogawa is socially and politically engaged rather than a detached observer; possibly his most famous films compose the "Fortress Narita" series (referring to *Narita: The Peasants of the Second Fortress* [Sanrizuka: Dainitoride no hitobito, 1971]), which were made in the late sixties and early seventies as part of the resistance to the forced selling of land for the building of Tokyo's Narita Airport. Second, he lives and works among his subjects, relating to them not as an outsider but as a friend and colleague. For the Chinese new documentary makers, being socially and politically engaged has never been an option because such movements are ruthlessly suppressed in the People's Republic. But Ogawa's quality of relating to his subjects has been shared by the Chinese from the first. Wu Wenguang's *Bumming in Beijing* is about people the filmmaker knows well and relates to as friends. Lu Wangping spent a year traveling around with the opera troupe he documents in *The Story of Wang Laobai*, and Li Hong spent two years befriending, living with, and returning home with the young women whose story she tells in *Out of Phoenix Bridge*.

This apparent self-censorship (conscious or unconscious) raises the other side of the question of working independently within postsocialism. Just as the market sector is dependent on the state sector in the economy as a whole, the independent documentary makers cannot operate without reference to the state sector. Indeed, for the most part they were trained within and worked within the state-owned television sector for years. Further, many of them continue to do so by making independent documentaries on the side while they earn their income in a television station. Shi Jian of the SWYC Group has been a powerful figure at CCTV all along, where he initiated the program *Oriental Moment* in 1992. Li Hong made *Phoenix Bridge* while moonlighting from CCTV and by borrowing station equipment.[24] Even those who, like Duan Jinchuan, have set up their own independent production companies continue to depend on the state-owned sector to some degree because there are no privately owned television stations in China and thus no other way to air their works. Duan studied at the Beijing Broadcasting Institute and then went to work at Lhasa Television Station for eight years in the 1980s before returning to Beijing. Even though all of his films in the 1990s were made independently, the main investor in *No. 16 Barkor Street South* was CCTV (which at the time of my last inquiry had not yet aired it) with a Tibetan company as a smaller financial partner. And the boom in television programming featuring the new documentary styles has given the new documentary makers opportunities for work that they have not passed up. Lin Xudong's *Diary of Tai Fu Xiang* and Lu

Wangping's *The Story of Wang Laobai* were both made for CCTV. In addition, Jiang Yue of *The Other Bank* has since made a video for CCTV called *A River Is Stilled* (Jingzhi de He, 1998) about the building of the Three Gorges dam from the perspective of the workers on the project.

This mutual implication of the "independent" documentaries and the state-owned television sector raises some complex questions. Put simply, what is the relation of these documentaries to the state? Are they a challenge or are they complicit? If the relation is not to be considered in such a binary way, do they function as a supplement that changes the system or as a co-opted token that props it up? These questions are impossible to answer in an absolute and generally applicable way. It is even difficult to give a simple answer in regard to any individual film. For example, *Crazy English* (Fengkuang Yingyu, 1999; dir. Zhang Yuan) is a cinema verité film that follows the celebrity Li Yang as he moves along the circuit of his mass English-teaching rallies. Mixing pedagogy and demagogy, Li yells out in English nationalistic business slogans about making money and outdoing the West, which the crowd then yells back at him in response. Li has been accepted by the authorities as a patriotic paradigm, and it seems that they also have accepted Zhang's film as a eulogy to this popular national hero. However, as I watched the film I could not avoid thinking that Li's mass teachings seemed deeply demagogic like perverse post-socialist mutations of Mao rallies. Given the use of the cinema verité mode, it is difficult if not impossible to detect the filmmaker's own attitude.

Questions surrounding television broadcasting illustrate how difficult it is to make clear-cut judgments about these issues. We need to ask if the television documentaries really do provide a voice for the ordinary people to speak back to power. Or does the fact that they are made within conditions of government control and censorship mean that actually they act as a way of fooling the people into speaking their minds, or of getting good information about public opinion for the government whose own officials ordinary people would be wary of? And if the latter is true, is this necessarily a bad thing? Does it promote positive government change or prop up the existing system and its problems?

Many more difficult questions can be posed as such, but the fundamentally unstable, tense, and ambivalent Gramscian hegemony that is postsocialism makes it impossible to provide definitive answers. Instead, only future developments and more research will determine how this period and these documentary makers are seen in hindsight as contributors to a struggle for gradual transformation from within or to the containment of tensions that later surfaced.

NOTES

1. Bérénice Reynaud, "New Visions/New Chinas: Video-Art, Documentation, and the Chinese Modernity in Question," in *Resolutions: Contemporary Video Practices*, ed. Michael Renov and Erika Suderburg (Minneapolis: University of Minnesota Press, 1996), 229–57.

2. For further discussion of the different uses of the term in the Chinese context and why I draw on Lyotard as opposed to some of the other usages, see Chris Berry, "Seeking Truth from Fiction: Feature Films as Historiography in Deng's China," *Film History* 7, no. 1 (1995): 95.

3. Michel de Certeau, *The Practice of Everyday Life* (Berkeley: University of California Press, 1984), 36–37.

4. Su Xiaokang and Wang Luxiang, *Deathsong of the River: A Reader's Guide to the Chinese TV Series "Heshang,"* trans. Richard W. Bodman and P. Wan (Ithaca, N.Y.: East Asia Program, Cornell University, 1991). Currently residing in the United States, Su has recently published his memoirs, *A History of Misfortune*, trans. Zhu Hong (New York: Knopf, 2001).

5. Many of the essays composing the Chinese debate about *River Elegy* have been translated into English and published in *Chinese Sociology and Anthropology* 24, no. 4, and 25, no. 1 (1992). For a critical analysis of the documentary's argument, see Jing Wang, "*Heshang* and the Paradoxes of the Chinese Enlightenment," in *High Culture Fever: Politics, Aesthetics, and Ideology in Deng's China* (Berkeley: University of California Press, 1996), 118–36.

6. According to Tony Rayns, the occasion, which he finds "tempting" to date as the birth of the "New Chinese Cinema," "was received with something like collective rapture" ("Chinese Vocabulary: An Introduction to *King of the Children* and the New Chinese Cinema," in *King of the Children and the New Chinese Cinema*, ed. Chen Kaige and Tony Rayns (London: Faber and Faber, 1989), 1.

7. Reynaud, "New Visions/New Chinas," 235.

8. Lu Xinyu, *Zhongguo Xin Jilupian Yundong* [The New Documentary Film Movement in China] (Shanghai: Shanghai Wenyi Chubanshe, 2003). I thank Professor Lu for sharing her ideas and parts of her manuscript with me.

9. Wu Wenguang, "*Bumming in Beijing—The Last Dreamers*," in *The Twentieth Hong Kong International Film Festival*, ed. Urban Council (Hong Kong: Urban Council, 1996), 130.

10. The remaining subject, a theater director called Mou Sen, was the focus of another early documentary, *The Other Bank* (Bi'an, 1995) by Jiang Yue. The video follows Mou Sen's eponymous workshop, which attracts youngsters from around

the country but neglects to offer any practical help beyond the experience of the modernist and experimental workshop itself. Lu Xinyu opens her book with an extended discussion of this film, which she sees as representative of the fall away from utopianism and self-criticism among the former avant-garde at the heart of new documentary.

11. Regarding job assignments, at this time students were on graduation still assigned work by the state.

12. For different opinions on this phenomenon in feature filmmaking, see Chris Berry, "Race (*Minzu*): Chinese Film and the Politics of Nationalism," *Cinema Journal* 31, no. 2 (1992): 45–58; Hu Ke, "The Relationship between the Minority Nationalities and the Han in the Cinema," in *Chinese National Minorities Films* [Lun Zhongguo shaoshu minzu dianying], ed. Gao Honghu et al. (Beijing: China Film Press [*Zhongguo Dianying Chubanshe*], 1997), 205–11; Zhang Yingjin, "From 'Minority Film' to 'Minority Discourse': Questions of Nationhood and Ethnicity in Chinese Cinema," in *Transnational Chinese Cinemas: Identity, Nationhood, Gender*, ed. Sheldon Hsiao-Peng Lu (Honolulu: University of Hawaii Press, 1997), 81–104; Dru C. Gladney, "Representing Nationality in China: Refiguring Majority/Minority Identities," *Journal of Asian Studies* 53, no. 1 (1994): 92–123; Esther C. M. Yau, "Is China the End of Hermeneutics? Or, Political and Cultural Usage of Non-Han Women in Mainland Chinese Films," *Discourse* 11, no. 2 (1989): 115–38; and Stephanie Donald, "Women Reading Chinese Films: Between Orientalism and Silence," *Screen* 36, no. 4 (1995): 325–40.

13. Here, I have noted the mimetic realist qualities found in some Fifth Generation films. For an interpretation that sees the non-mimetic qualities of these films as a form of "expressive realism" (or *xieshizhuyi*) also distinct from socialist realism's representational realism or *xianshizhuyi*, see Chris Berry and Mary Ann Farquhar, "Post-Socialist Strategies: An Analysis of *Yellow Earth* and *Black Cannon Incident*," in *Cinematic Landscapes: Observations on the Visual Arts and Cinema of China and Japan*, ed. Linda C. Ehrlich and David Desser (Austin: University of Texas Press, 1994), 81–116.

14. Gilles Deleuze, *Cinema I: The Movement-Image*, trans. Hugh Tomlinson (Minneapolis: University of Minnesota Press, 1986).

15. Gilles Deleuze, *Cinema 2: The Time-Image*, trans. Hugh Tomlinson and Robert Galeta (Minneapolis: University of Minnesota Press, 1989).

16. As Bill Nichols notes: "In a conventional mosaic, the *tesserae* (facets) merge to yield a coherent whole when seen from a distance . . . The *tesserae* or sequences of a Wiseman film are already coherent and do not merge into one impression or one narrative tale so much as supplement each other. The whole of a mosaic is almost invariably embedded in a larger architectural whole but such a larger whole is absent in Wiseman's case . . . the films . . . offer little overt acknowledgment that the institutions under study directly relate to a larger social context" (Nichols,

"Frederick Wiseman's Documentaries: Theory and Structure," in *Ideology and the Image* [Bloomington: University of Indiana Press, 1981], 211). Much the same could be said of Duan's film.

17. For more on Duan, *The Square*, and *No. 16 Barkhor Street*, see Chris Berry, "Interview with Duan Jinchuan," *Metro* 113/114 (1998): 88–89.

18. Lydia H. Liu, "Translingual Practice: The Discourse of Individualism between China and the West," *positions* 1, no. 1 (1993): 160–93.

19. On reportage as resistance, see Yingjin Zhang, "Narrative, Ideology, Subjectivity: Defining a Subversive Discourse in Chinese Reportage," in *Politics, Ideology and Literary Discourse in Modern China: Theoretical Interventions and Cultural Studies*, ed. Liu Kang and Xiaobing Tang (Durham, N.C.: Duke University Press, 1993), 211–42.

20. In addition to the spontaneous documentaries, nationalistic documentaries in the "special topic" *zhuanti* mode have also found new audiences on television and even in the movie theaters, where in 1996 the film *Test of Strength* about the Korean War, known in China as the War to Resist U.S. Aggression and Aid Korea, was an unprecedented box office hit in the cities. See Ye Lou, "Popular Documentary Films," *Beijing Review* 41, no. 26 (1998): 28–29.

21. For a more detailed discussion of Zhang Yuan's films focused on *East Palace, West Palace*, see Chris Berry, "*East Palace, West Palace*: Staging Gay Life in China," *Jump Cut*, no. 42 (1998): 84–89.

22. Although some may object to the statement that fewer films than ever are made directly by the studios, my understanding at the time of this writing is that the law requires that, at least nominally, films are made within the studio system and in conformity with the attendant censorship practices. This often involves "buying a studio logo" (*mai yige changbiao*) or paying a studio a fee for its nominal supervision.

23. Barbara Hammer's documentary *Devotion: A Film about Ogawa Productions* (2000) not only gives a useful background to Ogawa but also features historical footage of foreign documentary makers listening to the great Ogawa expound during a lecture. Among the attentive listeners is Wu Wenguang. Also noteworthy is the decision made by Ogawa's widow to invite the Chinese Fifth Generation feature filmmaker Peng Xiaolian to finish his final work, *Manzan Benigaki*, which was shown at the 2001 Yamagata festival.

24. Chris Berry, "Crossing the Wall," *Dox*, no. 13 (1997): 14–15.

II

THE POLITICS AND POETICS OF URBAN SPACE

tear down the city

Reconstructing Urban Space in Contemporary Chinese Popular Cinema and Avant-Garde Art

C hai-na (literally, the act of "tearing down") is truly the proper name for contemporary "China," as all Chinese cities have witnessed the destruction of old buildings and the construction of new structures. This process on a massive scale gathered great momentum throughout the 1990s with the infusion of transnational capital, and the process continues into the twenty-first century. Toward the end of Zhang Yang's domestic box office success *Shower*, a traditional Chinese bathhouse in old Beijing is torn down (*chai*) to clear space for the building of a new commercial district. The whole neighborhood is to be torn apart and all the longtime neighbors will be scattered to different corners of the big city. There will be no more leisurely gambling on cricket fights because, as one old neighbor complains, crickets can't live in an apartment building removed from the vital force of the ground (*di qi*). Water heaters in the new high-rises cannot compare with the warm touch and intimacy of the old bathhouse, where people can gather and chat. The bulldozers, hammers, shovels, and trucks herald the advance of capitalism to level and destroy the insulated community.

Chai is indeed the theme of much of contemporary Chinese visual culture. It points not only to the physical demolition of the old cityscape but also, more profoundly, to the symbolic and psychological destruction of the social fabric of families and neighborhoods. In this essay I explore the theme of the destruction and reconstruction of the city as depicted in multiple media in contemporary Chinese popular cinema and avant-garde photography and video. The transformation of a new sensory economy in contemporary Chinese cultural production, through what some critics have termed the "postmaterial" condition, is concomitant with the destruction of old spatial forms and the reconstruction of new cities.

Day-by-day and inch-by-inch the logic of capital and commercialization steadily takes over both public and private space in postsocialist China. As can be seen in the visual texts I discuss below, there is an acutely felt collision between culture and capital. In the formation of a global "singular modernity," what has transpired is more than the "becoming cultural of the economic, and the becoming economic of the cultural."[1] Culture and economy often stand asymmetrical, disjunctive, and antagonistic in relation to each other even as they may be partners in the global flattening of differences in accordance to the principles of the marketplace. In the Chinese case, residual traditional culture and socialist habits clash with the emergent capitalist economy. Whether it is a state-sponsored project or the injection of transnational capital, relentless modernization and homogenization has produced profound contradiction and discontent throughout the country. In the words of the sociologist Saskia Sassen, what is happening in the globalizing city in regard to the linkage of people to territory is "globalization and its discontents"; that is, the "unmooring of identities from what have been traditional sources of identity, such as the nation or the village. The unmooring in the process of identity formation engenders new notions of community, of membership, and of entitlement."[2]

There is clear distinction between the popular cinema's therapeutic or reifying effect of personalizing the demolition of the city space through melodramatic nostalgia, and a more radical exploration of the collision between private and public in avant-garde art. However, both the popular and marginal texts share an anxiety or discomfort with the linear temporality of modernization and globalization represented by the widespread phenomenon of demolition, and both offer critiques of postsocialist and capitalist commodification. In the current era of social and economic reforms, drastic changes in the public infrastructure of the city as well as in the private space of the home inevitably affect the interiority of the subjects whose sense of materiality in their living environs is rapidly changing. This distorted experience of being in the world is what is called "post-material" (*hou wuzhi*) by Huang Du, curator of the exhibition *Post-Material: Interpretations of Everyday Life by Contemporary Chinese Artists,* which was held at Beijing's Red Gate Gallery in October and November 2000. As Huang explains, post-material "implies an artificial manifestation of modern technology, distinguished from naturally produced or handmade objects."[3] Indeed, the world has entered the post-materialistic stage with the advent of new technologies and lifestyles.

Housing reform has been a major achievement in the recent transition of the Chinese economy toward a market mechanism. The socialist system of subsidized public housing has been largely suspended, and since the early 1990s residents have been encouraged to purchase "commodity houses" (*shangpin fang*). A privately purchased and owned home has turned from a space in which to dwell into a new fetish object among the populace as the boom in real estate has become a driving force in the growth of China's fledgling market economy. In 2000, commodity houses worth a total of 23 billion yuan (approximately US$2.8 billion) were sold in Beijing alone.[4] The commodification of housing, and consequently the commodification of the private home and the inner life of individuals and families, has created tensions in the transformation of intimacy and subjectivity for those people caught in the process of post-material public and private antinomies.

As city planners and municipal governments lay out grandiose projects to transform cityscapes by constructing new buildings and roads and by tearing down existing structures along the way, the impact on the psyche of city residents is far more contradictory and uneven. Daily reports about city constructions and related activities—such as building new roads and widening old ones, planting trees and grass, cleaning polluted rivers and canals, and residents moving into new apartments—fill up Beijing's newspapers. Brand-new streets and new neighborhoods annually increase in great numbers, and it is estimated that about three hundred new place names were added to Beijing's map in 2001. While old alleys and *hutongs* are torn down, most new places are named "gardens" (*yuan*), "plazas" (*chang*), and "malls" (*cheng*).[5] Among the results of Beijing's modernization efforts, housing space per capita in the city reached 16.2 square meters in 2000, and according to the new five-year plan (2001–2005), the figure will have increased to 18 square meters by

2005.[6] Here at the end of the twentieth century and the beginning of the twenty-first, the supreme goal of the Chinese nation has been the "all-out construction of a society of moderate affluence" (*quanmian jianshe xiaokang shehui*), a main component of which is the realization of the dream of acquiring the valuable asset of a home for each and every citizen. As per-capita housing space increases, the domain of memory and history diminishes proportionately for those who have lived in the past. While in their heads dreaming about the new, many citizens accustomed to established neighborhoods with communal space specific to traditional Chinese architecture and urban planning cannot so easily in their hearts let go of the old.[7]

A new generation of filmmakers, photographers, and video artists rightfully claim the modern Chinese city as their own. In representing the demolition and construction of urban space through their own media, they evoke the memories, intimacy, affect, and habits of life associated with the old city, and at the same time project new zones of hopes, desires, and dreams in the rapidly changing social landscape. The media they deploy and the cultural texts they produce enter into an uneasy, asymmetrical, and contradictory relationship with the teleologies of modernization, developmentalism, globalization, and social progress.

Both the popular cinema and the avant-garde photography and video examined in this essay address the restructuring of architectural and social space and the attendant psychological impact on people's everyday experience of contemporary China. These forms differ greatly, however, in terms of audience and manner of representation. Popular cinema's targeted audience is the vast number of average Chinese citizens, and its mood of presentation tends to be sentimental and reflectionist in nature. By focusing on the mundane and familiar scenes of family relationships, love affairs, and the resultant moral crises, these films easily relate to the daily life and spiritual state of ordinary Chinese people. However, the works of avant-garde photography and video aim at more critical, quizzical, and abstract interventions of everyday life and social space as they speak to a small circle of specialized audiences—art connoisseurs, intellectuals, cultural workers, and critics—who are trained to decode the form and message of this sort of art.

The kind of "popular cinema" that I focus on in this section is different from independent cinema. Popular films are largely produced and distributed through regular channels within China's film industry. They address urgent topical issues in contemporary Chinese society that strike a chord with regular moviegoers. Audiences usually will not find remarkable stylistic innovations or shocking revelations about culture and history in this kind of film. Rather, they are conventional heart-warming melodramas and moral tales aimed to capture the hearts of the majority of average urban dwellers.[8] Although some of these films have caught the attention of international film festivals, the primary audience of the popular film is China's domestic market, in which films must sell and make a profit by appealing to the sentiments and life-world of ordinary people. The strategy of this group of new urban filmmakers thus marks a significant departure from the so-called independent Sixth Generation directors, whose films are often not allowed publicly to be screened in China. Instead, international audiences are their primary markets. Because of their subject matter and style, such films do not enter the mainstream of Chinese cinema even if they pass the censors for initial release. The field of independent cinema is defined by the features commonly associated with these films, including marginal social groups (rock musicians, independent artists, squatters), "abnormal" sexual behavior, urban malaise, alienation from society, autobiographical narration, coming-of-age anxiety, the use of nonprofessional actors, and documentary style techniques.

For this essay I have chosen three popular films to use as case studies: *A Beautiful New World* (Meili xin shijie, 1998; dir. Shi Runjiu), *Shower* (Xizao, 1999; dir. Zhang Yang), and *A Sigh* (Yisheng tanxi, 2000; dir. Feng Xiaogang). My analysis of these works focuses on two interrelated issues concerning the clashing of old and new temporalities: the articulation of the everyday and the restructuring of spatial relationships in the contemporary Chinese city. These two elements account for the mass appeal of such popular cinema. The filmmakers depict mundane daily events in the lives of ordinary citizens and describe how identities and subjectivities are decisively shaped by the new configurations of urban space (in the forms of an apartment, a bathhouse, and a hotel, respectively). In one way or another, all of these films respond to the drastic transformation of the living space of the Chinese citizen as a result of the advent of a new capitalist commercial housing system (*shangpin fang*) in postsocialist China. Commodity housing based on the purchasing power of the people uproots and dislocates people from their habitual living environment long established under the old socialist system. At the same time, commodity housing raises the expectations of average citizens for a new world before they are psychologically and financially prepared for it, and the promise of a future home is often withheld or never delivered.

I begin here with *A Beautiful New World* (Imar Film Co. Ltd., with Xi'an Film Studio), a film set in Shanghai in the 1990s in which waiting for the future to arrive creates a collision of old and new social mores in the everyday life-world of ordinary Shanghai residents. The narrative of the film is framed by storytelling in the mode of a traditional Suzhou chanting-performance (*Suzhou pingtan*). This narrative structure of a story within a story is evident in the beginning and the end and is interspersed throughout the film. In a teahouse filled with an audience, the storytellers narrate the tale of Zhang Baogen (Jiang Wu), a young man from a small town who is lucky enough to win the lottery for a new apartment in Shanghai. The beginning of the film offers shots of the rivers in southern China (Jiangnan) leading to Shanghai, the dreamland of many rural Chinese. Baogen comes to Shanghai to claim the new apartment, but the promise of a new home seems to be perpetually deferred and withheld. The manager of the construction company tells him that his penthouse apartment is not yet ready because the entire building is still under construction. While waiting for the completion of the construction, Baogen stays at the home of a distantly related aunt, Jin Fang (Tao Hong), a lower-middle-class young woman who is stereotypically portrayed as a snobbish yet kind-hearted Shanghainese. Throughout the film, the viewer sees shots of the brand-new skyscrapers and glitzy neon lights of an ultramodern Shanghai, all of which stand in sharp contrast to the cramped, crowded house of Jin Fang and the narrow old lanes of her neighborhood.

Baogen, as the figure of the country bumpkin, personifies honesty, simplicity, and good nature compared to the urban attitudes of calculation and selfishness of the citizens of metropolitan Shanghai, who seem single-mindedly to seek status and wealth and are contemptuous of the lower social classes. Baogen's small-town, country mentality is markedly different from the wiles of Shanghai folks such as Jin Fang. But eventually, at the end of the film, a mutual appreciation, and even love, grows between Baogen and Jin Fang, and together under a downpour of rain they go to the construction site of the new apartment building. Baogen looks up at the sky, and tells Jin Fang that his future new apartment there will give him a most beautiful view of Shanghai. It is thus evident that the construction of new space is also the formation of new hopes and dreams. Perpetual waiting, dreaming about the future, and hoping for the materialization of a "beautiful new world" are the modes of living in the world for many urban dwellers in China's quest for modernization.

Another enormously popular film produced by Imar in association with Xi'an Film Studio is the aforementioned *Shower*, which provides a contrasting view of the same dilemma. If *A Beautiful New World* narrates the creation of new living space in Shanghai, *Shower* depicts the disappearance of old urban space in Beijing. The film begins with shots of a man taking a shower in a futuristic automatic shower machine, which needless to say is devoid of the intimacy found in the traditional Chinese-style bathhouse. Indeed, as we soon find out, such "futurism" in the film, as in *A Beautiful New World*, is illusory and misleading. After the shot of the futuristic shower the film cuts to the bathhouse and then proceeds to unfold a human story in a leisurely, slow pace. A steady stream of loyal long-standing customers live their lives in the bathhouse: they rest, chat, drink tea, play chess, bet on cricket fights, enjoy massages, and receive the cupping-jar treatment (*ba huoguan'er*)—a form of Chinese medicine used to release unhealthy body heat. In showing life at the bathhouse *Shower* reiterates and rehabilitates the Chinese father figure as compared to the parricide impulse of the rebellious Fifth Generation filmmakers. It upholds the wholesomeness of the traditional nuclear family and as such places the father as the head of a healthy institution. In contrast, in Chen Kaige's *Yellow Earth* (1984), the foundational text of the Fifth Generation, the Chinese father is seen as inept and unfit for the task of national modernization in the frenzy and fever of "historical and cultural reflection" (*lishi fansi, wenhua fansi*) during the 1980s. In *Shower*, under the protection of the good-natured patriarch, the bathhouse becomes an enclave of peace and tranquility against the pains, dangers, and violence stemming from the rapidly changing and modernizing outside world.

In a flashback sequence, the film establishes the important link between the father and water as both are precious sources of life. The father recounts his life story to his two sons. He originally comes from northern Shaanxi Province (Shaanbei), from "yellow earth," a barren land lacking water yet often seen as the cradle of Chinese civilization. We see the father's soon-to-be bride take a bath the night before her wedding; residents in impoverished northern Shaanxi can afford the luxury of taking a bath only a few times in their entire lives. Here the importance and vitality of water is emphasized by the father in his story, as it is throughout the film. The father, of humble rural roots, dies at the moment when his eldest son Daming rushes to pick up his ringing mobile phone, a call from his wife in Shenzhen, the state-delegated Special Economic Zone in the developing industrial and business sector of the Pearl River Delta region.

After the father dies, Daming takes his mentally challenged younger brother, Erming, to a mental hospital. Although Daming's intentions are good, the hospital environment makes Erming truly insane. Erming is used to, and content with, the daily rituals and tasks of the bathhouse: mopping, cleaning, scrubbing, and changing water. Heretofore he has helped the father run the bathhouse during the day, and in the evening they run and play games together in the old alley. As soon as Erming wanders too far from home, he is lost in the confusing outside world. He does not quite understand the world of his brother, even as he tries on Daming's suit in front of the mirror and toys with his mobile phone.

Three points about the film should be emphasized here. First, at the level of textual meaning *Shower* presents nostalgia for the old Beijing that is disappearing and offers a critique of the effects of modernization and globalization that uproot old communities. Second, despite the text's critique of globalization, the packaging of the film follows the logic of globalization in selling and marketing consumable images of an exotic, traditional China, where the "bathhouse" is made into another new icon of China for international audiences. Third, the self-conscious evocation of *Yellow Earth* wraps up and inverts fifteen years of New Chinese Cinema (1984–1999), not by dismissing the Chinese father as a backward figure in the nation's quest for modernity but rather by returning to him as the root of harmony and life much needed in the time of mindless commercialization and globalization. Thus *Shower* bears witness to how much China has changed from the beginning years of the nation's reforms to the beginning of the twenty-first century, as the country labors to advance from the backwater of the world market to the scene of active participation in globalization and modernization in its urban centers.

Beyond the new apartment and the old bathhouse, another kind of spatial form compounding the private and the public—the hotel room—is addressed in Feng Xiaogang's *A Sigh*. A highly popular film in China, *A Sigh* addresses the sensitive yet widespread phenomenon of extramarital affairs and divorce in postsocialist China, depicting in minute detail the dissolution of the "standard family" in the present time. In the film, the playwright Liang Yazhou (Zhang Guoli) is writing a screenplay for a TV drama. In order to concentrate on his work and not be distracted, he lives separate from his family in a hotel room in a seaport city. To speed up his writing and make his life more comfortable, his producer Liu Dawei (Fu Biao) sends to him an assistant, Li Xiaodan (Liu Bei). Although he is married, Liang Yazhou soon falls in love with his assistant—a beautiful young woman who adores him and admires his genius. As Liang Yazhou is entangled in the love affair with his assistant in the promiscuous space of a hotel room, his wife, Song Xiaoying (Xu Fan), unaware of her husband's infidelity, is busy decorating their newly purchased apartment—their dream home. After Liang Yazhou returns home he is again sent away by his producer to live in a hotel in the suburbs of Beijing, this time also in the company of Li Xiaodan, so that he may focus on his writing and be removed from daily family responsibilities. During a visit to his hotel, however, Song Xiaoying finally discovers her husband's extramarital affair. The couple is separated, and Liang Yazhou moves out to live with Li Xiaodan in another apartment.

In one scene, Liang and Li check into a hotel for one night's stay. As soon they walk into the room, the police arrive to conduct a routine "sweeping of prostitution" (*saohuang*). The lovers are asked to prove their marital status, which they cannot do. Along with other hotel guests who cannot prove their legal marital status, Liang and Li are rounded up, humiliated, and ordered to squat against the wall in the hotel. One male guest protests: "Isn't this a five-star hotel where people can do anything as they please?" A police officer replies: "A five-star hotel is still a hotel under the five-star flag [China's national flag]!" Toward the end of the film, Liang and Song Xiaoying reconcile and Li Xiaodan seems to have disappeared from Liang's life. In the final sequence, Liang takes his family to a seaport for a vacation, and the scenery returns to a beach in a warm climate just like the opening scenes of the film. Sitting alone in a hotel room, Liang receives a phone call from his former lover—what's going to happen next? And thus the film ends.[9]

Although *A Sigh* won the prize for best film at the Cairo International Film

Festival in 2000, it did not win any of China's Golden Rooster awards. While the film proved to be immensely popular among China's audiences, it appears that the subject matter was seen by the judges as too sensitive. It is evident that Feng Xiaogang and his generation's approach to filmmaking is decidedly different from that of the Fifth Generation. In this melodrama about life in contemporary Beijing, there is no elaborate display of ethnographic or anthropological details about an exotic China; nor is there any attempt at soul searching or roots seeking by returning to primitive, premodern, rural China. What it does instead is to tackle sensitive yet widespread social phenomena that are seen and felt by a large number of urban residents. In the words of one Western critic,

> *Sigh* is not a movie made to reinforce Western views of the mainland. No mandarins inhabit wooded courtyard houses with a gaggle of concubines; there are no stunning long shots of the Yellow River or of toothless peasants; nobody rides a rickshaw; no exotic women wearing cheongsams peek out from behind gaily colored fans. Representatives of the Communist government appear in only two scenes, neither of them negative.
>
> Instead, *Sigh* is a movie that provides Western audiences one of their first glimpses of the fast-changing, fast-paced city life in China. . . .
>
> Feng belongs to a new generation of filmmakers who have steered away from the deep thinking of the art-house directors and smirk at the party's heavy-handed approach. They want to do two things: tell stories and make money.[10]

This kind of film has done away with the self-orientalization, deep introspection, and the politicization of China used to arouse sympathy and indignation from Western audiences. Feng Xiaogang has been a master of popular films in China. The highest box office sales for domestic films in 1998–2000 were earned by his "New Year films" (*hesui pian*): *Part A Part B* (Jiafang yifang. 1998), *Be There or Be Square* (Bujian busan. 1999), and *Sorry, Baby* (Meiwan meiliao, 2000). Indeed, Feng Xiaogang's oeuvre best defines the path and nature of popular entertainment cinema in contemporary China.

In the three popular films discussed above, it is apparent that the transformation of affect, desire, and sociality of Chinese urban citizens goes hand in hand with the transformation of the spatial fabric of Chinese cities. The nexus of public and private space, and learning how to negotiate these new configurations, changed with the disappearance of the old forms of space, and the appearance of the new forms that border on the discreet and the open: hotel rooms, commodity housing, public bathhouses, and neighborhoods. In *A Beautiful New World*, the promise of a new apartment determines the "structure of feelings" for average folks in southern China. The delivery of a future home demarcates their zones of hope and longing. In contrast, the nostalgia for the quickly vanishing space in old Beijing—a public bathhouse, in *Shower*—is a lament for the destruction of a mode of productive, caring, collective life. Somewhere in the middle between these extremes, the characters in *A Sigh* hesitate between the old and the new. Love and marriage are forged and broken in the nexus between the pleasures afforded by the promiscuous hotel room and the security of the home—a dream apartment. The tenuous link between personal freedom and familial commitment is vividly sketched as the main character shuttles between the hotel room and his home, between his lover and his wife. The psychological confusions, moral dilemmas, and spatial dislocations in these films are symptoms of the larger processes of social transitions in the postsocialist state.[11]

Thus popular urban cinema has become a particularly important form of representation for addressing widespread "popular" phenomena and the attendant anxieties about change in Chinese cities. It is neither the official big-budget "main melody" (*zhu xuanlü*) film nor the outlawed, high-minded, low-budget independent or art film, but rather serves a unique social, artistic, and economic function. Popular urban cinema caters to the tastes, dreams, pursuits, and disillusions of a rising Chinese middle class, which is concerned less about politics and more about money and the breakdown of the traditional family structure in a time of socioeconomic shifts. These domestic commercial films are also, of course, complicit with the market economy of the Chinese film industry—and development sector—in transformation. Yet, while they themselves are commercial products and operate in accordance with the law of a "socialist market economy," these films at the same moment contain parodies of the commodification of life. In *A Beautiful New World*, the high-rise promises upward mobility, but the protagonist Baogen actually descends the social ladder. He eventually is reduced to becoming a homeless migrant worker in the city in a quest of the illusory commodity of a new apartment. In *Shower*, the dismantling of an antiquated bathhouse is supposed to be social progress, but this part of the modernization process makes the residents feel less secure than before. In *A Sigh*, the modern-style hotel is meant to create a room of one's own—a space of leisure, independence, and creativity. In the end, however, it turns into a desire-charged place that breaks apart the traditional family. In all of these films, the ambivalent sweet promise of a new home does not necessarily lead to happiness. While demolition destroys the family structure and the community associated with the traditional or the socialist city, the new commodity housing is threatening to the new-style middle-class nuclear family. Expanded, individualized, or commodified space creates separation and alienation. As seen in these films, the radical restructuring of spatial-social relationships could be discomforting and even traumatic to contemporary city dwellers.

REMAKING URBAN SPACE IN AVANT-GARDE PHOTOGRAPHY AND VIDEO

The theme of Feng's film *A Sigh* can be better understood by examining the broad spectrum of visual arts works by Wang Jinsong. Wang's photographic series *Standard Family* (biaozhun jiating) and *Parents* (Shuangqin) describe stable family ties and enduring marital relationships in the bygone socialist era. The *Standard Family* pictures are photographs of the standard three-member nuclear family under the one-child policy—a young couple and their child. The *Parents* series consists of photographs of old couples serenely sitting in their living rooms (including a picture of Wang Jinsong's own parents). This world of permanent relationships and a standardized lifestyle brings with it a peace and tranquility that shelters the protagonists of these images from the pain and destruction associated with the world of flux and change, but it also cuts them off from the excitement, thrills, pleasures, and opportunities of the "beautiful new world."

In a cross-cultural perspective, Wang's *Parents* calls for a comparison with similar works from the West, most obviously Janine Antoni's work *Mom and Dad* (1993–94). Antoni's piece consists of a set of three photographs of her mom and dad in the same pose. In these three pictures, with the help of makeup, her parents become a heterosexual couple, a gay couple, and a lesbian couple, respectively. Hence, *Mom and Dad* opens up a range of possibilities of upbringing, sexual orientations, lifestyles, responsibilities, and social obligations, all of which are unknown to the Chinese parents photographed by Wang, who live blissfully in their isolated environment.

Although photography and video art cannot compare with feature film in stretching the narrative potential of their media, they nevertheless depict aspects of public and private life in their own unique manner and excel in the immediacy and directness of their appeal. Photography has become a favorite and important mode of representation among China's avant-garde artists since the late 1990s.[12] In comparison to mainstream popular urban films, the works of avant-garde photography and video are mainly shown in privately owned galleries in Beijing (the Red Gate and Courtyard galleries, for example). They are viewed, consumed, and purchased by a small group of interested people. Instant appeal, the artistic conception, and the subject and manner of representation are factors that determine whether a work can grab the attention of the viewer in such mediums (photography and video). Popular film and the avant-garde thus speak to different segments of the Chinese population and occupy distinct public and critical spaces.[13] However, despite the differences in medium and approach, both popular cinema and avant-garde art tackle the central themes of urban transformation in our time.

Here I would like to focus on a few representative works by Wang Jinsong, Hong Hao, and the Gao Brothers (Gao Zhen and Gao Qiang). Wang Jinsong's photographic series *One Hundred Signs of Demolition* (Bai chai tu, 1999) epitomizes the theme of urban destruction in a most laconic fashion. It consists of pictures of the sign "tear down" (*chai*) that is seen everywhere in China, signaling the destruction of old walls, spatial enclosures, communities, and neighborhoods. Wang took one hundred photographs of the character "*chai*" that marked buildings for demolition. He numbered these pictures of "*chai*" from 1900 to 1999, significantly alluding to the course of modern Chinese history throughout the entire twentieth century. Although some viewers have noted that "Bai chai tu" reminds them of traditional Chinese paintings such as "bai shou tu" (one hundred pictures of longevity) and "bai fu tu" (one hundred pictures of prosperity), Wang's focus is on the relentless forces of change and destruction as opposed to the wishes for continuity and permanence. The old Beijing is being destroyed, while neoclassical simulations of both traditional Chinese and Western architecture line up the streets, such as the newly built Ping'an Boulevard (Ping'an dadao). In response, Wang's simple photographic work is the most direct, forceful representation of the disappearing old city.

Such avant-garde works document the loss of the familiar, the natural, the personal, and the material; evoke the feelings of living in an opaque, mediated, dematerialized world; and convey the anxieties of being dislocated from

Wang Jinsong, *One Hundred Signs of Demolition* (Bai chai tu), 1999.

tradition, roots, and home. In his writings, Huang Du describes this changing sensory-economy struggling with new reflections on the temporality of modern Chinese history:

> The age of "Post-Material" finds its unique expression in the visual reconstruction of contemporary Chinese society. The old system of the so-called "planned economy" is gradually being replaced by the market economy. This drastic transition is embodied by the massive expansion of China's modern cities. . . . Numerous buildings arose while the old Peking City was being torn down. The architectural space of Beijing is hitherto disordered and chaotic, which implies nothing but emotional uncertainty and insecurity of its urban residents. Hair salons, bathing centers and nightclubs compose the core physical structure of the city. The basic materialistic desire now motivates almost every action in the city, which used to be known for its glorious imperial past. . . . Now Chinese are struggling to build their own consumer culture while dealing with their loaded historical past such as thousands [of] years of cultural residue and the more recent political turmoil such as the Cultural Revolution.[14]

For Huang, the affluence of material objects is an indication of "spiritual paleness" in the present time. Thus he calls for the establishment of "new moral criteria" in radical response to the profound social changes. This avant-garde exhibition is "an effort to present a visual narrative of artists' redefining of the dialogue between art and life, and their attempt to reclaim a visual possibility of rebuilding a moral ideal."[15]

While Wang Jinsong's *Chai* series describes the disappearance of the old Beijing with almost an elegiac tone, Hong Hao's photographic pieces about the new Beijing offer a humorous, slightly satirical note on the subject. Hong Hao's solo exhibition *Scenes from the Metropolis* (Jing xiang) was held at Courtyard Gallery in Beijing in November 2000. While alluding to Zhang Zeduan's masterpiece by the same title from the northern Song dynasty (AD 960–1127), the *Spring Festival on the River* series (Qingming shanghe tu, 1999) is composed of images of the sprawling cityscape of the modern/postmodern Beijing made of glass and steel and of skyscrapers, hotels, shopping malls, office buildings, and highways. In *Spring Festival on the River No. 7* (2000), Hong Hao pastes bits and pieces of contemporary scenes onto the original work of Zhang Zeduan in an effect that is jarring yet comic. In the words of Meg Maggio, "The result is a jumble of parallel images which relay the confused and frenetic atmosphere of the new Chinese capital as it sprints forward at a break-neck pace toward the ever elusive goal of 'modernity.'"[16] Against the background of the ancient capital Bianliang (Kaifeng) of the northern Song dynasty, we now see colorful images and photographs of cars, motorcycles, trucks, and telephone booths. The original landscape is populated by contemporary street-strollers, foreign tourists, half-naked swimmers, golf players, and the artist Hong Hao himself, placed next to monks, merchants, peasants, soldiers, donkeys, and carts along the Bian River from the Song dynasty. Some of the series' numbered pieces are direct photographs of scenes of contemporary Beijing; for example, *No. 1* (2000) is a juxtaposition of sections of the original Song masterpiece and pictures of contemporary Beijing.

Hong Hao's *Beautiful Images in Focus* (Meili jing xiang, 2000) consists of photographs of rear views of women walking in the streets, with their buttocks in focus. The male gaze by way of the camera eye captures the voyeuristic pleasures of peeping urbanites and points to the sexual/sexist obsession of men in a city of desire. The *Beijing Tour Guide* (Youjing zhinan, 1999–2000)

Hong Hao, *Beautiful Images in Focus* (Meili jing xiang), 2000.

series features Hong Hao as a tour guide leading various groups of foreign tourists at famous sites of Beijing, such as Tiananmen, the Imperial Palace, and the Great Wall. The photographs highlight Beijing as a mecca of tourism and orientalist fantasy.

As opposed to showing grand panoramic views of the physical structure of Beijing, Hong Hao's self-portrait series depicts the subtle inward process of subject formation among city dwellers in the era of globalization. In *Mr. Gnoh, The Person Whom I Know Well* ("Gnoh" is the reverse spelling of "Hong"), the artist holds a mirror with a reflection of himself transformed into a Westerner with blond hair and blue eyes; in so doing he exposes the

fantasy of Westernization among China's young generation. In *Yes, I am Gnoh.* we see a picture of Hong Hao again with blond hair and blue eyes, talking into a mobile phone and wearing a Western suit. In the process of Westernization "Hong" becomes "Gnoh," an unreadable foreign name. In parodic self-portraits such as *Mr. Hong Please Come In* and *Mr. Hong Usually Waits under the Arch Roof for Sunshine.* Mr. Hong is Chinese and wears traditional Chinese clothes, but he also enjoys the luxuries afforded by the Western lifestyle (posh swimming pool, Western furniture, etc.). These images are both real and false reflections of the schizophrenic, fragmented self. They bespeak the follies and comedies of modernization and Westernization, and constitute travesties of the desire and wish fulfillment of ordinary citizens.

In spring 2001, Courtyard Galleries hosted an exhibition of the photography of the Gao Brothers (Gao Zhen and Gao Qiang), who were then based in

Hong Hao, *Beijing Tour Guide: Tiananmen* (Youjing zhinan, Tiananmen), 1999.

Jinan, Shandong.[17] In their works urban space is again the theme, in which the tortuous process of the formation and deformation of subjectivity is portrayed in adverse existential space. As such, their heavy style is a sharp contrast to the playfulness of Hong Hao's pieces. In the *Senses of Space* series (*Prayer, Anxiety, Pain,* and *Sleep*), naked male bodies are positioned in the cramped narrow space of partitioned bookshelves and cupboards, where they are curled up and not able fully to extend. Other objects in the images— candles, a Barbie doll, a dildo, a pistol, hammers, screwdrivers, and a bandage —serve as symbols and intimations of the existential(ist) struggles of the soul and the body. These signs of anguish, sexual deprivation, masochism, soli- tude, lack of communication, and absence of privacy betoken a pervasive urban malaise in China. *Chinese Noah's Ark No. 2,* which combines bits and pieces of *Senses of Space* into the shape of the Sistine Chapel, elevates the plight of daily existence to a spiritual, religious level. The overcrowded indoor living space as described by the Gao Brothers suggests the ineluctability of urban reconstruction in contemporary China. In contrast to the spatial con- finement in *Senses of Space,* however, *The Utopia of the 20 Minute Embrace* series takes us to vast outdoor space. At the bank of Yellow River or under a railroad bridge, strangers meet and embrace each other for a short period of time. These utopian sites of contact, communication, and intimacy build a "space of love," as it were, in a world full of conflicts and strife.

Here it is useful to examine video art in the sense that it provides the link,

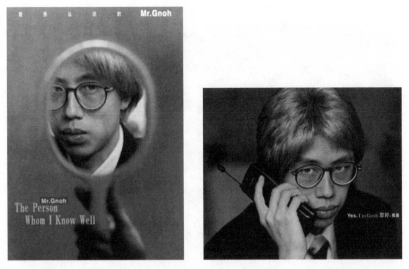

Hong Hao, *Mr. Gnoh, The Person Whom I Know Well* (Wo suo renshi de Mr. Gnoh), 1998.
Hong Hao, *Yes, I am Gnoh* (Nin hao, wo shi Mr. Gnoh), 1998.

and linchpin, between popular cinema and experimental photography. Chinese video artists have also gone to great lengths to probe the depths of drastic spatial transformations in China's metropolises. The six-minute video *Lady's* (Shuxijian, 2000), by the female Chinese video artist Cui Xiuwen, is a particularly noteworthy case, not only because of the video art form's border crossing from popular film practice to the avant-garde, but also because of its particular exploration of spaces that defy the label of either public or private in the libidinal market economy of today's urban China. The piece offers an intimate look into the sexualized, eroticized, and private space of women in a public setting, a zone of desires situated in the discos, bars, karaoke rooms, and nightclubs that have sprung into existence throughout the 1990s. In creating her work, Cui secretly placed a video camera that records women and their conversations in the women's restroom at the nightclub Passion (Tianshang renjian, literally "The human world in the heavens"). This club, located in the Great Wall Hotel, is an infamous place for meeting the priciest and reputedly most beautiful prostitutes in Beijing. Married or not, men come to the club to strike up casual relationships with women for the gratification of desires and bodily needs. Cui's video unveils these working women looking at

The Gao Brothers, *Sense of Space: Anxiety* (Ganshou kongjian: saodong), 2000.

themselves in the mirror, fixing their makeup and clothing in an effort to present themselves as sexually attractive as possible. The camera lens focuses on their hair, faces, underwear, breasts, and thinly veiled pubic hair because body, flesh, and good looks are used as means to exchange for cash in such space. Like Hong Hao's *Beautiful Images in Focus.* the private camera eye in Cui's work also indicts urban spectators/consumers as complicit voyeurs and peeping toms guilty of the commodification of women's bodies.

Cui's candid camera, as a shorthand cinema verité as well as docudrama, mediates the terrain between mass culture and avant-garde work, between the documentary impulse and the melodramatic, between the object and the subject. It vividly captures the emergence in postsocialist China of a new space that blurs the demarcation between the public and the private. The nightclub in a luxury hotel provides a public platform for the express purpose of satiating private fantasies based on the money principle. Indeed, karaoke rooms and bars have blossomed forth as new spatial forms in Chinese cities since the early 1990s. They constitute a mixed public/private space, heretofore unseen

The Gao Brothers, *The Utopia of the 20 Minute Embrace, I* (Yongbao 20 fengzhong de wutuobang zhi yi), 2000.

in Mainland China, outside the family, the work unit, the restaurant, and the teahouse. Indeed, a new social class has emerged—namely that of service girls who are addressed as *xiaojie* (miss). A large segment of the sex and entertainment industry is made up of *sanpei xiaojie* (literally "three-company miss"), who are paid to accompany male guests to drink, eat, and sing karaoke. These service girls are potential candidates for *disanzhe* (third person, or mistress) and *erniangzi* (second wife) for the wealthy and willing. As such, they shake the foundation of the socialist-style standard monogamous family. Large numbers of these girls come from the provinces, especially from Sichuan and the northeast (Dongbei), where the rate of unemployment and the number of laid-off workers from state-owned enterprises are the highest in the nation.

In 1989 the first bar in Beijing, Frank's Place (Wanlong jiuba), opened near City Hotel (Chengshi binguan); a decade later, however, there were about four hundred bars in the city.[18] Reserved karaoke rooms (KTV *baojian*), bars, mas-

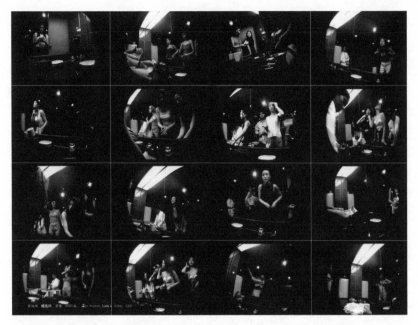

Cui Xiuwen, *Lady's* (Shuxijian), 2000.

sage parlors, beauty parlors, and clandestine hair salons (*falang*; or, more precisely, the salon's backroom) are new sites of socialization, indulgence, and transaction in the metropolis. As such, they erode and at times destroy the traditional social relationships built on the model of the "standard family" and the institution of marriage.[19]

Here again I borrow the term "post-material" in order to describe the problem facing hundreds of millions of Chinese. The present materialism in the form of commodity fetishism in an ostensive market economy may well be a reaction to and correction of the impoverishment, scarcity, and deprivation of material objects suffered under the name of the Marxist doctrine of materialism in a socialist planned economy during the Mao era. However, this obsessive and excessive impulse relating to material acquisition has also led to another kind of impoverishment by virtue of the success of more than twenty years of economic reforms in the Deng era and beyond. This impoverishment is the loss of being in touch with the materiality of things—namely with what really matters to urban dwellers in the soulful realms of the personal, the natural, and the private. Indeed, it is this phenomenology of the material, materialism, materiality, and post-material, as it were, that today's Chinese visual culture attempts to unfold and circumscribe.

NOTES

I thank Zhang Zhen for inviting me to present a paper for the series "The Urban Generation: Chinese Cinema in Transformation" at New York University in spring 2001. At that time I was spending the academic year in Beijing, and the conference invitation prompted me to sort out and write down what I saw, experienced, and wondered about when wandering in Beijing. This chapter has gone through several drafts, and Zhang Zhen's meticulous editing and numerous insightful suggestions have been most helpful in the revision process.

1. Fredric Jameson, "Globalization as a Philosophical Issue," in *Cultures of Globalization*, ed. Fredric Jameson and Masao Miyoshi (Durham, N.C.: Duke University Press, 1998), 60. See also Fredric Jameson, *A Singular Modernity: Essay on the Ontology of the Present* (London: Verso, 2002).

2. Saskia Sassen, *Globalization and Its Discontents* (New York: Free Press, 1998), xxxii.

3. Huang Du, ed., *Post-Material: Interpretations of Everyday Life by Contemporary Chinese Artists* (exhibition catalogue; bilingual edition in English and Chinese) (Beijing: World Chinese Arts Publication Company, 2000), 9.

4. Yu Meiying, "Qunian Beijing shangpin fang mai le 230 yi" [Last year commodity-houses worth 23 billion yuan were sold in Beijing], *Beijing qingnian bao* [Beijing Youth Daily], February 13, 2001, 34.

5. Zhou Jiawang, "Xin diming Beijingren zhao bu zhao" [Beijing residents can't find the new placenames], *Beijing wanbao* [Beijing Evening News], March 22, 2001, 1.

6. Liao Yan, Huang Dongjiang, "Duo jian jingji shiyong fang, ladong fangjia wang xia jiang" [Build more economic practical houses, bring down the price of houses], *Chen bao* [Beijing Morning Post], February 7, 2001, 1.

7. For a report on cherished old Beijing buildings in destruction, see Hong Jianshe, "Shi!" (Gone!), *Xiaofei zhe* [Consumer], no. 12 (2000): 48–49.

8. This orientation in popular cinema is fully discussed in Zhang Yiwu, "Zaidu xiangxiang Zhongguo: Quanqiuhua de tiaozhan yu xin de 'neixianghua' " [Reimagining China: The challenge of globalization and the new "inward turn"], *Dianying xinshang* [Film Appreciation Journal] (Taiwan), no. 105 (fall 2000): 35–43.

9. The events in the film seem to parallel director Feng Xiaogang's own personal experiences. Divorce is a rampant phenomenon in Chinese cities, and Feng himself went through the process. He left his wife and daughter and later married the

actress Xu Fan, who plays the role of Liang Yazhou's wife in the film. Also like the characters in the film, Feng and his family live in a huge, luxurious, exquisitely decorated apartment in Beijing.

10. John Pomfret, "From China's Feng Xiaogang, a 'Sigh' of the Times; Filmmaker Skirts the Censors—and Western Expectations," *Washington Post*, October 15, 2000.

11. The acute tension between traditional culture and the forces of postmodernization is the subject of Feng Xiaogang's new New-Year Films *Cell Phone* (Shouji, 2003) and *A World without Thieves* (Tianxia wuzei, 2004).

12. For an overview of contemporary Chinese avant-garde photography, see Li Xianting, "Dangdai yishu zhong de sheying meijie re" [The photography craze in contemporary art], *Jinri xianfeng* [Avant-Garde Today] no. 10 (January 2001): 136–47. In the same issue of *Jinri xianfeng* I offer an examination of the strategies of representation in contemporary Chinese avant-garde art; see "Gouzao 'Zhongguo' de celüe: Xianfeng yishu yu hou dongfang zhuyi" [Strategies of constructing 'China': Avant-garde art and post-orientalism], 148–61. A revised and expanded English version of this essay appears as "The Uses of China in Avant-Garde Art: Beyond Orientalism," in *China, Transnational Visuality, Global Postmodernity* (Stanford, Calif.: Stanford University Press, 2001), 173–92.

13. The question of public and private space in the Chinese metropolis as represented in avant-garde art is explored in Xiaoping Lin, "Discourse and Displacement: Contemplating Beijing's Urban Landscape," *Art AsiaPacific*, no. 25 (2000): 76–81.

14. Huang Du, *Post-Material*, 13.

15. Ibid., 14.

16. Meg Maggio, "Introduction," in *Hong Hao: Scenes from the Metropolis* (Jing xiang) (exhibition catalogue), ed. Meg Maggio (Beijing: Courtyard, 2000), 2.

17. See the exhibition catalogue *Gao Brothers*, ed. Meg Maggio (Beijing: Courtyard, 2001).

18. See the special section on Beijing's bar culture in *Xiaofei zhe* [Consumer], no. 11 (2000): 8–27.

19. I discuss the biopolitics and sexualization of life in contemporary China in my essay "Globalization, Biopolitics, China," forthcoming in *Third Text*.

tracing the city's scars

Demolition and the Limits of the Documentary

Impulse in the New Urban Cinema

YOMI BRAESTER

T
he new urban cinema (*xin chengshi dianying*), a term used to describe a prominent trend in Chinese film in the 1990s, is better understood as a critical approach that cuts across genres and generations. In this essay I explore not only the thematic interest in contemporary urban phenomena but, more importantly, the aesthetic concerns—especially what is called the "documentary impulse"—shared by the filmmakers at hand. I examine both art films and commercial productions and focus on their use of demolition as a symbol for the need to chronicle the city's transformation.

As a filmic trope, demolition does not simply reflect contemporary social issues but rather foregrounds the role of filmmaking in documenting the present. This essay is part of a larger project in which I look at the relationship between the cinema and city planning in the People's Republic of China (PRC) and argue that films have performed an important function in recording urban change. I argue that since 1949, a large portion of PRC films has been modeled after documentary productions. The documentary impulse in Chinese cinema started, however, with a prescriptive approach akin to documentary propaganda films, thereby shaping audience response as much as providing descriptive chronicles. Post-Maoist directors, and members of the

Urban Generation in particular, reacted to the prescriptive tendency by narrowing the documentary mission to matter-of-fact presentations that were sometimes lacking any narrative that might smack of subjective views. The documentary impulse in the new urban cinema became a vehicle of criticism —not only by placing a mirror in front of a numbed society but also by foregrounding the limitations of documentation in the face of inevitable and sometimes partly desirable urban development.

The salience of demolition in the new urban cinema may be better understood in light of the recent turn in the documentary impulse. Filmmakers are increasingly self-conscious of their role in preserving a record of the vanishing cityscape. Demolition sites are seen as timekeepers of urban history and cinema—that is, as an endeavor to retain the spatial repositories of personal and collective memory in effigy. The presence of the camera is not taken for granted, and filming the urban scenery is often part of the narrative. The films respond to the cities' spatial semiotics of memory, unearth the scars of urban development, and give visual form to the traumas connected with the change in landscape.

The significance of the documenting camera's presence may be exemplified by way of the concluding sequence in Huang Jianxin's *Stand Up, Don't Stoop* (Zhanzhi luo, bie paxia, 1992). The scene is seemingly a mere slapstick gag. A couple leaves their old apartment for a newly built condo. At the last minute, a photographer is called in to take a group picture of the residents. Stepping back, he slips on a banana peel, and the film ends with the resulting skewed view of the group through the tilted camera's lens, laughing at the falling man.

The scene is in line with the cheerful tone maintained throughout the movie; a tone that would pervade in many commercial hits describing urban life in the 1990s. In this case, the plot focuses on the quarrels among neighbors, yet the tension is diffused to allow the film to end in a more cheerful tone. With the help of good-humored post-Mao witticisms, all's well that ends well.

Despite the carefree atmosphere, the concluding scene also indicates a concern with the issues arising from rapid urbanization, and it shows an awareness of the social role of urban cinema. Photography and film are ascribed a role in recording the changing social conditions during the full swing of economic reforms. The camera is invited into the scene while the Gaos are in the process of moving. The transitions to modern city spaces are documented by the very people involved. The neighbor suggests that they should take a photo as a souvenir, demonstrating how the adjustment to the new environment is accompanied by real-time nostalgia, a longing for that which has barely changed or passed away. The residents thus pose for the camera in recognition of the importance of capturing the present. Yet the scene foregrounds the hapless photographer who appears at the end. The camera's intrusion, rather than simply trace the situation, becomes the ultimate object of the spectacle. Like the cameraman in this episode, the filmmaker chronicles the transforming cityscape not as an objective observer but rather as a participant physically present in and affected by the process.

THE BROAD LANDSCAPE OF THE NEW URBAN CINEMA

I chose to begin this essay with the scene from *Stand Up* because it challenges the perception of new urban cinema as the exclusive prerogative of the so-called Sixth Generation and its hard-hitting directors such as Lou Ye and Jia Zhangke. I have argued elsewhere that new urban cinema may also be traced to the melodramatic *Farewell, My Concubine* (Bawang bieji, 1992; dir. Chen Kaige), which pays homage to Beijing's vanishing cityscape.[1] Likewise, *Stand Up*'s director, Huang Jianxin, started working in film in 1979 and is associated with the Fifth Generation filmmakers. Yet Huang's trajectory is representative—and to some extent responsible for—the turn of Chinese cinema away from depictions of rural society. In *Stand Up*, as well as in the subsequent films *Back to Back, Face to Face* (Bei kao bei, lian dui lian, 1994) and *Surveillance* (Maifu, 1996), Huang depicts urbanization in his native city of Xi'an.[2] *Stand Up* provides a link between recent films and the often-neglected historical context of the changing cityscape. The new urban cinema, even during moments of light-hearted humor, resists official narratives. It turns its back on the drive for party-line film, encapsulated in Jiang Zemin's call of 1994 to foreground the "leitmotif" in arts. Recent independent films and commercial productions alike share sensibilities that can be traced to the late eighties. To understand the politics of the new urban cinema we must go back to early-1990s films such as *Stand Up* and *No Regret about Youth* (Qingchun wuhui, 1992; dir. Zhou Xiaowen), which I discuss later in this chapter.

For the new urban cinema directors, demolition sites indicate the threat that the city might change before it can be documented. Ning Ying explains that her films aim at leaving a record of today's Beijing; in ten years, she says, the city is likely to look like Singapore. In terms of film production she always tries to start shooting as soon as possible, fearing that the object of her interest might disappear.[3] In Ning's *On the Beat* (Minjing gushi, 1995), for example, a policeman is introduced to his new precinct. As he and a colleague pass through a large torn-down lot, they observe that some 600 to 700 households have been evacuated. They note in a somewhat rigid manner that the families must have benefited from the move to new apartment buildings, yet the next shot shows the two policemen dwarfed by heavy machinery bulldozing its way through the alley, followed by a shot where the camera tilts up to show high-rises hanging menacingly over the old district.

The image of the city demolished and rebuilt before one's eyes is featured in many films, and many plots come to a turning point as the disoriented protagonists either observe buildings to be demolished or waddle through the debris. This trope is featured in films as diverse in generation, genre, and style as Zhou Xiaowen's *No Regret about Youth*, Guan Hu's *Dirt* (Toufa luanle, 1994), Jia Zhangke's *Xiao Wu* (1997), Shi Runjiu's *A Beautiful New World* (Meili xin shijie, 1998), Yang Yazhou's *A Tree in House* (Meishi touzhele, 1999), Zhang Yuan's *Seventeen Years* (Guonian huijia, 1999), Jin Chen's *Love in the Internet Age* (Wanglu shidai de aiqing, 1999), Zhang Yang's *Shower* (Xizao, 1999), Zhang Yimou's *Happy Times* (Xingfu shiguang, 2000), and Huo Jianqi's *Life Show* (Shenghuo xiu, 2000).

In elevating demolition to a metaphor, urban cinema joins the concerns of other media forms in China in recent years. Wu Hung has noted the prominence of demolition in Beijing art of the mid-1990s: for example, Zhan Wang's *Ruin Cleaning Project* (1994) "restored" a building designated for demolition by giving a face-lift to the already half-destroyed structure, all the while knowing that it would be razed soon thereafter. The avant-garde artist Rong Rong captures torn-down structures in his untitled photographs, in which the focus is on pinup pictures eerily surviving, in mutilated form, in the debris. The vanishing urban spaces may be said to hold up against the viewer images that have already internalized their own ruin.[4] Wang Jingsong's work in the series *One Hundred Signs of Demolition* (1999) juxtaposes one hundred photos of the Chinese character for "demolition" painted on houses waiting to be demolished. As Wang explains: "It is as if the word 'demolition' were a borderline, left of which lies destruction and right of which comes rebuilding."[5]

The performance artist Sheng Qi has used well-known locales as backdrop for his provocative performances, and his recent work places demolition within a sociopolitical context. A collage that documents a never-performed part of his *Concept 21* shows the artist striking an operatic pose. He is wearing a police jacket and an AIDS ribbon, his head is covered with a red cloth, and a rope held by a policeman is tethered to his private parts. The awkward rapport between the Armed Police (a special branch formed after the events of June 1989) and the parodying artist-persona is enhanced by the location in the background. The two are standing in Tiananmen Square, photographed during its renovation in 1999. Sheng explains that he was amazed by the notion that even Tiananmen Square could be taken down overnight.[6] Tiananmen Square has come to symbolize the authority of the Chinese socialist state, and thus its demolition—compounded by Sheng's mocking pose—suggests the subversion of the power structure.

It should be noted that the multimedia works of these and other artists rely on photography, whether presented on its own merit, digitally manipulated, or as part of documenting performance art. Insofar as demolition sites encapsulate the ruin of memory, the camera becomes the only means of stopping or at least slowing down the process of forgetting. Demolition sites are also the scars in spatial form left by traumatic events, from the forceful evacuation of tenants to political oppression (Sheng Qi's photo of Tiananmen Square combines both—the site of the 1989 incident was torn up as part of renovating Chang'an Avenue for the PRC's fiftieth anniversary, a project that included the demolition of 75,000 square feet and the evacuation of 60,000 people).[7] Like other forms of visual art, cinema traces the city's scars and translates history into spatial representation; the photographic and cinematic documentation turns the city into an exhibition space for personal and collective traumas.

In their effort to convey social criticism, films from the PRC rarely use images of demolition as harsh as those expressed by similar images in the cinema of Taiwan.[8] As I will show, mainland productions often side with street-smart savvy or opt for tearjerker nostalgia. Yet as a whole, the new urban cinema portrays construction sites to foreground social issues and to argue for cinema's role in chronicling urban transition. While new urban films record landmarks, local idioms, and other specific characteristics, these allusions contrast with the ubiquity of construction sites in all of the cities filmed. These images denote and chronicle the disappearance of twentieth-century Chinese cities as known by their residents. In what follows I outline the developing concern with the changing cityscape in the 1990s through a reading of three films, namely *No Regret about Youth, A Tree in House*, and *Shower.*

THE CITYSCAPE AS A MAP OF TRAUMA

Among the first of the films to pay close attention to how demolition threatens to erase the past is *No Regret about Youth* by the Fifth Generation director Zhou Xiaowen. Earlier films exist that foreground the new cityscape: for example, *Young Couples* (Yuanyang lou, 1987; dir. Zheng Dongtian) starts with a crescendo of shots showing newly built condos, and *The Troubleshooters* (Wanzhu, 1988; dir. Mi Jiashan) begins with the images of new buildings mirroring even more recent construction sites. Other milestones include Xie Fei's *Black Snow* (Benmingnian, 1988) and Zhang Nuanxin's *Good Morning, Beijing* (Beijing, ni zao, 1990).[9] Yet *No Regret about Youth* redirects the focus away from the glitzy new edifices to older Beijing residences, along with the people who live in them and the people who tear them down.

The plot of *No Regret about Youth* is set in a Beijing suburb where a ramshackle alley, possibly dating back to the nineteenth century, is evacuated and demolished to make space for a modern shopping center. As in many urban films, the emphasis is on a younger couple. The story revolves around a construction worker, Jianong (Zhang Fengyi), and a nurse, Qun (Shi Lan), whose lives are connected through a web of mnemonic and spatial relations: she lives in a house that he is instructed to demolish; she administers the medical checkup for his severe headaches; she eventually becomes his lover. All of these relations are framed by a shared experience—a few years earlier, during the Sino-Vietnamese War of 1979, the two served in the same army unit. A bomb destroyed the structure in which they were taking shelter, and as Jianong shielded Qun his head was wounded. Jianong's description draws a parallel between his bodily injury and the building's collapse: "My wrist was broken . . . the building collapsed" (*shouwan dou guchai le . . . fangzi jiu ta le*). The incident results in Jianong's amnesia, so that from the plot's beginning the destruction of memory and the demolition of space are intertwined.

No Regret portrays Beijing in the throes of reconstruction. In 1979—simultaneous with the Sino-Vietnamese War—the capital was thrown into a construction drive that would change the cityscape drastically and, within sixteen years, add over a billion square feet of living space, which represents 3.5 times the growth of the previous thirty years combined.[10] In 1988 the reconstruction entered a new stage, with a plan calling euphemistically for the integration of new development and the "reconstruction" of old districts.[11] It was not a matter of scale alone, however; the makeover was radical in that its chief targets were the alleys (*hutong*) and courtyard houses (*siheyuan*) that define old Beijing. The 1950s had witnessed the demolition of the old city walls, a measure intended not only to facilitate traffic but also to signal the new government's challenge to the old power structure. Since the concomitant evacuations were part of government policy, public discussion about the human suffering involved was suppressed. Yet the sense in removing the wall and the new sweeping reconstruction were sometimes challenged. As one Beijing resident lamented: "Beijing's second city wall is in the process of being torn down. The alleys and courtyard houses are Beijing's second city wall!"[12] The collective trauma associated with the construction of the "ten monumental buildings" in the late 1950s was repeated in the late 1980s and 1990s, this time in conjunction with the drive to modernize the city's commercial infrastructure. Zhou Xiaowen's film portrays Beijing in the late 1980s as a doomed space, waiting to be rebuilt into impersonal high-rises, shopping centers, and other shrines to new capital.

Urban spaces appear in the film in two forms, either as not yet demolished structures or as yet to be completed new buildings. The protagonists' respective abodes represent the quasi-imaginary forms of space. Qun lives in an old house, yet her place does not and cannot carry a lasting significance. It is neither comfortable nor beautiful, and she never expresses any attachment to it. Her house bears the sign of its destruction—it is marked with the word *chai* (to be demolished) and thus is literally under the sign of erasure. Indeed, toward the end of the film we see it turn into rubble in less than a minute. In contrast to Qun's dilapidated house stands the apartment bought by her fiancé. It promises to be a modern high-rise condo, yet it is still under construction and looks surprisingly like the ruined district where Qun used to live. In both cases, the structures are indexes of time, the time of construction and destruction. The skyline is dominated not by the buildings but by the bulldozers and cranes that surround the structures like scavengers and birds of prey.

No Regret about Youth:
Facing trauma or willful
forgetting?

The third accommodation, Jianong's apartment, is the only place that does not change with time, yet it is even more transitory. It serves as Qun's way station from the demolished building to her fiancé's apartment, and Jianong's stay there is cut short too. In a telling scene, Qun stands in Jianong's place and looks at her old house through binoculars, then turns around and directs the binoculars at the sleeping Jianong. Both objects of observation are soon going to disappear—one will be torn down, the other is afflicted with a fatal condition and his days are numbered (in a preceding scene, he tells his friends to take away whatever they want from the apartment, thereby dismantling his own living space). The bulldozer operator is bound to vanish together with the buildings that he is engaged in demolishing.

By chronicling the process leading to the construction worker's demise and the death of the old city, Zhou's film resists the official policy, which in effect supports forgetting the city's past, repressing its traumas, and displacing its memory. Since the establishment of the PRC in 1949, the authorities have reconstructed and reconfigured urban space to signal their hegemony and instill in the citizens the desired ideology. As the revived capital, Beijing witnessed especially intensive attempts to suppress its pre-revolutionary past by transforming its spatial semiotics. Residential areas and public spaces alike were mobilized for that purpose.

A blatant example is the official use of Tiananmen Square, located at the capital's center. Since the founding ceremony of the PRC on October 1, 1949, the square has served as a marker of historical time to be remembered and commemorated. As Wu Hung argues, the space has often been used to control time—for example, a giant countdown timer was displayed in the square to signal the time of Hong Kong's annexation to the mainland in July 1997.[13] The effect of the so-called Hong Kong Clock, like the goal of other government-sponsored architectural endeavors (as well as "main melody" cinema), was to overwrite personal space and time with that of the state and the nation. The countdown clock and other "soft monuments," erected for specific occasions and dismantled at will, save the government the trouble of demolishing more permanent landmarks and allow it to control the fluctuating symbolism of urban spaces. *No Regret about Youth*, on the other hand, counteracts such underhanded reinventions of the city. Unlike the promise contained in the government's countdown clock, the dying Jianong is a human clock fast running out of time. The film demonstrates how both his work at the bulldozer and his amnesic illness divest him of memories.

Just as Jianong's amnesic and fatally afflicted brain can no longer function as a repository for memory, neither can Beijing's urban spaces contain their past. The city hurtles toward the final transmogrification presented at the film's ending—a year later, Qun and Jianong's divorcée meet at the new mall. Their exchanged pleasantries reveal to the viewer that Jianong died shortly after Qun had started taking care of him. Here also we are reminded of Dai Jinhua's observation that the same term, *guangchang*, is fortuitously used for both "square" and "mall"; the word associated with Tiananmen Square's revolutionary and dissident history has thus come to denote the new consumer culture, thereby presenting a linguistic and spatial symbol of the ideological change.[14] The mall erected on the site of Qun's old house contains no trace of her experience shared with Jianong. The new Beijing rises on the ruins of its former urban identity, yet through Zhou's lens it becomes the sign of its own obliterated memory. *No Regret about Youth*, like other films based on scripts by the immensely popular writer Wang Shuo,[15] portrays a city that fails to contain accurate memories. The protagonists are complicit in the project of forgetting—in a drawn and powerful shot the camera lingers on Qun and Jianong as they sit in the bulldozer and together pull the lever to tear down Qun's old place. Rather than an effort to face their common trauma, the scene suggests that the two have resolved to let go of the past. The film presents with exceptional candor the range of social problems associated with demolition, but at the same time it skirts any simplistic condemnation. Instead it documents the disappearance of spaces, of human life, and of memory itself, and draws its power from avoiding commentary on that loss.

THE ECONOMY OF DEMOLITION

Perhaps because of the plot's resonance with the personal life of the director Zhou Xiaowen, *No Regret about Youth* differs from most urban films of the early 1990s in its somber approach.[16] Its didactic tone sets it apart from later movies, which opt for a lighter or even cynical mood. In line with a growing urban savvy and with the need to compete with Hollywood blockbusters, many directors followed Huang Jianxin's lead in producing urban comedies. The mid-nineties also witnessed the appearance of independent filmmakers, often referred to as the Sixth Generation, whose neorealist aesthetics resulted in an impartial and often unflattering documentation of urban life. While the Sixth Generation's uncompromising attitude deserves much credit, it should not overshadow the fact that commercial directors have also found creative ways to represent urban sensibilities.

Thematically, urban films from the late 1990s reflect also the changing concerns among evacuated residents. *Stand Up, Don't Stoop* and *No Regret about Youth* already establish a symbolic economy of demolition, consisting of exchanging the old accommodations for newer ones, provided by the developers and the government (the common Chinese term *chaiqian*, "demolish and move," reflects the process). In *Stand Up*, a deal between Gao and Zhang stipulates that Gao's gain of a new space is contingent upon the demolition of his old one, and vice versa. *No Regret about Youth* juxtaposes Qun's old house with the new apartment building purchased by her fiancé. Both films stress the promise held by the new apartments as convenient modern spaces for which little is sacrificed in return.

A Tree in House, Yang Yazhou's solo directorial debut, takes the process of urban development a step further in recognizing the value of the old places that must be abandoned and demolished. Yang, who worked with Huang Jianxin on four of his previous films,[17] chose a script based on Liu Heng's entertaining short story *The Happy Life of Chatterbox Zhang Damin Pinzui* (Zhang Damin de xingfu shenghuo, 1998); enlisted the accomplished photographer Ma Delin; and cast the successful comedian Feng Gong (of *Stand Up*,

A Tree in House: Bending the rules of urban space.

Don't Stoop) in the lead role.[18] The result is a visually flowing, fast-paced, articulate, and amusing film. The plot is set in contemporary Tianjin and tells the story of the five Zhang siblings and their mother as they cope with increasingly tight living space. Feng Gong recasts Zhang Damin, portrayed in Liu Heng's text as an amusing half-wit, into a more sensitive and sensible character. The film's English title refers to Damin's resourceful solution to the cramped quarters, namely building an extra room in the inner yard around a tree that has grown there. Damin and his wife take the room as their nuptial chamber and decorate the tree that sticks up in the middle of their bed. Later, the son who is born in the room is named "Little Tree." Eventually the old place is demolished and the family moves to a new home provided by the government in compensation.

A Tree in House complicates the exchange of old spaces for new ones by showing the residents' attachment to the old abode. The film follows Damin in the process of reappropriating the yard by shaping it to his needs and personalizing it. To build the extra room, Damin first engages in his own version of demolition and tears down the outer yard wall, shifting its location farther into the alley. He claims the thoroughfare and privatizes the public space. The interior design, namely wrapping the tree trunk in festive cloth and adorning it with stickers, stresses the spatial reconfiguration. In the process, Damin strengthens community ties—at first his neighbor objects to the construction and even hits Damin, but later he helps him build the wall. The new space spares the family further conflict and provides room for a child. The name "Little Tree" insinuates that the courtyard ties together the people who live in it and shares their destiny.

Yet the promise of an organic bond between community and space is broken when the family is forced to move into a new apartment building. Although the film does not emphasize the human drama at this moment, Damin's first reaction when he visits the new place is typical of his seemingly idiotic yet meaningful chatter. He stares at the spacious condo and says only, "The tree is gone." Damin's disorientation represents a larger dislocation, which is insinuated in the concluding scene. Damin expresses his wish that his son will grow up without worries (he uses the colloquial phrase *meishi tou-zhele*, which also serves as the film's Chinese title). Yet after the move his son's name, "Little Tree," becomes an empty sign, the only reminder of the yard in which he grew up. Further, we are led to wonder how the dislocated name might reflect on the child's purportedly worriless future.

The film's plot touches directly on socially sensitive issues when Damin learns that his house is destined for demolition. He refuses to sign a letter conceding his rights to the place, and after a fight breaks out he is put under arrest. Here, the film strikes a raw nerve—in the late 1990s the evacuation process became increasingly tense as quasi-legal demolition enterprises disregarded the law and intimidated tenants. The number of lawsuits brought forth by residents rose sharply, and as the courts consistently ruled against the tenants social unrest grew.[19]

A Tree in House signals an awareness that the familiar city spaces have only very recently been irrevocably lost. That the film repeats the sentiments of *No Regret about Youth*, shot seven years earlier, demonstrates how Beijing's reconstruction keeps transforming ever-larger areas. In retrospect, 1992 saw only the beginning of a more comprehensive process, and the construction done in 1999 is likely to pale in comparison with the projects for the 2008 Olympics. Yet *A Tree in House* portrays the demolition in its time as the point of absolute rupture with the past. Damin leaves jail only to be informed that his old house has already been torn down. During his short incarceration everything has changed outside the prison walls. He never returns to the old site and instead goes directly to the family's new apartment. The sudden change is emphasized by the fact that we never see the demolition in progress. Instead, the film makes a jump-cut from the street brawl outside his house to Damin's release from prison, as the gate closes behind him and places him in front of a black background. The past is thus symbolically shut off forever and marked as an emptiness that must be offset by embracing the new spaces. A similar scene is found in *Seventeen Years*, where the protagonist returns home from jail only to find her entire neighborhood reduced to rubble. As Zhang Zhen has observed, the demolition site stands for a temporal void that corresponds to Deng's years of reform.[20] The old social structures vanish, leaving the protagonists with no access to their past.

Incidentally, both *A Tree in House* and *Seventeen Years* were filmed in Tianjin, which has suffered much demolition of its older neighborhoods. Author Feng Jicai has documented the destruction of the city's heritage and has waged a battle against the municipality's ongoing plans for urban transformation.[21] *A Tree in House* marks the recognition that official policies have failed to acknowledge the value of the spaces designated for demolition and the social alienation caused by moving into industrialized structures. The term "rebuilding in a new location" (*yidi qianjian*), applied to many cultural relics, has turned out to be a euphemism for the wholesale destruction of China's architectural heritage.[22]

It is interesting to compare the social criticism in Yang's film with other pieces that it inspired. Within a year of the film's release, Beijing TV produced a twenty-episode series bearing the title of the originary novel, *The Happy Life of Chatterbox Zhang Damin*. The storyline of the series is similar to that of the film, although the series adds episodes clearly inspired by Li Shaohong's *Red Suit* (Hong xifu, 1998). Yet the stretched and diluted melodrama of the TV style lacks the films' critical edge. Zhang Damin's house is in the series set in a Beijing that exhibits little local color. Further, the series ends with Damin's mother, suffering from memory loss, reenacting earlier scenes in her life. This saccharine conclusion, in which Damin's siblings are reminded of their past and recognize Damin's sacrifice, serves only to reaffirm the present. Although the family is scheduled to move to a new apartment, the last episode ends just before the possibly traumatic move.

A more interesting version is presented in the silver screen sequel to the series, *Ordinary People's Life* (Meili de jia, 2000; dir. An Zhanjun). The Chinese title, literally translated as "a beautiful home," is clearly sarcastic. Damin (played by Liang Guanhua) faces a series of setbacks, including leaking pipes, uncooperative neighbors, and a fraudulent remodeling contractor. Although the film suffers from the same slow pace and flat dialogues that characterize the TV series, it is successful in depicting realistically the problems faced by residents of new housing projects. This facet of urban reconstruction has arguably triggered the most vociferous protest, as residents have complained about finding that their new homes sometimes lack title registration or were poorly built. One newspaper ran an article under the headline, "A New House or an Unsafe House?" suggesting that the new houses were as unsafe as the old houses from which people had been evacuated.[23] An's film completes the portrayal of residents' travails; while, in the end *Stand Up, Don't Stoop* presents the difficulties associated with old housing, *No Regret about Youth* addresses the trauma of demolition, and *A Tree in House* implicates the longing for one's old spaces, *Ordinary People's Life* moves beyond trauma and nostalgia to the down-to-earth problems of living in new constructions built in a hurry.

THE NOSTALGIC CAMERA

The fast pace of change not only in the cityscape but also in the lives of urban dwellers is documented by filmmakers who are aware that they are working under the menace of disappearance and against the city's transformation. The challenge to the cinematic chronicling of the present is anticipated in *Stand Up, Don't Stoop*. The group photo of the residents, bungled by the slip on the banana peel, is taken after the Gaos's apartment has already been reappropriated and the workers have started tearing its walls down. In fact, the new tenant has the apartment wall hammered to dust even before calling the photographer. Like the new urban cinema, photography is already late in recording the makeover of city spaces.

The recognition that swift changes often take place before they can be captured in the camera's lens has led to diverging solutions for visualizing urban development. Some movies, such as *A Tree in House*, avoid showing the process of demolition or its aftermath. Others, such as *No Regret about Youth*, take great pains to portray each step as buildings are being razed to the ground. The latter approach foregrounds the presence of the camera and evidences the documentary impulse of urban cinema, in some cases by including the cinematographer inside the filmic frame. One of the more ambivalent portrayals of the camera's documenting role occurs in Zhang Yang's film *Shower*.

The film tells the story of a young man, Liu Daming (played by Pu Cunxin), who returns home to Beijing from the Shenzhen Special Economic Zone. On his return he is put in difficult situations, first in reestablishing rapport with his aging father (Zhu Xu) who runs a traditional bathhouse, and then, following the father's sudden death, in taking care of his mentally challenged younger brother Erming (Jiang Wu). The bathhouse (which resonates with the elderly people's club in Ning Ying's *For Fun* [Zhao le, 1992]) becomes a symbol for the charm of the Chinese traditional lifestyle. It is where people, mostly of the father's aging generation, come to socialize and relax. Daming, too, washes away his alienated Shenzhen businessman mentality when immersing himself in the hot communal tub. The mental healing power of old-style bathing is emphasized by comparing it to purifying rituals in the remote areas of Shaanxi and Tibet and by contrasting it with Shenzhen's (fictional) computerized car wash–like shower booths. The film strikes a nostalgic tone toward the end when the quaint bathhouse is torn down, presumably to give way to more modernized and impersonal facilities.

Although Chinese critics have been impressed by *Shower*'s flowing narrative, they often are irked by its nostalgia based on the tilted portrayal of Chinese tradition. Zheng Guoen and Qi Hong point out that private bathhouses were abolished after 1949 and that there is no reason to believe that the future will bring car wash–like showers, and they further note that the depiction of Tibet and Shaanxi also owes to myth. Nevertheless, Zheng and Qi claim that the factual inaccuracies help capture more truthfully the spirit of our time.[24] Spatial constructs such as the confabulated house-around-a-tree in Yang Yazhou's film can in context become meaningful symbols. The computerized showers present the fast-food mindset of coastal city businessmen, who lead a precisely timed and mechanized existence. The demolition of the fictional old Beijing bathhouse reflects the very real disappearance of the capital's familiar places in favor of alienated spaces. Yet *Shower* presents an affected image of the past (that is, any period before the late 1990s) as characterized by intimate interaction in nonindustrial settings and of the future as belonging to a lonely and superficial lifestyle. Along with the critic Hu Ke, we might note that unlike in the film, private establishments such as bathhouses are beginning to reappear now as an outcome of economic reforms.[25] *Shower* presents an imaginary city, both past and future, in order to mourn the bygone era. As such, the film parallels the growing industry of nostalgia that revives traditional-looking locales in Beijing, Shanghai, and other cities.

Ordinary People's Life: Trouble doesn't stop after moving to a new house.

The longing for a wholesome tradition, to the point of ignoring the harsh social issues associated with older modes of production and uses of space, stems from a rigid construction of "tradition." What is particularly troubling about such nostalgia, claims Yin Hong, is that it becomes complicit with "leitmotif" (i.e., government propaganda) films. Although *Shower* is motivated by market forces rather than by ideological doctrine, the movie offers reverting to "tradition" as a self-reaffirming panacea that covers up for the complexities of economic and social conditions in present-day China. If the Chinese people are truly living in Heaven, asks Yin, why do so many people look forward to demolishing old districts and moving into new housing?[26] In this light, the graphic demolition scenes in *Shower* do not help to document urban reality but rather support an escapist cultural imagination.

The film's dismissal of modern values, however, becomes in the end more contemplative and leaves room for thought for the spectator. The bathhouse patrons watch their haunt being torn down and are surprised to hear Erming sing loudly—"O sole mio"—oblivious to the havoc around him. The scene is a tearjerker, and it focuses on what seems to be the mentally challenged brother's passionate adieu to the spaces in which he grew up. Yet the conclusion also foregrounds Erming's uncertain future. Although he is assured of his brother's future support, it is unclear what form of social structure will shelter him. (A similar situation is featured in the original cut of Zhang Yimou's *Happy Times*, the last shot of which shows a blind young woman sitting in the middle of a demolition site, temporarily protected but with little promise of a better future.)

Shower: Residents document their disappearing city.

Shower's conclusion also drives home the limitations of filmic nostalgia. The sentimental sequence is framed by shots that show one of the bathhouse regulars using a camcorder to chronicle the demolition. The old customers are trying, with little success, to make sense of the event. In one shot, an elderly man peers right into the camera with a confounded expression. The man's gaze not only shows his stupefaction at the transformation of space but also seems to inquire into the intrusion of photography into the old locale. Filming, however, is all that the men can do. The camcorder's owner takes pains to ride in the back of a pedicab around the block being torn down. The preceding point-of-view shot moves unsteadily across the swath of debris. The tracking shot accentuates the impersonal magnitude of the demolition project, while the handheld camera effect evidences the fictional amateur cameraman's intimate familiarity with the territory. Like the group photo in *Stand Up*, the camcorder is used by the local residents for their own benefit, to provide a last memento of their neighborhood. The camcorder point-of-view shots identify Zhang Yang's lens with the camcorder's position. The cinematographer sympathizes with the residents and shares their documentary mission. The very last shot in *Shower* assumes yet again the camcorder's position, as it zooms in on Erming singing to himself. The film becomes an extension of the camcorder's homemade, intimate footage of the old Beijing neighborhood at the moment of its disappearance.

The uncanny convergence of a nostalgia that conceals social reality with the documentary impulse raises poignant questions about the aspirations of the new urban cinema. The attempt to fashion film as documenting the present has often led not to a growing realistic emphasis but rather to legitimizing a filmic erasure of history. *Shower* and *Happy Times* represent a growing tendency to use urban themes as a guise for focusing on the past and not privileging the present. The films demonstrate that the increasing accessibility of video technology and the proliferation of images might also be mobilized by a consumer society to repress the memory of its collective traumas. Rather than reflect and criticize the process by which city spaces have been manipulated by state ideology and consumerism, a certain strand of new urban cinema might also become complicit in perpetrating a similar dislocation.

NOTES

1. Yomi Braester, "Farewell, My Concubine: National Myth and City Memories," in *Chinese Films in Focus: Twenty-five New Takes,* ed. Chris Berry (London: British Film Institute, 2003).

2. For Huang's relation to Xi'an and to the Cultural Revolution, see his "Shenghuo jueding le wo de dianying" [Life decided my films], *Dangdai dianying* [Contemporary cinema], no. 4 (July 1997): 81–83.

3. Ning Ying, discussion with the audience after screening *On the Beat* at the Walter Reade Theater, New York City, February 2001.

4. Wu Hung, *Transience: Chinese Experimental Art at the End of the Twentieth Century* (Chicago: University of Chicago Press, 1999), 108–19.

5. Quoted in Huang Du and Bingyi, *Hou wuzhi* [The post-material] (Beijing: Shijie huaren yishu chubanshe, 2000), 62.

6. Sheng Qi, interview by the author, Beijing, July 16, 2001.

7. Fang Ke, *Dangdai Beijing jiucheng gengxin: Diaocha, yanjiu, tansuo* [Contemporary redevelopment in the inner city of Beijing: Survey, analysis, and investigation] (Beijing: Zhongguo jianzhu gongye chubanshe, 2000), 117.

8. I explore this topic in my " 'If We Could Remember Everything, We Would Be Able to Fly': Taipei's Cinematic Poetics of Demolition," *Modern Chinese Literature and Culture* 15, no. 1 (spring 2003): 29–62.

9. For a discussion of the early wave of post-Mao urban cinema, see Xiaobing Tang, *Chinese Modern: The Heroic and the Quotidian* (Durham, N.C.: Duke University Press, 2000), 245–72.

10. Zhang Jinggan, *Beijing guihua jianshe zongheng tan* [On Beijing's urban planning and construction] (Beijing: Beijing Yanshan chubanshe, 1997), 52.

11. The municipal government's new policy was called "one shift, one emphasis,

and four integrations" (yige zhuanyi, yige weizhu, sige jiehe). This bureaucratic language refers to the gradual shift of attention from developing new areas to integrated work on new development and rebuilding old districts; an emphasis on rebuilding old districts; and integrating reconstruction with the development of new districts, reform in residential policy, management of residential land, and preserving the old city. See Zhang Jinggan, *Beijing guihua jianshe wushi nian* [Fifty years of urban planning and development in Beijing] (Beijing: Zhongguo shudian, 2001), 178–79.

12. Quoted in Fang Ke, *Dangdai Beijing jiucheng gengxin*, 39.

13. Wu Hung, "The Hong Kong Clock—Public Time-Telling and Political Time/Space," *Public Culture* 9, no. 3 (spring 1997): 329–54.

14. Dai Jinhua, *Yinxing shuxie* [Invisible writing] (Nanjing: Jiangsu renmin chubanshe, 1999), 259–75.

15. *No Regret about Youth* is based on a subplot in a story by Wei Ren. It was reworked into a script by Wang Shuo at director Zhou Xiaowen's request.

16. On the autobiographical background in Zhou's film, see Chai Xiaofeng, *Xiaowen ye fengkuang* [Xiaowen too is mad] (Changsha: Hunan wenyi chubanshe, 1997), 49; and Lu Wei, "Shuoshuo Zhou Xiaowen" [On Zhou Xiaowen in brief], in *90 niandai de "diwudai"* ["The Fifth generation" in the 1990s], ed. Yang Yuanying et al. (Beijing: Beijing guangbo xueyuan chubanshe, 2000), 348.

17. Yang acted in Huang's *The Wooden Man's Bride* (Wu Kui, 1993); served as Huang's assistant in *Signal Left, Turn Right* (Hongdeng ting, lüdeng xing, 1996); and, with Huang, codirected *Back to Back, Face to Face* and *Surveillance*.

18. On Ma Delin's experience in photographing the film, see his "Meishi touzhe le sheying suibi" [Notes on the cinematography of *A Tree in House*], *Dianying yishu* [Film art], no. 3 (1999): 21.

19. See Fang Ke, *Dangdai Beijing jiucheng gengxin*, 51, 37.

20. Zhen Zhang, "Zhang Yuan," in *Fifty Contemporary Filmmakers*, ed. Yvonne Tasker (London: Routledge, 2002).

21. See Yomi Braester and Zhang Enhua, "The Future of China's Memories: An Interview with Feng Jicai," *Journal of Modern Literature in Chinese* 5, no. 2 (January 2002): 131–48; Feng Jicai's *Jiucheng yiyun: Tianjin lao fangzi* [Rhymes left by an old city: Old houses in Tianjin] (Tianjin: Tianjin Yangliuqing huashe, 1995); *Feng Jicai hua Tianjin* [Feng Jicai depicts Tianjin] (Shanghai: Shanghai wenyi chubanshe, 2000); *Shouxia liuqing: Xiandai dushi wenhua de youhuan* (Show leniency: The predicament of modern urban culture) (Shanghai: Xuelin chubanshe, 2000); and *Qiangjiu laojie* (Rushing to save an old street) (Beijing: Xiyuan chubanshe, 2000).

22. See Fang Ke, *Dangdai Beijing jiucheng gengxin*, 59–62.

23. See ibid., 45, 47.

24. Zheng Guoen and Qi Hong, "Jiadingxing zhong xunqiu zhenshigan" [Seeking a sense of reality from a false assumption], in *Zhongguo dianying meixue: 1999* [Chinese film aesthetics: 1999], ed. Hu Ke et al. (Beijing: Beijing guangbo xueyuan chubanshe, 2000), 292. All of the articles on *Shower* in this volume were originally published in a special issue of *Dangdai dianying* [Contemporary cinema] (no. 1, 2000).

25. Hu Ke, "Jingqiao de xushu yishu" [An ingenious art of narration], in Hu Ke, ed., *Zhongguo dianying meixue*, 278.

26. Yin Hong, "Chengren yishi: Quanwei yizhi yu dongfang zhuyi de shutu tong-gui" [A rite of passage: The convergence of authoritarianism and orientalism], in Hu Ke, ed., *Zhongguo dianying meixue*, 302–10.

scaling the skyscraper

Images of Cosmopolitan Consumption in

Street Angel (1937) and *Beautiful New World* (1998)

AUGUSTA PALMER

I
n the transnational China of the 1990s, nostalgic cultural products repro-
ducing urban images and architecture from the first four decades of the
twentieth century achieved an unprecedented popularity in the marketplace. The glut of nostalgic films and television series, novels, memoirs,
and coffee-table books with images of old postcards, advertisements, restaurants, and clothing has been remarked upon by both domestic cultural critics
and international China scholars.[1] These nostalgic products are a site where
the three-way tension between global, regional, and local identities is stretched
to its limit, imagined and reimagined, particularly in products that attempt to
re-create the cosmopolitan aura of pre-liberation Shanghai.

Beautiful New World (Meili xin shijie, 1998; dir. Shi Runjiu), a film set in
turn-of-the-millennium Shanghai, uses a nostalgic framing device that evokes
the intertext of 1930s popular culture and film to create continuity between
1930s Shanghai and 1990s Shanghai. The film envisions a former country
bumpkin as literally "upwardly mobile" as he stands on a future skyscraper's
girders pointing up at the sky. But this upward mobility also contains a
nostalgic linkage to the mythical past of the city of Shanghai. Although the
implicit intertext of 1930s popular culture is mobilized for the nostalgic appeal

of its glamorous surfaces, it is completely detached from the progressive politics and critique of consumption found in the class struggle narratives depicted in 1930s films like *Street Angel* (Malu tianshi, 1937; dir. Yuan Muzhi). In this essay I explore the way in which *Street Angel* and *Beautiful New World* make use of similar iconography, particularly the image of the skyscraper, to express entirely different ideologies about the nature and repercussions of cosmopolitan consumption. Despite the ideological discontinuity between the two films, the nostalgic framing of *Beautiful New World*'s contemporary story functions to erase the sixty-year divide between two eras of cosmopolitan consumption in Shanghai.

NOSTALGIA, CULTURAL IDENTITY, AND CONSUMPTION

Nostalgia is often viewed as a tainted version of memory and history, colored by longing for the past or anxiety about the future. Through nostalgia, a particular version of the past is often used as a means to construct or understand contemporary anxieties that undermine our sense of who we are. Thus, according to the sociologist Fred Davis, if any sociocultural group—such as a nation, an ethnic group, a religious sect, or even a family—is "susceptible to feelings of anxiety and concern for our future selves . . . by some untoward historic event or intrusive social change, it can be seen how at the most elemental level collective nostalgia acts to restore, at least temporarily, a sense of sociohistoric continuity with respect to that which had verged on being rendered discontinuous."[2]

In *Beautiful New World*, the "intrusive social change" is the advent of a consumer revolution and the intense rebuilding of the city of Shanghai as center for international trade, which necessitates a linkage with a pre-communist past that cannot be remembered by the film's characters or by much of its audience. Thus, this nostalgia created for a new generation of consumers smoothes over the discontinuity between the contemporary race toward individual financial success and the recent past's communist ideology. Arjun Appadurai notes that ersatz, or imagined, nostalgia "teaches" consumers to miss things they have never lost as well as eras they did not personally experience.[3] I would argue that if the consumer provides a facility for nostalgia in the form of a conditioned response to visual or narrative conventions created to evoke nostalgia, then these media images supply a type of "memory" and even a feeling of "loss" for the imagined past. Thus, the realms of fantasy, consumption, and nostalgia are inextricably linked in the plethora of popular texts that reference 1930s Shanghai. As Appadurai writes on the intertwining of these realms: "The fact is that consumption is now the social practice through which persons are drawn into the work of fantasy. It is the daily practice through which nostalgia and fantasy are drawn together in a world of commodified objects."[4] Fantasy, though often characterized as personal, may become part of a collective imaginary through shared media representation. Collective imagination, as Appadurai also points out, has a "projective sense about it" that "creates ideas of neighborhood and nationhood."[5] Thus, nostalgia weaves together fantasy, consumption, and an emotionally colored interpretation of the past to create a "new" yet seemingly continuous notion of identity.

In light of the radical economic and social transformation that China has experienced over the past fifteen years it is hardly surprising that many of the popular films made during the 1990s in the People's Republic of China invoked nostalgia for the past in order to examine and, to some extent, create new urban identities. Here I would contend that a discussion of nostalgic Chinese films made during the 1990s can benefit from a distinction between two separate types of nostalgia—namely, "fragmentary" and "totalizing."[6] Svetlana Boym, in her discussion of Russian culture after the fall of the Soviet Union, defines totalizing nostalgia as "reconstructive" and "utopian," in contrast to fragmentary nostalgia, which she sees as "inconclusive" and "ironic." She notes that the totalizing utopian form of nostalgia is more closely linked to the concept of *nostos*, or home, because it dreams of fully rebuilding a mythical authentic home. The second form of nostalgia, fragmentary, places more emphasis on the second half of the word, *algia*, referring to an ache or longing. This fragmentary form of nostalgia "acknowledges the displacement of the mythical place without trying to rebuild it."[7] Thus, the utopian totalizing form of nostalgia is more interested in bridging (or even erasing) a perceived gap between the past and the present, in "reconstructing the home and providing home improvements";[8] while the ironic fragmentary form of nostalgia is interested in bringing the displacement, or the gap between past and present, to light.

Notions of the totalizing and the fragmentary nostalgias may, of course intersect with one another. Emphasizing the break between two eras might also be seen as a totalizing (rather than fragmentary) nostalgic approach, as the concept of rupture could function to unify rather than fragment. Moreover, many films could be said to partake of both (rather than one) of these approaches. However, this pair of concepts does provide a useful schematic for identifying two distinct nostalgic tendencies in the Chinese cinema of the 1990s. Several films made during that decade create fragmentary nostalgic images emphasizing a complete rupture with the socialist past. *In the Heat of the Sun* (Yangguang canlan de rizi, 1994; dir. Jiang Wen), for example, provides a sunny portrait of the teenage Ma Xiaojun's sexual awakening during the Cultural Revolution. The film's final moments depict the present in black and white, a stark contrast to the hazy Technicolor past. And, though Ma Xiaojun and his thirty-something pals are depicted riding in a limousine drinking cognac, the hollowness of their contemporary existence is made clear when they drive by the neighborhood idiot, whom they frequently mocked in their teen years. Ma and his friends are dramatically different from their teenaged selves, but the idiot seems unchanged. He wears the same clothes and carries the same stick, but when he recognizes his tormentors, he calls *them* idiots. The observant viewer might think back to the film's opening, when Ma's voice-over narration asserted, "Beijing has changed so fast. In twenty years, it's become a modern city . . . Change has wiped out my memories. I can't tell what is real and what isn't." Thus, the rupture between a nostalgically inflected past and a stark—albeit more affluent—present seems not only entirely unbridgeable but also undermines the very possibility of truth and the veracity of memory.

How Steel Is Forged (Gangtie shi zheyang lian chengde, aka Zhangda chengren, 1998; dir. Lu Xuechang) also provides a fractured view of the relatively recent past. This film portrays the transformation of its protagonist, Zhou Qing, from a boiler stoker in the drab Beijing of the 1970s to a European sojourner in the early 1990s, and finally to a disenchanted rock musician in the Beijing of the late 1990s. While the 1970s are sometimes portrayed in a critical light, it is the immense changes that the protagonist experiences across the two eras that are at the center of the film. Moreover, the past depicted in the film is inherently ambiguous. The romantic idealism of Nikolai Ostrovsky's wildly popular Soviet novel *How Steel Is Forged*, which Zhou Qing reads as a boiler stoker, is projected onto the protagonist's own story to depict an earlier urban world that contains both a longed-for time of innocent adventures and a brutal, impoverished urban experience. The film's ironic ending allows Zhou Qing to daydream of righting past wrongs with a lethal butcher knife, but he eventually realizes that the past must be left behind. In the film's final moments, when Zhou Qing sets out to visit his former hero and to reunite with a girl from Lanzhou, it is clear that he is paying his respects to both his idealistic memories and the man his hero has become, and that the future and its connection to the past are both uncertain. This deeply embedded ambivalence about the carefully remembered individual past and the sense of discontinuity between the past and the present are what makes *How Steel Is Forged* a work of fragmentary rather than totalizing nostalgia.

It seems appropriate that the fragmentary nostalgia films mentioned above are set in Beijing, once the center of a relatively isolated party-centered China but now a city filled with Starbucks franchises, shopping malls, and highrises. The discontinuity between the socialist past and the commercial city of the present can easily be envisioned as a radical break, a shift from party-centered public life to individual-centered consumerism. Though Shanghai has also changed dramatically over the same time period, its entry into the global marketplace is often envisioned as a "return" to its cosmopolitan past. Significantly, nostalgia films set in Shanghai tend to refer to a pre-communist past rather than to the sunny, idealistic socialist past of the 1960s and 1970s. Thus, many films from the 1990s with a Shanghai period setting, such as Chen Kaige's *Temptress Moon* (Fengyue, 1995) or Zhang Yimou's *Shanghai Triad* (Yao a yao, yao dao waipo qiao, 1995), may be interpreted as totalizing in their use of Shanghai's cosmopolitan and chaotic past as a nearly mythical "Wild East" that can be linked—even if only obliquely—to the present character of the city. The luxuriant visual glamour of these films and their plots centered on crime and addiction remind viewers that both the pleasures and problems of consumer society have returned to China.

A more pointed example of totalizing nostalgia can be seen in *X-Roads* (Xin shizi jietou, 2000; dir. Shazon Jiang). This film was envisioned as a kind of sequel to *Crossroads* (Shizi jietou, 1937; dir. Shen Xiling) in which narrative repetition and footage from the 1930s film not only draw strong comparisons between past and present, but ultimately suggest that the characters from the Shanghai of the late 1990s can "complete" their parents' unfinished love story from the 1930s.[9] The indexical rapport of 1930s cinema and real life is exploited beyond logical limits in *X-Roads:* the film's director Shazon Jiang, who also provides the nostalgic voice-over narration, is the daughter of Bai Yang, the female star of *Crossroads*, while the male lead is played by Zhao Ming, the son of *Crossroads* star Zhao Dan. Portions of the 1930s film become the "memories" of the parents' of *X-Roads'* romantic leads. Notably, the politically progressive aspects of *Crossroads*, in which characters discuss labor conditions in the city and join hands in pledging to fight the Japanese invasion, are completely elided in favor of fantasy sequences and shots that capitalize on the nostalgia for vanished fragments of the urban past—like the fateful streetcar encounters between *Crossroads'* protagonists, which become the nostalgic emotional center of *X-Roads*. Selectively chosen glamorous surfaces from the romantic comedy that forms only one element of the 1930s film are separated from their narrative context to become fictional memories, which seem to unite past and present in a web of romanticized fate. Sampling from a 1930s intertext here creates a pastiche in which cinematic memory becomes personal and adds the veneer of historicity to a fairly tepid romantic comedy. It is the use of these nostalgic trappings of the past as a metaphor for the present and the forging of illusory continuity rather than a sharp divide between past and present that allows the nostalgia of films like *X-Roads* to be termed totalizing.[10]

Beautiful New World, through its use of a framing narrative related by *pingtan* singers seated in front of a sepia-toned image of the Bund, also makes totalizing allusions to a sanitized version of Shanghai's past in an attempt to create a historical precedent for the utopian image of the city as a cosmopolitan consumer's paradise. The Chinese film scholar Dai Jinhua has noted that the glut of media and consumer products using nostalgic imagery of Shanghai is significantly "extraterritorial and transregional" and attempts to (re-)create a contemporary urban Chinese identity that is part of the global scene. As she writes: "Thus, Shanghai becomes today's important 'immigration' city and yesterday's 'premier port of the East,' . . . It becomes the unconscious of contemporary Chinese history—a place in history that must gain its writing through forgetting."[11] Historical Shanghai therefore becomes "a cultural springboard that allows us to leap unscathed across cultural experiences and to express new freedom" in terms that are familiar,[12] but whose relevance and context may have been twisted or "forgotten" to make room for the "new freedom" to consume. The nostalgically inflected "history" of Shanghai that *Beautiful New World* draws upon is open to decidedly less utopian readings, one of which can be easily extracted from the plots of many films made in the 1930s. If the city of the 1920s and 1930s was a paradise for some, particularly Euro-American expatriates and Chinese millionaires, it was hell for many rural immigrants who labored for low wages in factories or dance halls when they were lucky enough to find work at all. Thus, the selective intertextual evocation of the world of films like *Street Angel* in *Beautiful New World* is a type of totalizing nostalgia, which invokes the past in order to forge continuity across fifty years of discontinuity.

RE-IMAGINING THE SHANGHAI OF *STREET ANGEL* AS A "BEAUTIFUL NEW WORLD"

On the surface, *Street Angel* and *Beautiful New World* seem to have little in common beyond their Shanghai settings and their use of the skyscraper as a symbol for the city's economic divide. Made in 1937, *Street Angel* is a beautifully shot early sound picture that draws on influences as diverse as the Russian avant-garde and early Hollywood slapstick comedies to form its own unique idiom. The film features the 1930s singing sensation Zhou Xuan as the ingénue teahouse singer Xiao Hong, and a young Zhao Dan as the dapper romantic hero and trumpet player Chen Xiaoping. *Street Angel* is the story of these two lovebirds and their small community of friends and family in Shanghai's "lower depths"—the world below the burgeoning skyline. The "angel" of the title is Hong's sister, Ah Yun, who has been forced by her adoptive father to turn to prostitution as a way to earn her living and provide for the family. When their adoptive father decides to sell Xiao Hong to a rich customer, her boyfriend Chen and his band of friends join together to help her escape. Ah Yun, who is despised by the idealistic Chen because of her profession, initially stays behind with their adoptive parents, but ultimately she is willing to sacrifice her own life for her sister's freedom. Ah Yun's bravery and her death as a result of her protection of her sister finally enable Chen to realize that he has been unfair to her. In this way, the characters are finally united in opposition to the powers that be, whose wealth is built on the exploitation of those unfortunate enough to inhabit Shanghai's lower depths. Yet unlike Zhang Baogen in *Beautiful New World* their upward mobility is certainly not assured by the film's end.

Made over sixty years after *Street Angel*, *Beautiful New World* is the story of

Zhang Baogen, a country bumpkin who comes to Shanghai filled with dreams because in a contest he won a high-rise apartment. When his apartment turns out to be only a construction site, Baogen is forced to move in with his distant relation Jinfang, a street-smart, money-grubbing Shanghai girl who looks down on his naiveté. Both Baogen and Jinfang struggle to make their living in the city, where they obtain and then leave jobs in quick succession. Finally inspired to go into business for himself, Baogen becomes a *getihu*, or self-employed vendor, and starts selling lunch boxes outside of Shanghai's stock exchange. Despite the financial success of his business, Baogen is ridiculed by Jinfang for his choice of an occupation so lacking in social status. In the end, however, the marriage of Jinfang's friend Ah Hui—for love rather than money—softens Jinfang enough to appreciate Baogen's honesty and diligence rather than focusing on his lack of money and style.

Though many would hesitate to identify the forward-looking *Beautiful New World* as a nostalgic film,[13] it contains significant echoes of the films of the past, which are most clearly visible in its narration through teahouse ballads. In *Street Angel*, Zhou Xuan's character sings in the type of teahouse that *Beautiful New World* uses for its nostalgic frame. Since the songs and image of Zhou Xuan herself have been repopularized as part of the nostalgia craze of the 1990s, sounds and images from *Street Angel* are an implicit inter-text for *Beautiful New World*. Thus, the *qipao*-clad singer and musicians sitting in front of a sepia-toned backdrop of the Bund in the 1990s create a nostalgic simulacrum of the teahouse culture presented in *Street Angel*. The character typology of *Beautiful New World* can also be linked to earlier Shanghai films: its use of easily recognizable character types such as the naive country bumpkin and the knowing city girl and its most basic narrative arc portraying a country boy's loss of innocence in the city appear frequently in films from the 1920s and 1930s. In addition, the portrayal of Shanghai as a flourishing global city with access to products from all over the world, and even its iconography that fetishizes the increasingly vertical cityscape, are all reminiscent of the Shanghai cinema of the 1930s. On all of these levels, *Beautiful New World* is in dialogue with *Street Angel*. Both films feature stereotypical characters: *Street Angel*'s helpless ingénue and idealistic male romantic lead seem not very far removed from *Beautiful New World*'s street-smart Shanghai native and backward country bumpkin. The two narratives offer fairly predictable stories of the struggle to earn a living in a glamorous metropolis.

Moreover, both films construct the city as spectacle and glittering playground. The opening and closing moments of both films prominently feature Shanghai's skyline and both use the skyscraper as a crucial motif to embody the wealth and power of the cosmopolitan city.

There is also a sociocultural and political "continuity" between the two eras in Shanghai's history. In a broad sense, both eras are noted for experiencing an economic boom under the shadow of political uncertainty. In the 1930s the threat of internal strife and external invasion would eventually crush profits, while in the 1990s the economic explosion could theoretically be halted at any time by political leaders in Beijing. Not surprisingly, in both eras there has also been an immense class divide as a result of newfound prosperity for a few. More specifically, in both the 1930s and the 1990s there was a massive immigration of the rural poor hoping to find fame and fortune in the city. What they most often found, however, was merely a different mode of subsistence. Finally, there is a further correspondence between these eras in that both economic booms have been built largely on international capital, which opens up the city to cosmopolitan experience with global products and a multinational citizenry. Thus, both in the Shanghai films of the 1930s and in some films from the 1990s a kind of cosmopolitan urban identity is being forged through the consumption of goods and media in the global city of Shanghai.[14] Yet, ultimately, the "results" and desirability of this influx of transnational goods and capital are configured quite differently in the two films.

Of course, to note such surface similarities between the two eras risks an ahistorical erasure of nearly half a century in which Shanghai and China were not enmeshed in global commerce. This type of historical blindness is certainly evident in films like *X-Roads*, which insist that the unfinished business of the 1930s can be completed more satisfactorily in the consumer-driven Shanghai of the 1990s. The return of the bar culture, for example, drives the male protagonist of *X-Roads* to seek his fortune by opening a bar with his American partner in the home inherited by the female protagonist. Thus the characters' fulfillment of their parents' thwarted love affair is intimately intertwined with the business of real estate and the exploitation of an old home for the purpose of selling two intoxicants, nostalgia and beer. The complexity of the larger historical frame, however, precludes this simplistic narrative of repetition and completion of the 1930s in the 1990s because of each era's historical and cultural uniqueness. Films like *X-Roads* and *Beautiful New*

World emphasize this link between the two eras precisely because the erasure of the fifty-year history of the People's Republic enables a sense of a continuity in consumption rather than a jarring disjuncture between the more recent communist past and the consumerist present.

In order to look at how surface similarities disguise two very different interpretations of the flourishing global city of Shanghai, I first want to explore the depictions of urban labor and consumption in *Street Angel* and *Beautiful New World*. The opening title sequence in *Street Angel* features a chaotic sea of rushing traffic, the silhouetted banks and hotels along the Bund, curtseying showgirls, and prominently displayed neon signs in both English and Chinese for nightclubs and multinational brand names like Frigidaire and White Horse Whisky. These frenetic images build an energy and excitement about the tantalizing cosmopolitan metropolis, an energy fueled by the promise of leisure and consumption. Leisure and the ability to consume are attained in *Beautiful New World* through diligence and hard work. In *Street Angel*, however, the link between work and the ability to consume is not a foregone conclusion. The difficulty of earning a living makes for deliriously funny comedy in *Street Angel* when one of Chen's friends is about to be forced out of his barbershop by his landlord. The group of friends band together to create a promotional event with Chen playing his trumpet to attract customers and the proprietor yelling out, "Two heads shaved for the price of one!" At this moment, however, a reverse angle shot shows that all the passersby on the street happen to be bald. When a man with hair finally appears, they forcibly drag him into the barbershop against his protests and begin to shave his head. Only when the landlord enters do they realize that the man, now with only random tufts of hair remaining, is a visitor for the landlord, who will now be even more likely to kick them out. Despite their best efforts, the friends are unable to get ahead. Thus, *Street Angel* derails the equation that work equals money, which equals the leisure to consume, by showing that its characters' hardest labor barely produces enough for survival, and not nearly enough to buy a Frigidaire, visit swank nightclubs, or drink imported whisky.

Moreover, consumption of anything luxurious is implicitly frowned upon in the film. When Xiao Hong innocently—and, we might add, gleefully—accepts a gift of dress fabric from the man who wants to buy her, Chen is furious and disgusted. He throws the fabric into the muddy street. Later, he visits the teahouse where Hong sings for her supper and drunkenly offers to pay for a song, which she is then forced by her adoptive "father" (who also functions as her manager and accompanist) to sing for him. The acceptance of the fabric and the payment of money for songs that were previously shared freely links Xiao Hong to her sister Ah Yun, whose work as a streetwalker has also been forced upon her by their adoptive parents.

Later in the film, the sullied fabric that Chen threw into the muddy street is replaced by a more modest gift from a more appropriate source—a smaller piece of plain fabric from Chen. Xiao Hong quickly makes this gift into a tunic that she proudly wears—unlike the earlier "gift," which, once it has caused a rift between the two lovers, disappears from the narrative altogether. The simple linkage of a piece of fabric to prostitution in *Street Angel* manages to divert the energy and excitement about consumption elicited by the neon signs seen in the opening titles. Like the barbershop's futile comedy, the narrative of Xiao Hong's dress subverts the image of Shanghai as a consumer paradise, thereby reforming utopic images of consumption to create a critique of the exploitation that lies at the root of all the hustle and bustle in *Street Angel*'s version of 1930s Shanghai.

In contrast, *Beautiful New World* is a virtual consumer primer, which links honest work to financial success and the enjoyment of an influx of international consumer goods. Though Jinfang and Baogen's struggle for financial success leads them both through a succession of jobs portrayed in wry montage sequences, only Jinfang's labor is ultimately unsuccessful. She and her friend Ah Hui can be seen as sanitized modern-day versions of *Street Angel*'s Ah Yun. Unlike the fictional Ah Yun and many real-life women in contemporary Shanghai, Jinfang and Ah Hui are not forced by anyone to sell their bodies, but instead actively seek their fortune by going on dates. Through the men they meet, the two women hope to find rich husbands or at least lucrative jobs so they can fulfill their dreams of luxurious weddings. Jinfang's jobs, however, are rarely lucrative and often demeaning. Dressed in a giant rabbit suit she tries selling balloons on the street, and she also goes door-to-door selling hospitality kits to hotel managers. In the latter job she is moderately successful, but only through bribery and sex appeal rather than hard work. She lives on credit, then borrows money to pay off her debts. Baogen initially has limited success on the job market, finding and then losing jobs as a construction worker and nightclub bouncer in quick succession. But when he finally finds his true calling selling lunches on the street, his hard work, ingenuity, and perseverance enable him to make enough money not only to survive but also to pay off Jinfang's debts.

Throughout the film, Baogen receives instructions on how to be a good consumer. First, he learns how to drink cognac from an affluent developer who tries to cheat him out of his luxury apartment. He also learns from Jinfang, whom he sees enjoying nightclubs and expensive cars and with whom he discusses the merits of the various products they see advertised on television. The viewer also learns that Jinfang and Ah Hui are avid consumers of clothes and are quite concerned with their looks and makeup as a lure to attract the men they believe will bring them financial success. Finally, Baogen learns from the television directly, which provides him not only with ads for new products, but also with his first glimpses of the stock market. The instructive power of entertainment media, specifically television, thus represents a distinct discontinuity from the 1930s. Its omnipresence in the homes of average- and low-income people provides a means of consumer instruction entirely missing from the world of *Street Angel*, whose poor characters do not have the means to join in the cosmopolitan consumption that drives their city.

Baogen's desire to consume may seem hyperbolic as well as largely based in fantasy, as when he pictures himself sipping brandy surrounded by a host of beautiful furnishings in a high-rise apartment with a spectacular view; but it is also a goal he strives for and may ultimately attain. Unlike in *Street Angel*, where the appearance and accoutrements of consumption are associated with prostitution and through self-sacrifice Yun must prove to Chen the inner goodness concealed by her war paint, the diligent Baogen must prove his worth to Jinfang by having the keys to consumption. His plain, less than affluent exterior and his pursuit of a "lowly" profession are obstacles to attaining her affection, which then are only removed by the revelation of his inner drive to attain financial success. Therefore, it is only the timing and mode of his labor and desire to consume that are portrayed as superior to Jinfang's overindulgence and fiscal irresponsibility. Baogen's entrepreneurial spirit is celebrated as a virtue. In *Beautiful New World* consumption itself is an attainable and desirable goal rather than a tainted diversion.

In order to explore another aspect of the two films' different treatments of capitalist consumption, I will address their opening and closing sequences, which prominently feature skyscrapers as emblems of economic hierarchy. Despite their differences, both films play on the contrast between the image of

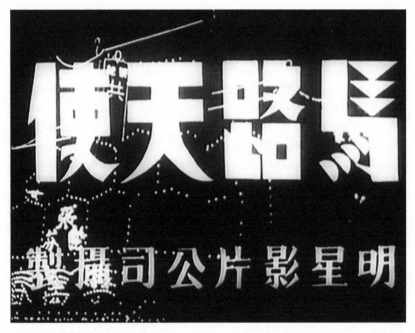

The neon world of *Street Angel.*

Shanghai as a bustling and glamorous global metropolis and the reality of daily survival in such a city. To this end, the openings of the two films stress the creation of a cityscape filled with modern beauty and excitement. *Street Angel*'s opening credits run over a kinetic montage portrait of 1930s Shanghai where multiple neon signs for nightclubs and international brand names are dynamically superimposed on opposite diagonals running across the frame. Scenes of urban leisure activities such as people strolling in the city's parks are quickly juxtaposed with scenes of rushing traffic. Looming church steeples are contrasted with the skyline of the Bund and its towering banks, hotels, and clubs. The sequence builds to an explosion of fireworks, neon, and curtseying cabaret girls, then the film cuts to the top of an imposing (model of a) skyscraper and displays a title that reads, "The year 1936." The camera pans down the height of the skyscraper and into the asphalt below to display another title, "Shanghai—the lower depths." The image cuts to feet marching on a Shanghai street, and the viewer is introduced to the film's major characters in the course of a cacophonous wedding procession.[15]

Beautiful New World also establishes the spectacular glamour of the city of Shanghai in its opening moments. The camera finds Zhang Baogen as he arrives in Shanghai on a night bus. It follows him as he asks directions and returns to the bus. The film cuts to three singers in a teahouse, the sound of whose singing has already introduced the viewer to the film's protagonist. The singers are pictured performing for an audience in front of a sepia-toned painting of the Bund. Then, inside the darkened bus, Baogen sees the glittering, unearthly blue skyline of Pudong, Shanghai's new development zone. This shot of the skyline from Baogen's point of view is followed by a close-up, back inside the darkened bus, of his face gaping in appreciation. A few moments later, another point of view sequence frames his first view of the legendary Bund before the bus moves on to drop him off at an older building reminiscent of those inhabited by the denizens of *Street Angel*'s "lower depths," and decidedly far removed from the glittering skyline. This building is Jinfang's home, the place where Baogen will plan his own urban success story. In contrast to the strictly vertical movement down *Street Angel*'s skyscraper, however, Baogen is able to move horizontally between the two worlds, thus presaging his access to upward mobility rather than emphasizing the hierarchical class divide.

In both films, the image of the skyline as a symbol for the city and the skyscraper as an embodiment of the city's wealth and prosperity is pivotal. It is used in the opening and closing moments of both films, which impresses the image more firmly in the eyes and memory of the viewer and serves as a linchpin of narrative and visual structure within the body of both film texts. The image of the skyscraper is a pervasive one in world cinema, perhaps because cinema came of age at the same time that the skyscraper did. The skyscraper was one of the first visual markers of the global metropolis, the home or office of the cosmopolitan classes who lived in a particular city but had the opportunity, through travel and culture, to move around the globe. As symbols of wealth, power, and status, skyscrapers in the 1920s and 1930s seemed to reach for the sky in an unnatural and certainly less than humble way, with a grasping verticality which could be construed as either grandiose or just plain greedy—such as in films like Fritz Lang's *Metropolis* (1927).

It's hardly surprising, then, that the skyscraper in *Street Angel* is portrayed as a towering art deco fortress.[16] The pan down the vertical height of an enormous skyscraper into the world of asphalt and dirt inhabited by the film's

Downward mobility:
the opening of
Street Angel.

难道你忽然间拾到了聚宝盆

Zhang Baogen, the country bumpkin, looks at Shanghai.

Zhang Baogen's vision of Shanghai.

central characters concretely embodies the divide between the world of the haves and have-nots.[17] After this early pan down the building, the world of skyscrapers and neon is entirely absent from the film until Chen and his friend Wang visit a lawyer in an attempt to protect Xiao Hong from being sold. This visit to the top of Shanghai provides comedic moments as the two men struggle to behave appropriately in front of the high-class lawyer and to manage strange modern conveniences like water coolers and cup dispensers. When they first arrive in the attorney's office, Chen and Wang get a dizzying point of view shot of the city below them. Wang remarks on the efficiency of the heating and declares the waiting room to be "heaven." Unfortunately, his utopian vision of life among the clouds is dashed when the two friends realize the immensity of the lawyer's fees and the impossibility of hiring him to plead Xiao Hong's case. After Chen and Wang's encounter with the lawyer, the film leaves behind any image or mention of the skyline in order to focus exclusively on the "lower depths." The characters have realized that the cosmopolitan life of skyscraper inhabitants—despite the building's close physical proximity to them—is completely inaccessible due to the financial and cultural divide that separates the residents of the two worlds. Despite the brevity of its appearance in *Street Angel*, this image of the inaccessible and oppressive skyscraper is central to the film because of its appearance in the crucial opening and closing sequences, both of which emphasize a particular relationship between the central characters of *Street Angel* and the inhabitants of the skyscraper world above them.

Beautiful New World paints a far more ambivalent and detailed portrait of the skyscraper than does its cinematic predecessor. Certainly there are surface similarities in the two portrayals, starting with the emphasis in both films on the skyline. *Beautiful New World* also features a scene of an awkward encounter between the world of the skyscraper denizen and a citizen from down below. Zhang Baogen's first entry into the skyscraper world is as a contest winner who is used contemptuously for free publicity by the developer. Then he is "taught" to appreciate cognac and Honduran cigarillos as the same developer tries to buy him off after admitting that the apartment on the thirty-seventh floor, which the press conference touted as the gateway to a "beautiful new life" for Baogen, has yet to be constructed. The developer suggests that Baogen exchange his deed to the high-rise apartment for an amount of money far lower than the purported worth of the apartment. Jiang Wu's wide-eyed comedic performance, in which he insists on discussing this matter with his parents in the countryside, brings to mind the slapstick bumbling of Zhao Dan in the lawyer's office in *Street Angel*.

However, images of the skyscraper and its inhabitants do not remain unattainable and alien to everyday life in *Beautiful New World* as they do in *Street Angel*. It is precisely the promise of an apartment in the skyscraper that brings Baogen to Shanghai and keeps him there even after he loses a succession of jobs and finds himself without a place to live. The film makes fun of Baogen's aspirations by picturing his daydream of sipping cognac in the stylishly furnished but still unfinished concrete shell of his skyscraper apartment. It also implicitly compares Baogen's gritty daily life underneath gray overpasses to both the present-day world of big spenders and the legendary 1930s prosperity depicted on the backdrop behind the teahouse performers. Ultimately, however, *Beautiful New World* affirms Baogen's dream of financial success as a definite possibility. Moreover, Baogen is not completely duped by the developer, nor is he permanently forced out of the skyscraper world. On his own, he makes the decision to refuse the offer of money up front rather than receiving an apartment in the future and thus retains the possibility of ascending again to the thirty-seventh floor. At the film's midpoint, the subterranean busker Ah Liang (played by real-life Taiwanese pop star Wu Bai) rebukes Baogen for complaining about his lost job and temporary homelessness because, unlike so many people in the city, he has at least the hope of (re)entering the skyscraper world. Overall, that world is far more accessible to the characters of *Beautiful New World* than it is for the characters of *Street Angel.*

The two images of the skyscraper, as oppressive and exclusionary or desirable and ultimately attainable, are cemented by the closing sequences of the two films. In *Street Angel,* after the group of friends has been united in grief over Ah Yun's death, the camera withdraws to the space outside of the room where they are gathered. Then the camera leaves them entirely to very slowly pan up the same skyscraper pictured in the film's opening moments, thereby implicitly placing the responsibility for Ah Yun's death on the world above, where money and power procured through the exploitation of those in the lower depths take precedence over friendship and family ties. The ultimate result of the group's unification is ambiguous: the spectator wonders whether they will fight together against the powers that oppress them or merely continue to live in their separate but far from equal world. What is clear is that the characters from *Street Angel* are excluded from the world above them by money and class. And, ultimately, the cold impassivity of the skyscraper and its physical separation from the characters' communal world below makes it seem unreachable and even undesirable precisely because it is both built upon their suffering and completely oblivious to it.

The final moments of *Beautiful New World,* by contrast, envision the heights of the skyscraper as not only desirable but also attainable. After attending the wedding of Ah Hui, Baogen and Jinfang, riding home in a taxi dressed in their best clothes and feeling a little tipsy, share a relaxed moment

Pingtan singers in front of a sepia-toned Bund.

Upward mobility: Zhang Baogen points to his home in the sky.

of giggling fun that prompts Baogen to finally show Jinfang why he came to Shanghai, a secret he has cannily kept from her for months. He pulls her, kicking and screaming, out of the cab and into the pouring rain. The camera follows as he leads her down into a construction pit and clambers up a pile of girders. He tells her of his thirty-seventh floor apartment and, when she laughs, Baogen points to the sky and demands that the pouring rain stop if he is really telling the truth. The vertical movement of Baogen's gesture and his striving for the "heaven" abandoned by *Street Angel's* Wang and Chen has an infectious momentum. But, when the rain stops suddenly, freezing Baogen and Jinfang in their skyward stare, their reverie is interrupted by the shouts of returning construction workers. The camera follows Jinfang and Baogen as they climb down from the pile of girders and scramble out of the construction pit. Then, just as it did at the close of *Street Angel*, the camera leaves them behind to tilt up into the surrounding skyscrapers. Yet unlike the end of *Street Angel* where the camera pans up a skyscraper in a completely separate space to indicate the alienation of the characters, *Beautiful New World*'s final camera movement is motivated directionally by the characters' own upward climb. And, though it reaches their purported goal without them, the viewer senses that Jinfang and Baogen are on their way up, too. In *Beautiful New World*, the image of the Shanghai skyline is the image of success—Baogen's own personal El Dorado. Shanghai and the success to be gained there are framed as mythical. The scenes inside the teahouse with its wall-sized image of the Bund, traditional costumes, and performances link the story of Baogen, albeit superficially, to an earlier version of Shanghai. The enunciation of his story through teahouse ballads places his striving for success in the big city within a historical and local trajectory of stories that have been passed down from generation to generation.

CONCLUSION

The evocation of the Bund and the pre-revolutionary city create a totalizing history, or a sense of continuity, for Baogen's drive to consume. In Mayfair Yang's words, this is part of an attempt to "(re)cosmopolitanize"[18] the Chinese metropolis. Nostalgia for the history of Shanghai as an international center with a specifically local culture is mobilized here not for the sake of remembrance but for the purpose of providing a local, historical precedent for cosmopolitan consumption. Clearly, this history is a selective one that ignores the crisis and chaos of the colonial city in favor of imagining a utopian future. *Beautiful New World* depicts a Shanghai that is "returning" to a set of roots that are not in the lower depths inhabited by the characters of *Street Angel* but rather in the sky above. Instead, it draws on the exhilaration and civic pride associated with the city's growth outward and upward. Though a film like *Street Angel* provides a scathing critique of this exhilarating upward progress, the utopian vision of the city of Shanghai's future can also be found by looking backward. In 1934, the novelist Mao Dun prophesied the creation of a

Beautiful New World when he wrote: "Shanghai will become the number-one metropolis in the world, a metropolis designed for consumption."[19] Neither Mao Dun's utopian vision nor the upward momentum in the closing scene of *Beautiful New World*, however, can obscure the fact that a nostalgic correspondence between 1930s and 1990s Shanghai masks not only the uniqueness of the two eras, but also the dark economic underside of their continuity. If Shanghai does become the "number-one metropolis . . . designed for consumption," will this achievement actually provide the upward mobility sought by millions of Zhang Baogens making their way to China's cities?

It seems more likely that the connection between the two eras is merely cosmetic. The function of the sepia-toned image of the Bund and the *pingtan* singers can perhaps be better understood through an excerpt from a more recent piece of fiction—Wei Hui's 1999 novel *Shanghai Baby*. In a chapter that opens with an epigraph of a song by Tori Amos, the novel's heroine Nikki describes a meeting with her publishers at a café on Shaoxing Road: "The café is called Old China Hand Reading Room in English, and is famous for its wall-to-wall library and its 1930s furnishings. The owner is a well-known photographer, Deke Erh, and his patrons include plenty of famous media types— journalists, publishers, writers, TV and movie producers, Chinese opera stars, and scholars from the West—who shine and sparkle like stars against its elegant backdrop. The books, jazz music, smell of coffee and antique furniture fit in with both Shanghai's erotic past and its consumer-oriented present."[20]

I would argue that nostalgic films set in or drawing upon popular culture intertexts from pre-liberation Shanghai often use these eras like *Shanghai Baby*'s "media types" use the Old China Hand Reading Room, as a beautiful backdrop that is ultimately obscured by the sparkling stars of the present. As in Wei Hui's description, this use of Shanghai's "erotic past" as window dressing reduces the historical city to only one of its many aspects. The pastiche of nostalgic images hints at a similarity between eras and pastes over the discontinuity of the communist past, but it also cuts and pastes the eroticized surfaces of the past into a discourse with its own contemporary consumerist agenda, thus separating these intertextual images from their narrative and cultural meaning in order to make the surfaces "fit" into the background of contemporary works. The cosmopolitan surfaces of 1930s films like *Street Angel* and *Crossroads* are completely severed from their narratives of collective political struggle to serve as advertising backdrops that "historicize" the individual struggle to obtain consumer goods portrayed in a film like *Beautiful New World*. This totalizing use of nostalgia serves as lens to focus the imagination of urban identity on continuity with the past rather than emphasizing the divide between communist past and consumerist present emphasized in films like *In the Heat of the Sun*.

Though film production in both the 1930s and the 1990s contains contradictory images of urban identity and political discourse, *Street Angel* and *Beautiful New World* can be considered as "representative" of particular cinematic trends in their respective eras. *Street Angel* uses the spectacle of the city's abundance as a harsh contrast to the realities of daily life. The film's concern with the absolute separation of the laboring classes and the elite necessitates the construction of an alternative social sphere that rejects individual consumption as a ladder to success and contentment. Instead, like many leftist films from the 1930s, the sacrifice of an individual character leads to the construction of a communal group capable of building a more equitable future. Though the end of *Street Angel* places more emphasis on tragedy than do some of the other leftist films of this era, it still can be said to contain the "bright tail" (*guangming de weiba*) typical of 1930s filmmaking. As Laikwan Pang succinctly describes this common technique, it consists of "a subtle hint of revolution at the end of the usually tragic story, promising a brighter future if further action is taken."[21] The fantasies created by these films projected a sense of "neighborhood and nationhood" constructed through collective political action. The closing scene of *Beautiful New World* also adds a "bright tail" to the narrative, but its emphasis on individual rather than collective action and the resulting financial success is more typical of the 1990s. As in many other commercial Chinese films from the 1990s, consumption, financial prudence, and romantic love must be balanced by the individual in order to attain contentment and to have a bright future. The reconfiguration of the motif of the skyscraper in *Beautiful New World* provides a shorthand visual and narrative symbol for the construction of individualized consumer identity through nostalgic fantasy in a (re)cosmopolitanized Shanghai. The collective consumption of films like *Beautiful New World* draws together the fantasy of an elite urban existence and the nostalgia for an earlier version of the city to imagine a utopian future for urban China, but the nostalgic fragments that the film pastes into its narrative can, upon reflection, elicit critiques of transnational consumption applicable to both the 1930s and the 1990s.

NOTES

1. See, for example, Dai Jinhua's "Imagined Nostalgia" in *boundary 2* (fall 1997): 143–62, special issue, *Postmodernism and China,* ed. Arif Dirlik and Zhang Xudong; and the chapter "Totalitarian Nostalgia" in Geremie Barmé, *In The Red: On Contemporary Chinese Culture* (New York: Columbia University Press, 1999), 316–44.

2. Fred Davis, *Yearning for Yesterday: A Sociology of Nostalgia* (New York: Free Press, 1979), 104.

3. Arjun Appadurai, *Modernity at Large: Cultural Dimensions of Globalization* (Minneapolis: University of Minnesota Press, 1996), 77–78.

4. Ibid., 82.

5. Ibid., 7.

6. Boym's discussion of nostalgia appears in *Common Places: Mythologies of Everyday Life in Russia* (Cambridge, Mass.: Harvard University Press, 1994).

7. Ibid., 284.

8. Ibid., 285.

9. The notion of repetition is made even more overt in the film's Chinese title, which translates as "New Crossroads."

10. Totalizing and fragmentary nostalgia are discussed in greater detail in chapter 3 of my dissertation, "Crossroads: Nostalgia and the Documentary Impulse in Contemporary Chinese Cinemas." In chapters 4 and 5 of the dissertation I go on to argue for a specific differentiation between a category of cinematic nostalgia that mobilizes the image of historical Shanghai to (re-)create a transnational Chinese past, and a second category of local, fragmentary nostalgia for specific urban youth cultures that attempts to resurrect specific urban experiences and environments in the interest of sustaining local identity and of emphasizing the disappearance of individual neighborhoods and urban experiences.

11. Dai Jinhua, "Imagined Nostalgia," 158.

12. Ibid., 158.

13. Indeed, a host of more overtly nostalgic films about Shanghai were made in the People's Republic during the late 1990s in commemoration of the fiftieth anniversary of the revolution and the liberation of Shanghai.

14. *Suzhou River* (Suzhou, 1999; dir. Lou Ye), for example, particularly foregrounds the self-construction of its ephemeral mermaid by her comparison to a blonde, Barbie-like mermaid doll.

15. The sequence that follows the credits has been meticulously explored from the perspective of leftist ideology in Ma Ning, "The Textual and Critical Difference of Being Radical: Reconstructing Chinese Leftist Films of the 1930s," *Wide Angle* 11, no. 2 (1989): 22–31.

16. For further discussion of this architecture, see Leo Ou-fan Lee's discussion of Shanghai's art deco skyscrapers in *Shanghai Modern: The Flowering of a New Urban Culture, 1930–1945* (Cambridge, Mass.: Harvard University Press, 1999): 10–13.

17. Ni Zhen refers to this opening sequence as crucial to the binary opposition between rich and poor (as well as evil and good) that is central to the mythology of 1930s leftist city cinema. See Ni Zhen, "Chengshi dianying de wenhua maodun" [Cultural contradiction in city films], in *Dangdai huayu dianying lunshu* [Discussion of contemporary Chinese-language cinema], ed. Li Tianduo (Taipei: China Times Press, 1996), 227–47.

18. This term is borrowed from Mayfair Yang, "Mass Media and Transnational Subjectivity in Shanghai: Notes on (Re)Cosmopolitanism in a Chinese Metropolis," in *Ungrounded Empires: The Cultural Politics of Modern Chinese Transnationalism*, ed. Donald M. Nonini and Aihwa Ong (New York: Routledge, 1997), 287–319.

19. "Shanghai de jianglai" [Shanghai's future], in *Xin zhonghua fukan* [New China magazine supplement] (Shanghai: Zhonghua shuju, 1934), 23–24, trans. by and quoted in Lee, *Shanghai Modern*, 343.

20. Wei Hui, *Shanghai Baby*, trans. Bruce Hume (New York: Pocket Books, 2001), 174.

21. Laikwan Pang, *Building a New China in Cinema: The Chinese Left-Wing Cinema Movement, 1932–1937* (Lanham, Md.: Rowman and Littlefield, 2002), 207. A more overtly optimistic "bright tail" can be seen at the end of many 1930s films. For example, the ending of *Big Road* (Dalu, 1935; dir. Sun Yu) features the dreamlike resurrection of characters killed in a Japanese bombing raid.

whither the walker goes

Spatial Practices and Negative Poetics

in 1990s Chinese Urban Cinema

LINDA CHIU-HAN LAI

rounded in a conviction to make sense of the materiality and visuality of the city, and a commitment to everyday creativity, *flânerie* and *dérive* ("drifting") are forms of spatial practice adopted, primarily among European intelligentsia, as subversive tactics to combat alienation in urban life in the West. The two terms mark a trajectory of subject positions. At one end lies the self-directed, purposeful, rational author: an often utopian presentation of a carefree (male) individual in the midst of the urban maelstrom, the typical modernist intellectual of authorial presence, the transcendental empirical subject, the active critic, the native who thinks and feels like a foreigner (as in the case of the *flâneur*). The gradation of these positions moves to the other end of the trajectory with the decentered subject who deliberately enters a series of digressions and breaks away from routines to rediscover, rather than reassert, his or her understanding of the urban space not fully known before (as in the case of drifting). But when these categories of "walking" become sheer metaphors, and when they can only be realized as textual strategies replacing material engagement with everyday urbanity, the radicalism implied is qualitatively undermined. I want to address this problem by discussing a number of representative contemporary Chinese films that, on various levels, embody the filmmaker's flânerie activities via unique visual aesthetics or by relying upon a walker/drifter as the main protagonist. They include a particular group of films by Huang Jianxin, often called the "urban attitude" series[1] and the so-called underground films, particularly Zhang Ming's *In Expectation* (Wushan yunyu, aka *Rainclouds over Wushan* [1996]), Jia Zhangke's *Xiao Wu* (1997), and Lou Ye's *Suzhou River* (Suzhou he, 2000).

The flâneur in Walter Benjamin's analysis was the character of urban myth living mainly in nineteenth-century novels (especially in France) and often the surrogate of the novelist, who was himself the walker in the streets (of Paris).[2] The walker is a discursive subject who at the same time articulates the authorial presence of the novelist and his fascination with the modern city. By the time the Lettrist International created the term "drifting" in the 1950s, the celebrative walker of the nineteenth century had already gone through an elaborate history to form a flânerie practice, which was negotiated with a growing critical emphasis by writers and artists of the twentieth century. By the time the Situationist International (SI) took up drifting in the late 1950s through the 1960s as a form of interventionist critical tactics, the term signified the refusal of symbolic transformation via poetry and called for the reinsertion of the personal subject into concrete lived space to materialize momentary changes.

My task in this essay is not only to differentiate the various modes of walking, but also to examine the implied mode of critical praxis. The discursive power of walking may end up as pure narrative practices, ready to be reabsorbed and dissolved into the endless game of discourse. Or, walking is discourse making and is praxis itself. In the case of the latter mode, narrative practices are no longer pure signification exercises in search of revised alternative meanings. Instead, narrative practices are lived intervention via engagement with everyday life practices and the creation of new spaces for self-articulation, such as breaking into the stronghold of established institutional norms and boundaries of cultural-textual production. Narrative practices as such contain in their core tactics the very social position assigned to a writer/filmmaker/poet. The distinction to draw between the two forms of walking can be expressed as that between affirmative (re-)articulation, that is, the taming of the world via the walker's insightful vision (flânerie), and walking by which the act itself is the violation of managed space, the breakaway from structured powers of containment by reopening settled meanings (drifting). In sum, in this essay my objective is to unravel the discursive construction of the Chinese city via an analysis of creative textual practices in selective urban films while, at the same time, redefine the preservation of a certain visual rhetoric of cinema in relation to the gradual materialization of a market economy in the Mainland. As a critical response, I raise the question of what really makes critical strategies critical, and I point out the limitation of filmmaking as an isolated activity to achieve radical critique.

MAPPING THE NEW CHINESE CITY, MAPPING URBAN CINEMA

The new Chinese city is an enigma that at first sight defies comprehension. It swarms with crowds and strangers who yet are bound by an unprecedented collective awareness of one another. The new Chinese city is the nation's key evidence of modernization as a celebration of progress and technological advancement, and yet there are more who find themselves left behind the march of change than those who catch up with it. The new city is an expansive, recognizable space marked by modern architecture, especially high-rises, and held together by networks of transportation. Yet the city is also endlessly sedimentary, where it is futile to attempt to separate the new from the old, the modern from the premodern, and what is Chinese from what is Western.

The new cities of China are best approached as *heterotopia*—that is, each city is a single space with multiple orderings, encounters, cores and planes; they are many places in one, of different levels of realities, and allude to many sites here and elsewhere; and they are the juxtaposition of incommensurate things, independent and yet collective, disrupting and at the same time layering upon one another.[3] Heterotopia, which suggests otherness, liminality, and hybridity, generates an alternative view of the new Chinese city that contrasts with many official, affirmative, laudatory accounts. The notion of heterotopia illumines the activity of walking comparable to that of "performance" or "speech act" in our understanding of language. Walking is like the act of speaking, while heterotopia provides an account of the diverse field of a lived urban system that embraces many incommensurable places, like the way the field of a linguistic system enables the diverse functions of the act of speaking.[4] From a different perspective, the notions of walking as speech act and heterotopia underline stylistic issues and remap aesthetic choices—both notions reject the easy generalization of aesthetic distinctive as generational differences that has marked most discussion of Mainland Chinese cinema in the 1990s.

In addition to its presence in the cinema, the walker is a vibrant category in contemporary Chinese literature found across many creative genres. A paradigmatic illustration of a Chinese city as heterotopia can be found in *Chang Hen Ge* (The song of long-lasting sorrow, 1996) by the Shanghai woman novelist Wang Anyi. The entire first chapter of Wang's novel is a complex spatial, materialist account of the city of Shanghai. This introductory chapter neither serves as the chronological precedent of an almost seventy-year saga of a Shanghainese woman, nor is it a retrospective portrayal of the spirit of the times. Rather, it stands out from the rest of the novel as a timeless characterization of a lived space. Wang's literary reproduction of Shanghai as a heterotopia is at once descriptive and discursive. Breaking down the chapter into five sections, Wang cuts through five very different planes of the city's daily reality: *longtang* (lanes, the typical Shanghai residential area), *liu yan* (rumors), *gui ge* (the maiden chambers), *ge zi* (pigeons), and Wang Qiyao (the name of the woman protagonist of the novel, who is the embodiment of the young maidens of Shanghai). These five sections produce as a whole many different levels of reality—architectural and spatial, spiritual and mystical, sociological, anthropological, personal and biographical. It is this basic set-up of a heterotopia against which the history of Wang Qiyao, also the history of Shanghai, unfolds.[5]

Wang's penetration into the city is multitropical, visual, and even "cinematographic," freely switching from a high-angle bird's-eye view of the entire city, a panoramic swish, to closer views of the interiors of the residential space from outside the windows, from encounters of everyday activities in the lanes, and to a microscopic study of the dirt and smell in the most secret corner. Furthermore, her authorial presence and omniscient journey into the interior and history of Shanghai is mystically embodied in the pigeons, which provide an aerial vision of the city. Pigeons, a fiendish presence throughout the novel, are the only conscientious, loyal, and caring yet fragile drifters in Shanghai. Only occasionally does the novelist draw attention to the almost invisible omnipresence of the pigeons, the "dumb witnesses" of the city's sufferings, reminding us that they have been enduringly watching, smelling the bad before any living being notices.[6] Wang's pigeons are the "surveyors" of material and spiritual Shanghai. They are not Wang, and yet they are the embodiment of her pathetic guardianship. *Chang Hen Ge* powerfully lends a fresh account astray of the dominant account of the legendary city of Shanghai. Zhang Ailing, one of the most internationally acclaimed authors of modern Chinese literature, has been cherished for her insights on the subtle relational politics of the "modern" Shanghai individual. By comparison, Wang engages in an even more complex way than does Zhang the material and emotive layers of Shanghai.

Filmmaker Huang Jianxin belongs, more or less, to Wang's generation. Huang's "urban attitude" films can provide here a cinematic counterpart to Wang's introductory passage to the actual story of *Chang Hen Ge:* both authors occupy the position of the compassionate intellectual who must see beyond what the ordinary eyes of others are capable of seeing. While Wang authorizes her real presence and guides us through the city via the highly fluid visualizing activity materialized in the narrativity of the written word, Huang's camera assumes a calculated mode that observes in a cool-minded way. And by relying heavily on the transparency of the photographic image, Huang's unambiguous empirical-realist method allows us to search the fictional episodes of everyday life as if we were studying the content of a tableau vivant, so as to see for ourselves the human interaction and speech exchange that often upholds sociological tenacity.[7] Huang's virtual walking through the city via the camera asserts a unified vision and single perspective that lacks Wang's consciousness of the necessity to articulate a place as heterotopia. In contrast, other films by independent filmmakers addressed in this essay are self-consciously working against a unified analytic vision. Via drifting, these films adopt a digressive method that allows the drifter to make random connections with events and people, thus taking us to experiences of diverse existential and material origins. The "place" thus formed in the mind of the viewers in these films is no more than the site of irregularities and enigmas. Drawing from the interpretive force of the notion of heterotopia, I suggest that films such as *In Expectation, Xiao Wu,* and *Suzhou River* contain, through their narrative method, "alternative modes of social ordering that are expressions of a utopic/dystopic spatial play."[8] These films, however, while in congruence with the idea of *heterotopia* that Wang upholds, deliberately defy her kind of prophetic vision as well as Huang's assumption of a filmmaker's position as a productive intellectual.

It is important here to emphasize that heterotopia is not just a metaphor that generates a convenient descriptive account of a place's multiplicity. In my reading, the term's adapted usage, starting with Foucault, is to open up new interpretive-critical paradigms that work against simplistic analyses that sacrifice complexities for narrative cleanliness in critical practice. It defies the easy separation of apparently incommensurate elements. It points to the peculiar and complex ways that individuals organize and map out their own spatial community—in cohabitation with, overlapping, and contradicting those of others within the same space. Foucault discusses heterotopia in relation to specific social places whose social meaning is out of place and unsettling within a geographical relationship of sites. Heterotopia therefore tackles the questions of what one may know about a place, and how one knows. It is not a definitive category but rather an open notion that sets off critical engagement.

The interpretive-critical implication of the term *heterotopia* also guards against rushed generalizations of a new China born by rapid changes and, instead, calls for the examination of the forces at work that transform the everyday life dramaturgy in recent decades. Urban construction and the effects of political relaxation only in the past twenty years started to butt through the thick walls of bleak socialism. In the new consumerist city culture, the political, economic, social, and cultural are often difficult to differentiate. To the critic, it is understandably tempting to grab any available cultural texts to derive a quick, encompassing view of urban development and consumerism in China. The desire (especially that of a non-Mainlander such as myself) to make sense of a complex historical process, and to conquer such a massive, often chaotic, experience of development following no universal regularities, tends to lead one to isolate, from the bulk of cultural texts, those that are reflective of the so-called spirit of the time or those that typify the demographic contours. A similar desire marks Mainland cultural practitioners who have sought all means to conquer urban realities via narrativity or, in Raymond Williams's terms, through "reading," that is, interpreting social practices, and "writing," the act of and struggle to maintain or challenge established/dominant meanings.[9] A sharp distinction between fiction and reality, discourse and fact, is in itself illusory—as is implied in the concept of heterotopia. The cognizance and the cognition of the city arise partly from the actual lived experiences of the material city by individuals, and are in part a product of discursive construction by people such as literary writers and filmmakers whose voice can be heard by many. In various ways, cultural practitioners have interpellated China's everyday arena since the late 1970s with different notions of a "new life," whether normative, projected, idealized, imagined, or fictionalized.

Based on the shifts in Foucault's later writings, I argue that heterotopia should best be understood in the performative sense of criticism. That is, a critic's task is less to identify what existing places qualify for a heterotopia based on a list of describable features than it is to actively interrogate the heterogeneity of a place. The use of the term does not ask, "Is this place a heterotopia?" Rather, the mobilization of the term begs the new discovery of a place to tease out human activities that articulate subjectivities—erasable in definitive accounts of a place, but accessible only when understood in multiple spatial-temporal terms. Thus heterotopia is approachable only in performative terms. Such usage to make sense of a place at once effectuates a critic's determination and concrete action to deconstruct established knowledge about the place in question, via (re-)reading and (re-)writing, and by begging multiplicity and heterogeneity. Heterotopia in this sense is a speech act. So, for example, in seeing and writing Shanghai in the way she does, Wang turns heterotopia into an action-concept with which she forces her way into Shanghai's conceptual/representational landscape, which already is crammed with familiar types and stereotypes. Following from this, bringing in Wang's literary attempt for the purpose of contrast with the film works discussed in this essay is a productive act. For the measure of the films lies not in the presence/absence of progressive themes and subject matters, nor in the formation of an alternative view, but rather in the deconstructive capacity of these works, such as whether narrative practice manages to keep open the signifier-signified chain.

THE METANARRATIVE OF THE CITY FILM AND
THE URBAN ATTITUDE OF THE NEW CITY DWELLER

In reviewing the bulk of films within the discourse of the "urban cinema" and the critical literature surrounding it, two characteristics stand out. First, the metafiction (metanarrative) of the city film's evolvement parallels a phasic narrative of political-economic changes in China. Second, the "new city experience" is often embodied in a fictional character, hero or antihero, who is a transcendental subject in action, and whose daily activities are conducted against the force of urbanity via a narrative that employs the "central conflict theory."[10]

In November 1978 when Deng Xiaoping announced the open door policy as a directive for China's future, other doors also opened gradually, including the influx of Western theories developed in the 1960s and 1970s, which brought forth socialist China's first wave of translation of Western texts into the Chinese language.[11] Together also came the relaxation of the orthodoxy of social instrumentalism in cultural, creative activities, including filmmaking. Indeed, a number of time markers have constantly returned as signposts signifying rapid progress in the country: 1978 (the beginning of economic reform and China's opening up to the West); 1987 (the implementation of economic reform in major cities; the release of Zhang Yimou's *Red Sorghum* and the subsequent popularization of the Fifth Generation's avant-garde aesthetics); 1988 (the conference "Contemporary Chinese Entertainment Films" held in December); 1989 (the disruption of freedom in cultural practices due to the June 4th massacre); 1995 (five Hollywood films reappear in China for public screening after an absence of over forty years); and 1999 (the beginning of China's negotiation for membership in the World Trade Organizations in November).[12] As more than pure coincidence, the discourse of the city in films, too, situates its beginning around the year 1978, following closely the timeline of economic changes. One example is the Mainland scholar Dai Jinhua's chronological-phasic discourse of the city in film representation since 1978, which roughly falls into three periods: the city as a counterpart to rural China (1978 to mid-1980s); the city as an independent center-stage (mid-to-late 1980s); and the age of diversity (1990s).[13]

The causal link between the political/economic (the context) and the cultural (both textual production and the conduction of everyday life) is somewhat presumed in many analyses. Such a view is based on a kind of permeation model reminiscent of the classical Marxian notion of economic determinism, which has been extended metaphorically into more generic models of determinism via base-superstructure analysis. The Mainland film theorist Li Yiming is most explicit in asserting such a model when he writes: "The years 1990 through 1995 formed a period of tremendous historic change in the ordinary life of China. It was also a period in which film aesthetics, film style, and investment modes and distribution systems went through revolutionary changes. The former is the overall social context, which foundationally determines the kind of changes taking place. The latter is a discursive system of a particular medium, a specific mode of articulation of its context."[14] Li continues with a detailed analysis of how the political, economic, and cultural contexts dictate the moves of the Sixth Generation filmmakers and their deviation from the Fifth Generation during this period from 1990 to 1995.[15] An interpretive model as such, which relies heavily on generalization, necessarily erases differences. In the end it does no more than affirm depoliticization and economic reform as a crucial impetus to changes in other domains of life—starting with the moment after Mao's death and the fall of the Gang of Four (around 1976–77). I do not intend here to deny the impact of economic reform and China's entry into the WTO, but the straitjacket accounts in the above generalizations can be misleading. What remains to be explained is how cultural texts function complexly. The employment of the idea of walking/drifting as a special lens is one way to break away from the economist's model in order to focus on the less-examined aspect of how traces of progressive cultural practice and the drive to preserve a serious cinema have sought to stay alive, and how they are very much at the core of an intelligentsia tradition, despite noticeable signs of commercialization. In brief, the condition of cultural production in China is far more complex than any simple deterministic model can adequately accommodate. Creative activities in China often strike the double string of "collectivity" in the arena of acculturation, sustained via elitist criticism, and "individuality" via the valorization of the author as individuated auteur. Films or other cultural texts may or may not have a broad reception among the public.[16] But the literate public of the People's Republic of China is most certainly heavily traversed by elitist readings and writings of the intelligentsia, which are in turn subject to the surveillance of higher bodies committed to safeguarding political correctness. Although the existing literature favors generalization, I insist that textual production should be taken as individual occasions of cultural practices, each embracing its own agenda in its unique circumstances.

The diagnosis of many filmmakers of the new urban condition results in the construction of the symptomatic city dweller who bears the scar of displacement or suffers from immense loneliness. The young protagonists in Zhang Yuan's *Beijing Bastards* (1994), for example, are typical aliens without hope and without voice who are suffering from an incurable sense of loss and separation from the new urban milieu. To them, the past is gone but the advocated "present" is not yet. By contrast, the Fifth Generation director Tian Zhuangzhuang also singles out the rock and roll kids (in *Rock and Roll Kids*, 1987), but he sees them as quasi-poets speaking on behalf of the younger generation. They begin as social deviants, but by singing and dancing they gradually reclaim their legitimacy in the urban order. Optimistic responses such as in *Rock and Roll Kids* were plentiful in the 1980s. Such films often feature dauntless new citizens who readily embrace the new economic era and breathe its new spirit. They are survivors shrewd in appropriation. In Zhang Liang's *Yamaha Fish Stall* (1984), the young protagonists finally recognize their proper place in the new metropolitan Guangzhou by injecting the premodern communal virtues (of agricultural China) into the market-driven capitalist structure of survival. The new urban young adults in Mi Jiashan's *Troubleshooters* (Wanzhu, 1988; based on Wang Shuo's eponymous novel) like to hang out on the busy streets of Beijing and ridicule the dogmatic ideals of the so-called meaningful life, and they set out to solve the ordinary people's everyday inconveniences of all sorts. They are positive participants whose "social" contribution consists of toppling social/moral proprieties. The new Beijing citizens in *Bianji bu de gushi* (The story of the editorial room) (TV series, 1991) are defined by speech: they adopt new local expressions and a new vernacular rhetoric. The most celebrative articulation is in Feng Xiaogang's *Be Here or Be Square* (Bu jian bu san, 1998), which takes for granted the global quality of the new Chinese subjects. His protagonists are casual global trespassers in the metropolis of Los Angeles who have no problems crossing cultural barriers and who are always able to manage.

In between the two celebratory types noted above are the isolated individuals whose subjectivity is affirmed by negating any impact from their milieu. In other words, the monumental influence of the new urban era on individual lives is undermined or denied. He Jianjun's young postman in *Postman* (1995) is one such example. The character roams through a certain borough in the city of Beijing as a daily obligation, trespasses the personal domains of strangers, and compulsively recoils from everyday routine into his private habitat. In all of these cases, except *Beijing Bastard* and *Postman*, the protagonists are active or even positive doers. In these texts, the city in the new economic era and the urban condition are imagined through psychologically driven characters who struggle, deny, resist, or adapt to changes. These willful protagonists are more or less the filmmakers' own surrogate. In line with the central conflict theory, the characters in these stories respond to the peculiar environment they are written into (the source of central conflict), and subsequently effectuate the film's main dramatic actions toward a personal solution (resolution in the denouement) almost always with a redemptive note.

By contrast, the protagonists in the independent films that are the gist of my analysis here are not action takers. They simply wander around, withdrawn from conscious engagement with any productive, meaningful activities in the normative sense. The main character in *Xiao Wu* is deliberately idling, while the one in *In Expectation* wakes up to find himself in an idling mental state. Perhaps the "invisible" protagonist in *Suzhou River*, whose presence is in the form of a point-of-view shot and first-person narrative voice only, is relatively more productive. But as he roams through the city of Shanghai with his video camera, he is more in restless search of something he does not know than he is engaging in self-assured pursuits—not to mention positive contribution to the new economy.

The focus on drifting and flânerie, especially the former, assumes a speech-act perspective regarding how one relates to the urban space. Michel de Certeau makes this most clear: "Walking is to the urban system what the speech act is to language or to the statements uttered."[17] According to speech-act theory, the point of posing an idea is not to ask questions of what the idea is made up of, but rather to describe it in order to perform and to produce some kind of response.[18] The very act of engaging in urbanity, therefore, singles out the "city" as a locus of meanings based on a specific performative intention. A city is not the total sum of its topographical features. A city is what it is only when it is being walked through. Walking is "a space of enunciation": the active appropriation of the topographical features of a place, "a spatial acting-out of the place" that establishes "relations among differentiated positions" via movement.[19] In Henri Lefebvre's terms, it is about how people actually engage in the production of space.[20] With a different emphasis, Ken Knabb points to the drifter's unraveling power when he says that dérive is to totality exactly what psychoanalysis is to language.[21] What matters is the present continuous, the here-and-now, the very act of and the actual moment of articulation or doing—in this case the on-going process of walking.

Lefebvre has offered us the most succinct argument that the urban space is not just a concept of the city but also concrete urban practices in the everyday settings. In his terms, walking is a form of spatial practice, the very act to make sense of space (make space meaningful) via the creation of activities and to prove that the individual is capable of doing it (conquering space). Spatial practice often combines the use of representational spaces (how one feels about a place in concrete forms) and related creative activities about them via spatial representation (such as mapping space via filmic representation). The cinematic spatial practices of the films in question share at least one thing in common: most of them open into the anonymous somewhere in the middle of a city, where the protagonist/director roams, making sense of space in different ways. The meanings of *walking* (and *not contemplating*) a city, and the deliberate choice to do so, should thus be further analyzed. "Walking" as an enunciative act can be a positive move to appropriate existing forms in order to generate new relations or as a deliberate act of negative subversion. The latter, which I call "drifting," has formed the manifest content of certain independent films. Walking is both the symptom and the main dramatic action of the protagonist, and it is a metaphor of the narrative materialization of the filmmaker's quest and critique of urbanity that amounts to the performative engagement with the idea of the city as heterotopia.

THE FLÂNERIE OF HUANG JIANXIN

The basic position that underlines Huang's vision of the city in many ways recalls the standard descriptions of a flâneur. Franz Hessel calls flânerie "the art of taking a walk" through the cities and spaces of modernity.[22] Flânerie is a response to the emergence of new dispositions resulting from accelerated capitalist development and urbanization. Flânerie is a mode of observation,[23] from which a number of rational actions follow—investigating, knowing, reflecting, and interpreting. Together these acts invoke a sense of history and the discovery (or, rather, the uncovering) of history that is mythical. Anke Gleber even suggests that "the flâneur is the precursor of a particular form of inquiry that seeks to read the history of culture from its public spaces." Flânerie in this sense is a "walking cure." That is, the seeing, understanding, and interpreting activities of the walk are to console the poet by his "returning to the past and anticipating the future." Its ultimate end is that of historical collection.[24] Flânerie affirms a transcendental subject who is at the perceptual core, exercising control, or taming the ever-changing material reality via reason. Gleber also affirms the ramification of the flâneur in various creative categories, breeding authors-as-flâneurs in film and literary practices: they walk and regard "images they see in the streets with a renewed sense of amazement." With less focus on the city's sprouting visuality and its impact on people's experience of reality, Huang Jianxin, then, "comes into being primarily as a figure of perception, as an epic camera, as a representative of the 'pure outside' of aesthetics in his modernity."[25] Huang is the camera-as-flâneur.

Huang's films open phenomenally with a cold, detached high-angle view of the city skyline that is analytical and almost minimalist, which then immediately cuts to the eye-level view of the human dwellings where noise, daily rituals, and concrete material living conditions draw the viewer into the web of relational drama. The narrative is then punctuated, or disrupted, at intervals by aerial shots that resituate the on-going micro-stories within the overall architectural space, thereby marking internal and external boundaries. (The intermittent return to the high angle is reminiscent of Wang Anyi's own perceptual presence embodied in the pigeons.) The camera work is calculated, with frequent use of the long shot. The city is a text awaiting Huang's excavation, and in it he encounters the "materials of observation in a new sphere of public exteriors."[26] Thus an impression of a contemplative, objective, unobtrusive analysis is achieved. But Huang is no manipulative poet who would explicitly designate meanings. Although his micro-epic camera trails along the most un-dramatic kitchens, living rooms, and offices to mark them for close observation, he offers no grand analysis of the condition he examines. In fact, through his show-not-tell rhetorical strategy, he deliberately dissociates himself from any explicit dominant discourse that lends him a "high-level" interpretation. Huang is not exactly the flâneur-historian like Franz Hessel;[27] nor do we find his films as affirmative of history and memory as in Benjamin's sense: in fact the latter's "lived moment into a citable experience" becomes, in Huang's case, the transgression of the burden of history.[28] Rather than mapping the contours of cultural history via a vertical chronology of the present from the past, Huang takes on a kind of typographical dissection of the city that looks at the horizontal network of relations instead. Huang is self-assured in his role as a reflective critic (of his city), a close analyst (of its architecture), an archivist (of events, scenes, and images), interpreter (of impressions into texts), and all-encompassing observer and reader-decipherer. Yet he implicitly situates his flânerie practice against monumental history-reading/writing. In response to his critique of politics and its infiltration into everyday life via the arrangement of space and management of relational ties, he detaches his narrative paradigm from the epic-historical to favor a sociological-anthropological dissection.

Huang's rhetoric is that of irony revealing, after all, a utopian view that upholds the role of the intelligentsia or cultural elite to enlighten the individual and to elevate the consciousness of the individual self. The city space is where Huang lays out the full paradigm of desirable and undesirable conduct to view the individual's presentation of self in the dramaturgy of everyday life. The narrative of these films shows how the intricate flow of interpersonal power vectors on the local level sustains an authoritarian rule, which in turn keeps everyone within its unbreakable cyclic effects. A strong sense of place is achieved in each of his films via isolating a particular site that is at once physical, institutional, and relational. *Stand up* (1992) penetrates into a certain neighborhood in Xi'an city. *Back to Back* (1994) lays open the Cultural Center of Xi'an in which the vacant position of the center's chief signifies the nexus of power influence of party politics beyond the center's own personnel structure. *Signal Left* assesses a driving school in which the consumer's mentality is detached from its normative economic context to be scrutinized under the lens of micro-relational networking. In *Surveillance* (1996), intertwining courses of events are gradually channeled to converge at a deserted watchtower, the embodiment of a strict, uncontestable paradigm of accountability, by which absolute blind power is upheld and the safety of the individual is subjugated to public security.

Huang's elitist guidance, through the laying out of paradigms of conduct and everyday behaviors, is ultimately tied to his assertion of "quality art" and the autonomy of the artist/filmmaker. Within the filmmaking community, Huang occupies an unrivaled fluid position as a director "within the film institution" (*tizhi nei*) while at the same time upholding the banner of avant-garde visions. *The Black Cannon Incident* positioned the director between the Fifth Generation and the Sixth Generation (the 1990s to the present) when cinema was subject to accelerating reorganizational measures to address a market-driven environment. Emblematic of an art cinema practice, Huang has through his career been uncompromisingly persistent on his autonomy in the choice of themes, subject matters, and creative treatment. To him, any film not produced by the criteria of public taste, popular mentality, and generic norms is an art film, and should be treasured for its unique vision.[29] Indeed, Huang's work is a rare case of a specially marked-out space to pursue serious cinema while remaining in the mainstream, a privilege that the other three directors discussed here do not share.

Huang firmly believes in the filmmaker's role of resignification, or meaning making. He believes in art and its enlightening power; he insists on the originality of the artist and her or his work; and he has continued to demonstrate his interest in film as a unique tool with new possibilities—all of which are the marks of a modernist conviction and film method in the West, which in China was coined "avant-garde" for the Fifth Generation filmmakers.

DRIFTING UNDERGROUND

The three independent films discussed here demonstrate a complete Icarian fall from the privileged viewing position,[30] as the filmmakers deliberately resign from the pleasure of seeing the whole from above—the opposite of Huang's privileged, total, cosmic, godlike vision. These filmmakers do not assume insightful knowledge of the city's psychic and relational interior, nor do they shuttle freely and intermittently between the macroscopic and the microscopic view. Instead, they would rather fall back onto the rugged space among the people. Their bodies follow the thick and thin of an urban "text" that they write through walking, feeling their way through and describing (via the camera), without necessarily being capable of comprehending what they describe. Their role as the enunciating subject shifts from "voyeurs" who lift themselves to an unusual height to see, to "drifters" who occupy the position of an ordinary city-dweller on the ground level.[31]

"Drifting" is not only an appearance or the warm-up part of a serious walk as in the case of flânerie practice.[32] To the Lettrist and the SI, drifting is existential. It takes as its core matter the present, the here-and-now, the very moment and process in which the walker opens up to architectural/spatial materiality. When a person drifts, she puts aside routines and the usual motives to allow herself to be carried away by her surroundings and new encounters. The drifter's discovery of a presence is not secondary to the study of "the precise laws and specific effects of the geographical environment." The new understanding of the urban space they open up is achieved performatively. In particular, drifting is regarded as the function of "psycho-geography," which is concerned with topographical elements, whether consciously organized or not, in light of their effect on the emotions and behavior of individuals. "Playful-constructive behavior," characteristic of drifting, implies a relaxed state of mind that allows more spontaneous emotive affect of the surroundings on one's subjectivity. No single location is definitely psycho-geographic based on a few spelled-out features or emotions invoked as a result, but "the variety of possible combinations of ambiances" gives rise to differentiated, complex feelings.[33]

The films *Xiao Wu, Suzhou River,* and *In Expectation* all have a drifter or drifters as their protagonists, or the film's narrative is organized around the notion of drifting. The main characters of these three films are highly unproductive, and thus diverge from mainstream urban discourse's "new city person." In all three cases, the protagonists wander around the city aimlessly doing very little, or digress into unplanned encounters by letting whatever comes by take them on the spot. They have no certainty about their place, nor will they invest effort in sorting out the mysteries that trouble them. It is almost irrelevant to think of whether these characters are marginal individuals or social deviants—at least not in the same sense that the young protagonists in *Rock-and-Roll Kids* and *Beijing Bastards* are judged.

Xiao Wu, for example, while roaming through the town, actively touches base with old acquaintances (who often reject him) and also makes new contacts. His nature is basically good, and he has his own norms of propriety. He is carefree; and while he does not lack compassion, every now and then while roaming around he commits minor misdemeanors. Drifting is the manifest content of *Xiao Wu.* For most of the 107-minute screen time, Xiao Wu drifts between his hometown and its neighboring areas somewhere around the Fenyang Prefecture of Shanxi Province. He allows all events that come to decorate his day—including happenings both big and small. A game of mahjong, unexpected romantic infatuation, a brief lockup at the local security bureau, chit-chatting from door to door, karaoke singing, stealing a bus ticket, and other such activities form the very empirical nodes by which Xiao Wu makes sense of the town for his own pleasure. Director Jia's cinematic spatial practice combines a soundtrack that seems to shower from above—propaganda messages calling for a crime-free town are broadcast over the airwaves in every corner of the city—with a unique assemblage of places and locations of either dilapidation, demolition, construction, and much that is in-between. The visual drama of uneventful drifting washed away by endless calls for good conduct prompts the cruel facts of underdevelopment in the age of a new economy.

The protagonists of *In Expectation* are permanently trapped in inertia. Like changes in the weather, unspeakable flushes of mood choke them in the midst of everyday banality. They are taciturn, indecisive, their minds constantly drifting. Not much happens. Nothing moves forward, but rather everything goes around in circles forever "in expectation"—of change, breakthrough, or even the stirring of a simple verbal utterance or a minor emotional outburst. In the film, director Zhang Ming turns the small town into a distinct psychogeography, a few meandering streets crisscrossing up and down the slope leading to the old Yangtze River—streets that transport more tourists than residents. Here and there, the suppliers of the accoutrements of modern life, along with the chance-takers, find themselves making transactions among household workshops and family-style stores. Across the river, the isolated lighthouse signifies for its guard Mai Qiang the site of distant watching and aimless desiring. In brief, the town is a map of unconsummated desires, on which Zhang's analytical camera work traces and locates repressed yearnings drifting through in futility. Romantic encounters vaporize. The air is moist, pregnant with trapped emotions. Showers come and go; thunderclouds are just behind the hill, about to roar and roll over any moment. Everyday life seems to be purposeless and the courses of events inexplicable. Human sexual agitations take on a different language—of the balance sheets in accounting, of loss and gain, and of reward and punishment.

Suzhou River opens with a ten-minute monologue in voice-over accompanying images of the Suzhou River and its banks in Shanghai. The sequence sets up the motif of drifting, literally. The camera work pans left and right with jump cuts here and there, resembling a drifter's random visual scanning of his or her surroundings. Images flick intermittently to parallel the sound of the camera shutter of the person who is delivering the monologue. The text-image relation is meant to remind us that a photograph is an open text, and that, in the words of Mary Price, "photographs without appropriate descriptive words are deprived and weakened" for the interpreter.[34] The opening sequence unmistakably underlines the authority of the speaking subject "I" (the one who interprets owns the meaning) and thus also the narrative in the

The site of drifting in *Suzhou River*: the neighborhood surrounding the river. (Courtesy of the Film Society of Lincoln Center)

An encounter in *Suzhou River*.

rest of the film, which is predicated on the object of one unified empirical subject occupying the perceptual center. The presence of this empirical "I" gives authority to the voice-over narrator who is also the photographer, and at the same time subjugates every story told afterward to his drifting activities. Almost the entire visual narrative after the opening sequence is delivered—via the unique grammar of the point-of-view shots—as the perceptual experience of the "invisible" drifter ("I") in his haptic space, and who exists throughout as a voice only. Or else, in scenes where the "I" cannot have been present, events and conversations are imagined vividly, still with the point-of-view style of shots, as if viewers are let into the mindscape of the invisible "I." In brief, the audience's narrative knowledge is acquired through the first-person voice-over and the point-of-view shots, which together form the film's external and internal narrative focalization.

The manifest text of aimless drifting in the film is paralleled by a subtext organized around the walking activities driven by seeing and visuality in general, the modernist core of flânerie. However, I argue that the use of a consistent perceptual center embodied in a drifting person does not result in a stable, unified vision of Shanghai. Quite the opposite, drifting at every step of the narrative destabilizes holistic meanings, driving the bodiless protagonist and the viewer into a continuous and restless process of revision of a knowledge of Shanghai and the personal events involved. The Shanghai experienced in the film is the Shanghai that the filmmaker, "I," walks through—subjectively, randomly, and partially. Through spatial poaching, *Suzhou River* maps out a unique psycho-geography that is peculiar to the drifter(s) of the film. It is the geography of fragmented memories and elliptical personal histories. The Suzhou River channels unspeakable desires. It is a fluid journey in which the boundaries between fact and imagination, fantasy and madness, dreams and desires, memories and history blur or collapse. Along this line, the autobiographical overtone of the film underscores the detached, melancholic lyricism of the drifter. Autobiography is not just a narrative construct, but also the material signifier of a decentered subject, carried via a voice that guides and confounds the viewer during the entire narrative process. In brief, drifting as presented in *Suzhou River* is decentering, chance-based, and performative in character.

Lou Ye's cinematic spatial practice isolates the Suzhou River from its surroundings and from the normal (economic) activities of Shanghai and then re-presents it as an assemblage of spectacles—as a sensorial whole of sensuous yet fleeting surfaces. The river is physically a penetrative strand of space that is at once alien and recognizable, which brings us back to the notion of heterotopia and, therefore, Lou's performative act to highlight a place as embracing incommensurable places. In Foucault's terms, the river is somewhere in between the heterotopia of illusion and that of compensation.[35] It is far from being utopic and yet it yields the innumerable possibilities of chance (human) encounters, especially romance. The river is not capable of yielding new real space, and yet it keeps open the space for new desires. Thus we hear the voiceover murmurs in the beginning: "If you watch it long enough, the river will show you everything." And toward the end we hear: "But I won't [run after her] because nothing lasts forever. So I'll just take another drink and close my eyes . . . waiting for the next story to start"—that is, to continue drifting. Does this lead us to the conclusion that the three "out-of-the-institution" filmmakers are more progressive than Huang's high-angle intelligentsia mode in getting closer to the politics of everyday creativity as intervention?

Much of what has been said about the three films fits a portrait of the postmodern poet offered by the Hong Kong literary scholar and poet Leung Ping-kwan (Liang Bingjun) in regard to his own works. In taking the subject-position of the poet as the enunciator, Leung differentiates between two kinds of poetics—the "poetics of discovery" as opposed to the "poetics of signification." To me, these two poetics parallel two kinds of spatial practice in the urban cinema of China, and are easily mapped onto drifting and flânerie practice respectively.

The poetics of signification, in close affinity with flânerie, refers to a creative mode by which the poet persistently states a vision of the world that she owns as a stable subject over time: a firm I-thou relationship is established between the creator and the world.[36] Wherever the poet is, and whatever she encounters, she sees her own well-formed vision once again reaffirmed. Contact with the external world often results in another occasion for the rearticulation of a self that exists already; only that in different instances the poet draws from a different set of raw materials (i.e., a different set of referents) for (re-)signification purpose. In the "poetics of discovery," with which Leung identifies himself, a poet does not seek to impose her subjective consciousness on her surroundings. Instead, the poet enters the world and finds herself in the middle of it, bewildered and carried away by the immanence of material existence and its fine details. She experiences, participates, and discovers spontaneously, grasping her momentary authentic presence and turning it into a poetic form with a heightened sense of immediacy. The poet upholds a kind of centrality that allows the enunciative self to freely extend in all directions. She is an empirical/interpretive agent but *not* an empirical/interpretive authority—the latter being the case with the modernist flânerie practice and the poetics of signification.[37]

The poetics of discovery materializes via a process-oriented narrative that is itself the unfolding of a journey—thus is the poet's full presence and her here-and-now engagement with events and happenings that emerge along the way. In this way, the postmodern text deconstructs the modernist norms of a closed text with coherent (re-)signification. The city in this sense is not a space endowed with fixed meanings but rather a space awaiting its visitors to read and write about its inexhaustible materiality and to step into unknown forms of dialogic invocation. The city in its material form becomes a space of chance encounter, whereby the "participant" discovers rather than reaffirms her or his view of life. As a form of spatial practice, the poetics of discovery connects what is out there in the urban space into a network of random collectibles, subject to the performative execution of speech acts in particular speech moments, which then results in works with automatic qualities materialized in momentary, fragmented utterances turned into a collage.

On one level, the poetics of discovery provides a handy narrative to capture my impression of the specific state of mind and manner of speech act in the three independent films I examine, all of which manifest a "real present continuous" speech mode in their narrative unfolding. In all three films, there is an unambiguous respect for "place" to let it assert its enchanting power on the human subject, the drifter. In *In Expectation,* the drifting motif forms the dual score of the characters' mental state as well as the director's discovering process of his perception of the town's psycho-geography. The key question, however, is whether decenteredness, spontaneity, randomness, and chance are the concrete manifestation of speech acts or are these same categories the results of managed impression and engineered effects through deliberate narrative construction? I suggest that in the three films, which demonstrate salient features of "poetics of discovery," the act of drifting and the surprise of unplanned encounters are objectives realized within a rational, coherent text that is neither open nor heterogeneous. Jia Zhangke, for example, makes explicit for *Xiao Wu* this enunciation of a postmodern gesture of, after all, a transcendental subject with an unmistakable modernist intention, by which positive meaning production is the ultimate goal. As Jia himself states: "On the one hand, my camera observes the material world but, in the end, it questions spirituality as such. . . . This is a film about our worries and our uneasiness. . . . It is a film about emotions. . . . It is a film about my native town and about contemporary China. . . . Above all, it is a film about some burning issues in our existence."[38]

Jia's words clearly articulate a creative method that begins with conception, which is the mark of the poetics of signification. This stands in contrast with the poetics of discovery, which prizes instantaneous perception and the very act of grasping it; the creative process begins with the citing of a situation and the employment of simple rules as point of departure. As Jia claims, *Xiao Wu*'s manifest content is *about* "the loss of framework in which feelings are possible"—but not the loss itself. That is, the "loss of framework" is represented and resignified within and via a solid narrative framework, but not realized in the overall strategy of the creative project's performative functions in its cultural context. Here, I suggest that *Xiao Wu*'s feature of drifting for discovery is a closed signifier, whereas the postmodern presumptions of the poetics of discovery cast into doubt any effort to settle on reassigned meanings by reinventing the relation between the signifier and the signified. There is only the act itself of signification and resignification, the recurrent chain of erasure and difference. My doubts for *Xiao Wu* apply to the other two films as well. In the long run, they are writing nihilism into the core of narrativity, affirmatively turning nihilism into an unambiguous signified. In sum, I argue that distinctions should be drawn between presenting "drifting" as an organizational, narrative strategy and the filmmaker's text as his own "drifting" practice in action, and that drifting in these three films belong to the former. The looseness and the spontaneity of action, whether mild or intense, are deliberate.

"Drifting" is one of the methods si uses to practice their critique of urban living and the resulting condition of estrangement (alienation). In Guy Debord's terms, "drifting" is a created situation, "a technique of transient passage through varied ambiances."[39] In this sense, "drifting," as a performative category, stands in opposition to deliberate projects of a preplanned story and the story-film tradition in general. It seems more likely that, if there is a story at all, it is only constructed in retrospect when the discovery journey is over. Similarly, when psycho-geography is reduced to a narrative formula (i.e., virtual drifting) or a pure object of representation, the critical energy of "drifting" and "psycho-geography" shrinks. What is left is little more than a special brand of narrative mannerism that draws its dramatic valence from an antidramatic grammar and, in the cases I address here, also exploits a melancholic lyricism.

Although I have questioned the progressive implication of discovery and deviation from routine as pure gesture, my discussion is not meant to renounce the significance of the films in question. Rather than dismiss them as pure narrative mannerism, I apply the term "negative poetics" to invoke a concentrated examination of the antidramatic rhetoric in these films. By qualifying the visual vocabulary of drifting as "negative poetics," I call attention to representational practices that subtract from, rather than build on, existing visual conventions. What I have called "drifting" can in the three films be understood as a deliberate effort to keep dramatic and expressive movements to the minimal in order to arrive at a kind of muteness of articulations, subdued emotions, and elliptical narrative unfolding with inconclusive scenes. These qualities culminate in the general suspicion of mainstream, goal-oriented narrativity. The (non-)actions in these films—that is, the act of city roaming and everyday trivialities—are the actual subject. The moments of roaming and unproductive activity are themselves the key dramatic events, displayed in long duration. Such a practice distinguishes these films from what Deleuze has called the "movement-image" convention, by which each shot or segment cannot be understood except in relation to what comes before and after it as part of a causal sequence. Many of the individual roaming events in the three films stand on their own merits, yet together they form the microcosmic overview of the city. The emphasis on the autonomy of the individual event foregrounds the materiality of the everyday. The resulting narratives are truncated and indecisive, emphasizing improvised inconsequential actions and defying the tenacity of logical, causal relations. Put in context, the employment of "negative poetics" is the act of deviating from mainstream cinema's demand for a coherent series of dramatic actions that follow from one to another with clear motivations. It is also the determination to react against the demand for psychologically motivated characters or unified transcendental subjects whose presence has an overarching influence over the state of events.

"Negative poetics" informs internal textual organization, but it also refers to the overall rhetorical strategy. Like drifting, which is to let go, to stray away, to disengage from "meaningful" pursuits, negative poetics also emphasizes a self-conscious choice of doubt and hesitancy. Not only do we have protagonists who are incapable of positive actions, but in each of these three films the filmmaker also consciously disengages himself from any active negotiation with the material signifiers of urbanity. Typical grand notions of urbanity such as consumerism, modernity, materialism, and alienation are bracketed. Token signifiers of urbanity such as construction sites, roads with heavy traffic in the city center, karaoke bars, and so on are there only to form the thickness of ordinary everyday life. These films, like those by Huang Jianxin, work against the "concept-city"[40]—a notion of the city as the rational-functional organization of space that privileges progress and has inflected cultural production in China since the late 1970s. The employment of "negative aesthetics" signifies these films' rejection of mainstream cinema's compromise with the official discourse's demand for the individual to engage in "meaningful" activities.

In Certeau's term, one measure of effective politics is whether or not a filmmaker situates his works outside the dominant discourse of urban cinema. In the end, what distinguishes Huang Jianxin's urban films from those of the three independent directors is not just their different reference to the flâneur, the well-intended walker, and the drifter of negative poetics. The distinction also lies between the two kinds of speaking positions. Huang is *inside* and *within* the institution; he may be ironic and skeptical, his discourse the inversion of the dominant discourse, but nevertheless he productively shuttles between the bird's-eye view and micro-mapping. The drifters, on the other hand, are basically *outsiders*. And they have chosen a very different path—namely, to remain outside the moral paradigms of signification of the so-called city film by staying away from any direct negotiation with or inversion of the category.

EPILOGUE: POSSIBLE PARADIGM SHIFTS?

Although the burden of the intelligentsia that marks Huang Jianxin's works seems to be less obvious in the three independent films discussed above, I argue that they nonetheless ascribe to the same set of creative principles comparable to the modernist tradition in the West. A number of questions thus arise. For instance, what kind of transactional and political values does a modernist method gain to signify differences, or is it pure gesture? Why is a modernist position still the most prominent attitude when it comes to the tactics of staying outside the dominant discourse? The failure to mobilize social change via poetry alone has been a constant critique of the modernist projects in the West. Indeed, where the Western modernists and the Fifth Generation Chinese directors both have failed is precisely in their omission of concrete everyday creativity that involves the body in their work of resistance

—which is also the failure to depart from elitism and to go beyond textual meaning making.

The critical force of the intellectual's bodily engagement in the urban space, and the very act of reliving the space via the here-and-now open violation of routine, is absent in much of this new urban cinema. A concrete engagement as such has been superseded by a linguistic/discursive exercise that effectuates no more than the defense for a serious cinema in the form of the reassignment of meanings. Perhaps "negative poetics" is discursively powerful. However, it signifies the possibilities of resistance and subversion only when read relative to what has been taken as the norm within mainstream cinema in the Mainland. In the end, I also cast doubt on the power of film production in general as a site of cultural resistance—there are limits to the progressive implications of film production that looks at resignification without working on the exhibition sector.

In the new era, public/official financial support for the arts is shrinking. As has been the case in most of the capitalist countries, in the final analysis the space of cultural production in China becomes the site of a discursive antagonism between movies for the "market" and movies to uphold the humanistic project of art. I have argued that it is questionable whether the modernist method's intrinsic speech value leads to acts of resistance. While there is no doubt that there is a desire to "change" or "improve" the quality of Chinese cinema, the notion of quality cinema is presumed but not spelled out, and therefore remains uncontested. The key issue is reduced to, and preserved as, the artistic autonomy of the individual, a token of the post–Gang of Four cultural arena. No matter what name the directors "outside" use to advance their pursuit, their projects to raise the consciousness of the new generation hinges on the scramble for their portion of social and cultural resources to sustain self-expression as a basic human right. Such implied self-interest and survival tactics, however, should not erase the validity of social cultural critique in the core of the projects in question here. Jia Zhangke, for example, was explicit about *Xiao Wu*'s engagement with society and culture: to him, Xiao Wu was meant to be "a character caught within human relationships during the large-scale societal changes brought about [in the] two decades of 'opening up,' " and such is Jia's creative and critical response to contemporary China's condition of culture.

The discourse of serious/art cinema is still very much alive in written accounts that seek to construct a genealogy of "the avant-garde tradition" in China to ensure its continuity.[41] Zhu Xiaoyi's account, for example, pinpoints the difficult yet affirmative survival of the avant-garde spirit in the 1990s, when even the Fifth Generation aesthetics were commodified and co-opted into the open free market. By comparison, however, there are many more accounts concerned with how Chinese cinema survives its new phase with the WTO arrangements. Accounts are also equally plentiful regarding the "amphibious" ability of the Newborn Generation directors to meet market taste while maintaining a recognizable degree of artistic achievement and a conscientious engagement with social reality. It is within such latter discourses that *Xiao Wu* and *In Expectation* are time and again cited as promising examples. *Xiao Wu,* in particular, has been complimented for its broad acceptance and the many awards it earned in international film festivals.[42] The outside-the-institution films discussed can be positioned as conscious attempts to preserve the continuously diminishing space for creative autonomy and the legitimacy of the artist as a proper social category in a new milieu when the rule of the market gradually dictates creative functions. After all, the cases I have outlined here revise the implication of the category of "creative autonomy"—not as an innocent humanitarian pursuit but as a discursive product. Creative autonomy capitalizes on the marking out of unique space to uphold the "spiritual leadership" of the artist by radically isolating him or her from commercial concerns. In the unique context of China, this is a response to the loss of status of the protected elite once offered by the Communist Party, as in the case of the Fifth Generation.

To conclude, I would like to draw a conceptual picture of a new species of filmmaking that transcends the binary tropes of modernist/postmodernist, signification/performativity, critique/intervention, and Fifth/Sixth Generation. All three of the films in this study share some common qualities. First, they are made both in and about the hometown or city of their makers: Zhang Ming's Wushan (in Sichuan Province), Lou Ye's Shanghai, and Jia Zhangke's Fenyang (in Shanxi Province). They are by various degrees works of auto-ethnography—often as attempts to capture the appearance of places on the verge of disappearance. Such ethnographic interest is obvious in the three films studied here, as well as in other recent films by the three directors: for example, Zhang Ming's *Weekend Plot* (Miyu shiqi xiaoshi, 2001), and Jia's

Platform (Zhan tai, 2000) and *Unknown Pleasures* (Ren xiaoyao, 2002). In *Platform*, the drifting motive in *Xiao Wu* is further developed for Jia's project of positively writing a "minor history" of the 1980s via a drifting journey, deploying the here-and-now present continuous mode of the empirical. Zhang's *Weekend Plot* was motivated by the urge to capture the look of a specific spot along the Yangtze River that because of development was to be submerged for good. He therefore unfolded the story of his characters on that space so that in the end the space itself becomes a main character.[43] Addressing the issue of disappearing, silenced, or suppressed space distinguishes these films from many other Sixth Generation films, whose concern is to herald a triumphant song of the new Chinese city.

Second, although I have repeatedly critiqued the works of the three young directors for falling short of actual intervention in the everyday, the performative value of these works is nonetheless unmistakable—notably in the phenomenal effort to "evoke emotions" in the present continuous tense. Lou Ye makes explicit that the foregrounding of emotions without explication or analysis is the main task of the *Suzhou River* project. In *In Expectation* and *Xiao Wu*, emotions are not only intensely evoked, but also turned into a focused performance via the employment of long-take and minimal actions. In all cases, the subdued productiveness of daily activities allows emotions to flow freely as a form of energy; emotions are the very subject of narrative exposition rather than simply an enhancing element or decoration of story information.

Third, the resulting aesthetics as I have qualified via the idea of "walking," "poetics of discovery," and "negative poetics" may have the discursive power of generating an identity of serious cinema, and thus subsequently qualify these films to unite with a genealogy of quality Chinese cinema with the Fifth Generation as their immediate predecessors. On the practical level, the aesthetics were very much a creative, spontaneous response to the specific problem of being disengaged from the official top-down supply of resources. In various interviews, both Lou Ye and Jia Zhangke described deliberate aesthetic principles as necessary choices in order to cope with a lack of funding and human resources. As Lou Ye explains the peculiar fluid quality of camera work in *Suzhou River*: "The jagged, loose-limbed style of the film was largely a function of economics. . . . We decided on a handheld camera because we didn't have much time to set up."[44]

Finally, we may see these films as engaging on various levels in a dialogic relation with creative communities outside Mainland China, by providing the supply of creative personnel, coproduction (cofinancing), or appearance in international platforms for film art. *Suzhou River* was the winner of the VRPO Tiger Award at the twenty-ninth Rotterdam Film Festival in 2000. *Xiao Wu* won the Wolfgang Staudte Prize at the Berlin Film Festival. These two films, as well as *In Expectation* and the three directors' next films, were also featured in various editions of the Hong Kong International Film Festival. In this sense, these films form a special brand of independent cinema that survives on foreign money and is relatively free from the burden of local film regulation, the pressure of local market interest, and even censorship pressure. The fact that *Xiao Wu* was a Hong Kong investment was an additional guarantee for creative freedom; as Jia notes: "My investor didn't care about the Mainland market, we didn't bother with the censorship process." And the problem of not having sufficient funds to shoot on 35mm also turned out to be a blessing, "According to the regulations, [a film shot on 16mm] means it's a non-commercial film."[45] The "fate" of not being recognized as a proper Chinese commercial film fit for theatrical release in the end allowed the work to travel freely internationally with a unique "art film" license. By comparison, however, Zhang Ming may not have been as lucky. Lacking the broad exposure in the West held by the other two films, and without any European film festival decorations, Zhang was only honored at the Hong Kong International Film Festival, where his works were faithfully listed in their special section of "Mainland independent."[46] Zhang described his situation as the "little fish in a big pond," in noting that "along with other like-minded directors who are trying to break the old boundaries, I am trying, under the scrutiny of censorship, to find a space in which I may create my film—at the same time having to manage the anxiety of creativity and the responsibilities of production. As a little fish in a big pond, all I can do is change a portion of my movie, and produce something with some character and with my own ideals."[47] This perhaps is a deliberately humble response to the Hong Kong film festival organizers against the backdrop of the difficulty of showing his work. Nonetheless, Zhang's stated goal to ride the anxiety of censorship in order to pursue aesthetic and thematic openness is pertinent to all independent filmmakers working today.

NOTES

1. They are *Stand up, Don't Grovel* (Zhan zhi luo bie pa xia; aka *Stand up Straight, Don't Drop*; *Stand up, Don't Bend*; and *Stand Up, Don't Stoop*, 1992), *Back to Back, Face to Face* (Bei dui bei lian dui lian, 1994), *Signal Left, Turn Right* (Da zuo deng xiang you zhuan), and *Surveillance* (Mai fu, 1996).

2. The nineteenth-century French novelists referred to here include, notably, Honore de Balzac, Eugene Sue, and Alexandre Dumas. See Rob Shield, "Fancy Footwork: Walter Benjamin's Notes on *Flânerie*," in *The Flâneur*, ed. Keith Tester (London: Routledge, 1994). For the earliest invocation of the idea of flânerie by Victor Fournel, see Anke Gleber, *The Art of Taking a Walk: Flânerie, Literature, and Film in Weimar Culture* (Princeton, N.J.: Princeton University Press, 1999), 3–5. For Benjamin's exposition on the flâneur, see his *The Arcades Project*, trans. Howard Eiland and Kevin McLaughlin (Cambridge, Mass.: Belknap Press of Harvard University Press, 1999), 416–55; and Howard Caygill, *Walter Benjamin: The Color of Experience* (New York: Routledge, 1998), 67–69. For "drifting," see Ken Knabb, ed. and trans., *Situationist International Anthology* (Berkeley: Bureau of Public Secrets, 1981), 50–54.

3. The term *heterotopia* is originally a medical term meaning "place of otherness" (in literal translation of the Latin word). The most prominent use of the term is that of Michel Foucault, who makes references to it as the metaphor of the social body as well as the nature of language and textual discourse, both often marked by unsettling meanings. Foucault's full elaboration of the term can be found in two of his works: "Of Other Spaces," *Diacritics* 16, no. 1 (1986): 22–27, and *The Order of Things* (London: Tavistock/Routledge, 1989). Some of the works that inform my summary of the term in this essay include the following: Pia Maria Ahlbäck, "The Road to Industrial Heterotopia," in *Technologies of Landscape: From Reaping to Recycling*, ed. David E. Nye (Amherst: University of Massachusetts Press, 1999), 254–66; Alejandro Morales, "Essay: Dynamic Identities in Heterotopia," in his *Fiction Past, Present, Future Perfect*, ed. Jose Antonio Gurpegui (Tempe, Ariz.: Bilingual Review Press, 1996), 14–27; and Kevin Hetherington, *The Badlands of Modernity: Heterotopia and Social Ordering* (London: Routledge, 1997), 7–12, 39–54. Morales uses the term *heterotopia* to describe how Los Angeles and San Diego/Tijuana together constitute a new urban model that combines "third worldness" and a north-bound, utopic vision of capitalist reality. Hetherington extracts from Foucault's term a more complex alternative to the idea of marginality and resistance as the binary opposites of core and submission. Ahlbäck applies the term to the study of a specific industrial plant, a technological icon that is part picture and part place.

4. Michel de Certeau, "The Practice of Everyday Life," in *The Consumption Reader*, ed. David B. Clarke, Marcus A. Doel, and Kate M. L. Housiaux (London: Routledge, 2003), 260.

5. Wang Anyi, *Chang hen ge* [Song of long lasting sorrow], (Hong Kong: Cosmos, 1996), 17–37. The novel portrays the life of the woman protagonist in Shanghai from the 1940s to the 1990s.

6. One of the most significant return of the pigeons is in the arrival of the Cultural Revolution (section 16, chapter four, part II [Cosmos edition, 272]). Without any depiction of the violence, bloodshed, or persecution that typifies most fictional accounts of those years, Wang confines her narrative activity on the surface appearance of the cityscape and the living spaces. In this section of the novel, the pigeons are harbingers of disaster, and the chorus of lamentation. The pigeons are described as "dumb witnesses" in the final paragraph of the novel.

7. For a productive discussion of Chinese cinema, the notion of realism should be, at the minimum, differentiated into the following categories: socialist realism, which calls for portrayal and critique of society based on socialist ideals; critical realism, after Brecht, which highlights the problems that cause the human suffering; social realism, after Lukacs, which upholds the typification function of novels in offering a general profile of society; and empirical realism, based on Bazin, which emphasizes, among other things, the camera's documentary power to capture and preserve the visible appearance and aura of what really exists or once existed, and, in relation to that, unified time and space.

8. Hetherington, *The Badlands of Modernity*, 12.

9. The terms "reading" and "writing" are used in the way that Raymond Williams redefines them, as discussed in T. G. Ashplant and Gerry Smyth, eds., *Explorations in Cultural History* (London: Pluto Press, 2001), 15–16.

10. I borrow the term "central conflict theory" from the Chilean-born director Raul Ruiz's writing in *Poetics of Cinema: Miscellanies*, trans. Brian Holmes (Paris: Dis Voir, 1995), 9–23. Ruiz offers a full exposition of the term in the first chapter to describe one form of dramatic construction perpetuated by American mainstream cinema, which also is prevalent around the world as the standard model. According to the "central conflict theory," a narrative is a system of credibility that only accommodates details that serve to address a central conflict. To Ruiz, the central conflict theory is an ideology: it encourages a cinema that is reductionist, that is purely at the service of entertainment, and that overemphasizes clarity and problem-solving—thus erasing the complexity of human existence and creative expression.

11. Chen Lai, "Sixiang chulu de san dongxiang" [The three directions of solution in thoughts], in *Zhongguo dangdai wenhua yishi* [Cultural consciousness in contemporary China], ed. Gan Yang (Hong Kong: Joint Publishing, 1988), 582–83. According to Chen Lai, the first list of translation projects was published on December 10, 1986, in *Guangming ri bao* [Guangming daily news]. The titles, which included Heidegger's *Being and Time* and Sartre's *Being and Nothingness*, among others, were part of a series called *Wenhua: Zhongguo yu shijie* [Culture: China and the world] edited by Gan Yang.

12. For 1987 and 1988, see Zhu Xiaoyi, "Zhongguo xianfeng yishu zhi huigu ji jiushi niandai Zhongguo xianfeng dianying" [A retrospective on China's avant-garde art and avant-garde films in the 1990s], *Film Art*, no. 276 (January 5, 2001), 81. For 1995 and 1999, see Zheng Dongtian, "To Be, or Not To Be?" from the feature series titled "Strengthen the Competitive Power of China Film by Acceding to WTO," *Film Art*, no. 271 (March 5, 2000), 4–8. One noted consequence of China's WTO membership would be to open up Chinese movie theaters in general to foreign films, beginning with a total of twenty in the first three years of membership, and/or shareholding rights of the cinemas up to 40 percent, with more in subsequent years.

13. Dai Jinhua, *Xie ta liaowang: Zhongguo dianying wenhua 1978–1998* [A broad watch from the slanted tower: Chinese film culture 1978–1998] (Taipei: Yuan-liou, 1999), 177–205, 319–38. According to Dai the first phase, from 1978 to the mid-1980s, looked at the city as the contrastive counterpart of agricultural China. Films such as *Neighbors* (Lingju, 1982; dir. Zheng Dongtian) and *Yamaha Fish Stall* (1984, dir. Zhang Liang) yearn for the realization of the premodern community and its ethics in the midst of the urban space. In the second phase, the mid-to-late 1980s, the urban space in China finally superseded "agricultural China" to become the very "stage" where cultural realities were unfolded. This phase witnessed the rise of the popular city culture. Urban physicality gradually took concrete forms: shopping facilities, the transportation system, highways, and other infrastructures along with an emphasis on interior decors and modern household facilities. At the same time, according to the discourse of the global village, Chinese cities have gradually lost their national/regional/local uniqueness, and soon will be like all other cities without character around the world. Films in this phase, Dai observes, bring queries of the new Chinese urban lifestyle into the foreground. Cited examples include *Rock and Roll Kids* (Yaogun qingnian, 1987; dir. Tian Zhuangzhuang), *A Little Sugar for the Coffee* (Gei kefei jia dian tang, 1987; dir. Sun Zhou), *The Sun and the Rain* (1987; dir. Zhang Zeming), *The Last Frenzy* (Zuihou de fengkuan, 1987; dir. Zhou Xiaowen), *Obsession* (1988; dir. Zhou Xiaowen), and *Black Snow* (Ben ming nian, 1989; dir. Xie Fei). The third phase, mainly the 1990s, is coined "the age of diversity." In it there is no more heroism but instead the affirmation of the ordinary everyday life; popular culture became the legitimate ideology; and even ideological correctness is turned into a commodity. Dai notes that many such films, especially those of Zhang Yuan and He Jianjun, dubbed "the cruel saga of the youth" [qingchun canku wuyu], are mostly the private stories of the anonymous ordinary people in the city.

14. Li Yiming, "Cong di wu dai dao di liu dai: Jiushi niandai qianqi Zhongguo dalu dianying de yanbian" [From the Fifth Generation to the Sixth Generation: Evolutionary changes in Mainland Chinese cinema in the first half of the 1990s], *Film Art*, no. 1 (1998): 15 (my translation).

15. Ibid., 15–22. For a similar kind of analysis, see, for example, Zhang Yiwu, "Fa-

zhan de xiangxiang: 1990–1994 Zhongguo dalu leixing dianying" [Imaginations on development: Genre films in Mainland China in 1990–1994], *Film Art*, no. 264 (January 10, 1999): 68–72.

16. A simple controlled interview survey (with six questions) reveals that in Beijing, only university students and the more educated people watch films regularly and in so doing have formed their own taste and preferences. The survey covers six types of targets: (1) university students and intellectuals, (2) white-collar workers in the city of Beijing, (3) employees in the service industry who are from outside Beijing, (4) ordinary employees (such as cab drivers, administrators, and shop-keepers), (5) people in the film industry, and (6) expatriates and overseas Chinese working in Beijing. The survey also found that people from outside Beijing or the agricultural areas don't care much about film. See Guo Xiaolu, "Zhongguo xuyao shenmeyang de dianying? Yi ci youguan dianying de tiaocha baogao" [What kinds of films does China want? A report on a survey on film], *Film Art*, no. 278 (May 5, 2001), 16–23, 70.

17. Michel de Certeau, *The Practice of Everyday Life* (Berkeley: University of California Press, 1984), 97.

18. Paul Cobley, ed., *The Communication Theory Reader* (London: Routledge, 1996), 18–22.

19. Certeau, *The Practice of Everyday Life*, 97–98.

20. Henri Lefebvre, *The Production of Space*, trans. Donald Nicholson-Smith (Oxford: Blackwell, 1991), 33, 38–42. Lefebvre differentiates the production of space into three kinds: spatial representation, representational space, and spatial practices.

21. Knabb, *Situationist International Anthology*, 372.

22. Gleber, *The Art of Taking a Walk*, vii.

23. Ibid., 138–39. Gleber compares the flâneur's seeing to the gaze of the camera.

24. Ibid., 136.

25. Ibid., 47.

26. Ibid., 3.

27. Ibid., 130.

28. Caygill, *Walter Benjamin*, 68.

29. Huang Jianxin, "Bu ke tidai de yishu dianying" [The irreplaceable art film], *Film Art*, no. 278 (May 5, 2001), 9–11.

30. Certeau, *The Practice of Everyday Life*, 92.

31. Ibid., 92–93.

32. As Gleber writes, the flâneur drifts along with the modern crowds, and yet at the same time he slowly "pursues [his] own trajectories, considering reality with [his] own careful gaze" (*The Art of Taking a Walk*, 3).

33. Debord, "Introduction to a Critique of Urban Geography," in Knabb, ed., *Situationist International Anthology*, 5–8 (originally published in *Les lévres nues*, no. 6 [September 1955]).

34. Mary Price, *The Photograph: A Strange Confined Space* (Stanford, Calif.: Stanford University Press, 1994), 2. Grounded on Wittgenstein's idea of "meaning *is* the use," Price advances the argument that a conceptual interpretation of photographs is not possible before naming what is seen in literal description, even if the conceptual interpretations are necessarily more interesting. Yet the act of naming can preserve the double vision of literal and conceptual instead of substituting for the abstract.

35. Ahlback, "The Road to Industrial Heterotopia," 256. Foucault draws a distinction between the heterotopias of illusion and the heterotopias of compensation. To him, the latter have the function of forming another real space.

36. Leung's discussion is directly quoted in Lo Kwai-cheng (Lo Guixiang), "Hou xiandai zhuyi yu Liang Bingjun 'you shi' (jielu)" [Leung Ping-kwan's *Wandering Poems* and postmodernism (extract)], in *Liang Bingjun juan* [Leung Ping-kwan collection], ed. Ji Si (Hong Kong: Joint Publishing, 1989), 356–61.

37. Ibid., 356.

38. *Proceedings of the Twenty-second Hong Kong International Film Festival* (April 1998) (Hong Kong: Urban Council, 1998), 65.

39. Guy Debord, "Theory of the *Dérive*," in Knabb, ed., *Situationist International Anthology*, 50–54 (originally published in *Internationale Situationniste*, no. 2 [December 1958]).

40. Certeau, *The Practice of Everyday Life*, 94–95.

41. For a full discussion of the survival of the avant-garde in the 1990s, see Zhu Xiaoyi, "Zhongguo xianfeng yishu zhi huigu ji jiushi niandai Zhongguo xianfeng dianying" [A retrospective on the Chinese avant-garde art and the Chinese avant-garde films in the 1990s], *Film Art*, no. 276 (January 5, 2001), 79–87.

42. For one example of this view, see Xie Fei, "Dui nianqing daoyan men de san dian kanfa" [Three views on the young directors], *Film Art*, no. 270 (January 5, 2000), 12–14.

43. See the first paragraph of the Chinese version of "Director's Notes," in *Proceedings of the Twenty-sixth Hong Kong International Film Festival* (March 27 to April 7, 2002) (Hong Kong: Arts Development Council, 2002), 80.

44. Ibid.

45. Jia Zhang, quoted in an essay online at http://www.beijingscene.com/v051023/feature/feature.htm. The essay carries direct quotations from Jia Zhangke in an interview format, but the author is not stated.

46. *In Expectation* (1996), Zhang's graduation film, was originally selected for the twenty-first Hong Kong International Film Festival (1997), but it was pulled out due to pressure from Mainland authorities. Zhang's next film, *Weekend Plot* (2001), was shown at the twenty-sixth Hong Kong festival in 2002.

47. See *Proceedings of the Twenty-sixth Hong Kong International Film Festival*, xliii. The quote is from the English version of the "Director's Note."

III

THE PRODUCTION OF DESIRE AND IDENTITIES

ning ying's beijing trilogy

Cinematic Configurations of

Age, Class, and Sexuality

SHUQIN CUI

The changing landscape of urban China has provoked the interest of film directors and prompted the genre of urban cinema. Ning Ying is one of the new generation of directors who has constantly framed the sociocultural space of her native city of Beijing in order to study the contemporary urban experience and turn it into cinematic representation. By taking urban space and city dwellers as my point of departure, in this essay I examine how Ning's urban trilogy presents the social life and geography of Beijing in a process of rapid transition. Due to the director's auteurist articulation and realistic approach, the trilogy stands apart from mainstream film productions. Its central concerns emphasize how ordinary city dwellers cope with extraordinary sociocultural transitions. In Ning's first film, *For Fun* (Zhao le, 1992), the love of Beijing Opera by elderly retirees relegated to the social margin suggests a cultural space that is about to disappear. Ning's second production, *On the Beat* (Mingjing de gushi, 1995), shows a social-political space of colliding forces as common police officers are caught between state and commercial imperatives. Finally, *I Love Beijing* (Xiari nuan-yangyang, 2001) constructs a gendered space where the interaction of a taxi driver with four women redefines gender relations and female sexuality in a metropolis overtaken by commercial culture. Seen together, the three films reveal the struggle of residents trying to adapt to Beijing's transformation into a vibrant, modern city.

Ning has attracted attention with her subtle vision of urban transformation. Nonetheless, one cannot easily label or categorize Ning or her films. For years she was the Italian director Bernardo Bertolucci's student and assistant director, yet her films show no evidence of his shadow. Ning is a member of the so-called Fifth Generation directors, but the absence in her films of national allegories and visual splendor has largely separated her from her peers.[1] Her films contribute to the emergence of urban cinema, yet they stand apart from those of the younger urban filmmakers.[2] Interestingly, although Ning is an important female director, her early films neither focus on women's issues nor show explicit feminist interest. When her camera finally frames gender relations against the urban milieu, it does so through the male protagonist's perspective. It is precisely her distance from mainstream production, her difference from other independent filmmakers, and her seeming lack of concern for feminism that make me ask whether Ning is consciously subverting or simply ignoring the major figures, trends, and conventions. This essay explores how Ning's Beijing trilogy expresses her love as well as her anxiety toward the city as it experiences accelerating change. As the familiar disappears and the unknown approaches, Ning's characters of different generations, classes, and genders nervously search for a secure destination against the uncertainties of ever-changing urban space.

HOMETOWN BLUES: BEIJING AND ITS ORDINARY DWELLERS

As the locus of Ning's films, Beijing's significance lies in its identity as both a capital and a city. For centuries, this social-political and urban space has experienced dramatic transformations: from imperial palaces to socialist bureaucracy to contemporary metropolis. At the close of the twentieth century, the capital city that had painfully endured sociopolitical upheavals, rampant industrialization, and a burgeoning population, again underwent radical change. This time, Beijing faced global market forces able to negotiate and divide its space. As a consequence, Beijing has became more cosmopolitan as it integrates with international economic currents and draws great numbers of job-seeking migrants. Under such circumstances, a capital city whose political dominance had overshadowed its commercial function recognized the need to attract and accommodate international business and capital investment. Monumental streets began to sprout luxury hotels and corporate office towers. The intrusion of commercial centers and business districts gradually erased the fundamental nature and structure of the ancient city. Urban dwellers, once confined within walled work-unit compounds or modest courtyard houses, moved into congested high-rise apartments. And the sea of bicycles retreating before the rising tide of private cars, became another significant sign of urban transformation. The remapping of the capital city by contemporary urban and economic development ruptured the boundaries between tradition and modernity, socialism and commercialism.

Against the setting of a city in the throes of extraordinary change, Ning's camera solicits the most ordinary urban dwellers as wandering flâneurs. Following them, we are led to a city in flux and urban life open to innovation. The gradual disappearance of familiar ways and the growing need to cope with a changing socioeconomic order become unavoidable in the daily lives of Beijing's residents. Indeed, the implications are prominent as waves of social change sweep over ordinary characters and their everyday routines. For example, the retirees in For Fun, relocated from the center to the periphery of urban society, seek a space where they can practice opera singing as an assertion of their social existence. The police officers in On the Beat, once an arm of the state apparatus, now must cater to the new commercial society, taking pains to adjust their identities and responsibilities. The taxi driver in I Love Beijing, with his roving wheel and rear mirror, reveals to viewers the Beijing streets filled with commodities and floating populations.

To discover and foreground the ordinary people (xiao renwu) is to make visible the unexplored city peripheries that have been either ignored by or exaggerated in the mainstream narratives. The representation of quotidian events emphasizes a common stratum of urban experience. By focusing on the ordinary in its multifariousness and immanence, theoretical and cinematic exploration can extend beyond the conventions of age, gender, and class. Moreover, the perception of the ordinary invites the audience to see the changing urban space from alternative perspectives. As Ning states, "I'm keenly interested in an ordinary character who is free from being exceptional, and in contingency. In this way, the film allows the audience to re-experience the essential meaning of life."[3]

Ning is remarkable for her ability to depict urban realities with satirical undertones. To show ordinary people grappling with social transitions, the director and her films mark a return to cinematic realism. Ning's view of realism follows that of Andre Bazin yet demonstrates a subjective approach. As she explains, "My films intend to seek a subjective reality, reality in my vision or from my point of view."[4] Thus she aims her camera to capture the drama of urban transition, leaving the familiar to memory and the unfamiliar to wonderment. Such a vision "also rejects any simple connection between reality and society and denies the use of realism for political ends."[5] "What matters most," Ning further emphasizes, "is not to verify but to lay open reality in its significance as well as its ambiguity."[6] In a time when traditional values collide with modern trends and ideological conventions face commercial pressures, Ning's films raise the significant sociocultural issues concealed in the wrap of everyday realities, yet only to subtly expose them to an ironical eye.

From the director's point of view, we begin to see Ning's cinematic vision. It is possible to say that in her film art she pursues "a profound realism which plumbs the depth of the real with the testimonial honesty of mise-en-scène."[7] To do so, Ning's camera frames spaces that are socially and cinematically excluded from other films. For instance, For Fun shows a typical residential area in Beijing where simple flats, a public bathhouse, and a coal-supply factory mark the street geography. The police officers in On the Beat patrol the city on their bicycles. The taxi driver's cab in I Love Beijing takes viewers to both the center and the periphery of the city. The familiar mise-en-scène of Beijing behind its affluent districts reveals not just places but a way of life undergoing transformation. For those familiar with this life, Ning's films create a bridge to the pre-filmic world. For viewers who cannot recall the old world, the experience of quotidian rhythms characterizes the city in its ordinary form, rich with detail. Such an approach corresponds to Lieve Spaas's study of Alain Tanner's films: "Beyond the screen there is not only another space which is evoked but there is also a hidden reality which traditional cinema avoids."[8] Thus the mise-en-scène and the space not only present a cinematic setting but also point to sociocultural issues.

Nonetheless, realistic mise-en-scène and familiar spaces do not suggest an absolute authenticity but rather an articulation of reality. In the process of re-presenting everyday life in Beijing, the director chooses documentary devices, such as location shooting, long-take cinematography, depth of field, and the use of nonprofessionals in the cast. Such means allow her "to respect the spatiotemporal integrity of the pre-filmic world."[9] Of particular importance is editing, which, in its authorial yet invisible form, shapes the viewing experience significantly. Ning's editorial practices do not try to impose an obvious reading of events. She prefers to lead the audience to sense rather than to seek the meaning embedded within the narrative. Different sensibilities bring about different perceptions. For instance, in an early sequence of *For Fun* cutting is barely visible where a long take with depth of field shows the old neighborhood in Beijing. The invisible editing allows the neighborhood to unfold without any interruption or intrusion. In *On the Beat* the disjunction between image and sound reinforces the contradictory roles of the police officers as agents of the state as well as of commercial interests. In *I Love Beijing*, a marriage and divorce sequence seen through montage editing connects the male protagonist to different women, thereby evoking gender issues in a changing society. Ning controls the articulation of her narrative and cinematic world and skillfully—through editing and other means—leads the spectator to observe rather than to become absorbed in daily urban events as these realities are framed on, off, and beyond the screen.

Finally, while focusing on the ordinary, Ning does not seem to consider gender and woman as central concerns. (This is especially true in *For Fun* and *On the Beat*.) Ning's films, therefore, suggest that gender as an interpretive approach should start not with the question of whether a man or a woman directed the film but with an analysis of how the film, its vision and structure, is constructed. As a director, Ning tries to see the urban world from a perspective free from established categories, whether gender differences or mainstream trends. The apparent absence of gender issues in *For Fun*, for instance, simplifies and heightens the central conflict between the new socioeconomic authority and the retirees. Gender implications do, however, exist off or beyond the frame. Similarly, the predominance of social rather than gender politics in *On the Beat* foregrounds the police officers' struggle to adjust to the uncertainty of the emerging consumer culture and the disappearing security of their socialist past. Brief cuts to a policeman's home and family, though, expose the spatial politics of gender. In her third film, Ning finally takes space and gender as her primary interest. But in so doing she selects the perspective of a male taxi driver to survey the urban scenes and map gendered spaces. This approach raises the question of the relation between female authorship and male perspective. In the following analysis of Ning's Beijing trilogy I will explore how social and cultural spaces may disappear, collide, or appear as gendered constructions.

A CULTURE OF (DIS)APPEARANCE

Ning Ying's camera anxiously captures vanishing cultural types and practices before they disappear from the urban scene. Aged retirees pushed to the edges of social life become the focus of her camera's solicitation. In *For Fun* we catch a glimpse of an old man, recently retired from his job in a theater, as he wanders in the street. In seeking a sense of identity in the aftermath of a loss of social status, the protagonist and his fellow amateur opera singers move from one place to another in an effort to organize their singing and regain their lost position. Their sense of space and identity, however, reinforces our anxiety about a culture teetering on the brink of disappearance.

Ackbar Abbas, in writing on Hong Kong cinema, architecture, and literature, raises the question of a "culture and politics of disappearance." In his view, the return of Hong Kong to China in 1997 marked a temporal and spatial rupture. The identity and global status of Hong Kong entered "a culture of disappearance" due to the arranged engagement between a postsocialist state and a postcolonialist metropolis.[10] Mainland China, too, has in its own way been making the transition from a totalitarian state to a socialist regime trying to steer a capitalist engine. The concept of a culture of disappearance is thus evident in Ning's films, primarily in how the forces of modernity and commercialism uproot and remove traditional practices. *For Fun* demonstrates how social and economic changes spread insecurity by dislodging people from their habitual posts. Old Han is a receptionist for an opera theater. He handles the newspapers, opens and closes the theater, and tends to other sundry duties. Although Old Han takes these tasks seriously he is asked to retire so that his job can be given to two young successors. As such the protagonist's new circumstances reflect the city's rush into an unknown future.

In the credits sequence, the tracking shots of the local setting, the Qianmen commercial district, capture an emblematic moment of transition in a cinematic spatial construction. Food and fruit markets, buses and bicycles, give the setting a local tone. A sign for the California Noodle Shop, however, announces the presence of international enterprise; the local scene contains the seeds of the global marketplace. In a different sequence, a long take with depth of field unveils a residential area located amid the old alleys. The garbage containers where residents dump their coal ash, and the off-screen sounds that suggest a public bathhouse, place the scene in the 1980s. The sidewalk packed with mounds of napa vegetables (cabbage) reminds the Chinese audience of the nuisance of collecting vegetables for winter storage. The reframing of the local space and lifestyle turns our vision toward a recent past; seen today the past becomes testimony, indicating at once the socialist planned economy and the emerging market for world trade. The change is so rapid that the lines blur between past and present, reality and memory. Only the space, framed onto the screen, reminds us and inscribes the change. As the credit sequence ends at a local Peking Opera house, the director's intention to document a disappearing culture is clear.

In positioning its protagonist against such social conditions, the film suggests the fading of both the old city and the old people. Old Han is stripped of his daily responsibilities—which he considers his profession—as well as of his "administrative authority." To a larger extent, the sense of loss describes an older generation, deeply tied to and manipulated by the socialist hierarchy, who see the system that once supported them now sinking. The ordinary retirees desperately seek a way to salvage their lost identity and social status. The film expresses this emblematic moment of transition in a cinematic spatial construction. The sign on the door to the reception office attracts our immediate attention—"Reception Office Staff Only"—and suggests an ironic contrast between the mundane space and the importance invested in it by its users. The mise-en-scène of the office, confined in a single frame, presents territorial space divided into different visual planes with a desk in the foreground and chairs and odds-and-ends in the background. At first, Old Han is positioned at the desk, a spatial symbol indicating his authority, as he instructs his apprentice on how to number the newspapers. The old man possesses the entire office space. He freely strolls around the room and complains about the young man's inappropriate behavior. As a close-up shot invites Old Han to address the audience, he declares that the theater will miss him after he retires.

The first day after his retirement, Old Han decides to visit his former assistant, only to discover that the space is no longer his territory. The young man welcomes Old Han but instructs him to take a side chair rather than sit at the desk: he must not interfere with the work of the office. The spatial arrangement, with the old man in the background and his successors in the foreground, clearly confirms the change in power relations. In addition, a wall calendar depicting a Western beauty and the young employees' conversation about current films signals a corresponding change that is foreign to the retired man. No matter how irritated, the old man cannot complain; he is confined to the edges of social space and cornered in a visual frame.

The question of where the elderly might resituate themselves after retirement becomes the film's primary concern. Pushed from their accustomed place in public life, the elderly feel vulnerable and adrift. In a society where everything is commodified, measured, and ranked, the old men cannot compete. With the loss of the iron rice bowl, the disadvantages of old age become more acute. In contemporary China, the categories of gender, age, and class also undergo a restructuring as the society moves from socialism toward a market economy. Young women, for instance, are encouraged to turn their beauty and youth into market commodities.[11] Former proletarians, poor peasants or the urban working class, at least have the possibility of changing themselves into private business entrepreneurs, whereas the old people who are let go from their accustomed posts find themselves shut out of the new economy. To relinquish one's position and return home (*gaolao huanxiang*) used to be a traditional honor for a retiring worker. The family or home that Old Han returns to, unfortunately, retains neither a traditional kinship nor a nuclear structure; instead, it is a space of emptiness and loneliness. The absence of a wife, children, family members, or any social network creates a daunting problem for him. A careful viewing of the film reveals how the concept of the look brings that absence into the discourse of gender and age. The next morning, the old man rises on time only to realize that he does not need to go to work. In assuming his perspective, the camera pans the room and stops at his deceased wife's photo on the wall. This point-of-view shot links the man's vision with the woman's image. Her presence as an image yet absence as a woman indicates personal loss as well as the cultural disappearance of traditional values and family structures.

The film further exposes the alienation of the family and the loneliness of the elderly when the group of amateur Beijing Opera singers responds to a journalist's interview. Facing the camera and therefore directly addressing the audience, one man complains about the "child emperor" who rules at home. Another man whines that no one at home likes the "noise" of his singing. They all share a passion for opera singing, such that their feet feel "itchy" if they miss one day of practice. As the film concentrates on the neglected elders and their passionate attachment to the opera, it becomes evident that the aged retirees and the dying opera reflect each other, signifying a social group and an art form threatened with disappearance. To capture that moment, Ning's camera follows the old men as they wander through different social-urban geographies. The process of transforming social geography into cinematic space enables the ordinary elders to try to find a new niche. Driven to the periphery of social and family life, the men search for solace by trying to find a space where they can practice singing opera and in so doing restore their ignored self-identity.

Place is conflated with identity as the men attempt to return from their social banishment. The sound of ballroom dance music attracts Old Han and his mentally retarded friend to the local cultural activity center. They begin to negotiate a possible place for the group to practice opera. The head of the activity center speaks in the language of officialdom as the old man bargains. Here, the voice from the margins is insistent and cannot be ignored. The old man and his young friend finally win over the space. Surprisingly, the success in gaining social acceptance results in a power struggle among the elders themselves. First, the members vote to "institutionalize" their club and formulate regulations. Old Han, as the head of the club, kindly encourages everyone to enjoy singing, yet he stubbornly exercises his "power of authority." As a result, the chance for a turn to sing and the decision about whose turn it is produces a power distribution among individuals. Such an outcome in a group of ordinary characters is not only narrative satire but also a comment on a social-political inclination deeply embedded within everyday reality.

The film reveals the power play through the mise-en-scène of a divided frame. Inside the activity center, members of the club indulge themselves in their opera performances. One member arrives late and asks Old Han for a turn to sing. As the head of the club, Old Han keeps to the regulations and rejects the member's request. Conflict emerges as a result, and the camera focuses on and tracks the arguing characters while leaving the others off-screen. Thus a single shot establishes a contrast that marks a social division: the sound of opera from off-screen suggests a stable institutional order while the drama framed on-screen shows a chaotic power struggle. The member insists on his right to the "stage" but Old Han uses his authority to deny him the space. When this member finally forces a chance to sing, Old Han, calling on his superior knowledge of opera, frequently disrupts the man to correct his mistakes. The competition for space therefore turns into a confrontation between discourses of power and knowledge. The ability to speak "expert discourse" and exercise administrative power enables Old Han to shape the course of events. The resisting member must discipline himself according to the rules.

The opera club's cooperative management fails to function and the group disbands. Why do the elderly, dismissed from social-political hierarchies, return to and inscribe the very system in their everyday community life? In response to this question, Ning explains: "A retired person should finally assume freedom after release from the work unit. Yet the idea and long experience of social hierarchies have left their mark on the men. Thus, they try to reproduce a social-political collectivity with its institutions, regulations, and disciplines. This hopeless dependence under an extraordinary historical transition can result in tragedy. There is no free and ideal alternative."[12] The tentacles of power and bureaucracy reach deep into the everyday social life of citizens in China. Few alternatives remain available. The predominant structure, oppressive but familiar, serves not only as the governmental apparatus but also as a consensus mechanism to determine who has access to a desirable good. As Michel Foucault explains the concept of power: "Power doesn't mean a group of institutions and mechanisms that ensure the subservience of the citizens of a given state."[13] Instead, power is only a certain type of relation between individuals.[14] As a measure of how people relate to each other, the power relation is a negotiating process where power remains the central nexus as the competitors keep shifting their positions; an elite member of one social-political environment could be oppressed in another, or vice versa.

Ning's narrative satire and social critique demonstrate such contradictions. On the one hand, the increasing prominence of modernity drives the elders away from the mainstream and into the margins. On the other hand, any possible return to the center will replay the bureaucratic power struggles on a small scale. Ning's satirical device, as Jerry White points out, "exposes just how deeply engraved the propensity for power struggles is within human nature, not to mention Chinese society."[15] The film ends where it began with a contrast between the group and the loner. Failing to maintain his administrative power, Old Han has left the opera club and the remaining members have returned to the park for their daily activities. An extreme long shot seizes the moment when Old Han attempts to rejoin the group. He first sits at a distance, listening to them sing; then he finds the courage to walk toward the group. A possible reunion remains uncertain, however, as a freeze-frame seizes the character in the distance and isolates him from his desired community. This open ending keeps the negotiations between center and margin over a cultural remnant lingering.

SPACES IN COLLISION

On the Beat stresses China's social, political, and economic transitions as it takes the police bureaucracy and its officers as a primary subject. The opening credits end with a time marker: 1994, the year of dog. The social and political connotations of the time become evident in a voice-over narration delivering a speech on police reform. Viewers then are invited to follow two police officers on their bicycle tour of the city. Their journey and our vision pause at a mise-en-scène of high-rise buildings looming behind lines of flat houses, shown in a single frame. Clearly, socioeconomic forces are remapping the urban geography. In a technique similar to that in For Fun, social-political implications are conveyed through the narrative of the protagonists' everyday routines. The daily responsibilities of the police ironically include chasing dogs, searching for household pets, and interrogating "criminals"—the likes of which include a card gambler who cheats customers, a peddler who sells posters of female nudes, and a dog owner who has a bad attitude toward the police. The film reveals not merely the boredom of today's police but also the paradoxical situation in which they do not know how to adjust. Caught between the old status of working as an instrument for the party dictatorship and the new realities of law enforcement, the ordinary policeman on patrol is confused.

As the nation-state undergoes economic reforms, the nature of police work inevitably shifts. The concept of the criminal changes from that formed of politically oriented counterrevolutionaries to a new criminal class that is economically defined, and the absolute power of the police begins to crumble. As Michael Dutton explains: "[The] politico-moral methods once used under

Mao to improve police performance would give way to a series of money-based bonus systems, responsibility systems, and contractual arrangements."[16] For instance, the film begins with a bicycle tour, where the senior officer introduces the residential area of responsibility to the new officer. The film ends with an announcement of a suspended bonus because the senior police handled a case extra-legally. The concept of money is the connection between the police and the "criminal." The number of dogs the police should collect and kill is a contractual assignment, and the extinction of one rabid dog brings honor and a bonus to the whole station.

A scene of catching and killing dogs occurs in an abandoned imperial palace. When the dog, pursued by the police, chooses the palace as a hiding place, the film's satirical tone becomes apparent. The ancient building has witnessed various social-political transitions, but the drama of police officers chasing and killing a street dog is an absurd fall from past splendor. While reforms change the system of policing and the image of the police, the old and familiar ruling structure has not yet disappeared. The coexistence of the old and the new creates a series of satirical moments. The film first punctures the notion of whether the policing system can be independent from both the government and the local customs. As the film shows, the neighborhood committee composed of aging retirees still functions as a mass-control organ. Seven older women oversee almost every single corner of the residential community. They firmly and proudly state that living together without marriage is illegal and that tracking the numbers of pregnancies and abortions is their duty. The film then ridicules the contemporary police. A charge is brought against a man who owns a puppy that bites. Yet when the police interrogate the "criminal," they drone on with questions of family class origin and political status, along with requests for information about family members and social relations. They fail to realize that the police apparatus from the past can no longer assume complete control over the masses. As the puppy's owner finally bursts out in anger, cursing the police as dirty dogs, the interrogator loses his composure and slaps the man's face. The film continues the satire by showing the police officers in their jeep patrolling the neighborhood on a late rainy night. The criminals they are searching for are not counter-revolutionaries but rather residential pets. The scene might be amusing or satirical, but the question is penetrating: How can the police be respected when their legal function is to collect and kill dogs?

Yet Ning is not interested merely in the odd spectacle of policemen chasing dogs or old men singing operas. She pursues an autonomous way of constructing representation and selecting angles of view. As she self-consciously stresses: "When I write about or film the elders, I actually search for myself and for the question of how to represent those characters from my perspective."[17] I see this as a personal vision and critical pursuit of authorial subjectivity and cinematic aesthetics. Indeed, the singularity of Ning's films is due in part to characterization but in larger part to her handling of the mise-en-scène and the editing. *On the Beat* begins with the opening credits rolling along with a voice-over narration. As the image lures the viewer through a long take, we see a meeting room where the police chief is reading a political document while his officers are buried in cigarette smoke. The topic is how to coordinate police reform with the changing economic policies of the party. The film ends in the same setting, with the same voice-over. But this time the chief announces an administrative and financial punishment against the senior officer. Subjective editing gives the familiar mise-en-scène different connotations with significant implications. The ideology of police reform that the officers have been faithfully following seems betrayed. As the reform policy leads to absurdity, the chief police officer feels confused and caught in the contemporary socioeconomic parody. The police do not benefit when dogs and puppies become the unfortunate "criminals" of urban society. "What are we doing here? I haven't been home for a whole week, only chasing dogs and dealing with this shit." The voice of confusion and indignation brings the narrative to a close by mocking the results of police reform.

Clearly, women are not Ning's central concern here; indeed, they emerge occasionally in this film. A subtle female consciousness or feminine vision, however, does impose a gendered implication. Again, the director's careful editing raises the spatial politics of gender relations. After the sequence in which a group of policemen beat a rabid dog to death, the film cuts directly to a domestic scene with a police officer's family. The question of whether the editing attempts to moderate or reinforce the contrast between violence and tenderness remains ambiguous. The familial sequence occurs on an ordinary Sunday, with the whole family playing a game. At the request of her young son, the mother tells him a story. In her made-up tale, she manages to "allegorize" her husband as a big tiger and the boy as a little tiger. She then complains about how patriarchal the big tiger is, since he refuses to do any housework. Thus the film enables the woman to insert her voice to indicate the inequity of contemporary social conditions. The contrast between the policeman's public duty and his home life is elaborated in another sequence. After the police finish their task of rounding up residential dogs, the film cuts again to the family. It is early in the morning, and the returning policeman disturbs his family. When his wife tries to express how hard it is to be a police officer's wife, the husband shuts her off as if he were interrogating a criminal. In a third scene, the film does not use a cut but reveals how abruptly the officer hangs up on his wife's phone call as he responds to another assignment.

The brief associations of the police officer with his family concisely reveal the conflict between public affairs and domestic interests and the husband's continuing authority over his wife. Indeed, Ning does not need to centralize her female character to make a feminist statement. Her camera work and editing uncover the domestic place and gendered space where a woman lives. The articulation of the simple cut and a woman's voice exposes the family as a socially defined space where gender difference comes into view as editing controls the screen time. First, we see the family, and the wife is able to deliver her story. Next, she can hardly finish her words as her husband yells at her to stop. Finally, the film mutes her voice and erases her presence because her domestic matters are interfering with public affairs. The camera's alternating glimpses of familial scenes thus convey the woman's subordinate position as well as her expected multiple responsibilities.

GENDERED SPACE AND MALE PERSPECTIVE

In the film *For Fun*, a horizontal dimension of Beijing in the 1980s is displayed in a number of tracking shots. *On the Beat* reintroduces Beijing in the early 1990s with police officers patrolling the city on their bicycles. In contrast, *I Love Beijing* opens with a succession of bird's-eye shots of a traffic intersection jammed with streams of cars, buses, bicycles, and pedestrians. The vertical dimension and the density of the traffic, as accelerated by montage editing, intensify time and space to show the frenzied pace of change in Beijing. As the crane shot zooms out, its extreme high-angle view of the city, along with the background sounds of car-radio news, locate the metropolis in the late 1990s. A wedding photo session then fades in: responding to the photographer's question, the groom introduces himself as a taxi driver and his bride as a working girl from Henan. The following cut to an office scene shows the same taxi driver but with a different woman, now undergoing the divorce process. The officer of a local street organization, off-screen, questions the couple in a voice-over. Her intimate questions and concealed position indicate how the state apparatus, now an invisible force, still interferes in the personal lives of citizens. The narrative montage of marriage and divorce suggests gender relations under different social, cultural, and economic conditions.

Thus Ning's *I Love Beijing* finally turns her investigation to issues of gender and space. In this film, a taxi driver takes us on an intimate tour to observe the changing landscape of Beijing. His point of view and interactions with four female characters raise gender issues including a problematic relation between female authorship and the male perspective. The taxi driver resembles a flâneur, although he is not a metaphor for the modernist artist. He is, however, an observer of the ever-changing urban culture who remains both engaging and detached from the city crowd. More important, he is not a sidewalk stroller but rather the operator of a motor vehicle. The public function of the vehicle enables this contemporary Chinese flâneur to observe, participate in, and translate urban experience into various narratives. The rearview mirror—the lens of his vision—frames passengers of all social classes, who together make a composite image of contemporary Beijing. The wealthy man and his female companion, for instance, demonstrate how a thriving capitalist economy has made a commodity of female sexuality, while the passenger unable to pay his fare exemplifies how the lower economic class struggles in the new commercial environment. A businessman rehearses his welcoming remarks to foreign guests in awkward English, reiterating, "Peking duck, Peking duck." As the rearview mirror frames the passengers on the back seat, the taxi takes us to every spatial corner of the metropolis. Nightclubs or karaoke bars present the space where men can hire a female escort (or *sanpei xiaojie*; literally, Miss Company who offers three kinds of service) for sexual service. The high-prestige club is the place where only foreigners and Chinese elites gather together. Shopping districts or restaurants speak for the prosperity of a newly flourishing consumer culture.

The course of the male cab driver and his vehicle maps public spaces and defines public spheres. The film, while creating such a figure to establish a viewing position and perspective, demonstrates his social-economic subordination. Working in a service industry, the taxi driver plays a role in, as well as a witness to, the exchange of commodities. His mobility and access to so many diverse spaces is a response to the desires and money of his customers. He shares the public space not as a consumer but as an attendant, watching local elites and foreigners wining and dining, or the "winners" in the new economy appropriating female sexuality. The film thus presents a cab driver as the observer of China's contemporary commercial culture: a male figure who possesses a vision of urban space.

We cannot help but wonder why Ning, a female director, relies on a male flâneur and a male perspective for her exploration of urban experience. Do women not now have access to urban modernity, and can they not assume the roles of either observer or participant? In Elizabeth Wilson's expansion of Benjamin's concept of the flâneur, she describes "a man who takes visual possession of the city, who has emerged in postmodern feminist discourse as the embodiment of the male gaze . . . [who] represents men's visual and voyeuristic mastery over women . . . the flaneur's freedom to wander at will through the city is essentially a masculine freedom. Thus the very idea of flaneur reveals it to be a gendered concept."[18] Yet the flâneur as a gendered concept remains partially defined unless a woman's place in the urban land-scape is taken into consideration. In this film, the interactions between the cab driver and four women shape the primary narrative structure and bring into discourse such gender issues as marriage, divorce, and female sexuality.

An understanding of these contrasted female figures in relation to the male protagonist begins with the relationship between women and space. For in-stance, the divorce narrative in the beginning sequence is spatially specific. From the couple's arguments we learn that she was one of his passengers, and that he first wooed her by following in his car as she walked along the street. After the marriage, however, he keeps her at home while he goes out to make money. This is not, however, a simple matter of the woman confined in her domestic space while the man freely roams the public sphere. Dichotomies of public and private, man and woman, must be set in their commercial, cultural environment. The woman is neither a housewife nor a mother. She is a fashionable city woman and a modern individual, deciding to leave her hus-band's home. The idea of separate spheres is out of date. So the woman rejects such spatial restrictions and emotional ignorance, and asks for a divorce. The wife shares the apartment flat with her mother-in-law. The day she departs, the mother-in-law verbally and physically harasses her in public. As the film

I Love Beijing: The taxi driver, Derzi. (Courtesy of Eurasia Communications)

I Love Beijing: A marriage in trouble. (Courtesy of Eurasia Communications)

displays the drama of women's conflicts, the spectacle visually explains how the traditional cliché of a mother-daughter complex remains persistent. We hear the urgency of her voice requesting a divorce, and we see her leaving the man's house, but we do not see the wife or her fate clearly, since we see only the fragments of a woman's story from the man's vision.

The question thus arises of how to read the "social map" of gender as the urban geography in China undergoes drastic change.[19] In a society inscribed simultaneously by the persistence of post-socialist politics and an emerging commercial economy, gender difference means spatial renegotiation. The cab driver transforms his vehicle and male labor into a commercial mechanism subject to market regulations. His income allows him to keep his wife at home, consuming fashion and cosmetics yet yearning for a more satisfying relationship. By placing the woman in the home not as a mother or housewife but as a commercially confined "property," the film narrative represents a social-cultural environment where everything and everyone is valued and exchanged in commercial terms. Whereas the male protagonist is at least able to navigate in the urban milieu, the woman, released from work and given leisure at home, is ambivalent about her possible place and space. The divorce is her resistance against domestication. Yet where can a woman turn when she is not defined in terms of production or reproduction?

Further, the changing economic climate in China has created a floating population of millions of workers seeking jobs in urban regions. Among the migrants are many country girls, emerging onto the urban scene in search of a better life and material comfort. They dream of participating in the thriving urban space but instead typically end up as "migrant working girls" (*dagong mei*). The spatial transformation from country to city might emancipate the girls from rural poverty only to relegate them to a similar urban form of confinement. The taxi driver's girlfriend, Xiao Xue, came to Beijing from the northeast and works in a restaurant. His later bride-to-be came from Henan and serves in a student cafeteria. These migrant working girls are neither occupants nor consumers of public space; they are labor commodities in the relation between customers and business owners. The working girl cannot claim any space as her own. Again, it is the roving vision of the cab driver that leads us to view the working girls as a specific gender group in Beijing. Xiao Xue, for instance, oscillates between the restaurant and a rented apartment. At work, she must conform to business regulations; in her apartment, family members from back home occupy every square inch of space. Finally, she commits suicide for reasons that are not clear; although the trauma of sexual violation by family members is suggested, the filter of male vision obscures the woman's story and the matter is left unexplained.

Suicide extinguishes the migrant woman's dream of securing a place for herself in the city. Marriage to a Beijing resident presents another possibility. The taxi driver's fiancée appears briefly in the film. Their first meeting occurs inside his car, where the country girl expresses her desire to take wedding photos if he agrees to marry her. This migrant from the countryside, bereft of identity and place, dreams of herself as a city woman in a wedding dress. To emphasize the identity transition and spatial relocation through marriage, the film shows the wedding photo session twice, at the beginning and at the ending of the film. The first time, the woman in bridal gown conceals her identity as a working migrant from the countryside. The urban identity she tries to project, however, remains superficial—only an image coded by the dress. The photo session at the opening of the film demonstrates a spatial and gendered negotiation, where country and city, groom and bride, transact urban space in commercial terms. In the wedding photo sequence seen at the end of the film, however, the bride remains a working girl but the groom decides to marry her after a series of unpleasant incidents on his driving routes. The desire to embrace the rural province as reality, embodied by the country girl, indicates that the male city drifters are troubled and longing for a secure identity. It is significant that the wedding photo sequence opens and closes the film: we can infer that the constant negotiation for urban space and thereby social-cultural identity is ongoing.

After juxtaposing different female figures and their fragmentary narratives, the film inserts one more such juxtaposition to pursue the issue of female sexuality. A young woman is strolling along the street, looking for her destination. The cab driver trails her as his prey and successfully lures her into his car. They begin a verbal fight; this educated woman, a university librarian, curses the man, "*liumang*,"[20] and the driver displays the power of his money. The dispute between the woman and the cab driver ends when he invites her to have an ice cream and then pays for it. The film extends the narrative rather unconvincingly when the woman invites him to engage in sex in the apartment she shares with her parents. Her invitation for a sexual encounter in a spatially and socially confined environment is obviously gratuitous: the sexual

I Love Beijing: A woman strolls along the street, followed by a taxi driver.
(Courtesy of Eurasia Communications)

exchange results from the fact that the man covered an "expensive" bill. The
audience is left confused about what the woman wants in terms of sexuality
and whether this scene is meant to represent the sexual fashion of the modern
urban milieu.

This sexual engagement suggests that gender and class differences extend
beyond conventional social and spatial boundaries. The apartment belongs to
the university, so the young woman invites the taxi driver to trespass on an
institution of higher education. The one-night stand mocks institutional conventions as it exemplifies the profound effects of commercial culture. By asking
the man to her apartment rather than going out, the librarian temporarily
controls her body as well as the space. In so doing, the young woman's sexual
life, though still under her parents' watchful gaze, is no longer a taboo but an
experiment and adventure. The deal made between the two, however, doesn't
last long. The walls of the university finally separate the educated woman from
the taxi driver, indicating their differences in social-economic status.

As the film presents the cab driver's encounters with different women, it is
not apparent that the vignettes add up to a linear woman's story or represent
women's experience. The film appears to raise gender issues only to leave

them unexplored. An explanation begins with the film's narrative structure—the fragmented women's stories linked by the male vision. The cab driver is an urban spectator with a mobile gaze that further renders women as passing images. The driver and his vehicle provide access to urban space and its spectacle. The rolling car and its rearview mirror take the audience on a tour through the city, where the possession of vision enables the male discourse to set spatial and temporal boundaries. The unfolding of domestic problems with the wife, for instance, as well as the adventure of chasing girls in the street and various scenes with passengers in the backseat, become possible only as consequences of the driver's access to mobility through urban space and his moving gaze. Female figures are selected from the crowd, framed within the vision, their time and space measured for the linear construction of man's urban experience. The fragments also suggest how the new market economy has not necessarily brought about meaningful change in women's position in society, despite the surface appearance of liberation and mobility.

Finally, *I Love Beijing* is marked by the contradiction between a female directorship and a male perspective. While the film reveals aspects of Beijing's socioeconomic transition through gender relations, the male perspective limits the exploration of gender issues. Although the film offers female voices—requesting divorce, revealing sexual violation, desiring marriage—the voices are brief, the images fleeting. The decision to shoot the movie through a "male filter" prevents female flâneurs from occupying the urban center and enjoying a freedom of spatial and social mobility. This film raises the question of to what ends should we still inquire into the subject of a women's cinema. As Teresa de Lauretis comments, "To ask whether there is a feminine or female aesthetic, or a specific language of women's cinema, is to remain caught in the master's house and to legitimate the hidden agendas of a culture we badly need to change."[21] She further proposes that "feminist theory should now engage precisely in the redefinition of aesthetic and formal knowledges, much as women's cinema has been engaged in the transformation of vision."[22] Ning achieves a personal vision, however, either by rejecting sexual difference as a narrative focus or by adopting, though not endorsing, a male vision for the perception of gender issues. Her films, while forcefully illustrating the effects on ordinary residents of Beijing's extraordinary social-economic changes, do not provide an easy answer to the question of why this woman director has not delved into the consciousness of gender construction.

Ning's Beijing trilogy employs the experiences of diverse city dwellers struggling to make sense of their rapidly changing world. The elderly retirees in *For
Fun* signify the disappearance of cultural tradition. The police officers in *On
the Beat* wrestle with the conflict between the state apparatus and an emerging
consumer culture. The young taxi driver shows how sex and labor are commodities in flux in the new urban landscape. Old men, cops, and cab drivers
are the contemporary Chinese flâneurs, strolling through the streets, observing the crowds, taking in the urban scenes. Their methods of strolling—first
walking, then bicycling, and finally driving—indicate different stages of urban
transition. Old or young, individual or collective, we notice that the urban
strollers are men. As a result, problems occur when female flâneurs attempt to
share the urban space. The urban woman cannot move freely in the streets,
unimpeded and unintimidated. We need a conscious female vision and a
female subject of urban discourse in Chinese cinema.

NOTES

1. For biographical information on Ning, see Yuanying Yang, "Conversations with
Ning Ying," in *Their Voices: Autobiographies of Chinese Women Directors* (Beijing:
Zhongguo shehui chuban, 1996), 270.
2. For a discussion of China's young independent film directors, see Shuqin Cui,
"Working from the Margins and Outside the System: Independent Film Directors
in Contemporary China," *Post Script* 20 (winter/spring 2001): 79.
3. Literary translation from Shen Yun's "About *For Fun* and *On the Beat:* Conversation with Ning Ying," in *The Fifth Generation of Chinese Filmmakers in the 1990s*,
ed. Yang Yuanying, Pan Hua, and Zhang Zhuan (Beijing: Broadcasting Institute
Press, 2000), 398.
4. See Yang Fan, "Ning Ying: Wozai chengshizhong xunzhao lingleigan" [Ning
Ying: In the city seeking alternative feelings] *City Pictorial* (August 2, 2001), available at http://vogue.sina.com.cn/f/r/2001–08–02/10848.html.
5. Quoted in Shen Yun, "About *For Fun* and *On the Beat*," 401 (my translation).
6. Ibid., 401.
7. See Robert Stam, "The Phenomenology of Realism," in his *Film Theory: An
Introduction* (Malden, Mass.: Blackwell Publishers, 2000), 76.
8. Lieve Spaas, "Center, Periphery and Marginality in the Films of Alain Tanner,"
in *Spaces in European Cinema*, ed. Myrto Konstantarakos (Exeter, U.K.: Intellect,
2000), 153.
9. Stam, "The Phenomenology of Realism," 76.
10. Ackbar Abbas, *Hong Kong: Culture and the Politics of Disappearance* (Minneapolis: University of Minnesota Press, 1997), 7.

11. Zhang Zhen, "Mediating Time: The 'Rice Bowl of Youth' in Fin de Siecle Urban China," *Public Culture* 12, no. 1 (2000): 93–113.

12. See Shen Yun, "About *For Fun* and *On the Beat*," 401 (my translation).

13. Michel Foucault, *The History of Sexuality*, trans. Robert Hurley (New York: Vintage, 1990), 92.

14. Michel Foucault, *Politics, Philosophy, Culture: Interviews and Other Writings, 1977–1984*, ed. Lawrence D. Kritzman, trans. Alan Sheridan et al. (New York: Routledge, 1988), 83.

15. Jerry White, "The Films of Ning Ying: China Unfolding In Miniature," *CineACTION* 42 (1997): 5.

16. Michael Dutton, "The End of the Mass Line? Chinese Policing in the Era of the Contract," *Social Justice* 27, no. 2 (2000): 62.

17. Yuanying Yang, ed., *Their Voices: Autobiographies of Chinese Women Directors* (Beijing: Zhongguo shehui chuban, 1996), 277.

18. Elizabeth Wilson, "The Invisible Flaneur," *New Left Review* 191 (1992): 98.

19. Alison Blunt and Gillian Rose, in their introduction to women's colonial and postcolonial geographies, cite Shirley Ardener's concept of a "social map." Ardener describes a social map of patriarchy that "created ground rules for the behavior of men and women, and gender difference was thus seen as inscribing spatial difference" (*Writing Women and Space: Colonial and Postcolonial Geographies*, edited by Alison Blunt and Gillian Rose [New York: The Guilford Press, 1994], 1).

20. The term *liumang*, as Geremie R. Barmé explains, has a venerable pedigree in modern Chinese urban life. It appeared as early as a century ago when it was first used to describe the rootless rowdies and petty criminals who plagued the growing port city of Shanghai, where a rich underworld culture developed in the first half of the twentieth century. This definition was expanded to include people guilty of a large range of sexual misdemeanors, giving the term its most common range of meanings today. In legal terms, a *liumang* crime denoted anything from premarital sex to gang rape. The usage "to play liumang" (*shua liumang*) is used in everyday speech to describe overt sexual suggestions or harassment of a woman by a man. See Barmé, *In The Red: On Contemporary Chinese Culture* (New York: Columbia University Press, 1999), 64. I would add that the term *liumang* is a gendered concept that women often use to defend themselves from potential male threats, both sexual and criminal.

21. Teresa de Lauretis, "Rethinking Women's Cinema: Aesthetics and Feminist Theory," in *Multiple Voices in Feminist Film Criticism*, ed. Diane Carson, Linda Dittmar, and Janice R. Welsch (Minneapolis: University of Minnesota Press, 1994), 144.

22. Ibid.

zhang yuan's imaginary cities

and the Theatricalization of the Chinese "Bastards"

BÉRÉNICE REYNAUD

Zhang Yuan's first feature film, *Mama* (1990)—awarded the FIPRESCI Prize in Edinburgh—was hailed as "the first genuinely independent movie made in China since the communists took power."[1] Cinephiles were also fascinated by the experimental aspect of its texture, which combines black-and-white 35mm footage for the narrative (the poignant story of the tender yet difficult relationship of a young librarian, Liang Dang, with her mentally handicapped son), video for talking-head interviews (of real mothers in similar situations), and 16mm color film for the documentary footage taken at facilities for handicapped children.[2] For its audiences, the intimate mise-en-scène of the fictional part of the film brought to mind both Italian neorealism and the socially conscious films produced during the "golden age" of the Shanghai studio system. On the other hand, the implied social criticism of China's lack of policies to help the families of mentally handicapped children, as well as the oppositional mode of production of the film, suggested guerrilla filmmaking at its political best. Critics pointed to "the movie's keen sense of street level reality" and reading it as the harbinger of a new cinematic movement, identified as the "Sixth Generation."[3]

"Urban realism" was thus to be the salient trait of post-1989 cinema, and as such it stood in sharp contrast to the nostalgic fictions of the Fifth Generation. In 1993, three Sixth Generation films seemed to confirm this diagnostic—Wang Xiaoshuai's *The Days* (Dongchun de rizi), He Yi's *Red Beads* (Xuan lian), and Zhang's second feature, *Beijing Bastards* (Beijing zazhong). Wang Xiaoshuai, one of Zhang's classmates at the Beijing Film Academy, set his film *The Days* in the aftermath of the 1989 crackdown, where it follows the daily lives and interpersonal conflicts of a married couple, both of whom are impoverished painters (actors who are playing themselves, in semi-improvised performances). A former assistant of Zhang Yimou and Tian Zhuangzhuang, He Yi (aka He Jianjun), shot *Red Beads* in a mental hospital, mixing realistic and dreamlike elements. Shot illegally, these films were banned in China, yet all were shown in international festivals. In 1994 Zhang, Wang Xiaoshuai, and He Yi were in Rotterdam when the Beijing Film Bureau asked seven media makers to withdraw their work from the festival. Faced with their collective refusal, the bureau banned them from filmmaking. The stage thus was set to turn Zhang into a "cultural hero" persecuted for bringing to the screen and presenting to international audiences the "hidden reality" of China's growing urban subculture.

Zhang's career is, however, more multifaceted and contradictory than this brief overview suggests, and the issues are made more complex by his decision to work "above ground" after 1999. When his films were invisible in China, Zhang was able to show them to an international, sophisticated audience of filmgoers and potential financiers while developing an original directing style. What lies at the core of his mise-en-scène is the relationship between fiction, character development, and specific urban spaces. Yet, from film to film various kinds of spaces are explored and (re)constructed following a different logic in its shifting register of realism, hyperrealism, and surrealism. First, there is the minute rendering of cramped dwelling spaces, such as Liang Dang's apartment in *Mama*, the compound in *Sons* (Erzi, 1996), and the nurse's dormitory apartment in *I Love You* (Wo Ai Ni, 2002). Then there are spaces that are fluid, evolving, or, to borrow Ackbar Abbas's fortuitous expression, *déjà disparu*—such as the urban landscapes in *Beijing Bastards, The Square* (Guangchang, 1994), *Seventeen Years* (Guo nian hui jia, 1999), and *Crazy English* (Fengkuang yingyu, 1999). This fluidity and uncertainty pertaining to the object of representation in turn opens up toward imaginary spaces that Zhang restages (*remet-en-scène*) through his passion for Chinese architecture and opera—as in *East Palace, West Palace* (Dong Gong, Xi Gong, 1996) or *Jiang Jie* (2003).

Abbas defines the *déjà disparu* in the specific, postcolonial context of Hong Kong as follows: "The feeling that what is new and unique about the situation is always already gone, and we are left holding a handful of clichés, or a cluster of memories of what has never been. It is as if the speed of current events is producing a radical desynchronization, the generation of more and more images to the point of visual saturation going together with a general regression of viewing, an inability to read what is given to view—in other words, the state of reverse hallucination."[4] While Abbas's analysis is quite specific to the situation of Hong Kong, it is somehow applicable to the perception of the current Chinese "reality" that is held by the post-1989 generation in China, and by Zhang Yuan in particular. It is "China" itself that becomes a problematic entity, once it is "presented and represented in terms of the old *binarisms* whose function is to restabilize differences and domesticate changes, for example binarisms like East and West, or tradition and modernity."[5]

In this essay I examine the apparent contradiction that runs throughout Zhang's work—between the "realistic," semidocumentary impulse and the theatricalization of the contemporary urban experience. The cities inhabited by Zhang's camera are not "invisible" (to borrow Italo Calvino's phrase), but they are mostly imaginary—hybrid spaces caught between the past and the future, incessantly (re)shaped by the fears, desires, memories, and projections of the protagonists. In light of this examination, I will outline the complex dialectic woven by Zhang between realism and amnesia, theatricality and memory, and, ultimately, the male and female perspectives on the new Chinese urban spaces. The constant shift of registers created by his mise-en-scène forces the spectator to raise questions about the nature and direction of the gaze and its structuring relationship to desire and space. If the father's gaze is one of the vanishing points of Zhang's oeuvre (in the sense that it is already disappearing), the woman's gendered gaze may be another (as a structuring element in a tableau).

Zhang Yuan's cinema emerged at the same time as underground Chinese documentary, which was aimed at giving a voice to the dilemmas of the post-1989 generation. In the film *I Graduated!* (Wo biye le, 1992) made by the

Structure, Wave, Youth and Cinema Experimental Group, a young man says: "The motherland I love is the China of my imagination . . . I like to call it China, not PRC." On the one hand, the imaginary China alluded to here is pure virtuality—a China that never was, the untapped potential of the post-1911 republican era whose move toward a capitalist form of modernization (which might have been able to gracefully combine local culture and the achievements of the West) was cut short in 1949. On the other hand, in 1988–1990 those individuals in their twenties were "longing for a strong and influential China" as it had existed in the past.[6] Not only did the post-1989 generation feel displaced, uprooted, and victimized, it was also as if reality itself were missing. The power apparatus crushed and misrepresented the aspirations of thousands if not millions of citizens and was clinging to outdated modes of government and economic management while claiming to still believe in the virtues of socialism—a form of politic fiction—as if the Chinese were still lost in the monstrous dreams of a mummy.

Zhang Yuan's own discourse on the issue of "realism" reveals a certain ambivalence. In an interview shortly after the first screenings of *Mama*, he declared:

> We graduated in 1989 during the June 4th incident. . . . Most of the Fifth Generation directors are intellectual youths who've spent time in the country, while we're urbanites . . . Tian Zhuangzhuang and his peers all went through the Cultural Revolution and they remained kind of romantic. We didn't. . . . I make films because I am concerned about social issues and realities . . . I don't like being subjective, and I want my films to be objective. *It's objectivity that'll empower me.*[7]

In 1996, with a few films under his belt and thus more media savvy, he stated:

> For too long, China has not had any real documentary film . . . The only films made [by] the documentary studio since 1949 are political propaganda pieces. So what we lack most are works which record contemporary reality. *This is because China has not dared to face reality for a very long time.* Also, I didn't want that perspective of looking down in judgment; that perspective still tinged with the political. I prefer *my view from the edges of society, the perspective of an ordinary guy looking at people and society* . . . I'm a marginal kind of director myself. Being an independent director in China is an absolutely marginal activity . . . I think all these people on the margins, including myself, have something in common.[8]

The Hong Kong filmmaker Stanley Kwan in his documentary *Yang and Yin: Gender in Chinese Cinema* (Nansheng Nüxiang, 1996) asks Zhang the reason for his interest in marginalized people—single mothers of mentally challenged children, drunken rock musicians, and homosexuals cruising public parks at night. In response, Zhang states: "Marginal families and individuals are in conflict with society; through them you can see how society is changing."

The "reality" presented in Zhang's films is seen from his (subjective) point of view, which because it comes from the edges/margin rather than from the center or from above can be defined as a sidelong glance. It is a partial, sympathetic gaze: the director is pointing his camera at a reality in which he is a part. The sidelong glance is also at odds with mainstream representation ("mainstream melody").[9] Not only does it aim at representing society as it is, but more importantly as it is becoming. It is a fragmented gaze, shifting back and forth between the objective and the subjective, as the point of view of the observer/filmmaker evolves at the same time as that of society.

ROCK AND ROLL, AMNESIA, AND THE DÉJÀ DISPARU

Beijing Bastards is a keen example of Zhang's partial, fragmented, intimate, and self-reflexive gaze. The film was shot in real locations, so that the camera's lens is often blocked by unmovable obstacles (walls, the narrowness of the room, traffic in the street), thereby opening a limited field of vision. As such there are no grand vistas or master gaze; because the camera is mostly hand held and many locations allowed only one or two angles, the focus is on intimate details. Shooting was done on the run while dodging the police, and thus some of the footage, underexposed or out of focus, was not usable. The film's protagonists/actors were Zhang's personal acquaintances from his underground rock/art milieu—for example, the rock star Cui Jian for whom Zhang had shot a series of music videos. Cui is credited as co-producer and co-screenwriter of *Beijing Bastards*, in which he plays himself.[10] The main character, the musician Karzi, is played by Li Wei (aka Xiao Wei), a self-described "rock promoter" who reappears as himself in *Sons*. His mother, Fu Derong, is seen briefly in *Beijing Bastards* where she scolds him for not getting out of bed before noon. In mixing improvisation, concert footage, and semi-scripted sequences the film follows a loose narrative thread. At the beginning, Karzi and his girlfriend Maomao bitterly argue about whether she should have an abortion. When Maomao disappears, Karzi vaguely attempts to find her as he drinks, parties, and engages in casual sex and brawls that eventually land him in jail.

Most commentators, even when praising the film's "gritty realism," agree that it quickly departs from reality. *Beijing Bastards* has been described as "a seemingly free-form portrait of rock-generation kids in the city . . . gliding from documentary to fiction to fantasy";[11] and as bent on exploring "the imaginary spaces, created and occupied by disaffected young male Bohemians in Beijing in the 1990s."[12] Zhang notes that his goal was to "reflect the state of mind of young people in contemporary China. A state of mind that can be described as the global outcome of a bastardized contemporary culture."[13] The film's locations—bleak tenement buildings with broken elevators, unheated rehearsal spaces and makeshift concert halls, neighborhood dives, construction sites, railroad tracks, cramped apartments, dark back alleys littered with parked bicycles, and large avenues clogged with traffic jams—are "urban generic"; that is, they contain no famous landmark, no exotic vista, no picturesque corner. The architecture is an unappetizing mixture of postindustrial Western functionality and third world squalor—as "bastardized" as the lives of the protagonists, which are "neither communist nor capitalist, neither eastern nor western."[14]

The vector through which *Beijing Bastards* first attracted Western attention was its depiction of a nascent rock scene in China. For Chinese authorities rock music was a "sign of unhealthy spiritual pollution from the West . . . that by its very nature [remained] incompatible with Chinese culture"; Deng Xiaoping himself condemned "capitalist living styles [for] corrupt[ing] the younger generation with the declining culture from the West."[15] On the other hand, because of the subversive, oppositional quality associated with rock music and the lifestyle it generates (sexual license; drug taking; "creative" fashions and hairstyles), Western spectators have been understandably titillated to discover the existence of an underground rock culture in Beijing. These new Chinese revolutionaries are more like figures from the West; they listen to the same tunes, wear the same sneakers, dance to the same rhythms while fighting the "old, repressive" order—in short, they are like rock lovers all over the world.

Chinese rock has to strike an uneasy balance between a desire to be simultaneously young, Chinese, and cool and the increasingly commodified production of transnational rock culture—a dilemma that Cui Jian poignantly, if somehow cryptically, articulates in the song he performs toward the end of *Beijing Bastards:*

> I'm walking straight into the wind, anger in my soul . . .
> I don't care how far I go. Dunno where this rage comes from
> but it inspires me. Don't wanna think about the past.
> Year after year the wind blows, changing form but never going away.
> I want to find the source of that rage, but I can only walk into the wind.

The bitterly cold, sweeping wind may be a metaphor for the brutal changes of Chinese history ("revolution after revolution . . . how much pain to how many people") or for the advent of the global market. Either way, it threatens to engulf the singer/walker, who, as a result, has no place to go and thus keeps on walking because it is the only thing left for him to do. Times are, indeed, changing, and globalization threatens the indigenous space of creativity, which, in turn, has to be renegotiated within rock culture itself. This negotiation between the local and the global forces the subject to exist, according to Ang Ien, in "a borderland, a crossroads . . . where the boundaries between inside and outside are blurred."[16] The bastardization of the space and that of the subject overlap, creating shifts in register between what is constructed as "the real" and what is experienced as "fantasy." A specific form of theatrical mise-en-scène is born out of such blurring of boundaries. Rock musicians are performance artists, and their concerts, as well as their lifestyle, are subjected to elaborate forms of hybrid/bastardized staging. The international ideology of rock consists of allowing both performers and audience to intermingle in a no-man's land (made more or less porous depending on the performers' fame and the bodyguards, promoters, and publicists who surround them), where shirts, guitars, and memorabilia are thrown to the public, who in turn send mementoes and so on back to the performers, and where singers descend into the audience while some fans are allowed backstage. The allure of Cui Jian's "provocative" lifestyle is due to the uncertainty of whether it is "real" or the result of unconscious posturing or a well-orchestrated publicity stunt. The "bastardization" of Chinese culture hinges on this hybrid form of theatricalization specific to the later stages of capitalism and best described through the concept of Debord's "society of spectacle,"[17] in which every act, public and private, is commodified.

Zhang Yuan directs on the set of *Beijing Bastards* (Courtesy of the Film Society of Lincoln Center)

It can be argued that, traditionally, Chinese society is structured around a different concept of "privacy" than that of the West. In China, the structure of domestic architecture, family life, and politics allows for people's most private moments to unfold under the always curious, sometimes caring, and sometimes judgmental gaze of neighbors, relatives, and local committees or party officials. From the onset, Zhang's films have paid keen attention to the way the urban space is structured by the curious/desiring gaze of the spectator, and how the subject is aware of this gaze. One of the most touching scenes in *Mama* involves the little boy, Dongdong, gazing intently at his mother while she is putting on makeup (lingering over the operation, as if for his benefit). This follows an interview with the real mother of a mentally challenged child, who describes the curious gazes of onlookers in the bus as a means of turning her son's mental illness into a "spectacle," a source of wonderment and maybe entertainment. What is different in *Beijing Bastards* and in the films that follow is that by stressing the blurring of boundaries between reality and fantasy, Zhang equates the process of (post-Debord) theatricalization with the situation of hybridization/bastardization in which he places his characters.

His mise-en-scène tends to focus not so much on the "reality" of urban space but on the desiring logic through which it is (re)organized. Space is a state of mind.

The mind that looms over the film *Sons* is that of the crazed, incompetent father, Li Maojie a ballet star who marries his dance partner, but then after retirement is reduced to a state of paranoid, mean, blundering alcoholism. Here, the "bastardization" of Xiao Wei and his brother Touzi is related to their filiation: If your father does not really act as a father, then what kind of son are you? The concept of bastardization emphasizes and questions the father-son relationship, taking the mother-son bond for granted.[18] What remains are the histrionics and wanderings of the man who would not be father. Although Li Maojie is no longer active as a dancer, he never stopped being a performer— even a ham. However, his "stage" has been reduced to modest proportions, as he displays his antics in the courtyard at the center of the apartment compound—an echo chamber for his stentorian voice, a glass bowl in which he is subjected to the neighbors' gaze. In addition, Zhang Yuan brings himself into the glass bowl: his voice introduces the film, describing the Li brothers as his downstairs neighbors, and later he has a brief cameo appearance as a patient in the mental hospital where the father is finally brought.

The topology of the compound awakens distant echoes of the classical Chinese architectural form of the *siheyuan*—a cluster of small buildings around a quadrangle courtyard—brought to the attention of the West in films such as Zhang Yimou's *Raise the Red Lantern* (Da hongdenglong gaogao gua, 1991). Originally a feudal/rural construction in northern China whose design follows feng shui and concepts of Confucian patriarchal hierarchy, siheyuan gradually became a staple feature of urban design in Beijing, where it could be seen in every *hutong* (small lane or alley) in the central part of the city. Shared by several families, the quadrangle courtyard is the center of social life, with children playing together, gossip being exchanged, old people playing mahjong, women helping each other with chores, and "private life" unfolding under a plurality of gazes. With the acute housing crisis in Beijing, however, traditional hutong and siheyuan are being demolished and replaced by high-rises. Still, old habits die hard, and many of the new constructions involve some form of shared courtyard or a common space between buildings.[19]

The apartment compound in *Sons* belongs to this hybrid/bastardized style of architecture (not traditional, yet not truly modern), which was used in

Beijing in the 1980s before the major "urban renewal" of the 1990s. Only four stories high, the structure has a gatekeeper controlling the entrance—so the Li brothers prefer to climb over the wall rather than face the gatekeeper when they come home late. The film starts with a medium-long shot of the entrance of the compound—a functional, ugly building of the type seen in any working-class or lower-middle-class urban area in the world. This opening shot is followed by shots of Xiao Wei looking at family pictures as well as close-ups of the photos themselves as frozen traces of a happiness long gone: snapshots of the smiling family, his mother and father dancing together or embracing. The introduction thus shifts from the "set as narrative" of an urban drama to the symbolic space where the family romance is projected (family pictures).[20] Zhang's voice-over presents the Li brothers' ambivalent position: "The Li brothers . . . asked me to make a film about their family. [They] wanted the family members to act as themselves in it . . . In this compound, their family was the coolest. Their father was the best dancer of his troupe, the mother was his best partner . . . People didn't like the father because he drank too much. But when he didn't drink, he was a very bright man, a genius of art. I asked them why they wanted to name the film *Sons*. They said all men are sons, but not all men are fathers."

While the brothers pay perfunctory respect to their father as they talk to Zhang, they do not express such feelings when addressing Li Maojie. Similarly, the family, together yelling at him when he becomes too obnoxious, forms a united front against a stranger who tries to warn them that drinking might impair his mental state. Such strategies of denial are common in alcoholic's families; more interesting is the refusal by the sons to identify not only with their actual father but also with the paternal function—that is, the symbolic father. At the end of the film, Zhang reports a conversation he had in the mental hospital with Li Maojie, who was lamenting the lack of love in his family: "They didn't give me much love either." This could be deciphered as: "They did not hear me (that's why I had to scream); they did not see me (that's why I had to drink)."

Abbas's concept of "reverse hallucination" ("an inability to read what is given to view") may be useful here to further develop the analysis.[21] The sons refuse to see their father for what he really is—an alcoholic with a heavy heredity (his own father was given to drinking, gambling, and philandering) and a hidden, tragic history. When Li Maojie tries to express his own sense of abjection, and his "reasons for drinking" to his elder son, the long-haired Touzi, the latter downplays the issue by saying with cool cynicism that "alcohol is a happy thing at your age." Having written the original story on which the film is based,[22] Touzi imbues it with the amnesia often characteristic of the "rock generation" ("Don't wanna think about the past") and makes no attempt to uncover the processes that had brought the parents to the point where they are now. Li Maojie is déjà disparu because his presence is the symptom of past traumas, the remnant of a recent history that the brothers' lust for "modernity" wishes to deny and eradicate. We learn that the Li parents were married in 1962. As classical ballet dancers, were they persecuted during the Cultural Revolution?[23] Touzi was born in 1963, but Xiao Wei came seven years later. What happened during these seven years? Were Li Maojie and Fu Derong sent into separate exile or jailed?

Li Maojie looks more like a bum than a retired ballet star, and his wife supports the family by teaching in a small dance school, where she is also asked to give workshops in places as far away as Kunming (the capital of Yunnan Province). Faced with such a "role model," Touzi and Xiao Wei are unemployed, hard-drinking, hard-partying slackers who can be found vomiting in the street, getting into fights, or mistreating their girlfriends. And, due to the housing shortage, they still live at home. About twenty-five minutes into the film, Li Maojie drags Fu Derong into the Residential Committee office and boisterously obtains a divorce. The next shot shows them back home, the woman cooking, the man eating, while he states in a self-satisfied tone: "The regulation says that before I remarry I am entitled to live here." Xiao Wei then arrives and gobbles his food without even saying hi, and the scene ends with a close-up of Fu Derong's hands doing the dishes. The sons remain unaware of their parent's divorce until much later, when, rummaging through their mother's things to steal money, they find the legal papers.

Cohabitation proves, in the long term, to be impossible; the ersatz siheyuan becomes the stage and the symbol of this impossibility. Touzi and Xiao Wei have to escape more than once to avoid conflicts with their father. Married or divorced, Li Maojie continues to scream out his wife's name throughout the compound—apparently to scold her, but the effect is more like a lovelorn suitor or a child looking for his mother. Is it the remnants of love, or is it travesty? His wife's name—once uttered in the heat of erotic passion, a name that shared top billing with his—is all that's left of his former splendor.

One evening, Xiao Wei finds his father sleeping on makeshift bedding he brought into the courtyard. Zhang shoots the scene with a mobile camera, going from medium shots of the son—who, in his frustration, walks in circles while trying to reason with his father—to circular panning shots around Li Maojie on the ground. The camera movement is slightly out of synch with Xiao Wei's steps, as if finding it impossible to keep up with him. Li Maojie complains that sleeping at home makes him nervous, and we learn that he's been trying to find a flat for himself, but none can be found.

It's nice sleeping here. Nice dreams . . .
Nice dreams? We have nightmares. Your sleeping out here makes us nervous in there.
Didn't you drive me out?
Who drove you out? The big bedroom is yours. We three sleep in the small one, all right? Haven't other people seen enough of our family business?

The family dysfunction comes to a climax when, coming home late one night, Touzi finds that his father has made Fu Derong drink until she is stuporous. Furious, he breaks a stool over Li Maojie's head. Zhang then cuts to an extreme close-up of the old man's bloody face; looking sad and suddenly sobered up, he says twice: "I thank you, my good boy." As Touzi takes him to the hospital, he goes from his drunken antics to a melancholy assessment of the situation: "A son who beats his old man. The gods will be mad. An impious son is the father's fault."

The symbolic killing of the father allows the sons, after a few moments of vague guilt, to take over. Despite his protests, Li Maojie is locked up in a mental hospital where he becomes what he was always afraid of being—invisible. At the end of the film his family no longer comes to visit him. Abbas connects the denial and rejection involved in déjà disparu with a certain version of the family romance—namely, "the fantasy that some children have that their parents are not their real parents."[24] This certainly applies to the brothers' relationship to Li Maojie, whom they perceive as an embarrassment to them, an obstacle to their "upward mobility" within "hip" Chinese society. By assaulting him, Touzi breaks the filial bonds. And indeed, after the father is put out of sight, the brothers leave their state of bohemian stasis and enter full speed into a concerted strategy of urban renewal. They become entrepreneurs, and open a trendy Thai restaurant in one of Beijing's most famous

Beijing Bastards: rehearsal space.

hangout areas, Sanlitun ("Bar Street"), near the embassies where *au courant* urbanites mix with foreigners.

THE THEATER OF URBAN MEMORIES

Zhang's découpage of specific urban spaces in Beijing in his first three narrative films created a subtle dialectic between the progress of the diegesis and the sense of entrapment experienced by the protagonists. Shot in collaboration with the video documentarist Duan Jinchuan—a master of verité techniques[25]—*The Square* opens up ironic vistas in these claustrophobic surroundings. As Zhang and his assistant, Wang Ping, were operating the 35mm camera, and Duan was recording the sound, the three-men team walked around Tiananmen Square filming ordinary scenes—tourists and school children attending the flag-raising ceremony, people flying kites, young mothers taking their children for an outing, policemen and soldiers patrolling the square, and a camera crew filming. The overall impression is one of a precarious equilibrium between the fluidity and unpredictability of the mass of bodies that flock onto the square and the rigidity and constraints of crowd control exerted by the authorities. Visually, the horizontal lines of the square suggest a vast yet enclosed, space, and at key moments the perspective is blocked by well-known icons such as the giant portrait of Mao Zedong with a lone policeman standing guard. The square is the stage of a well-orchestrated yet subdued mise-en-scène. The icons of power are exhibited for the benefit of the onlookers, who, in turn, become a "spectacle" for each other as well as for the police in a silent exchange of gazes. It is the sound that carries the restless, untamed, fluid character of the crowd, whose voices resonate, are amplified, and rebound as many invisible presences—whispering, laughter, children's voices, rambling conversations. While remaining on the bland surface of the present, the film suggests past tensions between the spontaneity of the crowd and the iron fist of power witnessed by the square on May 4, 1919, October 1, 1949, and June 4, 1989.

Zhang's specific zeitgeist is his ability to make use of such tensions—which, throughout his work, is also translated as a contradiction between what critics have called a "realistic rendering of urban spaces" and a more theatrical/operatic form of mise-en-scène. *East Palace, West Palace* (which perversely alludes to the gender-bending tropes, the melodramatic situations and the high-pitched melodies of Kunqu opera)[26] as well as *Jiang Jie* (a straightforward, subtly ironical staging of a classic revolutionary opera) exist as stage and film productions.[27]

The most efficient "music videos" of all time may have been the revolutionary or model operas (*yangbanxi*) of the 1960s—a source of entertainment for urban teenagers and, strangely enough, a distant origin for today's youth culture in China. "In the 1970's," one commentator remembers, "revolutionary Beijing operas were like our cartoons."[28] Barbara Mittler has underlined the links between the yangbanxi and contemporary forms of urban culture—from "urban novels" to pop music to the hybridization/Westernization (or "bastardization") of Chinese culture.[29] Zhang himself has acknowledged the emotional and sexual impact that *The Red Detachment of Women* (Hongse nianzi jun) had on him.[30]

Zhang's joyful interest in using Chinese opera as an inspiration subverts two tired clichés. The first is the depiction of the years of Cultural Revolution as uniformly bleak and cruel and their cultural output as trite, ridiculous, and forgettable—while for a generation of kids too young to be "sent down" the era is fondly remembered as exciting and fun.[31] The second cliché is the rupture between the classical operatic tradition and the yangbanxi, which, as challenged by recent scholarship such as Mittler's research, shows aesthetic and semantic elements of continuity between the two. Zhang's restaging of *Jiang Jie* stresses such a link. Created in 1964 for Mao Zedong by the Navy Art Troupe, the original opera recounted the life of a revolutionary heroine shot by the Kuomintang. For the title part, Zhang cast Zhang Yuoding, who is a fine example of the revival and continuation of classical opera in China. Trained in performing male roles, Zhang Yuoding is a member of the China Beijing Opera Theater, which was founded in 1955 and whose first president was the famous female-impersonator opera star, Mei Lanfang.[32]

Like fairy tales, yangbanxi repeatedly tells slightly different versions of the same story, with simple plots, broad characterizations, and Manichean oppositions between good and evil. Like MTV, yangbanxi have a "concert version" (ballet or opera) and a "film version," in which three different types of spaces (the original, "real" space of the diegesis; the abstract theatrical space; and finally its retranslation into an abstract cinematic space) are collapsed into one. For example, *The Red Detachment of Women* was originally a film directed in 1961 by Xie Jin that recounts the heroic deeds of women who joined the Red Army in Hainan Island. The original (exotic and bucolic) diegetic space then was transposed (through lighting, choreography, and decor) onto an abstract proscenium for the ballet version, collectively created by the National Dance Company.[33] In 1971, this theatrical space was then transposed back into a cinematic space by Pan Wenzhan and Fu Jie, who codirected the ballet film of the same name.[34] Then, a year later, Cheng Ying created an opera version. The stage performances and their filmic versions offered young, urban spectators a representation of the faraway countryside in which these legendary struggles had taken place—but reduced to a set of abstract relations (spatial, visual, rhythmical, ideological). Zhang grew up in a world in which a theatrical version of the countryside was brought to him—in a reversal of the classical Maoist paradigm: instead of having the city go to the country (in search of class consciousness and proletarian education) it was the country that came to the city, restructured and rearticulated by the tropes of sophisticated urban cultural production. As seen in *Sons*, but also in Zhang's own statements about realism, different memories from the Cultural Revolution are creating a sharp divide within the Chinese population—depending on whether these years were spent in the countryside or in the city—triggering generational conflicts between father and sons, as well as between the Fifth Generation and the Sixth.

All these influences coalesce in *East Palace, West Palace*—Zhang's subversive response to *The Red Detachment of Women*. Dealing with the intimate connection between eroticism and power, the film brings to light the sexual subtext foreclosed by Cultural Revolution productions (and the era's official puritanism). Following an operatic mode, it involves masks and performances, and, like the yangbanxi, takes "a true story" as its departure point. Zhang was inspired by a newspaper article about a new AIDS research institute that, because it lacked data on the lifestyle of homosexuals, asked the police to give detailed questionnaires to the gay men they arrested. He cowrote the screenplay with the novelist Wang Xiaobo, who, with his wife, Li Yinhe, had written the first sociological study on the male homosexual scene in China.[35]

Having thus anchored his film in "reality," Zhang again departs from it. The title becomes a vector allowing him to shift between several registers. In Beijing gay culture, "East Palace, West Palace" refers to two public bathrooms on either side of Jingshan Gongyuan Park, located just behind the Forbidden City,[36] that are used for cruising and brief sexual encounters. However, the nostalgic and imperial connotations of the phrase bring the viewer to another plane, onto which imaginary identifications can unfold. The film is in fact highly successful at suggesting the unreal quality of gay life in Beijing—a theme that has since been further explored by the nascent "queer underground film movement"—as in the digital video work of Cui Zi'en.[37] While the latter encapsulates his surrealist narratives in neorealistic representations of Beijing urban spaces, Zhang stages his parable on a sound stage. This change of strategy on the part of an auteur noted for his "gritty realism" has often been interpreted as a result of censorship because it would have been impossible to shoot such a film in real locations. Yet the Sixth Generation directors are quite adept at shooting "guerilla-style," and thus (without totally eliminating the role of censorship) it seems that Zhang's decision was motivated by a desire to make an opera film of sorts—one that might be titled "How Xiao Shi arrested A Lan and was seduced by his stories in the moonlight." In staging the encounter between a gay writer and a policeman, the film unfolds a series of role playing. At first Xiao Shi (Hu Jun)[38] is a straight cop embodying authority and A Lan is the captured delinquent. But then the tables turn as A Lan states his desire for being arrested, his love for the policeman, and his fetishistic attraction to the symbols of his macho authority (the black leather jacket, the handcuffs). Through flashbacks, A Lan recounts sexual encounters that become more and more sado-masochistic, in which the place of his sexual partner, at first empty, is filled by the shadow, the hands, and the back of a man who looks very much like Xiao Shi.

Formally, the film proceeds through the denaturalization of well-known, familiar urban spaces: pagodas, lakes, and pavilions in Jingshan Gongyuan Park, public restrooms, a police station, a classroom, a school hallway, and abandoned industrial buildings. A few documentary-style establishing shots appear and disappear as in a dream. The park is first shown through a series of brief shots accompanied by opera music mixed with the screeching of insects, and in so doing it is not the reconstruction of a "real" place but rather a stage on which policemen and gay men play cops and robbers. Then the "supporting cast" disappears, and the space in which the interaction of the main protagonists is choreographed gradually takes on a surreal quality.[39]

This shift from reality only increases as A Lan's stories unfold in flashbacks. Childhood memories as recounted through partial, fragmented images: a staircase in the brick building of a factory housing, a close-up of the mother's hands at her sewing machine, and so on. When he starts retelling his sexual adventures, a discrepancy is introduced between the soundtrack and the image. When A Lan describes, in lavish detail, the plush house of a rich lover, we are shown a sordid, dirty, semiabandoned bathroom. Retroactively, this casts a doubt on the rest of the "story." Are these two men really in a police station? Aren't they playing erotic games at home? A Lan's narration is fractured, as he gradually interweaves elements of a love story between a female thief and the guard who captures her. At key moments, opera singers in full makeup perform mysterious, elliptical scenes, like ghosts coming out of the shrubbery.

By locating the diegesis in one of the most famous and most identifiable places in Beijing, Zhang, rather than trying to eradicate the specific "Chinese" aspects of the metropolis attempts instead to stress their local color. Jingshan Gongyuan Park is a place inhabited by history (the last Ming emperor is rumored to have committed suicide there) yet is reworked to suit the needs of a nascent gay counterculture. Zhang's strategy aims at embedding homosexuality in Chinese history, while the official party line is that it is a Western import, as un-Chinese as rock and roll.[40] *East Palace, West Palace* points at the transhistorical connections between the tradition of female impersonation by male singers in Chinese opera; the repressed eroticism of the relationship between citizen and the state as it reached an apex during the Cultural Revolution; and the new gay underground. And it is the complex contemporary state of Chinese architecture in which centuries-old buildings coexist with modern, Western-inspired constructions that provides the setting for these connections.

In the film, these architectural spaces only exist through imaginary representations because the link with the past is tenuous and marked by the unavoidable distortion of nostalgia—a feeling that has become "a pulse of the not inelegant urban noise," an integral component of urban culture.[41] Moreover, the "new" Chinese city does not really exist any more than does a full-blown Chinese gay subculture. Both are willed by the concerned subjects in their desire for modernity—both are imaginary projections. The idea of the modern city is based on the desire to repress a certain past (the difficult, unglamorous years of socialism in which peasants and workers were the "model classes") while reconnecting a different version of it (imperial splendor and/or the bustling and slightly corrupt modernity of urban centers in the Republican era). Thus, urban renewal follows contradictory principles of rupture and continuity. China's adoption of transnational urban architecture eventually reveals a "return of old spatial concepts" marked by a vision of the world in which China was at the center. As Anthony King and Abidin Kusno observe, "The city that China desires as a model is not really London, New York or Tokyo . . . but rather Singapore. . . . Chinese post-modernity is constituted . . . as . . . a synthesis of different claims, from Mao's ideas of 'socialism with national style' to the imperial ethics of Confucianism a la Singapore and Western concepts of growth."[42] Imaginary identifications with the West reveal a desire to reoccupy a central position in East Asia.

WANDERING FROM THE AMBIGUOUS MARGINS TO THE LOST CENTER

This desire to reoccupy the center may give us the key to decipher Zhang's decision to get back into the fold of officially sanctioned productions.[43] Working illegally meant being entirely dependent on the Western gaze—that is, being in a marginalized, decentered position. Making films in China for Chinese spectators is a way of repositioning oneself at the center. However, the sidelong glance still has a strategic value. As making officially sanctioned productions means being subjected to a two-tier censorship system, a direct approach to reality is even more problematic, and ironical distance, metaphors, and double entendre become all the more necessary.

In 1999, Zhang Yuan submitted two productions to the Film Bureau. The first, *Crazy English*, is a fascinating documentary about the unorthodox method designed by a businessman, Li Yang, to teach English, in which he gathers masses of people in public spaces and makes them scream sentences from the top of their lungs. On the one hand, the students want to get "in sync" with the modern world; on the other hand they strive to resolve age-old Chinese issues (lack of self-confidence, shyness, fear of failing one's parents/ancestors/country, suspicion of foreigners). The bastardized Chinese subject here exists simultaneously on two planes—regional and transnational. Li's genius is to provide a highly ritualized and theatrical outlet to the discomfort caused by this ontological dislocation.

The second project, the narrative feature *Seventeen Years*, is roughly divided into three parts.[44] It starts with the portrayal of yet another dysfunctional family—living in a traditional neighborhood of winding, narrow hutongs. Yu Zhenggao and his wife Tao Airong, each with a teenage daughter from a previous marriage, keep quarrelling about trifles. The daughters—Yu Xiaoqin, a studious, scheming, hypocritical beauty, and Tao Lan (Liu Lin),[45] a vivacious, devil-may-care sixteen year old—can't stand each other and compete for their parents' attention. The film courses through the events of a missing five-yuan note, a family feud, sibling rivalry, and then tragedy when Tao Lan accidentally kills Xiaoqin. In showing the architecture of the hutong, Zhang, liberated from the constraints of guerilla shoot-and-run style, experiments with sweeping camera movements, starting with a birds-eye view over the grid of back alleys, and then descending to show Yu Zhenggao carrying the body of his daughter back home, the entire neighborhood following him with a mixture of curiosity, sympathy, and respect. In the safety of the *East Palace, West Palace* sound stage, Zhang had already used such camera movements in his establishing shots. Unlike his earlier style, which demonstrated proximity with his subject, this more aestheticized mode of shooting suggests a certain distance—as if looking at something already lost.

When, seventeen years later, Tao Lan is granted her first furlough to spend the New Year holiday with her family, the year is 1998. By implication we infer that the prologue must have taken place in 1981—the year that Jiang Qing

(Mao's wife) was sentenced to death, the Cultural Revolution ended, and the Deng Xiaoping reform era was in full bloom. Severely disturbed from 1968 to the mid-1970s, regular schooling had in the late 1970s resumed and most of the universities had reopened.[46] However, the lines that Xiaoqin had uttered have a strange anachronistic ring. She wants to "go to college and get out of here, go as far as possible." Such language is more likely to come from a hip teenager of the 1990s than from a (female) hutong dweller of the early 1980s. The melodramatic tension—will Yu Zhenggao be able to forgive Tao Lan and welcome her home?—involves the viewer in a suspense that sweeps away issues of historical accuracy. In fact, the different parts of the story may have to be read as symbolically simultaneous (a feeling of simultaneity that is enhanced by the total elision of the seventeen years spent by Tao Lan in jail).[47] Abstraction is used to convey an essential dimension in contemporary Chinese experience: the coexistence of several types of urban spaces that belong to different periods of time—like collage in postmodern architecture. As a dislocated subject, Tao Lan navigates between several moments of history and is anchored in none.

The second part of the film is a road movie of sorts—one that uses the means of transportation available to the ordinary Chinese subject: bus, foot, pedicab. From the Tianjin prison to the old neighborhood of He'an (now transformed into a pile of rubble) to the new urban zone of Chengguan where her parents have been relocated,[48] Tao Lan, helped and sweetly nudged along by a young female warden, Chen Jie, floats in spaces she can't recognize—stopping here in a police station, there at a small dumpling stand. As Zhang avoids landmarks and focuses on touches of uniform pan-Asian modernization—large avenues, busy intersections, advertising billboards, smokestacks, makeshift shelters, deserted streets on the outskirts, gray housing projects—the spectator is as disoriented as the protagonist.[49]

In the third part of the film, Zhang returns to the enclosed space of melodrama and stifling family romance, the nuclear-family apartment. Tao Lan's parents now live in a modern but cold building, with sharp angles, straight walls painted off-white, Western-style furniture, and running hot and cold water—but the sense of entrapment remains. Family love is as much a prison as an actual jail. Being forgiven by Yu Zhenggao, Tao Lan will be able to live at "home" after completing her sentence, but it is as if another door had been shut—which may explain why, after leaving alone in the dark, the young warden Cheng Jie cries.[50] The disappearance of tradition is not so much the loosening of family bonds but rather the loss of a community (old urban neighborhoods; extended families with several generations living under the same roof) that helped to collectively manage the pressure caused by these bonds. Nuclear families are now isolated, stuck together in cramped spaces and at each other's throat. Urban families may be, in essence, dysfunctional.

EPILOGUE: THE WOMAN IN THE CITY

I Love You—an adaptation of Wang Shuo's novel *Get a Kick and Die*—explores the split caused within the Chinese subject by urban modernization at the same time that it makes a giant leap in the depiction of female desire. The young protagonists are "bastardized" subjects treading uneasily between the claustrophobic, cramped quarters of the domestic sphere and the open, unpredictable spaces of the modern city. Both are dangerous. In the secret of their home, years ago, Xiaoju's father killed her mother; in rooms lacking privacy, hurried sex leads to unwanted pregnancy; physical proximity can be mistaken for emotional closeness and passionate declarations of love are whispered in the middle of the night; the cohabitation of a newly married couple in a nurse's dormitory apartment turns into a living hell. When they go outdoors, Xiaoju and her peers are ill prepared to deal with the changing city. No matter how hard they try to get the "user's manual" for urban life (at the beginning of the film we see them taking driving lessons), they realize that they "don't belong." This leads them to behave like smugglers, for which they are tragically caught. Xiaoju, her first fiancé, and a friend decide to sneak into a swimming pool at night. In the dark the young man takes a dive—and crashes onto the concrete floor. In their naiveté, the intruders had not expected that the swimming pool might be in the process of being cleaned.

As a quintessential Zhang's character, Xiaoju (Xu Jinglei) inhabits a space she does not control or understand but still tries to remold according to her fears and desires. Xu Jinglei had started her career with a brief part in *Beijing Bastards*. Ten years later, she comes back with a vengeance as the desiring subject—she becomes the predator (as A Lan was in *East Palace, West Palace*) when she "takes" Yi and tries to turn him into the object of her fantasy. In one of the most disturbing scenes of Zhang's cinema, she repeats to him, word for word, the seductive lines that had "worked" on her first fiancé. Out-

The depiction of female desire in *I Love You*. (Courtesy of Zhang Yuan)

doors, Xiaoju is a lost child; indoors, in a space theatricalized by the antics of her hysteria, she performs a play whose lines she has apparently written, and in which she has given herself the best and most difficult role—that of the madwoman.

Not over-educated but bright, not sophisticated but emotionally complex, prone to irrational feats of anger and instances of deep generosity, Xiaoju is Tao Lan's little sister, a product of China's new urban environment. Like Tao Lan she lives a double, hybrid life in an imaginary city that does not yet exist—and in a very old city that is already no longer. However, the film that *I Love*

You most resembles is not *Seventeen Years* but *Sons*. Both films ride a fine line between script and improvisation, between theatricality and realism. In the domestic scenes between Yi and Xiaoju, which are filmed in tight close-ups to heighten the sense of claustrophobia, Zhang wanted to document the relationship between the two actors. This was done not because they were emotionally or sexually involved (they were not), but rather simply to show how a body reacts to another body in given situations and in a certain kind of space. Thus Zhang gives the actors a certain amount of freedom, from which emerges a raw, moving quality in their performances.

However, this freedom was confined by the parameters of the original screenplay, written in collaboration by Wang Shuo, Zhang Yuan and Xia Wei—not entirely unlike the way Li Maojie, while "improvising" his own lines, was actually following a script. *Sons* was indeed based on Li's life—while, similarly, the screenplay of *I Love You* is a fictional transposition of Xu Jinglei's personality. Xu is married to Wang Shuo, and the original novel that inspired the film is a thinly disguised transposition of the couple's passionate and "crazy" relationship—the way that Elia Kazan's novel *The Arrangement* (which he turned into a film in 1969) was inspired by his relationship to his wife, the actress Barbara Loden. Xu was luckier than Loden—while the latter lost the role to Faye Dunaway, the former was cast to play "herself" in *I Love You*.[51]

The original question—who wrote the lines uttered by Xiaoju in moments of madness or passion?—is now posed with greater urgency, for Wang Shuo occupies a key position in the consciousness of the Urban Generation of filmmakers. Like Zhang and Cui Jian, Wang Shuo became famous by offering an alternative, oppositional vision of China, taking into account the collapse of the socialist master narrative, the blasé, amoral, and self-destructive behavior of many urban youths and the disintegration of the traditional texture of society. Wang Shuo's protagonists float from city to city or between tenements and jails, toy with delinquency, prostitution, and even murder, and actively seek sex and lose money. His hooligan or punk literature (*pizi wenxue*) quickly captured the attention of filmmakers such as Huang Jianxin, Mi Jiashan, or Jiang Wen.[52] It is, however, a male-centered fiction, in which women function as troublemakers or enigmas.

With the stunning exception of *Mama*, the urban spaces depicted by Zhang in the first part of his oeuvre are male territories. The city is a place where women disappear, like Maomao; where they are dispensable commodities, like Li Wei or Li Touzi's girlfriends; or where they are marginalized in the diegesis, like Fu Derong. In *Seventeen Years* he attempts to construct a narrative driven by female desire and anxieties and to present the urban geography through the eyes of a woman—yet the vanishing point of her journey remained the gaze of the father. In an intriguing, short documentary partially shot in digital video, *Miss Jin Xing* (2000),[53] Zhang shows the modern Chinese city through the point of view and romantic fantasies of a male-to-female post-op transsexual, who is a former Red Army ballet dancer. While the subject, a noted choreographer and countercultural star, is not exactly a woman, Zhang is clearly fascinated by the volatile, unsteady dialectic between femininity and the urban space. Similarly, in a more recent film that marks an interesting, yet problematic, development in his oeuvre, *Green Tea* (Lü Cha, 2003), the female protagonist (played by the pop idol Zhao Wei) is involved in a schizoid masquerade because she plays two different characters—a stuck-up graduate student and a pianist-cum-high-class hooker. Yet it is her male suitor (Jiang Wen) who ends up being lost in the meanders of her imaginary—and it is she who takes him "places," ranging from the stark designer's decor of the South Silk Road Restaurant to the plush carpets of the Grand Hotel Hyatt.

Xiaoju is more grounded in everyday life than is the heroine of *Green Tea*, but in all of his films Zhang seems to perceive the dialectic between urban development and subjective fantasies as more problematic for women than for men. On the one hand, the enigma of femininity and the intricacies of the city function as a mirror for each other: they are ungraspable, multifaceted, and forever changing. On the other hand, the city is a dangerous, sometimes forbidden place for women. They can't go walking in the wind with anger in their heart, like their male counterparts. As Giuliana Bruno remarks, "The full expansion of women's territorial horizons is a journey in slow motion,"[54] and it is closely related to urban development. City living represents for women a greater freedom of movement and lifestyle but also the increased possibility of getting lost. The dangerous theatricality that Zhang attributes to some of his heroines is a way of "acting out" their sense of loss. They have lost their grounding in domestic spaces that have become "too small" for them, yet they are still "visitors" in urban spaces whose modus operandi escapes them. Zhang is particularly astute in describing the precarious, ambiguous relationship of these women to their "home." Maomao leaves the apartment she shared with Karzi; Fu Derong has to vacate the best part of her apartment for the benefit of her drunken exhusband; Tao Lan can't wait to leave home but, once released from prison, has no other place to go; and Xiaoju's housing depends on her job, thus limiting her privacy and the free run of her domestic theatrical performances.[55]

As he has consistently staged the relationship between space and desire, it is not surprising that Zhang's recent work addresses the issue of the gendered gaze and constructs femininity as a model for the new kind of hybridity that defines the "bastardized" Chinese subject. The content and mode of production of Sixth Generation films have become increasingly more gender-specific, in ways that may be disturbing. In spite of their difficulties with censorship, Fifth Generation films were supported by a system of education and production that, give or take, was upholding the socialist belief of equality between the genders; so there has been outstanding Fifth Generation female directors who have addressed issues of contemporary urban development (Ning Ying, Li Shaohong, or Peng Xiaolian). On the contrary, Sixth Generation films must rely on the market and, more often than not, on the "old-boys" network to find sources of financing. As a result, there is a limited number of women in the director's chair: Emily Tang's *Conjugation* (Dongci bianwei) and Li Yu's *Fish and Elephant* (Yu he daxiang) were only completed in 2001. Equally disturbing is the proliferation of male-directed Sixth Generation films that reinsert the prostitute (or its many incarnations, from karaoke hostess to hairdresser)[56] at the center of the urban landscape, such as Wang Xiaoshuai's *So Close to Paradise* (Yuenan guniang, 1998); Jia Zhangke's *Xiao Wu* (1998); Tang Danian's *City Paradise;* Zhao Jisong/He Jianjun's *Scenery* (Feng jing, 1999); Wang Chao's *The Orphan of Anyang* (Anyang de guer, 2001); and Zhu Wen's *Seafood*. A woman who walks by herself in the city often risks being identified as a "streetwalker."[57] From a male perspective, then, urban development is often equated with the rise of prostitution—an alluring cliché that plays a capital role in the fictional or pictorial representations of the city.

With the exception of *Green Tea* (in which, however, prostitution is presented as the schizoid fantasy of the female graduate student rather than as reality), Zhang has stayed away from casting his female protagonists as whores—which is an index of the oppositional and complex modernity of his work. His city women are lost but not fallen, hard working but not selling their bodies, sometimes out of control but always with a certain direction in their mind. They may be mistaken about their object of desire, but they know what they want, and will do anything to get it. As cities are the recipients of the collective fantasies of their inhabitants, they contribute, in dialectic contradiction with the male protagonists, to shape the outlines of the new urban landscapes in China.

NOTES

1. Tony Rayns, catalogue for the Vancouver International Film Festival (Vancouver: Vancouver International Film Festival, 1992), 26. The FIPRESCI Prize is the award of the Fédération Internationale de la Presse Cinématographique (International Federation of Film Critics). Produced with private money, the film was not, however, illegal—unlike all of Zhang's films until 1999. Zhang Yuan sold it (or, more appropriately "gave" the rights to it) to the Xi'an Film Studio so that he could show it in China. See also Chris Berry, "Zhang Yuan: Thriving in the Face of Adversity," *Cinemaya* 32 (1996): 41.

2. The screenplay of the fictional part was written by the actress Qin Yan, who had a handicapped child in her family.

3. Rayns, Vancouver International Film Festival catalogue, 26.

4. Ackbar Abbas, *Hong Kong: Culture and the Politics of Disappearance* (Minneapolis: University of Minnesota Press, 1997), 25.

5. Ibid., 26.

6. One of the hard-rock bands, created in 1988, was called "Tang Dynasty." See Jeroen de Kloet, " 'Let Him Fucking See the Green Smoke Beneath My Groin': The Mythology of Chinese Rock," in *Post Modernism and China*, ed. Arif Dirlik and Xudong Zhang (Durham, N.C.: Duke University Press, 2000), 256.

7. Interview with Zhang Yuan, catalogue of the seventeenth Hong Kong International Film Festival (Hong Kong: Urban Council, 1993), 67 (italics added).

8. Berry, "Zhang Yuan," 42.

9. The slogan "mainstream melody" [*shehui zhuyi zhuxuanlü*] was coined during the 1995 Changsha (Hunan) conference to urge filmmakers to celebrate the courageous struggles of workers, peasants, soldiers, and intellectuals in the construction of socialism.

10. The credits list three screenwriters: Zhang Yuan, Cui Jian, and Tang Danian. A 1989 graduate of the Beijing Film Academy, Tang penned *Good Morning Beijing* (Beijing nizao, 1990), directed by Fourth Generation filmmaker Zhang Nuanxin, which at the time was considered a minor breakthrough on the festival circuit. Tang Danian also wrote and directed two feature films, *Jade* (Yu, 1998) and *City Paradise* (Dushi tiantang, 2000), and collaborated on the screenplay of Wang Xiaoshuai's *Beijing Bicycle* (Shiqi sui de danche, 2000).

11. Rayns, Vancouver International Film Festival catalogue, 33.

12. Stephanie Hemelrik Donald, *Public Secret, Public Spaces—Cinema and Civility in China* (Lanham, Md.: Rowman and Littlefield, 2000), 107.

13. Zhang Yuan, catalogue for the Locarno International Film Festival (Locarno: Locarno International Film Festival), 1993, 43.

14. Rayns, Vancouver International Film Festival catalogue, 26.

15. De Kloet, " 'Let Him Fucking See the Green Smoke Beneath My Groin,' " 241–42. Cinema was also suspected of being a foreign import and "not being Chinese enough," at least in its cosmopolitan Shanghai version, and that the efforts of the post-1949 government in that domain were to bring about a "sinification" of Chinese cinema. See Paul Clark, *Chinese Cinema: Culture and Politics since 1949* (Cambridge: Cambridge University Press, 1987). As I discuss below, homosexuality is still considered to be a form of spiritual pollution from the West.

16. Ang Ien, "Doing Cultural Studies at the Crossroads: Local/Global Negotiations," *European Journal of Cultural Studies* 1, no. 1 (1998): 24, quoted in De Kloet, " 'Let Him Fucking See the Green Smoke Beneath My Groin,' " 271.

17. See Guy Debord, *La société du spectacle* (Paris: Buchet-Chastel, 1967), translated as *The Society of the Spectacle* by Donald Nicholson-Smith (New York: Zone Books, 1994).

18. This may be why in both *Beijing Bastards* and *Sons* the role of the woman as mother is foreclosed, while the girlfriend/sex object is a simple commodity. See Donald, *Public Secret, Public Spaces,* 106–16.

19. Even high-rise housing projects involve some kind of common space—as is humorously shown by Zhang Yimou in a scene of *Keep Cool* (You hua haohao shuo, 1997) when the main protagonist hires a thug to shout, through a megaphone, "I love you!" to his runaway girlfriend from the plaza below her apartment.

20. The term "set as narrative" here is quoted from Charles Affron and Mirella Jona Affron's *Sets in Motion: Art Direction and Film Narrative* (New Brunswick, N.J.: Rutgers University Press, 1995), where L. C. Ehrlich defines "set as narrative (as opposed to the set an embellishment, artifice or mere punctuation)" as creating a place "in which what happens . . . cannot be separated from where it happens" (9).

21. Abbas, *Hong Kong,* 26.

22. The screenplay was cowritten by Li Ji (Touzi's official name) and Ning Dai (see Abbas, *Hong Kong,* 25–26).

23. The Cultural Revolution lasted from 1966 to 1976, but the ban by Jiang Qing's (Mao's wife) on classical ballet and theater started as early as 1963.

24. Abbas, *Hong Kong,* 25

25. As one of the major voices of the Beijing-based "New Documentary Movement," Duan Jinchuan has directed video documentaries such as *Highland Barley* (Qingke, 1986), *No. 16 Barkhor Street South* (Bakuo nanjie shiliuhao, 1996), and *The Secret of My Success* (Linqi da shetou, 2002).

26. Founded before the Ming dynasty (1368–1644) in South China, Kunqu opera

precedes Beijing opera and is considered softer, and more refined and poetic—favoring romantic stories over military or acrobatic feats. Suppressed during the Cultural Revolution, Kunqu is now enjoying a revival.

27. *East Palace, West Palace* was performed in Brussels, Rio de Janeiro, and Paris; *Jiang Jie* was presented as part of the Theater der Welt in Germany.

28. Yang Ruichun/Zhu Lin, "Revolution Is Also Rock," *Beijing Today,* April 5, 2002, online at www.ynet.com/bjtoday/047/47%5ED0405E1208.htm.

29. Barbara Mittler, "Cultural Revolution Model Works and the Politics of Modernization in China, an Analysis of *Taking Tiger Mountain by Strategy,*" *The World of Music* 45, no. 2 (2003): 58–81.

30. "The color red (dominant in these operas) had a highly charged sexual meaning for me." Author's interview with Zhang Yuan, quoted in B. Reynaud, *Nouvelles Chines, Nouveaux Cinémas* (Paris: Cahiers du cinéma, 1999), 73. Other excerpts of this interview also appear in Reynaud, "Gay Overtures: Zhang Yuan's *East Palace, West Palace,*" *Cinemaya* 36 (1997): 31–33.

31. For alternative accounts of growing up a mischievous kid during the Cultural Revolution, see Wang Xiao-Yen's *The Monkey Kid* (Hou Sanr, 1995) and, above all, Jiang Wen's *In The Heat of the Sun* (Yanguang canlan de rizi, 1994), which was inspired by Wang Shuo's novel *Ferocious Animals.* See also Xueping Zhong, Wang Zheng, and Bai Di, eds., *Some of Us: Chinese Women Growing Up in the Mao Era* (New Brunswick, N.J.: Rutgers University Press), 2001.

32. On Mei Lanfang (1894–1961), see Wu Zuguang, Huang Zuolin, and Mei Shaowu, *Peking Opera and Mei Lanfang* (Beijing: New World Press), 1984; see also Chen Mei-juin's documentary *The Worlds of Mei Lanfang* (2000). In *Jiang Jie,* Zhang creates another link with the past by casting in a supporting role the great female singer Wang Jinhua, who had graced such classical operas as *Women Generals of the Yang Family* (Yangmen nüjiang), which was brought to the silver screen by Cui Wei and Chen Huai'ai (Chen Kaige's father) in 1960.

33. The ballet version was presented in a festival of revolutionary ballets in Shanghai in 1965.

34. On the different film versions of *The Red Detachment of Women,* see Clark, *Chinese Cinema,* 102–3, 105, 128, 142. On the ballet film, see "Le ballet chinois suit un brillant développement," in *Cahiers du cinéma,* no. 236–237 (1972): 76–81.

35. This book, titled *Their World,* was published in Hong Kong but not in the People's Republic. Born in 1952 in Beijing, Wang Xiaobo was "sent down" to Yunnan during the Cultural Revolution, after which he worked as a teacher and a factory worker before entering People's University in 1978. He studied in the United States between 1984 and 1988. His most famous book, *The Golden Age* (Huangjin shidai [Beijing: Huaxia Chubanshe, 1994]; published in French as *L'âge d'or* [Versailles: Éd. du Sorgho, 2001]) was banned because of its controversial descriptions of, in the words of Dai Jinhua, "loyalty and betrayal . . . chastity and promiscuity" during the Cultural Revolution ("Imagined Nostalgia," 214). Wang Xiaobo became a cult figure in both China and Taiwan. He died of a heart attack in 1997 at the age of forty-five.

36. *Behind the Forbidden City* was the original English title of the film.

37. As a professor at the Beijing Film Academy and a noted gay activist, Cui Zi'en wrote the screenplay of (and starred in) Liu Bingjiang's *Men Men Women Women* (Nan nan nü nü, 1999). In 2001, he started directing low-budget experimental digital video features such as *Enter the Clowns* (Choujue Dengchang, 2001), all of which have enjoyed an international cult following. In 2001, he organized the first Gay and Lesbian Film Festival in Beijing, which was closed by the authorities after the first weekend. This was the first public screening of *East Palace, West Palace* in China.

38. Hu Jun reappeared to play the older lover in Stanley Kwan's *Lan Yu* (2001), which depicts a homosexual relationship in Beijing.

39. As Zinaid Meeran wittily puts it, in a paper written for my graduate seminar on Chinese cinema at the University of California in Los Angles, "The police station, for example, has the lavish curlicue ironwork, plush carpets, drapes, ornate paper screens and full-length mirrors of a concubine's chamber or the boudoir of a favored wife."

40. Among the growing literature devoted to Chinese homosexuality, the following texts are notable: Chris Berry, "Sexual DisOrientations: Homosexual Rights, East Asian Films and Post-Modern Post-Nationalism," in *In Pursuit of Contemporary East Asian Culture*, ed. X. Tang and S. Snyder (Boulder: Westview Press, 1996, 157–82); Bret Hinsch, *Passion of the Cut Sleeve: The Male Homosexual Tradition in China* (Berkeley: University of California Press, 1990); and Gerard Sullivan and Peter A. Jackson, eds., *Gay and Lesbian Asia: Culture, Identity, Community* (Binghamton, N.Y.: Harrington Park Press 2001).

41. Dai Jinhua, "Imagined Nostalgia," 206.

42. Anthony D. King and Abidin Kusno, "On Be(j)ing in the World: 'Postmodernism,' 'Globalization,' and the Making of Transnational Space in China," in *Postmodernism and China*, ed. Arif Dirlik and Xudong Zhang (Durham: Duke University Press, 2000), 59, 60, 62.

43. "I hope I can end this kind of life which consists in making a film in China and then going to Germany, France, America etc. . . . to show it. I want to have the chance to show my films in my own country, where I live." Zhang Yuan, interviewed in Solveig Klassen and Katharina Schneider Ross's documentary *My Camera Does Not Lie* (Meine Kamera lügt nicht, 2003).

44. The film was cowritten by Zhu Wen, Yu Hua, and Zhang's wife, Ning Dai. A talented writer, Zhu is the author of the story that inspired Zhang Ming's *Rainclouds over Wushan* (Wushan Yunyu, 1995)—the plot of which revolves around whether or not a middle-aged hotel receptionist was raped by a shy lighthouse keeper or if the sex was consensual. Since 2001, Zhu himself has turned to directing with *Seafood* (Haixian, 2001) and *South of the Clouds* (Yun de nanfang, 2004).

45. Lin Liu wrote the music for another urban film, Wang Xiaoshuai's *So Close to Paradise* (Yuenan guniang, 1998).

46. In 1968 schools and universities were closed, and while some reopened in the early 1970s they were under control of the People's Liberation Army. The entrance exams for college were replaced by a system wherein leaders of work units were to recommend hard-working individuals with perfect political credentials.

47. The phrase "seventeen years" also has a hidden meaning referring to the years between the founding of the People's Republic (1949) and the official launch of the Cultural Revolution (1966).

48. Zhang had demonstrated his interest in issues of urban displacement a year before, when he directed a TV documentary titled *Relocation and Dislocation* (Dingzi hu, 1998).

49. Reviews and program notes locate the diegesis in "a northern Chinese city"— meaning either Beijing or Tianjin. In fact, the film was shot in Beijing, with the exception of the prison scenes, for which Zhang was granted access (for the first time in Chinese cinema) to a real women's prison in Tianjin.

50. Another, undeveloped subtext in *Seventeen Years* is that of the repression of female sexuality; because the film was an "approved" production it had to abide by censorship rules, which therefore forecloses the sexual liberation that Cheng Jie may have represented for Tao Lan. As Zhang notes: "I had hoped that the two women would fall in love . . . But I stopped dreaming and thought . . . that I had to hand out the script to the censorship bureau and that if I wanted the film to be screened in China there was no way to make them love each other" (Zhang Yuan's speech at the first Gay and Lesbian Film Festival in Beijing, recorded in Klassen and Ross, *My Camera Does Not Lie*). Yet, Zhang does insert subtle signs alluding to this possibility. The rule "homosexuality is forbidden" is uttered by an inmate over a very alluring medium shot of Cheng Jie. The two women bond when the warden helps Tao Lan pick up a lipstick she had dropped on the floor.

51. The similarity does not stop here. Both Loden and Xu decided to write, produce, and direct their own films, in which they also starred. Barbara Loden's *Wanda* (1970—a cult film in some circles, especially in Europe) and Xu Jinglei's *My Father and I* (Wo he baba, 2002) and *Letter from an Unknown Woman* (Yige mosheng nüren de laixin, 2004) are interesting, original, and powerful character studies of women who are both rebellious and lost.

52. The Fifth Generation director Huang Jianxin was the first to adapt a novel by Wang Shuo (*Emerging from the Sea*) with his epoch-making *Samsara/Transmigration* (Lunhui, 1988). That same year, Mi Jiashan directed the smart urban comedy *The Trouble-Shooters* (Wan zhu, 1988) from a script cowritten with Wang Shuo. Jiang Wen's *In the Heat of the Sun* was also an adaptation of one of Wang's

novels. In 1997, Wang Shuo directed *Papa*, based on his novel of the same title. The film was banned but resurfaced briefly to win the Golden Leopard award at the Locarno International Film Festival in 2000. A few of Wang's novels are available in translation, including *Playing for Thrills* (New York: Penguin Books, 1998), *Please Don't Call Me Human* (New York: Hyperion, 2000), *Feu et glace* (Arles: Editions Philippe Picquier, 1995), and *Je suis ton papa* (Paris: Flammarion, 1997).

53. Commissioned by the 2000 Chonju Film Festival in South Korea as part of an omnibus film composed of three digital shorts, the film includes 16mm footage that Zhang Yuan and some of his friends shot during Jin Xing's sex change operation. This footage is montaged with digital scenes in which the new Jin Xing, now a woman, restages her life.

54. Giuliana Bruno, *Streetwalking on a Ruined Map: Cultural Theory and the City Films of Elvira Notari* (Princeton, N.J.: Princeton University Press, 1993), 51.

55. One morning Yi wakes up to find out that Xiaoju has tied him up and is threatening him with a knife. At that moment, another nurse knocks at the door, saying that Xiaoju's services are urgently required. Xiaoju has to go, leaving the situation unresolved (for her it was "a game"), which eventually causes the final break-up of the couple.

56. As massages are offered to customers who want a haircut, hair salons often have a back room in which sexual services also are offered. Many hairdressers are unskilled young peasant women who are considered "not pretty enough" to work as karaoke hostesses.

57. See Anne Friedberg, *Window Shopping: Cinema and the Postmodern* (Berkeley: University of California Press, 1993), esp. 32–38; Susan Buck-Morss, "The Flaneur, the Sandwichman, and the Whore: The Politics of Loitering," *New German Critique* 39 (fall 1986): 99–140; and Bruno, *Streetwalking on a Ruined Map*.

mr. zhao on and off the screen

Male Desire and Its Discontent

XUEPING ZHONG

I n 1998 I watched *Zhao Xiansheng* (*Mr. Zhao*) on video in a smoke-filled meeting room at a publishing company in Shanghai. I was instantly struck by how different in style and content *Mr. Zhao* was from any recent Chinese films I had seen.[1] Like most of the new and independent urban films made in China, *Mr. Zhao* has not been formally released either in China or in the rest of the world, nor has it been possible for the general public to watch it on the big screen.[2] The lack of these films' public release made my accidental encounter with *Mr. Zhao* a rather pleasant surprise. What I did not realize at the time, of course, was that this would be my first encounter (albeit belated) with what is now known as the Urban Generation of filmmakers whose work is characterized by a low-budget, documentary-like quality and by their concern, for the most part, with displaced or marginalized urban groups and individuals.[3] At the same time, however, unlike most of the films examined or discussed in this volume, *Mr. Zhao* is directed by Lu Yue who is a member of the so-called Fifth Generation filmmakers, and thus is most well known for his cinematography in several films directed by Zhang Yimou. As such, he stands out among this group of urban filmmakers as somewhat different both in his sensibility and his cinematic style, while at the same time his own style and concerns are far from the emblematic pseudo-ethnographic films that, fairly or unfairly, have come to symbolize the Fifth Generation.

What makes *Mr. Zhao* different from both the Urban Generation and Lu Yue's own Fifth Generation counterparts is precisely what I will explore in this paper. At the heart of the film is a unique representation of a middle-aged well-educated man—a man of a generation that grew up during the Mao era—whose personal world is intertwined with China's recent rapid economic and sociocultural transformations,[4] thereby creating a temporal dimension that adds to the complexity of a seemingly simple film. Indeed, to push this comparative point a bit further, we can say that Lu Yue's shift to the mundane and to a more explicit and direct take on issues of male desire helps shed light on the male figure—the filmmaker—that used to hide behind the camera. With its portrayal of Mr. Zhao, the film has in effect transported that male figure onto the screen. Along with many other cultural products, this move signifies a shift in the mode of representation of male desire from the high modernist ethos of the 1980s to that of the consumer culture milieu of the 1990s.

In terms of the temporal dimension, I want here at the outset to consider the film's last image of Mr. Zhao, in which he sits in a wheelchair with a smile on his face but without any reaction to the people around him. Mr. Zhao is at this point incapacitated and not able to commuicate verbally, and yet this is also the only time in the film when he is serene and no longer bothered by the noisy world. Is he a tragic figure, or a redeemed one? If neither, what does he signify? Does he represent a desire to arrest time or, conversely, a gesture of letting go, thereby becoming free (and if so, from what)? What does it mean, in other words, when the film ends with this figure seemingly frozen in time?

There are several periodizing terms with which critics identify contemporary China, such as the post-Mao/post-Deng era, the new era, the post-new era, and so forth. The term that is seen as the least controversial and most straightforward to both Chinese and Western identifications is, interestingly enough, "economic reform era." However, it is precisely what is assumed and yet never clearly spelled out in this term that makes today's Chinese social context so complex. Economic reforms in China are in essence a process in which China has changed from a Leninist state to an authoritarian one,[5] and with the rise of a market economy the capitalist logic—in terms of production and consumption—is rapidly becoming an assumed, accepted, and often unquestioned reality. What is not immediately visible in that reality is a form of capitalism that, in the words of Gilles Deleuze and Félix Guattari, is "born of the encounter of two sorts of flows: the decoded flows of production in the form of money-capital, and the decoded flows of labor in the form of the 'free worker.' "[6] Undoubtedly, much remains to be debated about the nature of the market economy in China: about what is actually meant by the qualification of "socialist" (as in "socialist market economy"); about the social changes and consequences brought about by the economic reforms and the capitalist logic identified therein (i.e., liberalism); and, last but not least, about the gender and cultural politics informed by these changes in China.

In raising these issues at the outset, I make the familiar move of situating the production and reception of *Mr. Zhao* in a historical context. I do not pretend to use this film to address the issues raised above. Nevertheless, I insist on the need to recognize the linkages between the two, so that we can fully appreciate the relationship between the cinematic and the social manifested in *Mr. Zhao* symbolized, among other things, by the final, frozen, image of the protagonist incapacitated. Within the specific historical context in which the film is made and the story is situated, how do we understand the relationship between rapid economic development and the displacement of the individuals, especially individuals who grew up in an age of idealism? How, in other words, do these two forces encounter each other in the Chinese context, and what happens when they do? What kind of human stories confront us today in a society that tries to absorb the flows of these two forces on a temporal and spatial dimension whose implications are yet to be fully comprehended? And how do we understand the desire produced and consumed under such determinate conditions?

MR. ZHAO ON AND OFF THE SCREEN

Ever since first viewing *Mr. Zhao* I have been struck by the outpouring of cultural products dealing with subjects similar to that of the film. These products include TV series such as *Holding Hands* (Qianshou, 1999) and *Comings and Goings* (Lailai wangwang, 2000); a recent film called *A Sigh* (Yisheng tanxi, 2000; dir. Feng Xiaogang), which even caught the attention of some Western journalists; and stories published in various literary magazines. The subject they share is that of men's extramarital affairs. In contrast to the sexual repression theme commonly found in the literature of the 1980s, these cultural texts suggest that Chinese men are finally sexually liberated.

As I suggested in the afterword to my book *Masculinity Besieged*, the set of men's issues introduced in the 1990s await further analysis.[7] Indeed, one of the most notable issues is found in the cultural texts that openly express male sexual desires. Since the early 1990s, China's rapid economic reforms have not only created developmental miracles but also have unleashed an explosion of sexual energy. And this has been happening against the ever-weakening official ideology that has lost its power to either contain or channel such energy (in spite of the state's periodic crackdown on pornography, prostitution, and even extramarital affairs).[8] If the cultural products and the state's behavior are any indication of society, it is not an exaggeration to suggest that post-Mao China is going through an undeclared "sexual liberalization" of sorts that no single set of moralities—Confucian, Maoist, or otherwise—can contain.

However, to celebrate this "liberalization" for its political implications and for individual freedom is in my view a bit misguided. Too many things have happened and are happening in China such that the social and political divide is no longer simply between the state and the individual (which even before the onset of reforms has never been simply a divide). Likewise, against those who lament such changes or are even nostalgic about either the power of Confucian ethics or the Maoist puritanism that kept China "clean," I argue that such a liberalization is not and should not be viewed simply as the return of a culture of "vices." Nor does it mean that the "sexual liberalization" necessarily operates on a different premise from that of sexual repression, especially when it comes to an issue such as male desire.[9] What China is going through, I believe, is a complex process in which globalized capitalist social and desiring production is being rapidly recoded into its economic and social fabric and into people's daily existence, all in the name of modernization (but with little room for public debate about its direction and consequences).

The cultural interest in the subject of extramarital affairs provides a useful entry into the maze of today's Chinese urban space, where men and women caught in a society in rapid transition are compelled to make quick sense of it. Indeed, with the rapid spread of the idea (and logic) of a market economy into almost all levels of society, coupled with the state's retreat from most of the private domains of people's lives, men and women in urban China have stepped into a wide, often uncharted, social space woven with changing relations and permeated with newly released pent-up desires. Rapid economic and social changes have also altered the nature of the relationships between the state and society; between the individual, the state, and society; and between men and women. It is in recognition of these social changes that I argue that we must understand the implications of the post-revolution sexual liberalization beyond seeing it as an allegorical symptom of individuals resisting the state or official ideology. In fact, part of the irony here lies in the fact that in a supposedly value-confused society, this "liberalization" is one that tends to follow the motto of money, power, and sex, which just happens to be the unspoken dominant ideology sanctioned by the state in the name of economic reforms. In today's China, in other words, the unleashed sexual desire is quickly being coded into the logic of a market economy and its production and consumption.

By focusing on one man's desire and its discontent as represented in *Mr. Zhao*, I will explore the ways in which such a representation helps raise interesting questions. How, for example, has China's post-revolution and pro-market social mobility made it possible for men (and women) to live out their desires? How do they fare in such endeavors in a fast-changing urban world where the once-familiar sociocultural references, or codes, have lost their clarity or meaning while the new ones appear alluring and yet offer little assurance? And how do we understand the relationship between their daily pursuits and discontent in conjunction with the rapid economic changes that supposedly are bringing China into the world of the modern or the "global family?"

The plot of *Mr. Zhao* is a simple one. The protagonist—Mr. Zhao, or Zhao Qiankun—is a college teacher of Chinese medicine. He has a wife, a son, and also a lover. The wife discovers his affair, and she demands an explanation. The lover meanwhile tells Zhao that she has become pregnant, and she demands to know what he plans to do. While Zhao hesitates, the mistress decides to get an abortion, but when Zhao finally rushes to stop her he is too late. As he waits for her in the hospital, he is harassed by one of her friends. Unable to stand the man's unrelenting questioning, Zhao leaves—but the man follows him out to the street. When Zhao tries to run away from the man he is hit by a truck and goes into a deep coma. In the end, he is completely incapacitated and becomes an invalid (*feiren*) sitting in a wheelchair.

To some extent, the story is one that follows a familiar dramatic pattern: the man has an extramarital affair; the wife discovers it; both wife and mistress demand a solution; the man is caught in-between until something happens to him. Although this formula is relatively common—found, for example, in the aforementioned *Comings and Goings* and *A Sigh*—*Mr. Zhao* stands out from these in terms of its plot structure, cinematic style, visual representations, and most of all its intriguing ending. Unlike other visual texts that glamorously represent successful men's extramarital affairs, *Mr. Zhao* deals with an ordinary college teacher and his mundane circumstances. But in doing so in such a mundane fashion, it provides fresh insight into the intricacies of desire and social relations that characterize contemporary China. *Mr. Zhao* offers a look into the psyche of urban individuals, especially those who are middle-aged and well educated, as they strive to stay afloat in a city that is going through radical changes. And it takes us into the microcosmic world of Mr. Zhao in which those radical changes are themselves simultaneously manifested through his desire, fantasy, and physical destruction.

The film opens with the scene of Mr. Zhao's wife revealing his affair. In so doing, it peels back the intricate layers of sociocultural and gender relations embedded in the ensuing human interactions and their tensions. The first shot is of a woman getting into a taxi and asking (in Shanghai dialect) the driver to follow the car ahead of them. As the car moves along the road, we hear on the soundtrack a discussion on the car radio about the stock market and we see the city of Shanghai passing outside the window. Immediately, as if taking a ride with the unseen characters in the scene along the freeway, the viewer gets a glimpse of the modernizing city noisily interwoven with desire for money and with the freeway that channels flows of desire into various unknown directions. Meanwhile, as the camera shoots from the back seat, capturing both the conversation coming from the radio and the movement of the car on the freeway, the film projects a sense of an ordinary moment in the busy city of Shanghai along with a not-so-ordinary moment in an individual woman's life. In both cases, the shot indicates that the vision is focused and yet limited and blocked by the steel frame of the moving car. From the outset, the film sets up a tension between the city in rapid change and the individual caught in the web of changes and desires. Indeed, the layered space in this scene—that of the interior of the vehicle moving on the freeway in a one-way direction alongside a maze of high-rises—as well as the simultaneous conversation about the stock market in the soundtrack both signify a kind of "confinement on the move," in which an individual appears to indulge in the freedom of movement and yet what facilitates her movement also conditions the direction she is taking. At the same time, it does not cancel that what is captured in that moment is a personal, indeed a local, experience.

The film then cuts to a scene in which a man gets out of a taxi and proceeds to walk into an old city lane while the woman, her taxi stopping behind, hurriedly follows him. Without noticing her, the man continues along the lane until he walks into an old Western-style apartment building and disappears into a room on the second floor. The woman follows him into the building and sees him disappear behind the door. She hesitates and leaves. A few cuts later, we see a close-up shot of someone turning the key in a door lock. The door opens and the same woman walks straight to the bathroom where she finds the man, Mr. Zhao, her husband whose upper body is naked. Disgusted, she turns around and rushes out.

This entire pursuit sequence has little, if any, verbal exchange. Visually, however, it manages to establish the relationship between the man and the woman via the woman's body language and emotion. It assumes her point of view and captures visually the flow of both characters' energy that leads toward the explosive moment in which the man's desire gets cornered, both literally and figuratively, in a dark little bathroom. From the beginning, the film establishes the tension between a dark little corner and a city that is noisily expanding. At the same time that the city expands and desire has no boundaries, the film brings us into the micro-universe of individuals like Mr. Zhao and his wife as they follow the flow of desires produced by economic and social changes. In the rest of the story, the film takes the viewer into Mr. Zhao's life as he struggles to walk out of his dark little corner, and ultimately fails.

Upon the "discovery" of his affair, emotional conflicts inevitably follow in which Mr. Zhao is forced to face both his angry wife and his demanding lover. Indeed, following the opening sequence described above are two exceptionally long scenes. Visually, each long scene takes place in one singular interior—that of Mr. Zhao's home and his lover's apartment, respectively. The tight frame in each scene and the film's relentless refusal to cut away from the setting creates a sense of confinement. In fact, much of the film takes place in a similarly visually confined mise-en-scène: in addition to the first two scenes, for example, are the scenes in the hospital waiting room, the hospital bed to which Mr.

Zhao is confined after the accident, and, of course, the wheelchair to which he is confined at the end. Together, these "confinement" scenes further symbolize Mr. Zhao's cornered position relentlessly dramatized by the first two long scenes.

In the first long scene, Mr. Zhao is confronted by his wife at home; in the second he is pressured by his lover in her apartment when she tells him she is pregnant. His wife accuses him of having a lack of conscience. Years ago, it was she who supported the family when Zhao attended college.[10] Then, she expresses her disgust at the fact that the lover is one of his former students, asking (in the Shanghai dialect) "Nong hesi laosi le?" (ni haishi laoshi ne; Are you not a teacher?), which she follows by demanding an explanation of the nature of the relationship. Finally, she asks what he is going to do: "Nong zenbei naneng bei la" (ni zhunbei zengme ban; What are you going to do?). Annoyed, and unable to give her a satisfactory answer, Zhao moves to their son's room to sleep. His wife follows him there, once again demanding a solution to the problem. And once again Zhao manages to dodge the question by repeating that he is not serious about the girl and will stop the affair soon. Even though he refuses to answer the question, from this moment on Mr. Zhao will be frequently made to face it.

The film then cuts to his lover Tian Jing's apartment. In a livelier and more playful atmosphere, Tian Jing tells Zhao she is pregnant and asks him what he thinks she should do. He tells her that he is considering divorcing his wife but that it will take some time because he has to consider her and his son's welfare first before asking for a divorce. Tian Jin says that the child she is carrying is his, so he should also consider its welfare. When Zhao is unable to come up with an answer Tian Jing becomes emotional, and in response Zhao flees her apartment.

From a gendered perspective, it is hard not to notice the politics embedded in the representations of these women and their relationships with Zhao. The women are depicted in a stereotypical manner: the wife is jealous and vicious; the young lover is selfish and demanding. And both of the women are irrational and prone to behaving erratically. At the same time, Mr. Zhao is shown as being somehow victimized by these women's irrational behavior. He tends to speak in a meek manner in which he tries always to be agreeable, and he constantly implores the women to be "reasonable." And in each case, it is the woman's irrational emotions that drive him away. As noted earlier, both of these scenes of confrontation are very long, where each couple is placed in a tight frame and let go at each other. In addition, the unglamorous setting, lighting, color, and overly emotional acting of the wife and the under-emotional reaction of the husband in one setting, and the seemingly indulgent lover's insistence on Zhao leaving his wife in the other, have the effect of making the viewer long for a break or relief. When the relief does not come soon enough, however, the viewer is inclined to be irritated by each of the women for they are the ones who refuse to relent. The film thus echoes the long-held prejudice against women by reinforcing their supposedly irrational propensity. And the viewer is encouraged to identify with Mr. Zhao and his embattled position rather than the other way around. The sympathy generated not only encourages a negative reaction toward the women but also promotes the view that Zhao is their victim. In its efforts to humanize Zhao, the film subscribes to traditional gender politics.

The film's inability to step out of the male-centered view of Zhao's relationships with the two women reflects the post-revolution and pro-market nature of China's gender politics. Increasingly, women are shown as emotional beings whose reason for existence depends on whether or not men love them. And, more than being simply emotional, women are also shown as potentially dangerous. At the end of the film *A Sigh*, for example, the main character is in the process of returning to his wife and child. They are on a beach where the wife and child are playing and the man sits nearby watching them. Then, as if sensing something, he turns around and looks into the camera, his eyes wide open. This shot gradually fades, and the film concludes. Given what leads up to this scene, the viewer is meant to guess that this end indicates the approach of his lover, whose presence directly threatens the harmony of his family. Thus *A Sigh* clearly shows from a man's point of view the peril of having a lover who refuses to disappear. Needless to say, China's gender politics continue to be sexist despite "liberalization."

What is also in common in many of these narratives is the way in which they naturalize male desire either as a "need" once a man has money and power or as a "lack" when a man does not have these things. Such assumptions, as noted above, operate within the same male-centered ideological stance that informed the male desire in search of masculine identity commonly found in the literature of the 1980s. The difference between the two decades is that yesterday's lack has become today's need. What remains invisible here is the seemingly counterintuitive argument that the sexual repression during the Mao era was in essence itself (in Deleuze and Guattari's words) a "desiring-production" that operated on the principle that "desire produces reality."[11] Indeed, the historicity of this irony lies in the fact that it was the production of the male "lack" through repression that made the return of male desire and fantasy appear to be its natural result.

MALE DESIRE AND ITS DISCONTENT

Although *Mr. Zhao* operates within a male fantasy, it appears less comfortably situated there. Indeed, as a film named after its protagonist, it is curiously less enthusiastic about Zhao's position as a desiring male subject. Not only does it "expose" him in a little dark corner from the beginning but, more interestingly, it ends with him being turned into an invalid. In face of a social reality in which male desire is celebrated for its glorious return, why is Mr. Zhao defeated in this way? Or, conversely, is it a defeat as such? To consider these questions, I turn to the two scenes that lead to the end of the film. One involves Mr. Zhao's encounter with his lover's friend whose pursuit in turn leads to his accident, and the other is a flashback while Mr. Zhao lies in the hospital gradually falling into a coma. For the purpose of my argument here, I will begin by first examining the second scene.

The flashback scene is preceded by a short scene in the hospital in which the doctor tells the family to keep talking to Zhao in order to keep him awake (so that his brain will not end up being permanently damaged). However, in spite of the efforts of his wife and of his lover Zhao gradually sinks into a coma. It is at this moment when the film reveals further surprises. The camera first focuses on the face of Mr. Zhao as he struggles for his life. It then cuts to the florescent light on the ceiling, but as the camera moves down we see Mr. Zhao moving a piece of furniture in a room. Soon we realize that the scene is a flashback to the time when after his quarrels with his wife and his lover Zhao has moved out of his home to stay temporarily in the school's faculty dormitory. It is during this time that Zhao has a brief romantic encounter with a woman who accidentally walks into his life. What follows is a long sequence of Zhao's interaction with this woman, but the sequence is interrupted now and then by the camera cutting back to Zhao lying on the hospital bed, occasionally uttering unintelligible sounds.

In the flashback sequences everything seems to happen naturally, thereby offering "romantic relief" from the earlier long, single-setting scenes. The dorm's hallway provides the setting for Zhao's encounter with the woman, where she appears to be in need of help. She is on her way back to her hometown of Bengbu after attending a conference in Ninbo, a city south of Shanghai. She has only one night to stay in Shanghai and she wants to visit her friend, a colleague of Zhao's. When her friend fails to make their appointment, Zhao invites her to go out. First they go to a cinema where they watch an old film on video. The scene then cuts to a scene in which first they dance through an underpass that has temporarily been turned into a dancing hall for old people and then have wontons in a restaurant. As they eat, she jokingly asks him to tell her the worst thing he has ever done. He laughs and vaguely says that he has done lots of bad things, but then he changes the subject to talk about the film that they have just seen. When they return to the dorm, her friend has returned, and the woman gathers her things and says goodbye to Zhao. After a short while, however, there is a knock on the door and the woman stands outside, apparently having decided against going to her friend's room. The film then cuts to the next scene in which Zhao and the woman are on a bus with the woman resting her head on his shoulder. In the next cut, we see Zhao helping the woman board a train, after which he stands outside her window. He then gives her a piece of paper with his phone number on it, and she asks whether he would have been willing if she had wanted sex the previous night. Zhao smiles without saying anything. The film then cuts to the present in which Zhao sits in a wheelchair pushed by his wife with their son walking alongside. It is a grim scene, but there is a smile on his face. Shortly thereafter, we realize that both his wife and his lover, Tian Jin, are on their way to clear the dorm room for him. It is there that they both hear the messages that the third woman has left on the answering machine. In the first one, she thanks Zhao for the one evening in Shanghai and invites him to visit her. In the second one, she hesitates, obviously unsure if he will answer. As the telephone rings again, the screen goes blank. We continue to hear the phone ring followed by the busy signal, once, twice, and three times—and there the film ends.

Structurally the flashback sequence is periodically cut as the film returns to the hospital bed on which the injured Mr. Zhao lies. The sequence is set, in other words, within Zhao's coma—and thus is the reference to a "romance in a coma" where two individuals temporarily step out of their usual social roles and environment and connect to each other in a brief (and yet seductive) moment. Perhaps also it echoes a narcissistic fantasy about (Chinese) men's sexual prowess and what that leads to. But by framing the romantic moment within the coma, the film also connects such fantasy to its discontent. The double timeframe—the flashback and the hospital ward—suggests a complicated twist of tension within Zhao's life. The romantic moment can be both simultaneously liberating and (potentially) nightmarish, especially when we realize that it will end by permanently pulling him away from "reality." While the hospital ward with the two women by Zhao's side might allow him to exist in "real time" (if he does not fall into a coma), it is nevertheless already shown to be his "confinement."

The contrast between the two worlds in the film is, therefore, more than incidental. When the film repeatedly cuts back to the "present" scene, the two women try to keep Zhao awake. When it then cuts to the romantic flashback we cannot but sense a further retreat by Zhao from his "real" world represented, once again, by the two women. Conventionally, such a move is easy to interpret. It is only "natural" for a man to enjoy a moment with an attractive woman, especially when the two women on the other side have not made his life easy. But the irony here is that the pleasure of the romance has also pulled Zhao further into his "coma" and in turn has left him permanently in the place where he exists as an invalid. Is this, then, a liberation or punishment? Can we interpret the concluding "romance in a coma" sequence as a symbolic castration that suggests that "sexual liberalization" can be a double-edged sword? Does it, in other words, suggest that Zhao is a casualty of men's newfound sexual freedom, with Zhao as a silent observer of the noisy modern world where more casualties like him will occur? Or is it symbolic of Zhao's inability to face such a question as "What are you going to do?" in a society where well-educated men—by extension, intellectuals—like him are now challenged to face difficult questions regarding their own desires and the consequences? The film, I think, answers yes to all of these questions, thereby signaling its multiple implications in representing, once again, the tension between and ironies within male desire and its discontent in today's China.

At this point, where the question of Mr. Zhao's invalid position turns enigmatic, is where we need to take another look at the film's representation of him. Here, I turn to the scene mentioned above in which Mr. Zhao encounters the "questioning man." While the film itself may not overtly subscribe to a particular set of moral standards vis-à-vis Zhao's affairs, its choice of Mr. Zhao as a college teacher is not entirely accidental. Nor is the fact that throughout the film he is repeatedly asked certain questions until he is incapacitated. Indeed, one of the first questions asked of him by his wife is "How can a teacher do this?" In the scene with his lover's friend, Mr. Zhao is also asked "What kind of teacher are you?" In both cases his social position as a teacher is brought to the fore, but for the film the point of such questioning does not lie so much in a moral judgment as in revealing the tension and contradictions in Mr. Zhao's overlapping positions, both as a teacher and as a man (with an emphasis on his sexuality).

In this regard, of course, contemporary China does not lack cultural texts that place a well-educated male in the position of striving to exert his sexual prowess. One good example is Jia Pingwa's novel *Fei Du* (The Abandoned Capital, 1993). The novel collects a group of so-called contemporary men of letters (*dangdai wenren*) in the ancient city of Xian and graphically depicts some of their sexual liaisons and affairs.[12] The difference in Jia's case, however, is that the novel was written against the context of sexual repression and is in more than one way a male fantasy. Furthermore, the novel is obviously conceived within the shadow of the well-known classical novels such as the mid-sixteenth century *Jin Ping Mei* (The Golden Lotus) and the mid-eighteenth century *Hong Lou Meng* (The Dream of the Red Chamber) and tries to reach a cultural "sublime" (that of decadence as sublime) via a sexual route. Although it was published in the early 1990s, the novel was written in the ethos of the 1980s in which many male writers were obsessed with Chinese men's (lack of) masculinity. In Jia's case, the belief appeared to be that by returning "decadence" to men of letters they would be able to regain their "masculinity." And for him, the display of the men's sexual prowess is "naturally" coded with traditional learning, thereby revealing his own—a modern man's—desire to reach the sublime via evoking the ancients and their (supposedly) stylized decadence. In *Mr. Zhao,* however, what we find is an anticlimax, or indeed a discontent, of Jia's fantasy world.

In Jia's novel, the protagonist Zhuang Zhidie's major flaw is his insatiable sexual appetite. And given the theme of the book—the return of decadence as a badge of honor for "men of letters"—the novel is actually a celebration of such a "flaw." In the film *Mr. Zhao,* on the other hand, a well-educated man's promiscuous behavior is neither to be idealized nor condemned. Rather, it is the aftermath of the promiscuous behavior that is examined, and through which questions about Mr. Zhao's social position are raised. And nowhere in the film do we find this "questioning" more acutely represented than in the "interrogation" scene between Mr. Zhao and his lover's friend.

The scene takes place in a hospital waiting room where Mr. Zhao stumbles into a friend of Tian Jing's who insists on having a conversation with Zhao. Seeing him reluctant to talk, the man grows suspicious and finally figures out that Zhao is Tian Jing's lover. He begins to ask Zhao the question that the others ask him, "Nong zenbei naneng be la?" (What are you going to do?). After realizing that the man will not stop questioning him, Zhao stands up, gives the man a hard push, and leaves the hospital. The film cuts to the next scene in the street where the man continues to pursue Zhao for an answer. Zhao starts to run, and shortly after he runs out of the frame, we hear a loud braking sound of a vehicle. Upon seeing what has happened, the man, who remains within the frame, quickly runs away.

Shot from behind, this "interrogation" scene in the hospital is uncomfortably comical. By focusing on the back of their heads, the camera manages to create a claustrophobic feel in spite of the fact that the conversation takes place in a rather large public area. In addition, in shooting from behind the film suggests that wherever Zhao goes he will be pursued by those who ask him the question that plagues him. At the same time, his back toward the camera also suggests that Zhao himself will always have trouble facing those questions. This time, however, when he runs away, tragedy happens, leaving these repeatedly asked questions—"How can a teacher do this?" and "What are you going to do?"—permanently hanging in the air.

In the "interrogation" scene the key is when the man realizes Zhao's identity. "Zhao Xiansheng," he says—with an emphasis on the word *xiansheng*, which in addition to "Mr." also means *laoshi* or teacher. Indeed, in the film Zhao's wife and his lover's friend repeatedly evoke the word *lao shi* as in (Shanghai dialect) "Nong heisi laosi le" (ni hai shi laoshi ne; "But you're a teacher") or "Laosi naneng kuyi geneng ge nei?" (laoshi zengme keyi zheyang de ne; How can a teacher be like this?). Needless to say, such evocation is possible mainly because of the traditional moral implications that the word denotes; in spite of the Cultural Revolution's degrading and sometimes brutal treatment of teachers, laoshi has continued to generate a set of moral codes and cultural implications. "Wei ren shi biao," or "Teachers are role models," is something derived from the Confucian tradition that continues to resonate in modern China. And so the film touches upon one of the contemporary social ironies in China: the dislocation or disjunction between the cultural meanings and the complex social and economic positions of teachers (and, by extension, of intellectuals), and between the moral implications embedded on the one hand in the notion of teacher, and on the other hand in the teachers' own economic and social standings and their daily choices.

During the reform era, teachers, especially college teachers who represent the learned elite, have borne the brunt of the reforms when their social positions suffered a downward turn in a society where money, as opposed to knowledge, is gaining respect and sometimes even blindly worshipped. Even though certain forms of knowledge have increased in monetary value (such as Mr. Zhao's knowledge of Chinese medicine, which takes him into the hotel rooms of traveling businessmen), the traditional connotation of laoshi complicates the social position of the teachers. They continue to be expected to embody the morals or ethics of a society in a way that few other social groups are expected to do, and yet this is a social group that has a hard time fulfilling its moral obligations. Indeed, in the film it is very telling that Zhao never appears in a classroom or in a social setting where he functions as a laoshi. It is as if his social position as a teacher has become peripheral in relation to his other roles such as masseur, husband, lover, and friendly stranger, and thus Zhao "Xiansheng" is not so much a teacher as a man to whom the moral implications of laoshi do not always apply. Such an internal split in rapidly changing urban China is indicative of the paradoxes embodied by Mr. Zhao, and by extension, Chinese intellectuals.

THE POLYPHONIC AND THE SPEECHLESS

The internal split in male roles may also reflect the complexity of the increasingly varied nature of urban development, in which cities like Shanghai are being rapidly transformed into a mosaic of spectacle where people from different parts of China and elsewhere in the world are vying to capitalize on changes in the city. Cinematically in *Mr. Zhao*, however, all of these changes do not receive a "spectacle/spectacular" treatment. Instead, they are captured in an interestingly arranged relationship between sound and image—for example, the simultaneous soundtrack of the city noise and the car radio conversation about the stock market that accompanies specific shots of the city. Another such example is the curious combination of Shanghai dialect along with Mandarin that is spoken in many of the dialogues.[13] For Chinese viewers, this aspect of the sound undoubtedly affects their viewing experience. In addition, given the fact that Mr. Zhao ends up losing his ability to speak, the film's choice of language becomes all the more intriguing. Realistically speaking, of course, the fact that Zhao and his wife speak different dialects is unlikely and hence does not quite ring true. The question, then, is why is there a linguistic difference in this case? In my view it should be understood in conjunction with the position of Mr. Zhao and what he can be seen as representing (i.e., the ambivalent and conflicting position occupied by contemporary Chinese intellectuals). But before I continue with this point, I would like briefly to consider the use of Shanghai dialect.

As noted above, the exterior of the city is barely shown in this film, thus the use of dialect is one major indicator that the setting is the city of Shanghai. In the film, Shanghai does not seem so much to be seen as heard. What does it mean, then, for us to "hear" Shanghai, especially in the film medium whose primary language is visual? Perhaps the answer is simply that the director wants the viewer to "hear" Shanghai by way of watching Zhao's story, to sense the city not just visually but also to see how language structures the relationships between the city and the people who reside in it.

In recent years, Shanghai has commanded a sizable amount of scholarly attention, especially regarding its history and popular and political culture during the period between the late Qing dynasty and 1949. Meanwhile, in the post-Mao era, especially since the early 1990s, the radical changes in Shanghai have among the city's elite brought back sentiments of the city's old glory, and a number of books have been published in an effort to restore the essence of this old glory. The love affair with the "old Shanghai," both in the West and in contemporary Shanghai itself, helps stage the city once again onto the world, not necessarily without its old halos of "the whore of the Orient" looming somewhere in the background, urging the rest of the world to look at it again. In all of this scrutiny, however, the city itself is barely being heard, especially in its own terms. Most scholars, relying on written materials, tend to forget the sociocultural and political implications when it comes to what I would call the internal linguistic transactions within the city.

Indeed, the dialect/discursive side of Shanghai is much more complex than is generally recognized. In the film *Mr. Zhao* the difference in social position between the husband and the wife is shown through the dialects they use: the wife who from the working class "naturally" speaks Shanghai dialect, while Mr. Zhao as a college teacher (and a modern-day mandarin of sorts) "naturally" speaks Mandarin, the use of which indicates that he is educated. The dialect as spoken by the wife, a worker, and Tian Jing's friend, a self-styled *curen* (or "crude man"), conveys a feel of the rawness of the city, a degree of its earthiness mixed with a degree of "shrewdness" that Shanghai city dwellers are commonly (and negatively) known for. This, I argue, is what is overlooked by most nostalgic views of the old Shanghai and its decadence and much of the contempt toward its 1949–1990s period. By giving a voice to Shanghai, the film *Mr. Zhao* imbues the city with character, making it appear more colorful and complex. Hou Hsiao-hsien, in his film *Flowers of Shanghai*, also tries to give a voice to Shanghai even though his efforts leave much to be desired owing to the poor quality of the sound work and dubbing. Of course, Hou's interest and preference in using dialects other than Mandarin has much to do with his ambivalence toward Mandarin and the official culture it represents. Still, his efforts are laudable in trying to capture the linguistic flavor conveyed in the novel on which the film is based. There, the Shanghai dialect is even spoken with different accents, thereby further enhancing the city's unique characteristics.[14]

In some ways we can say that *Mr. Zhao* turns the tables on the "northerners" by showing the character flaws of the Mandarin-speaking Mr. Zhao. In many popular culture products of the 1980s, the designated speech pattern of the weak-spined educated man is that of a southern-accented mandarin, or an educated man. Indeed, in China, the flawed characteristics of the *zhishi fenzi* (intellectuals) have been so habitually associated with someone from the south that it is hard for most Chinese to imagine any hero who does not speak Mandarin or a northern-based dialect. Mr. Zhao is perhaps the first Mandarin-speaking educated man who is shown, in relation to southerners, to be indecisive and flawed, although by contrast he is far less caricatured than his southern-dialect-speaking counterparts. The interesting question remains of what it means for this Mandarin-speaking educated man to be turned into an invalid incapable of expressing himself.

Indeed, to return to questions raised earlier, do we know how to interpret the implications of Mr. Zhao's invalid status now that we see the ironies embedded in his social position? Is it a punishment, an escape, or a liberation? Before I offer some final thoughts on these questions, I wish to raise another point in light of a question put to me by a friend regarding the male writers I discuss in my book. She wondered if the anxiety that the male writers demonstrated about Chinese male identity was caused by the fact that "they don't have anything better to do." My answer to her was no, partly because these writers were "rebels with a cause"—that of searching for the "sublime" (and by extension, their masculinity) in the face of the supposed decline of Chinese culture. However, if we ask her question in terms of the characters found in the Urban Generation films, the answer is likely to depend on what is meant by "better," because its meaning increasingly depends on whom you ask.

If we come back to Mr. Zhao, for example, we can see that for him a better choice is not to make any choice. And yet, in so doing, he causes grief to his family and his mistress. Likewise, a better choice for Zhao's wife is for her to stop his affair by forcing him to break up with the mistess in front of the three of them. Instead, she discovers more than she bargains for when the lover says she is pregnant, and so the "better" choice backfires on her. When pressed by the man, Mr. Zhao chooses to leave the hospital, for the choice appears to be a "better" one than to stay. And yet that choice violently backfires on him when the man decides that his "better" choice is to follow Zhao and insist on getting an answer from him. The circles of "better" choices thus appear to be viciously endless until Mr. Zhao drops out of the chain of circles. My point here is to suggest that what we find in the Urban Generation films in general and in *Mr. Zhao* in particular is a move toward recognizing the disappearance of one singularly "better" thing to pursue and the appearance of a multitude of many seemingly better choices and their consequences. What is also revealed in such a move, then, is a social and existential reality open to the operation of the capitalist logic that, in the words of Deleuze and Guattari, "axiomatizes with one hand what it decodes with the other," infinitely decoding what has just been coded and recoding what has just been decoded.[15]

Visually in *Mr. Zhao*, such reality is at the same time represented as a local existence that is subtly, or not so subtly (as in the use of the dialect), captured in the mise-en-scène. As noted above, in the film the city of Shanghai is not shown as a spectacle but rather as a locale with lived experiences, all of which are represented through an array of fragmented visual elements including the interior of a taxi, old lanes and old apartment buildings, the 1980s-looking interior of Zhao's home, a hotel lobby and room, the corner of an old factory where Zhao's wife stands in a worker's uniform, and the old reference room in the college with its shelves of reading materials and furniture serving as stands for unused musical instruments. The juxtaposition of the "new" and "old" constitutes the daily experience of the locals. Further, the "old" things—the about-to-disappear state-owned factories, the reading room and musical instruments in disuse, and the books that are forgotten and perhaps soon to be discarded—were once and in various ways continue to be part of "local" lives. In the film they are quietly but surely on display, adding a touch of the local that may nevertheless soon disappear with the onset of the latest wave of globalization and modernization.

In considering the college room scenes Zhao's presence there begins to take on additional meaning. Perhaps he truly belongs to a different era, even though that era is being relentlessly pushed to the background and even though he himself tries hard to escape it. By running between home, hotel rooms, and his lover's apartment, Mr. Zhao appears to be pursuing what the new-found freedom promises. At the same time, however, his pursuit also places him in the little dark corner "exposed" by his wife. His "alternative" space, interestingly enough, is the abandoned reference room in the college. Even though it is there where he encounters his last romantic fling, it does not provide an escape from his cornered position. By the time the woman from the college calls again, he is already in the hospital. By the time her messages are played, Mr. Zhao sits outside under a tree completely oblivious to the world around him. The woman's messages have become irrelevant, just like the abandoned reference room and everything else in it. When the film ends with the ringing sound of the telephone and the clicking sound of the answering machine but with no more human voice, the film itself appears by turning itself speechless to have dissolved into the last image of Mr. Zhao. In this sense, *Mr. Zhao* the film becomes one with Mr. Zhao its protagonist, as an ambivalent transitional figure in China's pursuit of modernization at the end of the twentieth century.

If we remember Deleuze and Guattari's argument that "the truth of the matter is that social production is purely and simply desiring production itself under determinate conditions," then what we face in China is such a production in which China's century-long quest for modernity is on the one hand being rapidly structured into the global economy, and on the other hand chaotically permeated into the individual's daily pursuits.[16] What is being vacated, as symbolized by Mr. Zhao's loss of language ability, is the cultural or humanistic domain where the addressee—a well-educated man—is facing what appears to be insurmountable difficulties in trying to answer the question "What are you going to do?"

Perhaps what is actually implied in the last image of Mr. Zhao is a big void—an "exterior limit" or the "schizophrenia," to invoke Deleuze and Guattari again—in today's China, a void symbolized by Mr. Zhao's loss of language, which in turn signifies the embattled and sometimes confused position of the male intellectual. And it is perhaps because of this that the last image of Mr. Zhao is so haunting. Will the intellectuals themselves ever be able to recover from their "deep coma" in order to transcend the position of the injured and silent observer and tackle the questions put to them? Or, conversely, does the film imply that the "deep coma" is the best escape for them? Suffice it here to say that in giving us the silent Mr. Zhao, the film *Zhao Xiansheng* does not provide a clear answer to either possibility.

NOTES

1. In the years since my first viewing of the film this point still holds; indeed, even today this film remains difficult to equal in terms of its unique style and sensibility.

2. To my knowledge, the only time when this film was shown on the big screen in the United States was as part of "The Urban Generation: Chinese Cinema in Transformation" film series held in March 2001 in New York City, Boston, and Washington, D.C.

3. Among scholars of Chinese cinema it is well known that the film industry in China is going through a difficult time financially. Cinema attendance decreased by two-thirds between 1988 and 1998. Due to a lack of interest, many films are not distributed, while others do not pass censorship and thus are not given permission for release. This does not mean, however, there are fewer film directors than before. Indeed, due the growing number of independent filmmakers there now may be more directors than ever before. However, these independent films often are not released to theaters, or even if they are released they may not be able to draw popular attention.

4. When this essay first was presented at New York University in March 2001, the head of the panel challenged the panelists with an interesting question: Are the changes taking place in the post-Mao reforms era necessarily unprecedented? What makes the presenters think that this particular period is unique in Chinese

history when great changes also occurred in many earlier historical moments? Even though I understood the underlying caution against seeing contemporary China's transformation as a singularly unprecedented historical moment, I would still argue that such caution does not change the specific historicity of the transformations taking place in this day and age, which, in turn, conditions the specificity of the experiences that the changes entail.

5. I owe this argument to Lin Chun and Cao Tianyu.

6. Gilles Deleuze and Félix Guattari, *Anti-Oedipus: Capitalism and Schizophrenia* (Minneapolis: University of Minnesota Press, 1983), 33.

7. Xueping Zhong, *Masculinity Besieged? Issues of Modernity and Male Subjectivity in Chinese Literature of the Late Twentieth Century* (Durham, N.C.: Duke University Press, 2000), 171-72.

8. During 2000, for example, there was news from Guangdong that the provincial government made illegal the practice of financially providing for a mistress by equating it with polygamy, a practice outlawed by the first marriage law issued in 1950. Nationwide, debates were generated by a proposed legislation in the People's Congress calling for a revision in the marriage law by adding an item to penalize the spouse who is involved in an extramarital affair.

9. Nor, moreover, is it a locus for possible social reform. A full exploration of this issue, of course, exceeds the scope of this essay.

10. This refers to the first two classes of college students, generally referred to as the class of '77 and class of '78, who entered college by passing entrance examinations after the Cultural Revolution. Many of the students were already married and had children.

11. Deleuze and Guattari, *Anti-Oedipus*, 30.

12. The novel was published in 1993 and generated much publicity and debate about its sexual content. Ever since then, no literary text has been able to draw as much public attention as did Jia's novel.

13. Throughout much of the Chinese film history, dialects were rarely used in filmmaking until the late 1980s. In the 1990s, dialects began to appear in both film and television drama. The Urban Generation filmmakers addressed by this volume are particularly interested in using dialects and dialect-inflected Mandarin.

14. Zhang Zhen reminded me that Hou Hsiao-hsien also used Shanghai dialect in other films, notably *City of Sadness*.

15. Deleuze and Guattari, *Anti-Oedipus*, 246.

16. Ibid., 33.

maintaining law and order in the city

New Tales of the People's Police

YAOHUA SHI

I t is striking that so many of the Chinese directors who emerged in the mid-1990s chose to cast police officers—sometimes literally—in central roles in their films. Ning Ying's *On the Beat* (Minjing gushi, 1995), Zhang Yuan's *East Palace, West Palace* (Donggong xigong, 1996) and *Seventeen Years* (Guonian huijia, 1999), and Zhang Ming's *In Expectation* (Wushan yunyu, 1996) immediately come to mind. This partial inventory does not include films in which the police make brief but significant appearances—such as *Xiao Wu* (1998; dir. Jia Zhangke) and *So Close to Paradise* (Biandan guniang, 1998; dir. Wang Xiaoshuai). What is the reason for this sudden convergence of interest in the police among the Urban Generation of directors? These directors' works do not constitute a genre of "cop films" or "cop and gangster films" (*jingfei pian*) in the sense of a familiar category of narrative feature films with clearly identifiable typological features. Indeed, what sets *On the Beat, In Expectation, Seventeen Years,* and *Xiaowu* apart from Zhou Xiaowen's cop-and-gangster films of the mid-1980s is precisely their nongeneric nature. One of the elements common to all of these Urban Generation police films is that they are anchored in instantly identifiable locales and periods. With the possible exception of *Seventeen Years*, these films deliberately eschew glossiness and pursue what might be called an aesthetic of the real.[1]

Is it a mere coincidence that so many films within such a short time span feature members of the Public Security Bureau or the "People's Police" (renmin jingcha)? If not a coincidence, how do we account for this cinematic phenomenon? Modern police forces and film both were Western products introduced to China at roughly the same time in the late nineteenth century. Both film and police are intimately linked to the city. Cops, guns, crime, and violence seem a natural subject for film with its ability to record fast-moving images and exciting sounds. Indeed, the relationship between the police and film seems almost to be symbiotic—for example, both share some of the same technological apparatuses.[2] The camera and sound-recording mechanism are as indispensable to film as they are to the modern police, and for both groups new technology is eagerly embraced.[3] In addition to the use of technology, film and police have parallels in terms of technique. The ability of the police to condense a suspect's life into a legible profile is perhaps not dissimilar to a filmmaker's capability to make sense of a cityscape through, for instance, an aerial shot.

Cop movies are, of course, a staple of world cinema. In Hong Kong, cop and gangster movies constitute a major genre that is the bread and butter of the local film industry. Jackie Chan's Police Story series was a huge hit at the box office both in Hong Kong and abroad and are now eagerly watched by millions of Chinese on pirated VCDs and DVDs. In contrast, in Mainland China before the mid-1990s cinematic representations of the police were few and far between. Except for several films in the 1950s and in the 1980s, it is difficult to find a body of films with the police as the main point of interest.[4]

In what follows I examine the recent crop of Urban Generation police films as a way of exploring the complex dynamics between an often antagonistic triad: the city, police, and film. In what sense are the three implicated in one another? How do the cinematic representations of the Chinese police in the 1990s differ from the classic socialist cinema of the 1950s? What can we deduce about the Urban Generation of directors, who train the camera squarely on the police? Does the intense scrutiny of the police represent a shift in the power balance between film and the police—that is, between film as a potential centrifugal force and the police as a state instrument of control? To what extent does the camera angle and the shot composition and selection constitute a surveillance of the police, a return of the oppressive gaze of the state on the part of the filmmaker? Before I attempt to wrestle with these questions, I will begin by reviewing the way in which the modern police and film were introduced to the Chinese urban space.

FILM AND POLICING THE CITY

In English, the word "police" is derived from the Greek *polis*, meaning city or city-state. While the etymology of the Chinese word for police has a different history, the link with the city is also indisputable.[5] Yuan Shikai is usually credited with the introduction of a modern police force to China around 1900. The newly created police forces were charged with the responsibility of surveillance and the maintenance of law and order.[6] In northern China, Yuan Shikai's reform efforts were driven by national and imperial interests. In the semicolonial city of Shanghai, however, the rise of modern police forces in the International Settlement and in the Chinese city was dictated by more immediate local exigencies. The meteoric rise of Shanghai from a sleepy, insignificant county seat in the lower Yangzi Valley to a world-class metropolis created severe strains on sanitation and on law and order. The relative security of the International Settlement and the French Concession turned Shanghai into a haven for successive waves of refugee populations fleeing political instability.[7] However, the authorities in both the foreign settlements and the Chinese city alike saw the deracinated refugees as threats to stability. In the eyes of the establishment these *liumin* (migrants) were capable of metamorphosing into *liumang* (criminals) at any given moment. As early as 1854 the Shanghai Municipal Council of the International Settlement organized a formal police force. By 1898 the local Chinese gentry had established a Patrol and Arrest Office (*xunbufang*) and started to recruit policemen to patrol the Chinese quarters.[8]

It was against this background of explosive urbanization and rampant crime that film was first introduced to Shanghai and the rest of China. A quintessentially urban product, film quickly edged out traditional opera, shadow-puppet theater, storytelling, and so on as the most popular form of entertainment in China's most modern city. Movie theaters quickly became permanent fixtures in Shanghai's landscape and thus emblems of its modernity.[9] Along with cabarets, nightclubs, teahouses featuring "sing-song" girls, gambling

dens, and brothels, movie theaters catered to the libidinal needs of the denizens of the semifeudal, semicolonial city of Shanghai.[10] In a notoriously congested city, such quasi-public spaces as the cinema became an extension of the
bedroom, where the fantasies of Shanghai urbanites were indulged both on
and off the screen.[11]

Regardless of its origin of manufacture, film was seen as a symbol of moral
degeneracy. In a city already overwhelmed by crime, policing the entertainment industries became a high priority. The authorities cast a wary eye on the
popularity of films. According to Frederic Wakeman, the police were given
sweeping powers to "regulate every aspect of popular culture, from movies
and funeral arrangements to astrologers, fortune tellers, and even neighborhood gossips."[12] The police forces mediated between the anarchic drives unleashed by rapid urbanization and the official desire for social order. As part
of the city's wayward id, film was subject to watchful surveillance by the police
in its role as the state's normative superego. Film and the police, which almost
simultaneously became part of the Chinese urban landscape, immediately
entered into an antagonistic relationship.

The triangular dynamics between the city, film, and the police were camouflaged after 1949 under a totalitarian regime. Under the new regime, which
essentially was anti-urban in its history and orientation, urbanization came to
a standstill; indeed, at times the government even sought to de-urbanize the
country. As a result, film production came under tight control. The concept of
the dictatorship of the proletariat along with periods of political turmoil
obscured the old social contradictions and reduced the reliance on formal
policing powers.[13]

The unmistakable marks of this period can be seen in two films from the
1950s with policemen as the central characters. The first, *This Life of Mine* (Wo
zhe yi bei zi, 1950; dir. Shi Hui), belongs to a transitional period in Chinese
political and film history.[14] Produced by the private studio Wenhua, it is a val-
entine to the newly founded People's Republic. The script was adapted from a
novella by the well-known writer Lao She.[15] Directed by (and starring) Shi Hui,
the film covers the life and career of a policeman who lives through the seismic
events in modern Chinese history from the collapse of the Qing dynasty to the
Communist triumph in 1949. The horrific social conditions responsible for the
series of calamities that befall the policeman are the leitmotif of the film. Only
the Communist victory—represented by a striking montage of a proud and

ecstatic soldier of the People's Liberation Army holding the army flag superimposed over a map of China—promises a better future. When the anonymous protagonist first appears on the screen, he is in street clothes and is dying of starvation. The title *This Life of Mine* with its suggestion of temporal sweep and intellectual retrospection, together with the film's extended-flashback structure, conveys the "truth" that "only socialism can save China" (zhi you shehuizhuyi neng jiu zhongguo). Both the title and the narrative structure (as literal hindsight) serve as powerful epistemes encapsulating a life crowded with misfortune and its attendant hard-earned lessons.

The fact that the protagonist is a policeman seems almost incidental to the narrative. We are told that joining the police was one of the few career options for a semi-illiterate, unskilled man in the last days of the Qing dynasty. As much as anything else, *This Life of Mine* is about the impossibility of policing under oppressive and corrupt regimes. The anonymous protagonist comes across as an impotent bystander unable to stop the atrocities taking place under his nose.[16] Not coincidentally, the culprits in the film are never unruly elements among the inhabitants of the city but rather are rapacious soldiers passing through the capital or evil members of the ruling classes. There is no question about how the protagonist aligns himself—it is as a member of the oppressed masses rather than as an agent of the state that the protagonist evokes the viewer's sympathy,[17] and the cinematography of the film is quite telling in this respect.

This Life of Mine begins with a long sequence of panoramic shots of the Forbidden City and other famous landmarks of the seven-hundred-year-old imperial capital. This sequence is accompanied by the protagonist's voice-over. With their suggestion of visual mastery, the aerial shots indicate that the point of view cannot be that of the indigent first-person narrator. The ideological content of the film—expressed through the apparent visualization of the subject's consciousness—is structured over this disconnect between sound and image. The coupling of the panoramic shots of the former imperial palaces and the narrator's deictic references to them points to the disembodied voice of ideology.[18] As the camera pans around the vast palace complex of the Forbidden City—the Summer Palace, Beihai Park, the Temple of Heaven—the message of alienation of the impoverished ordinary people from the imperial grandeur and splendor is brought home. It is also worth noting the incongruity of the barely literate policeman's role as a knowledgeable tour

The People's Policeman in *It's My Day Off*.

guide. More than an eloquent raconteur, the old policeman assumes the guise of a wise historian, delivering his lecture in perfectly grammatical and neatly turned sentences in a carefully modulated tone of voice.

A decade after *This Life of Mine* was released came the film *It's My Day Off* (Jintian wo xiuxi, 1959; dir. Lu Ren)—a tenth-anniversary gift for the founding of the People's Republic of China, as it were. A comedy about a kind-hearted young policeman named Ma Tianmin, the film is as upbeat as *This Life of Mine* is tragic. Like *This Life of Mine*, *It's My Day Off* is a paean to socialism as well as an exemplar of "socialist realism" and "socialist romanticism," the officially endorsed new aesthetics of the People's Republic. The Chinese society that emerges from *It's My Day Off* is one that basks in "the warmth of the socialist big family." It is a socialist utopia free from strife or tension. There are no signs of social unrest or serious threats to law and order. The only disruptions to the harmony in the film are a few minor traffic infractions and the occasion when a farmer's hogs run amuck. There is no influx of migrants; the farmer is not a refugee figure fleeing rural poverty but rather a provider of sustenance for the city. The altruistic protagonist who is ready at any moment, even on his day off, to extend a helping hand to those in distress personifies a protective, parental state. He symbolizes the spirit of the socialist new man, truly worthy of the name "People's Police."

It's My Day Off has been described as exemplary of new contemporary comedy films made in the 1950s in China.[19] The qualifier "new" is important here: there is little romance of the old-fashioned kind in *It's My Day Off*. Indeed, as much as anything else, the film is about the postponement of romantic fulfillment in the name of higher duty. Ma Tianmin, the very embodiment of the socialist superego, does not allow his libidinal drive to get in the way of being a people's policeman—not even on his day off. Although he succeeds in getting his girl, the setting cannot be more prim and proper. The formal meeting when it finally happens has all the trappings of a traditional arranged marriage with Ma's mentor playing the matchmaker and Ma's future father-in-law, an older farmer, putting his stamp of approval on the prospective son-in-law.[20]

THE RETURN OF THE POLICE: FROM SOCIALIST REALISM TO POSTSOCIALIST HYPERREALISM

Relative to *This Life of Mine* and *It's My Day Off* as bookends of the 1950s, the renewed interest in the police since the mid-1990s marks the end of a cinematic absence of almost forty years.[21] A historical or sociological explanation for the sudden emergence of interest in the police can be found in the parallels between the New Era and the late Qing. Both periods are characterized by the unleashing of centrifugal forces, the loosening of central control, the decision to open to the West under internal and external pressures, the acknowledgment that the old ways are bankrupt, and explosive urbanization. The urbanization of the late nineteenth century was concentrated in a few coastal cities, notably Shanghai. In the late 1980s and 1990s, after five decades of policies aimed at freezing population movement, migrants from China's vast hinterland were once again flocking to the cities in search of employment and better economic prospects.[22] Their very transitory status is once again regarded with suspicion by the authorities as well as by the permanent residents of their not-always-welcoming host cities. Urban migration, a nonissue for five decades with the stringent urban residency permits introduced after the founding of the People's Republic in 1949, has resurfaced as a pressing concern.[23]

Needless to say, with the rapid urbanization process sweeping through China, the transformation in the 1990s of Chinese society in nearly all significant sectors of life has had a major impact on Chinese cinema. Indeed, films portraying the People's Police in the 1990s provide unique opportunities to examine a host of issues. No longer odes to socialist utopia, the new tales of the People's Police bring to the fore the potential conflict between ordinary people and the police as agents of the state rather than their harmonious coexistence. Chinese society, particularly Chinese urban society, is shown to be fraught with tension caused by massive reconstruction, population migration, the urban/rural divide, and changing sexual mores.

Films like *On the Beat* and *In Expectation* offer rich texts for studying shifting power relations, not only between the state and ordinary people, but also between different socioeconomic sectors. The image of the police and Chinese society seen in the recent films is also far more ambivalent than in their predecessors. In the 1990s even the policewoman in *Seventeen Years*— Zhang Yuan's gig as a "main melody" chorus member—does not come off totally unblemished. Never before has there been such a close view of the nitty-gritty of police work and its milieu.[24]

The cinematic return of the police in the 1990s is accompanied by a radical representational shift from socialist realism to what has been variously called postsocialist "hyperrealism" or "documentary realism" (*jishi zhuyi*). We would be hard pressed to find class-determined "typical" characters or highly formulaic plots in the recent crop of police films. The Stalinist-infused classical Hollywood practice that characterizes classic Chinese socialist cinema is highly removed from the preferred representational modes of the Urban Generation of directors.[25] Instead of lighting, costumes, and sets that are designed to sanitize reality, films like *Sons*, *Xiaowu*, and *On the Beat* seem to dwell on brute reality. Long takes, on-location shooting, the use of nonprofessional actors, synchronous recording rather than post-production dubbing, tracking (sometimes more specifically trucking) shots instead of the traditional two-shots, and a stationary camera, became the stylistic signatures of the 1990s.[26]

This new brand of realism is equally distinct from the cultural-national allegories made famous by the Fifth Generation directors. Socialist realism and/or socialist romanticism as exemplified by *This Life of Mine* and *It's My Day Off* had become in any case distant memories for the group of directors who came to their own in the 1990s. Their immediate predecessors, erstwhile rebels themselves, had become the elder statesmen of the Chinese film world. The rejection of grand narratives in the mold of Zhang Yimou and Chen Kaige was almost inevitable as the newcomers consciously or unconsciously sought to overcome their "anxiety of influence" to borrow Harold Bloom's phrase. In lieu of grandiloquent metaphysics, the focus shifted to the concrete quotidian lived experiences of ordinary Chinese people. The chronotope of the new generation of directors became firmly anchored in the here and now. Furthermore, the desire to "get real" mirrored the general psycho-intellectual change of the country in the wake of the traumatic events at Tiananmen Square in 1989 and the subsequent pragmatic embrace of the market instead of abstract ideals.[27]

As noted above, the pursuit of the real occurred in conjunction with the New Documentary movement of the 1990s.[28] Zhang Yuan, for instance, is well known for being a practitioner of both genres. His first feature *Mama* (1991) includes documentary sequences of real-life mothers of handicapped children. His first feature-length documentary, *The Square* (Guangchang, 1994; codirected with Duan Jinchuan) was completed barely a year before *Sons*, thus further blurring the line between documentary and feature film. Jia Zhangke's 1999 film about a traveling performing troupe parallels two documentaries covering similar subjects—Jiang Yue's *The Other Bank* (Bi'an, 1994) and Wu Wenguang's *Life on the Road* (Jianghu, 1999).

This new kind of film practice, particularly as seen in the documentaries, has been described as "intersubjective" and "democratic."[29] When the camera focuses on the police and their work in a feature film such as *On the Beat* and presents the result—seemingly unmediated—to the audience, the attention becomes inevitably subversive. The film not only demythologizes the People's Police but, more importantly, it highlights the mechanism of police surveillance and control. The self-conscious documentary-style film technique meant to obscure the director's presence and the carefully scripted shot selections and scenarios enacted by real-life policemen enlisted by the director make for a complex mix of fiction and reality. It is interesting to note that Ning Ying frankly acknowledges the highly personal nature of her work when she describes her approach as "subjective realism."[30]

The unrelenting focus on the police and on police work constitutes a form of (counter) surveillance. Tracking shots, long takes, and stationary camera work subject the police to close scrutiny. Indeed, *jingcha* (literally "vigilant observation") is not only the subject of the films but also their stylistic modus operandi. The director deliberately and effectively blurs the distinction between her subject and its representation by casting real-life policemen. The hyperrealist emphasis on specific chronotopes—or, to use the term preferred by many of the directors of the New Documentaries and feature films of the 1990s, *xianchangxing*—has unexpected consequences when the subject is the police. Shot on location, often in real time, the films become analogous to evidence acquired "at the scene" (*xianchang*) by the police.

It is not difficult to see where the power balance tips at the representational level. Far from being the enunciating subject, the police—both real policemen in addition to professional actors portraying police—speak words scripted by the director either directly in the form of memorized dialogue or indirectly, thereby seemingly arising organically from the premeditated scenarios. The issue of agency becomes highly pertinent in the subject-object relationship between the director and the police. In a film like *On the Beat* the contrast between a preponderance of trucking shots, which in fact highlight the presence of the camera and by extension the director, and the almost total absence of police point-of-view shots is emblematic of the loss of control by the police.[31] The film ends with the protagonist literally losing it and hitting the intractable suspect. Similarly, in *East Palace, West Palace* it is the gay writer hauled in for questioning, A Lan, who determines his narrative, dictates the course of the interrogation, and wears down the policeman in the end. The marginal artist, the unyielding suspect, assumes the term occupied by the director at the representational level. Meanwhile the spectator, the third dimension of this triad relationship, is positioned to identify with the camera and thus to serve as a witness to the police's deeds and misdeeds. Far from a simple celebration, the love affair with the police on film is fraught with ambiguity—as complicated as A Lan's relationship with his object of desire.

ROMANCING THE POLICE: *EAST PALACE, WEST PALACE* AND *SEVENTEEN YEARS*

East Palace, West Palace, billed at international festivals as the first film from Mainland China to broach the sensitive subject of homosexuality, revolves around the encounters between the young gay writer A Lan and a policeman.

The event of a roundup of gay men cruising in a park in Beijing becomes the beginning of an unlikely romance *of*—if not exactly *between*—the captive and the captor. With his daring plan of seduction, A Lan clearly hopes to turn a nightlong interrogation into something of a one-night stand, perhaps even more.

At least in some respects the film could be read as similar in structure to the late imperial drama form of *chuanqi*. There is no attempt at documentary realism—an aspect often said to characterize *On the Beat* and much of the Urban Generation's work in general. Creative writing or fiction is very much at the heart of the film. A Lan firmly believes in the transforming power of narrative to elevate life from the merely pedestrian. Much of the dramatic tension in the film derives from A Lan's recounting of his sexual history and its impact on his interrogator. A Lan's accounts—with their large doses of sadomasochism—comprise the lurid flashbacks that make up the film's center. Much like Tang *chuanqi*, with its emphasis on the extraordinary (*qi*) or paranormal through its descent from the *zhiguai* of the Six Dynasties, *East Palace, West Palace* dwells on "aberrant" or transgressive behavior and the ambivalent reactions to it by an apparently straight-laced, normative system symbolized by the policeman, who is at once instinctively repelled by and uncomfortably attracted to A Lan. Rhetorically, *East Palace, West Palace* also resembles *chuanqi* with its characteristic plot twists and turns and colorful descriptions.[32]

On first viewing, the almost baroque elaborateness of *East Palace, West Palace* stands in stark contrast with the hyperrealism of *On the Beat*. The interplay between image and sound and the use of traditional Chinese architectural and musical motifs obliterate temporality, thereby linking the protagonist's narratives to a mythical past. The park with its covered walkways resembles a stage set. The intricate weaving of Chinese opera as well as Western-influenced instrumental music; the flashbacks to the protagonist's past; the enactment of an ancient story of a beautiful woman captured by a jailor; and the elaborate mise-en-scène make for an extraordinarily complex film. Unlike *On the Beat*, *East Palace, West Palace* is extravagant rather than spare.

Despite their obvious stylistic differences, however, *East Palace, West Palace* and *On the Beat* share a fascination with the police and the nature of surveillance and control. It is no accident that interrogation informs both films. By including extended scenes of the police questioning their suspects, who are intransigent and even openly defiant, both films interrogate the police and the state power's policing of what it considers transgressive of normative boundaries. *On the Beat* features a man taken into police custody for selling pornographic pictures on the streets. The suspect obstreperously challenges the official definition of pornography. To him the distinction between artistic nudes and dirty pictures is nebulous and therefore arbitrary. The stationary camera, at the same time coolly detached and intensely involved, draws the spectator in to scrutinize and judge.[33]

It is tempting to draw parallels between the independent or "underground" filmmaker and the delinquents represented in the films. Both the pornography peddler and the homosexual writer can be seen as the independent filmmaker's alter egos. Like members of the Urban Generation, they exist on the margins of Chinese legality. As one critic points out, "China has no law against either homosexuality or independent film-making, but anyone practicing either vice is highly vulnerable to censure from the neighborhood police, the Public Security Bureau or any of the country's many other agents of control."[34] The cinematic romance with the police refracts the problematic relationship of the filmmakers with state power and censorship in the age of "transformation." Both *East Palace, West Palace* and *Seventeen Years*, for instance, can be viewed—at least in part—as a response by the director to the Film Bureau's crackdown on him and six other filmmakers in 1993. Though vastly different from each other vis-à-vis their representation of power and control, Zhang Yuan's two police films cannot be separated from a consideration of the director's precarious relationship with the Chinese state and its policing body of the film industry, the all-powerful Film Bureau.

Just as A Lan's advances toward the policeman carry overtones of aggression—one might as well characterize his assaults on the (straight) policeman as a form of *tiaoxi* ("taking sexual liberties") with its suggestion of irreverence and play—the love affair between the independent filmmaker and the police is not unmarked by gestures of defiance. In the context of the film, A Lan's allegory of the female prisoner and jail warden and his declaration of love for the policeman are more suggestive of insolence than masochism.[35] It is A Lan who dictates the terms of the romance, writes to the policeman, declares his passion, and engineers his own arrest. Faced with his impudence, the policeman can only express incredulity and impotent fury. And it is A Lan who sets the course of the nightlong interrogation by constantly ignoring the policeman's questions. He is the master of his own narrative, determining both what he wants to narrate and how to narrate it. "I didn't ask you about that" is his interrogator's constant refrain.

Likewise, the effrontery of a director like Zhang Yuan, who deftly negotiates the murky, unpredictable world of Chinese filmmaking while somehow managing to be the toast of the international festival circuit and winning a measure of recognition at home at the same time, is noteworthy. When he turns out a "positive" film like *Seventeen Years*, the Chinese government welcomes him like a long-lost prodigal son. Whereas the director's earlier *Sons* is a bleak, unflinching study of a family's slow and painful disintegration, *Seventeen Years* ends with the restoration of a broken family and a convict's reintegration into society. The reception of the two films could not have been more different. *Seventeen Years* won a Golden Rooster award for the actress playing the policewoman, whereas the director's previous film, *Sons*, never passed censorship.

Yet even *Seventeen Years*, with its hopeful humanist message of forgiveness and rehabilitation, has a dark side. The painfully frank depiction at the beginning of the film of a dysfunctional family rife with jealousy and distrust is reminiscent of *Sons*, a docudrama inspired by the real-life story of the director's neighbors, a family plagued by the father's alcoholism and mental illness. The relationship between the former convict and the policewoman inevitably reminds the viewer of the allegory of the female prisoner and the jail warden in *East Palace, West Palace*. The young policewoman, who is closely identified with the penal and reform (*laogai*) system, is the modern reincarnation of A Lan's mythical jail warden. The former convict's infantile dependency on the policewoman—a direct result of her incarceration and indoctrination, is as twisted as the female prisoner's love for the jail warden in A Lan's allegory. Tao Lan is as much reformed (*chongxin zuo ren* in *laogai* rhetoric) as she is deformed by the penal system. The precedence of *Sons* and *East Palace, West Palace* makes an intertextual reading of *Seventeen Years* all but inevitable. In Bakhtinian terms the director's two previous films relativize the apparently celebratory message of *Seventeen Years*.

It could be argued that the politics of the Urban Generation's cinematic love affair with the police amounts to not only narrative mastery but also a provocative tease of state authority and state discourse.[36] In the case of *East Palace, West Palace*, romancing the police entails subjecting them to narrative

Seventeen Years: The convict returns. (Courtesy of the Film Society of Lincoln Center)

or fictive invention—hence the film's parallels with Tang *chuanqi* or romance. In many ways the director's alter ego, A Lan, is above all a *fictor.* Far from being a mere passive, masochistic object of police persecution, A Lan's insistence on being the enunciative subject turns his captor into a captive audience. Mailing and dedicating amorous manuscripts to Shi Xiaohua—"his love"—is but the first frontal attack on the object of his "affection." A Lan's romancing of the policeman also reverses the stereotypical role assignment in erotic pursuits. It is the weak, effeminate artist who chases, and in the end overpowers and thus emasculates, the macho policeman. The same dynamic is replicated at a different level between the filmmaker and the state. By taking on controversial topics of his own choosing rather than being content with those sanctioned by the state, or what in Chinese is called *mingti zuowen* (compositions on assigned topics), the director seizes the creative initiative. His unsolicited, often unwelcome, attention to the police (as well as the handicapped and the marginalized) is a potent sign of his independence.[37] With *Seventeen Years* Zhang Yuan seems to have come out of the wilderness as an "underground" filmmaker. His extraordinary survival skills—his almost feline tenacity—have enabled him to live several lives. At the same time, the apparent contradictions not only in *Seventeen Years* but also in his seemingly complete transformation from pariah to officially celebrated director make a mockery of state censorship and control.

REFRAMING THE POLICE: NING YING'S *ON THE BEAT*

Compared with Zhang Yuan, Ning Ying's trajectory as a filmmaker is far less dramatic. Her films about ordinary people living their ordinary lives seem singularly free of the kind of drama that characterizes Zhang Yuan's films. *On the Beat* follows two policemen—a seven-year veteran of the Public Security Bureau, Yang Guoli, and a rookie, Wang Liangui—as they meander on bicycle through the mazelike alleyways or *hutong* in their precinct in Beijing. The all-nonprofessional cast, the unobtrusive original music score by Su Cong, and the minimal use of technical wizardry complement a seemingly unremarkable story of the People's Police, as unadorned and prosaic as the original title of the film, *Minjing gushi*. The director relies on the tedium and absurdity of the routine of police work to provide narrative interest and occasional comic relief. The hunting down of a rabid dog in the neighborhood gives some shape to an otherwise loose, rambling narrative—a shaggy-dog tale, so to speak. Instead of the crisp, carefully articulated Mandarin painstakingly acquired in drama schools, the nonprofessional actors speak in the boggy dialect of Beijing hutong alleys. The blurring of fiction and reality hits home when the final credits roll and the viewer discovers that several of the characters play themselves.[38]

Despite the critical acclaim for its docudramatic realism and spontaneity, around the seemingly amorphous structure at the middle of *On the Beat* is a neatly symmetrical framework. The film begins and ends with a meeting in the same cramped conference room at the police station with the same group of policemen. As the opening credits roll, a roll call is heard off screen, followed by an announcement that the section chief will read from an official document. The opening shot of the film is a medium frontal shot of the chief sitting at the head of a table in a position of authority, from which he is reading aloud a document defining the nature of the public security organization. A roomful of policemen huddle around the police chief, furiously taking notes. The police chief's bland, steady tone of voice matches the formal, abstract language of the document, which emphasizes the unique importance of the public security organization as an indispensable component of the "people's democratic dictatorship." The directive stresses that the primary task of the public security bureau is to protect national interests and ensure national security. The Central Committee of the Chinese Communist Party demands the highest degree of loyalty, professionalism, and discipline.

It is against this official discourse that the rest of the film unfolds. The urgency with which the lofty goals outlined in the directive must be accomplished hints at the discrepancy between reality and ideals in the official view. Between hunting down the rabid dog and questioning drunkards, cardsharps, pornography peddlers, and sexual deviants, tempers are frayed. By the end of the film, the overworked, ill-paid police reach a breaking point. Even the police jeep—the only modern transportation that the police possess—breaks down. *On the Beat* ends with Yang Guoli's supervisor announcing the official disciplinary decision against him. The formality of the language echoes the directive at the beginning of the film. As the party secretary reads aloud the eight drawbacks of unprofessional conduct, the contrast of this somber last scene with the film's opening cannot be more stark. The ending cannot but show up the hollowness of the official vision of a highly professional, disciplined, and well-equipped police force charged with protecting state interests. The irony of the gap between theory and praxis, between the government's pretentious rhetoric and absurd, sordid "reality" embodied in the center of the film, is brought home. Indeed, a silent but eloquent commentary on the People's Police is offered in the movement from the controlled environment at the beginning of the film to the messy police precinct threatened by rank sexuality, massive urban reconstruction, uncontrollable migration, and the urban-rural divide and then back to the same meeting room at the end, with one of the members of the exhausted, overextended police being disciplined for violating its own rules.

Framing the narrative in this way—effected through editing as opposed to the long takes characteristic of the body of the film—makes visible the hand of the editor, who also happens to be the director of the film. While the rest of the film seeks to obliterate all traces of fiction through the use of locations, accents, real-life policemen, and so on, the frame reveals the film's subjective nature. The frame contains the narrative and defines its hermeneutic boundaries, informing the director's otherwise apparently unstructured "slice of life." The beginning and end of *On the Beat* is to the spectator one of the clearest signs of the film's mediated nature, that it indeed is a story (as is announced in the original title in Chinese) narrated from a certain point of view. Indeed, the opening and end of *On the Beat* do not belong to any of the characters' points of view. They are recorded by the camera as a surrogate for the director for the sole visual possession of the spectator, who sits in judgment of the content of the shot and its significance. Rather than relying on a second shot to realize its meaning, the opening shot appears as a complete statement. Unlike in the socialist realist cinema exemplified by *This Life of Mine* and *It's My Day Off*, there is no second shot in *On the Beat*; the policemen in *On the Beat* are dispossessed of their vision. Both the frame and the body of the film visibly belong to the director, while spectatorial pleasure and power derive from a close identification with the camera and the director.

Framing in *On the Beat* occurs not only at the macrodiegetic or structural level but also, albeit in a slightly different sense, in terms of shot selections and plot development. Although it appears to the contrary, the film is carefully plotted.[39] The police are framed, set up, "incriminated" even, by the director, who goes to great length to pass what is staged as seemingly or almost real. The most obvious example at the level of the plot is police violence. When a man is brought into the police station for having verbally abused the rookie policeman Wang Liangui, the questioning quickly deteriorates into a personal battle between the man and the veteran policeman Yang Guoli. Instructed by his supervisor to take the brazen civilian down a notch, Yang Guoli is bent on breaking down the man insolent enough to challenge the prestige and authority of the police. As it becomes clear that the man is not about to buckle, insisting on rights and proof, Yang Guoli gets increasingly agitated. When a ruckus breaks out downstairs and the man tries to leave the detention room forcibly, Yang Guoli finally loses control and gets into a fistfight with the man.

The misdemeanor for which the veteran policeman Yang Guoli is disciplined at the end of the film is part of the "story" plotted by the director, who plays with the spectator's sense of staged drama and reenactment of real life through a host of devices that effect maximum *vraisemblance* (semblance of reality). The police routine unfolding on the screen is shot in long takes (frequently in real time). In so doing it assumes a semblance of reality that has a profound impact on the spectator's view of the People's Police as they are "caught off guard," "inadvertently" exposing themselves in front of the camera. However, despite the nonprofessional cast, the use of dialects,[40] on-location shooting, long takes, and improvisational dialogue, the film does not try to erase the director's presence. In fact, the opposite is true. Through framing and tracking the police and "their story," the film calls attention to the director's interventions.

The disappearance of the actor, the mise-en-scène, and the dramatic plot—key factors for André Bazin's analysis of Italian neorealism—seems equally applicable to a film like *On the Beat*.[41] What makes *On the Beat* a drastic departure not only from socialist realism but also neorealism, however, is the director's distance from her material. Whereas an Italian neorealist director like Vittoria De Sica is said to have "inexhaustible affection" for his characters, Ning Ying is characterized by a cool detachment from her subject. Perhaps this is why one critic described *On the Beat* as "anthropological."[42] The director-cum-anthropologist/ethnographer follows the People's Police in their "natural habitat"[43] with camera in tow to observe and record every move of the police. In fact, *On the Beat* can be thought of as an extended tracking shot as the camera follows the police around their beat. That the police are placed or willingly entrapped in a naturalized rather than natural environment is one of the film's biggest ironies.[44]

The paradox of the film's hyperrealism is most apparent in the director's use of the tracking, or rather "trucking," shot. The symbolic transition from official discourse to "ground reality" at the beginning of *On the Beat* is a series of long takes of Yang Guoli and Wang Liangui winding their way on bicycle through the streets and hutong alleyways of Beijing. Yang Guoli has taken Wang Liangui under his wing and is teaching him the ropes of neighborhood policing. The approximately eight-minute sequence is composed of eighteen shots, which range from a minute to thirty seconds, using largely but not exclusively the forward trucking shot.[45]

The first forward trucking shot shows the duo jostling with other cyclists and vehicles for space on the street. The shot moves from right to left as Yang Guoli reminisces about his rookie days and his own mentor. At this point a subtle shift in language is noticeable. Unlike the chief who delivers the directive in standard Mandarin with little trace of the Beijing patois, the two policemen pedaling their bicycles speak in the mushy dialect of the inner city. Their diction is casual and colloquial. This first shot, which is about a minute long, is interrupted by a yellow minivan, which cuts in front of the camera.

The second forward trucking shot—again about a minute long—also moves from right to left. Yang Guoli continues to reminisce about his mentor. The break in visual continuity is "sutured over" by dialogue. Yang Guoli asks Wang Liangui for his name. The rookie is embarrassed about his rustic-sounding name. The veteran says that his name is dated, too. A young mother is seen crossing the street with her young son behind the two policemen. The boy stares into the camera. Several seconds later a middle-aged man comes into the sight line and looks into the camera, his feet grazing the ground. A truck blocks the two policemen. The shot comes to an end.

Shot three is another forward trucking shot in which Yang Guoli quizzes the rookie on his knowledge of police work. Wang dutifully recites what he learned in the police academy: the work of the public security bureau is based on managing household registration and centers on maintaining order (*yi huji guanli wei jichu zhi'an wei zhong xin*). The veteran immediately brings the rookie down from the pretentious rhetoric. With the exception of the bodily functions of the twenty-three hundred residents in their precinct, which consists of six alleys with nine hundred households, everything else—marital squabbles, disputes between neighbors and so on—is their business. The veteran warns his protégé that the largely uneducated inhabitants of the low-rises near the old city wall are a quarrelsome lot.

The remaining shots in the sequence are as follows:

Shot four—Yang Guoli continues to describe his tedious duties.

Shot five—The two policemen turn a busy street corner. There is a lull in the conversation. The camera becomes stationary as the two turn the corner; the forward trucking shot becomes a following shot.

Shot six—A medium shot where the camera moves from right to left. The two get off their bicycles. The camera becomes stationary as the two policemen prepare to cross the street into a narrow hutong. The forward trucking becomes a following shot.

Shot seven—The two pedal along the hutong. Yang Guoli continues to describe the residents of the precinct.

Shot eight—A long shot wherein the two pass by a vast, freshly demolished neighborhood of traditional courtyard houses. The camera moves from right to left.

Shot nine—The camera moves from left to right showing a huge neighborhood freshly razed to the ground. Six or seven hundred households were relocated, according to Yang Guoli, whose voice is heard off-screen.

Shot ten—A forward trucking shot in which Yang Guoli registers his approval of the wholesale urban reconstruction that is threatening to obliterate Beijing's past. It certainly makes his work much easier. Occupants in highrises have less cause for dispute, thus saving him the headache of mediating conflicts between neighbors.

Shot eleven—The camera moves left to right. The two turn left.

Shot twelve—Huge bulldozers block the way of the two policemen. Yang Guoli and Wang Liangui get off their bikes and wait for the bulldozers to pass.

Shot thirteen—Bulldozers are seen moving forward toward the camera. The bulldozers soon fill up the entire screen.

Shot fourteen—A short following shot of the bulldozers.

Shot fifteen—A close-up shot of the immense, ominous wheels of the bulldozers.

Shot sixteen—Another close-up shot of the bulldozers.

Shot seventeen—An aerial shot of the two policemen threading through the remaining hutong alleyways. The camera pans up to reveal medium- and high-rises on the horizon encroaching on the traditional neighborhoods.

Shot eighteen—The two policemen disembark from their bikes and prepare to enter the neighborhood committee compound.

This extraordinary sequence of mostly forward trucking shots adds great depth to the film as the camera moves across multiple planes.[46] The rambling dialogue, which resembles a series of musical miniatures, acts as a counterpart to the shots. This multilayered sequence, which can be viewed as the director's commentary on police neighborhood control and changing urban form, among other things, once again seeks maximum documentary realism while at the same time revealing the director's hand.[47] Far from obscuring the presence of the camera, the "in-your-face" forward trucking shots foreground it. Instead of being followed or tracked seemingly unaware of the camera, the policemen move toward it. The real-life policemen pretending to be fictional policemen pretend to ignore the camera. However, by inserting themselves between the policemen and the camera, the curious onlookers call the spectator's attention to it.

Indeed, the spectator is made aware of the camera throughout the film. The camera anticipates the movement of the police and moves in tandem with them. However, as the characters become still, the camera seems to become reactive. A stationary camera is used in the three interior interrogation scenes. The first and last one involving a card hustler and a defiant suspect, respectively, are composed of extreme long takes. The first take of the first interrogation runs about three minutes; the first take of the last interrogation runs about six minutes. In the first scene, the camera lies in wait as Yang Guoli and the card hustler enter the room. The camera only moves when Yang Guoli orders the card hustler to stand up and show him his card trick. After a close-up of the trick, the camera backs up to its original position and becomes stationary again. The voyeuristic movement of the camera in the interior scenes, therefore, contrasts with the quasi-exhibitionistic exterior scenes.[48] In either case, the spectator is made to identify with the prying, coercive eye of the camera.

RETURNING THE GAZE

From *It's My Day Off* and *This Life of Mine* to *On the Beat, East Palace, West Palace*, and *Seventeen Years*, the transformation of Chinese cinema cannot be more drastic. A comparative study of *It's My Day Off* and *On the Beat* has much to teach about the shift from socialist realism to hyperrealism in Chinese cinema. More than a higher degree of unmediated realism, hyperrealism is an effective strategy, a license, a cover for the filmmaker to put the police under the microscope and show them "warts and all." As varied as their representations of the police are, directors like Zhang Yuan, Ning Ying, Jia Zhangke, and Zhang Ming demystify or demythologize the People's Police by placing them in mundane quotidian situations. Wu Gang, the boyish-looking policeman in Zhang Ming's *In Expectation* would sooner focus his energy on getting a bargain price for a new refrigerator than on investigating an alleged rape case. The avuncular policeman in *Xiao Wu* speaks in the same impenetrable (for the audience) dialect as does the delinquent whom he tries to steer from a life of petty thievery.

Accustomed to the constant scrutiny of the state, which through its proxy the Film Bureau vigilantly polices errant would-be "independent" directors, the Urban Generation turns the table on the state by subjecting to the gaze of the camera its supreme instrument of control and surveillance. Whereas the eye of the camera in *This Life of Mine* seems disembodied, it is constantly obtrusive—even invasive—in *On the Beat* and is clearly identified with the director. When the man accused of peddling pornography in Ning Ying's *On the Beat* challenges the police to come up with a clear and convincing distinction between dirty pictures and artistic nudes, it is the state that is made to struggle to answer what defines the acceptable boundaries of art.

The social, economic, and institutional changes engulfing China since the late 1980s gave rise to an independent or quasi-independent cinema such as had never before been possible. The intermittent relaxing and tightening of state control created (limited) interstices for errant energies—including artistic energies—to come to the fore. The accelerated urbanization and globalization process thrust the city back to history's center. The city with its inherent anarchic impulses and the state instrument designed to reign in these destabilizing forces inevitably came to a head in film, the quintessential urban product. Rooted in the city and international in orientation, the wayward Sixth Generation directors tell new tales of the People's Police that call into question the mechanism of state control. Hyperrealism, the favored representational mode in the 1990s, aligns the spectator on the side of the director, whose camera returns the gaze of the omnipresent, all-seeing "proletariat dictatorship" and its agent—the police.

NOTES

I'm grateful to Zhang Zhen for her comments and for pointing me to several references. I'd also like to thank the two anonymous readers for Duke University Press for their critiques of an earlier draft of this essay.

1. As Paul Clark has noted in his *Chinese Cinema: Culture and Politics since 1949* (Cambridge: Cambridge University Press, 1987), 94, glossiness and glamour are characteristic of Chinese films of the 1960s. Clark links the tendency to glamorize reality to the strictures of socialist realism and the lingering influence of traditional Chinese aesthetics. The pursuit of glossiness and glamour persists into the 1980s, as is evident in Zhang Yimou's early works and some of Chen Kaige's films, notably *Farewell, My Concubine.*

2. As Tom Gunning points out, "Just as cinema itself developed from technology designed to analyze the flow of bodily motion into calculable segments and observable poses, . . . [an early film like] *Une erreur tragique* shows that motion

picture's succession of images can also be stilled, fixing an image of guilt" (Gunning, "Tracing the Individual Body: Photography, Detectives, and Early Cinema," in *Cinema and the Invention of Modern Life*, ed. Leo Charney and Vanessa R. Schwartz (Berkeley: University of California Press, 1995), 41.

3. The policemen in Ning Ying's *On the Beat* avidly watch the American TV cop show *Hunter* and try to figure out the model of the American police cars. They also note with envy that their American counterparts are allowed to carry guns.

4. Examining the situation in republican China is beyond the scope of this essay. A cursory search of Cheng Jihua's history of Chinese cinema reveals several films with the police as central characters. Among them is the 1945 film *Jing hun ge* directed by Tang Xiaodan with a script by Li Shizhen, an official at the nationalist government's Central Police Academy. The production of the film is said to have been ordered by Jiang Jieshi. See Cheng Jihua, Li Shaohong, and Xin Zhuwen, *Zhongguo dianying fazhan shi* [History of the Development of Chinese Film], vol. 2 (Beijing: zhongguo dianying chubanshe, 1998), 131.

5. It was the Japanese who first adopted the Sino-Japanese compound *keisatsu* when the Meiji government introduced a modern police force following French and Prussian models. The Tokyo metropolitan police was created in 1874. For more on this topic, see Walter L. Ames, *Police and Community in Japan* (Berkeley: University of California Press, 1981), 10. On the new nomenclature, see Oura Kanetake, "The Police of Japan," in *Fifty Years of New Japan*, vol. 1, ed. Okuma Shigenobu (New York: Kraus, 1970), 281. The Chinese subsequently took over the term from the Japanese; on this issue, see Frank Ki Chun Yee, "Police in Modern China," (Ph.D. diss., University of California, Berkeley, 1942), 1. Frank Ki Chun Yee was Jiang Jieshi's point man on the form of the police during the Nanjing decade (1927–1937), and he was responsible for reintroducing modern police forces into the cities. For more on Yee, see Stephen MacKinnon, "A Late Qing-GMD-PRC Connection: Police as an Arm of the Modern Chinese State," *Selected Papers in Asian Studies, New Series* (Western Conference of the Association for Asian Studies), no. 14, (1983): 5.

6. Yuan Shikai called the police the government's "responsible eyes and ears." Because of the Boxer Rebellion, surveillance and information gathering became matters of primary concern. See Stephen MacKinnon, *Power and Politics in Late Imperial China: Yuan Shikai in Beijing and Tianjin, 1901–1908* (Berkeley: University of California Press, 1980), 512.

7. Statistics vary considerably. According to Rhoads Murphey, the Chinese population in the foreign settlements increased from 500 in 1852 to 20,000 in 1854 to 500,000 in 1864; see Murphey, *Shanghai: Key to Modern China* (Cambridge, Mass.: Harvard University Press, 1953), 10. Others put the figure at 150,000 for 1865; see Zou Yiren, *Jiu shanghai renkou bianqian de yanjiu* [Research on population changes in Old Shanghai] (Shanghai: Shanghai renmin, 1980), 15. The exponential increase in the Chinese population in the 1850s occurred as a result of a local

uprising connected with the Taiping Rebellion in 1853 and 1854. The population was to swell periodically in response to political upheavals in the rest of China: the Sino-French War in 1884–1885, the Boxer Uprising in 1900, the Republican Revolution in 1911, the First World War and the Japanese intervention in Shandong between 1915 and 1918, the Northern Expedition between 1926 and 1927, the Japanese attack on Shanghai in 1932, and the Anti-Japanese and civil war from 1937 to 1949.

8. See William Crane Johnstone Jr., *The Shanghai Problem* (Westport, Conn.: Hyperion Press, 1973), 74. Yuan Shikai may not, after all, get the credit of introducing modern police to China. The picture is more complicated than MacKinnon realizes; however, it is no doubt accurate to say that Yuan Shikai's reform represented the first official Qing government attempt at creating a modern police force. According to Frederic Wakeman, in 1898 the Shanghai circuit intendant, Cai Junjian, hired a Japanese police officer to set up a police post in Yangshupu, but the effort came to naught following Cai's removal after the Hundred Days of Reform movement was aborted; see Frederic Wakeman Jr., *Policing Shanghai, 1927–1937* (Berkeley: University of California Press, 1995), 19.

9. In 1908 Antonio Ramos, a Spaniard, opened Shanghai's first cinema, the Hongkew Theater. By the time he left China in 1926, he had come to own more than half of the cinemas in the city; see Cheng, Li, and Xin, *Zhongguo dianying fazhan shi* vol. 1, 12. For an overview of the cinema building frenzy in Shanghai in the 1920s and 1930s, see Leo Ou-fan Lee, "The Urban Milieu of Shanghai Cinema, 1930–1940: Some Explorations of Film Audience, Film Culture, and Narrative Conventions," in *Cinema and Urban Culture in Shanghai, 1922–1943*, ed. Yinjing Zhang (Stanford, Calif.: Stanford University Press, 1999), 75.

10. Shanghai's reputation as "Sin City" is well known. Almost from the very beginning, the city became synonymous with moral depravity. The Duke of Somerset of England called the city "a sink of iniquity" after his visit in 1869 (quoted in Murphey, *Shanghai*, 7). Condemnations of the city came from both Christian missionaries and Confucian moral stalwarts.

11. As one Western observer noted: "The real salvation of the Shanghai suitor is the moving picture theater" (Elsie McCormick, *Audacious Angles on China* [New York: D. Appleton and Company, 1923], 98). The association between cinema and luxury and sensuality is also made equally clear by a Shanghai writer, who stated: "In the future, Shanghai would have movie houses equipped with hot and cold running water; in addition to showing movies of "fragrant and voluptuous sensuality" (quoted in Wakeman, *Policing Shanghai*, 3). The theaters would feature international dance troupes demonstrating the latest fox-trot steps in the nude.

12. See Wakeman, *Policing Shanghai*, 92.

13. See John D. Brewer et al., "People's Republic of China," in *The Police, Public Order and the State* (New York: St. Martin's Press, 1988), 191.

14. For an overview of this transitional period in Chinese film history, see Jay Leyda, *Dianying* (Cambridge, Mass.: MIT Press, 1972), 181–98.

15. A decade after he published *This Life of Mine*, Lao She wrote a play, *Chaguan* (Teahouse), which also features a policeman. The play was filmed in the 1980s. In 2001 Lao She's story was adapted for television and made into a twenty-episode series.

16. A particularly gruesome scene depicts him witnessing the brutal killing of his neighbor and mentor, Uncle Zhao's only son, at the hands of mutinous soldiers. He also bears silent witness to the corruption with the police force through the collaboration of the police chief with the Japanese.

17. The policeman is depicted as a totally benign figure. Soon after he joins the police force, we see him assisting the urban poor by giving them directions.

18. The aerial shots of the various landmarks of Beijing are "contradicted" by the narrator's use of the demonstrative pronoun *zhe* ("this") in his descriptions; "*zhe shi*" ("this is") suggests an eye-level point of view.

19. Ma Ning cites *It's My Day Off* as an example of romantic comedy, which together with new social comedy constitutes the two main categories of comedy films made in the 1960s; see Ma, "Satisfied or Not: Desire and Discourse in the Chinese Comedy of the 1960s," *East-West Film Journal* 2, no. 1 (1987): 33.

20. As Ma Ning points out, in the new romantic comedy "love is more often than not a reward to the positive characters for their altruistic endeavors" ("Satisfied or Not," 33). The highly decorous, almost "feudal," character of the courting ritual is a recurrent feature in many of these kinds of "romantic" comedies. Ma Ning analyzes the date scene in *Satisfied or Not* (Manyi bu manyi, 1963; dir. Yan Gong) in terms of the disguised return of the repressed—the traditional arranged marriage (46). Since that tradition itself serves to regulate sexual drives within a socially sanctioned context, the return of the repressed is also the return of the repressor.

21. Although Zhou Xiaowen had made two films in the late 1980s featuring the police—*Desperation* (Zuihou de fengkuang, 1987) and *The Price of Frenzy* (Fengkuang de daijia, 1988)—they were knockoffs of the Japanese and Hong Kong cop-and-gangster genre. The success of the films gave rise to imitations such as *Bloodshed at Dusk* (Dixue huanghun, 1989; dir. Sun Zhou). The plots of these films were sensational and the settings generic. There was little pretense that the films were anything but entertainment. The police have at their disposal not only helicopters but all sorts of advanced telecommunications equipment—equipment about which the low-tech police in *On the Beat* could only dream.

22. It is interesting to note that the language describing the migrants, *liudong renkou* (floating population), is reminiscent of an earlier term used in Shanghai in the late nineteenth and early twentieth century—*liumin*, or floating people.

23. That China lags behind other developing countries in urbanization is today viewed as a sign of the country's backwardness. The government has announced plans to reform the household registration system and loosen restrictions on rural migrants seeking residency in small towns. This policy shift is a radical departure for the Communist Party, which sought to de-urbanize the country decades earlier.

24. The 1959 comedy is significantly titled *It's My Day Off*. The notion of a policeman unable to police is the central paradox presented by *This Life of Mine*, made a decade earlier.

25. See Chris Berry's summary of the thematic and stylistic characteristics of socialist realism in his "Chinese Urban Cinema: Hyper-realism versus Absurdism," *East-West Film Journal* 3, no. 1 (1988): 76–77.

26. I use the term "trucking shot" instead of "tracking shot" in my analysis of the beginning of *On the Beat* because "trucking shot" refers more specifically to a shot from a moving vehicle. The opening sequence—indeed the whole film—was shot on location as opposed to on a studio lot on tracks.

27. See Chris Berry's essay in this volume.

28. In addition to Chris Berry's essay on the subject in this volume, see Dai Jinghua, *Wu zhong fengjing: Zhongguo dianying wenhua, 1978–1998* [Spectacles in a fog: Chinese Film culture, 1978–1998] (Beijing: Beijing daxue chubanshe, 2000), 400–4.

29. See Zhang Zhen's introduction to this volume.

30. Ning Ying has used the term on several occasions; for instance, at the Urban Generation symposium at New York University in February 2001.

31. The rare exceptions in *On the Beat* are when the rookie policeman is being introduced to members of the neighborhood committee.

32. See Lu Xun's well-known description of the generic characteristics and evolutionary history of the Tang *chuanqi* in his groundbreaking work on Chinese fiction, *A Brief History of Chinese Fiction*, trans. Yang Hsien-yi and Gladys Yang (Beijing: Foreign Languages Press, 1964), 85.

33. Ni Zhen makes a similar point in his essay "Jishixing dianying he geren fengge de wanshan: Ping *Minjing gushi* [The perfection of docu-dramatic film and personal style: A critique of Minjing Gushi]," in *Jiushi niandai de "Diwudai"* [The "Fifth-Generation" of the Nineties], ed. Yang Yuanying, Pan Hua, and Zhang Zhuan (Beijing: Beijing guangbo xueyuan chubanshe, 2000), 431.

34. Tony Rayns, "Provoking Desire," *Sight and Sound* 29 (July 1996): 26. In his interview with Chris Berry, Zhang Yuan expresses his empathy for homosexuals and other marginalized social groups. The director's previous films, *Mama* and *Beijing Bastards*, feature handicapped people and rebellious rock musicians. See Berry, "*East Palace, West Palace*: Staging Gay Life in China," *Jump Cut* 42 (1998): 84.

35. On the allegorical dimension of the film, see also Zhang Zhen's essay on the director in *Fifty Contemporary Filmmakers*, ed. Yvonne Tasker (London: Routledge, 2002), 424.

36. It is interesting to note that *xishuo* (playful, irreverent narration) seems to have become one of the preferred narrative modes in Chinese popular culture since the 1990s, as attested by the numerous TV dramas bearing the word *xishuo* in their titles—particularly those dealing with authority figures such as dynasts.

37. According to *Yangzi wanbao* [Yangzi evening news], the Ministry of Public Security issued a directive discouraging cop and crime films and TV dramas (*jingfei ju*) on the grounds that they had an adverse effect on national security and social stability. As Chinese administrative directives go, this one was characteristically vague. It did not specify the harmful effects of cop and crime films and TV dramas, especially those based on serious cases (*zhongda xingshi anjian*). The ministry's directive went on to warn producers of using the real names of the people involved—it is not clear from the newspaper whether the directive meant the criminals or the police. The news story was carried by the *Jiefang ribao* [Liberation daily] on August 22, 2001. Many of the cop and crime films and TV dramas (mostly the latter) that the Ministry of Public Security alluded to were driven by commercial considerations and do not necessarily share the same thematic or stylistic concerns of the Urban Generation. Nevertheless the ministry was uncomfortable enough to try to reign in the popularity of the genre.

38. Wang Liangui and his comrade Li Jian are played by themselves. Another policeman, Wan Jun, is played by Wan Jianjun. The closing credits are preceded by the announcement that the cast consists entirely of nonprofessional actors.

39. In an interview, Ning Ying criticizes documentary realism as practiced by [other] Sixth Generation directors as lacking in structure. She stresses the amount of work she puts into her scripts. See Shen Yun, "Guan yu 'Zhao le' he 'Minjing gushi'" [About *For Fun* and *On the Beat*], in Yang, Hua, and Zhang, eds, *Jiushi niandai de 'Di wu dai,'* 402. The interview first appeared in *Dangdai dianying* [Contemporary Cinema] 3 (1996): 33–38.

40. The use of dialects adds a great deal of sociological information to the film. One of the suspects in Yang Guoli's custody, a card hustler from Shaanxi, speaks in a thick dialect, which is a source of great annoyance to the big-city policeman even though his own Mandarin is heavily Beijing accented. His sense of superiority, however, is quickly deflated when he finds out how much more money the unkempt provincial can make in an hour than he can on his policeman's salary.

41. See André Bazin, *What Is Cinema?* vol. 2, trans. Hugh Gray (Berkeley: University of California Press, 1972), 58. Ning Ying's Italian connection—having studied editing and directing in the Rome Film Laboratory Center and served as Bertolucci's assistant director on *The Last Emperor*—makes this comparison with Italian neorealism almost irresistible. In an interview, Ning Ying frankly acknowledges her admiration for and debt to Italian neorealism (see Shen, "Guan yu 'Zhao le' he 'Minjing gushi,'" 401).

42. See Jerry White, "The Films of Ning Ying: China Unfolding in Miniature," *Cineaction* 42 (1997): 7.

43. Some Chinese critics have used the term *yuan shengtai* (literally, original

habitat; but the term can also mean a raw or unprocessed state of things) to describe the director's relationship to "life" (see Ni Zhen, "Jishixing dianying he geren fengge de wanshan," 431).

44. Astonishingly, the film was made with the full cooperation of the Beijing Public Security Bureau. Members of the Beijing police department appear in the credits as consultants.

45. On the basis of the shooting script, Li Yiming calculates that there is a total of 218 shots in the film. The average length of the shots is twenty-eight seconds. About twenty shots last more than a minute; five shots last more than two minutes. These long shots make up more than 10 percent of the total number of shots. See Li Yiming, "Shenme shi dianying?" [What is cinema?], in Yang, Hua, and Zhang, eds., *Jiushi niandai de "Diwudai,"* 416.

46. For an interesting contrast, see Godard's use of the tracking shot in *Weekend*, which, according to Brian Henderson, flattens bourgeois reality (Henderson, "Toward a Non-Bourgeois Camera Style," *Film Quarterly*, 24, no. 2 [winter 1970–71]: 2–14).

47. As Li Yiming points out, the most important performance in the film does not come from the nonprofessional cast but instead from the camera and the director's editing ("Shenme shi dianying?" 418).

48. The best example of the voyeuristic camera takes place in Yang Guoli's home. As the exhausted policeman comes home after a night shift, there is a shot of the wedding photo on the wall. The camera then backs up to show Yang Guoli's wife in bed asleep.

urban dreamscape,

Phantom Sisters, and the Identity

of an Emergent Art Cinema

ZHANG ZHEN

t the Shanghai Film Festival in October 1999, *Lunar Eclipse* (Yueshi), Wang Quan'an's directorial debut and an independently produced art film, made quite a splash at the otherwise lukewarm event. Chinese critics were impressed by the film's sophisticated camera work and editing, in addition to the nonlinear story that, despite its contemporary urban setting, has an otherworldly dimension inhabited by a pair of phantom or "virtual" twin sisters who live in two parallel universes situated within the city of Beijing. It was indeed unusual for an art film, let alone a debut, to receive such enthusiastic acclaim in a country where experimental or art cinema has always been regarded with suspicion, if not conspicuously repressed by the official film apparatus for its potential subversive power. In 2000, Wang took the film to the Moscow International Festival, where it received the FIPRESCI prize. That same year, Lou Ye's *Suzhou River* (Suzhou he), another noir-type film featuring a female double, this time set in contemporary Shanghai, emerged on the international art film circuit. The many festival awards bestowed on the film include the Tiger award from Rotterdam and the Best Film award from the Paris International Film Festival (which also gave the rising star Zhou Xun the Best Actress award). The film was subsequently shown in the New Directors series at the Museum of Modern Art in New York and selected as one of the ten best films of 2000 by *Time* magazine. *Suzhou River,* produced by an independent German company, now has a U.S.-based art cinema distributor (Strand). It has been exhibited and received favorably in a number of art houses in the United States, Europe, and Japan, yet it remains out of the purview of the Chinese audience except in a VCD format released in Hong Kong.[1]

Besides the figure of the female double as a central narrative device, *Lunar Eclipse* and *Suzhou River* share a film language rarely seen in previous Chinese cinema—that of fission, nonlinear narrative, jostling camera movement, jump cuts, discontinuous editing, and noir-style lighting and mise-en-scène. The latter in particular stresses the rough streets and a sinisterly nocturnal ambience enhanced by rain and mist. The two young directors, both born in the mid-1960s, seem to be at pains to cultivate an individual style modeled after the by-now canonized international art cinema (ranging from the French New Wave to Bergman, Mizoguchi, some of Hitchcock, Tarkovsky, and Kieslowski, and more recently, and closer to home, Wong Kar-wai and Iwaii Shunji). At the same time, these directors try to put a personal touch to their China-based stories. It is thus not surprising that the two films, along with those by their peers (Wang Xiaoshuai and Jia Zhangke, for instance), were readily welcomed by the international art cinema circuit, which had been eagerly anticipating a younger and more energetic cinema after Zhang Yimou and Chen Kaige's epic-scale art cinema that thrived on cultural allegory and glossy exoticism.

The new generation of filmmakers, unburdened by the baggage of the Cultural Revolution and the mission to create a distinctive national cinema marked by a "timeless" Chineseness in order to stand out on the international stage, is more readily cosmopolitan in their professional conduct as well as cinematic expression. They consciously align their practices with the international art film and independent tradition. At the same time, their engagement with the contemporary transformation of Chinese cities and daily life therein, as seen in the documentary proclivity of their works as a whole, foregrounds the localizing vernacular that is a critical component of their cosmopolitan vision.

Lunar Eclipse and *Suzhou River* appeared within the span of one year on the threshold of a new century. Why did these two young filmmakers choose to work with the same motif and a similar storytelling mode at nearly the same time? Why are both so fascinated with the intertwining of the real and the fantastic, the mundane surface of everyday life and its violent and uncanny undercurrents? As each film is set in a Chinese metropolis and deals with urban physiognomy as much as with its psyche, what then is the meaning of the phantom sister in today's rapidly transforming Chinese city? On the formal level, how can we explain their eclectic yet innovative film styles, in which with great ease elements are blended from, on one hand, conventional genres such as melodrama and ghost films that have a long tradition in China, and from a wide spectrum of international art cinema, on the other?

Clearly both Wang and Lou are exploring new domains of film form in conjunction with forms of moral and affective economy and the possibility of sensory revivification (hence the figure of the double and haunting) in an era of radical social dislocation and perceptual upheaval. More visibly than other Urban Generation films, *Lunar Eclipse* and *Suzhou River* explicitly materialize what Gilles Deleuze has described as the "time-image" and a tactile "cinema of the body," not least because time is key to these films that center on vanished bodies and resuscitated memories and senses. In a film culture dominated by official propaganda films and commercial fast-food productions, the avowedly "personal filmmaking" (*geren dianying*) practice echoes that of the international auteurs of the 1960s whom Deleuze celebrated as the harbingers of a "modern cinema" in the postwar period. The preoccupation with the social and epistemological status of the body; the fractured narrative, or "dispersive" time (in which "chance becomes the sole guiding thread");[2] the "glorification" of marginal people;[3] the ubiquity of mimetic machines; the noir-tinged discourse of the uncanny (city); and above all the palpability of social unevenness and its repression mark Wang's and Lou's films as noteworthy efforts in the making of an alternative cinema that is locally grounded yet globally engaged.

The absence of a strong art film tradition in China, however, does not preempt the existence of art film spectators who have come into contact with various kinds of international art cinema through multiple channels, particularly since the early 1990s.[4] At the festival in Shanghai, even Wang Quan'an himself was surprised by the warm reception of *Lunar Eclipse*, noting that "[Chinese] audiences actually understood the film, and may in fact be more prepared to accept a wider range of film grammar."[5] The question, then, is why the space allotted for art cinema in China should be so limited given the ready audience. With the structural changes taking place in the Chinese film industry, including the weakening since 1993 of the China Film Corporation (the central film distribution and exhibition monopoly) and the fragmentation of the official studio system, are there possibilities for the emergence of a more multifaceted film culture that will include independent or semi-independent art cinema?

In this essay I present a preliminary effort to tackle this question, although my primary concern is with how the films' theme of the female double articulates a particular urban experience and cinematic vision. To address this issue I employ the method of motif analysis inspired by Kracauer's study of Weimar cinema, and delve into both the context of production and the textual as well as intertexual space of both *Lunar Eclipse* and *Suzhou River*.[6] This effort entails an invocation of an early Chinese sound film, *Sister Flowers* (Zimeihua, 1933), which also is centered around two look-alike sisters, in order to tease out some key issues related to the social and aesthetic status and historical significance of an emergent Chinese art cinema. The overwhelming presence of photography and videography in both contemporary films can in this regard be seen as evidence of the filmmakers' self-projections about the identity of an alternative film practice within a politically as well as commercially volatile film structure in China at the turn of the century. The uncertainty of this identity, socially and cinematically, is suggested by the ambiguous figure of the female double as well as by the male photographer or videographer. The invocation and diegetic deployment of both pre-cinematic and post-cinematic representational technologies, however, paradoxically revivifies cinema's capacity for remembrance and collective innervation. This is achieved above all by each filmmaker's cultivation of an affective regime and a tactile aesthetic. Despite their settings in two different cities, both films obsessively dwell on the question of urban youth's place in a changing society as much as on the epistemological status and cultural function of the photographic image in the age of paradigm shifts in film and media culture.

THE SHADOWY BUSINESS OF MAKING ART FILMS

In the early 1990s, the so-called Sixth Generation filmmakers began to emerge from the shadows of the political turmoil of the late 1980s as well as from the "anxiety of influence" of their Fifth Generation predecessors.[7] Wang Quan'an and Lou Ye are both graduates of the Beijing Film Academy, the artistic cradle for towering figures like Zhang Yimou, Chen Kaige, and Tian Zhuanzhuan. Lou was assigned to the Shanghai Television Station in 1990, while the Xian'an Studio employed Wang after he graduated from the acting department at the academy in 1991.[8] Lacking the kind of opportunities and the initial enthusiasm that greeted the Fifth Generation directors, who were taken under the secure wings of provincial studios, the new generation found themselves having to learn their trade in a circuitous way and to be resourceful on their own. Many of them took up MTV, TV, and commercial production, which also pushed them into the expanding realm of popular culture and its expressive possibilities.

Lou Ye, like his classmate Zhang Yuan, the maverick figurehead of the young generation, worked on MTV and other media productions when he was not working on film. His first feature, *Weekend Lovers* (Zhoumuo qingren, 1993; released in 1996), about a group of disillusioned Shanghai youth, is a kindred spirit of Zhang Yuan's *Beijing Bastards* (Beijing zazhong, 1992) and Guan Hu's *Dirt* (Toufa luanle, 1994)—two early Sixth Generation manifesto-like works. Unlike Zhang's entirely independent production, both *Dirt* and *Weekend Lovers,* bearing at least the label of an official studio, were eventually allowed for public release after heavy cuts. Unable to make films that interested him within the studio after his experience with *Weekend Lovers* and another feature, *The Girl in Danger* (Weiqing shaonü, 1995), Lou ventured into independent projects, taking advantage of the flexibility and mobility created by the economic and institutional reforms.

The production history behind *Suzhou River* is instructive. It testifies to how artistically innovative Chinese films are made across borders today, often through a combination of local and transnational guerrilla tactics. The film is technically a China-Germany joint production, released by Essential Films and Dream Factory. It was in fact started as part of an (unfinished) television series called *Super City* (Chaoji chengshi) produced by Lou Ye and sponsored by the Shanghai Studio.[9] Initially consisting of two thirty-seven-minute episodes shot on 16mm, the version for TV was reedited and polished after the Berlin-based producer Philippe Bober joined the project and made it possible to turn the footage into a unified feature to convert to 35mm. The hand-held cameras (by the first-time cinematographer Wang Yu) and the jigsaw-like style (features typically associated with an art film) in part are a result of a shoestring budget and a tight schedule for location shoots.[10] Although over-seas financial backing is not uncommon for the Fifth and Sixth Generation films alike (albeit with the Fifth Generation's epics often getting the big figures from business giants), it was a novelty that an unassuming project for Chinese TV inadvertently turned into a cosmopolitan art product. However, because of its label as a China-German production, *Suzhou River* has yet to be distributed in China.

What *Suzhou River's* production history suggests is that while it is possible to get art films made in China in the absence of structural support, there are formidable challenges in trying to give a film a life after it leaves the editing table or the censor's screening room. The directors, increasingly left to their own devices to shoulder virtually all financial and political responsibilities, find themselves forced to undergo a self-taught crash course in professional-ization and reconceptualization of what it means to be a director, especially an independent one. Previously, the system included only official studios em-ploying officially appointed directors who received a monthly salary no mat-ter how much or how little they accomplished. Despite the stringent finan-cial rewards, the directors belonged to the cultural elite and benefited from a nepotistic genealogy.[11] The studios held exclusive rights to the films and also took responsibility for their distribution. With the dissipation of such a tightly controlled yet secure system along with the proliferation of inter-national coproductions and TV productions, virtually anyone can become a director as long as he or she has a script and a producer.[12]

Wang Quan'an is one of these self-made directors. No longer interested in working as an actor,[13] Wang devoted himself to writing scripts as a way of embarking upon a director's career. In moving back to Beijing in the mid-1990s, he practically had to invent that career on his own. For *Lunar Eclipse* he was fortunate in raising five million yuan (about US$520,000), which came from an (unrevealed) source of "social funds" (*shehui zijin*). Despite its 100 percent unofficial investment, Wang was able to secure a release label from the Beijing Studio, which would significantly increase its chance to be seen in China. Having passed the censors, he became in fact "free" to find a distributor himself, a difficult task, however, in a chaotic market. This freedom is a mixed blessing because the studio, relinquishing all of its financial responsibilities on a film, also frees itself from the respon-sibility to market it.

In most instances, independent features are art films because of their propensity for innovation in film language and their audacious treatment of sensitive materials, such that their filmmaking is habitually called "exploration cinema" (*tansuopian*), a term first applied to some Fourth Generation and early Fifth Generation works in the 1980s that departed from the officially sanctioned socialist realism. The narrow space allotted to these emerging, often self-appointed, directors and their experimental films has ironically spurred a strong desire to explore new resources and dimensions both inside and outside of China. At the same time, they are not losing sight of the possibility of cultivating a domestic art film audience (if not market, quite yet). Wang Quan'an, who spent a good deal of time in France observing its healthy art house industry, and was encouraged by the warm reception of *Lunar Eclipse* in Shanghai, is particularly enthusiastic about connecting with an emerging art house enterprise in China.[14] Two years after its completion, during which *Lunar Eclipse* was screened at several festivals or in special programs in Asia, Europe, and the United States, Wang's film finally found a place in China's emerging art film market. In 2002 the film reportedly became the first feature booked by the newly founded A-G (short for avant-garde) distribution company (a subsidiary of the Zijingcheng Company) specializing in art cinema. It was shown at the Dahua Cinema in the Dongdan area in Beijing, which served as a location for a key reflexive scene about cinema in the film (discussed further below).[15]

These sketches of the production history behind *Lunar Eclipse* and *Suzhou River* are not meant to present the whole picture of the Urban Generation filmmakers, but rather should be seen as indicators for mapping out the shifting contours of an emergent independent art cinema. In its resistance to the "leitmotif" cinema but in dialogue with popular cinema, this "minor" cinema, in a Deleuzian sense, is conscious of its constant deterritorialization and possible reterritorialization in relation to both the domestic film industry and the international art film circuit. This instability generates anxiety as well as energy among the young filmmakers who have to play hide-and-seek games with both the authorities and the market forces, while also negotiating between artistic aspirations and social engagement. This situation has produced a breed of self-sufficient independent filmmakers who are "nomadic" in straddling different media, administrative units, and underground and above-ground operations. Rather than acting with a tragic aura as doomed self-exiles from the center, they are deft performers and dealers in producing and marketing an alternative cinema.

After seeing *Lunar Eclipse* and *Suzhou River*, it is hard not to think of Hitchcock's *Vertigo*, or of the more recent work by Kieslowski titled *La double vie de Veronique* (1991)—a "metaphysical thriller" about the related fate of two look-alike women in the shadowy aftermath of the cold war.[16] A typo in the publicity slogan that Wang coined for his film—"Two stories, one woman, or, *two woman*, one story" [English original]—is revealing about the filmmaker's conscious or unconscious desire to emulate and transform either the Hollywood classic or an art film by two European masters. Some Chinese critics have hastily dismissed these recent films as mere copies of Hitchcock, Kieslowski, or Iwaii Shunji (*Love Letter*, 1995), and hence without any merits of originality. What interests me here is not so much the degree of "originality" of these films about doubles or copies but rather how they perform this transnational "double take" and, in the process of metamorphosis and synthesis, create a culturally and historically conditioned film experience.

In his erudite work on the "culture of the copy," Hillel Schwartz outlines a taxonomy of the copy and proceeds toward a new understanding of the prevalence of twins, doppelgangers, and replications in the modern age. Notwithstanding the biotechnological and psychological findings about the "innate" twinhood at the root of each human life, Schwartz argues that the vanishing (or disappeared) twin in the industrializing society serves as "mute testimony to vanishing kin" in an epoch of massive social dislocation and "fading networks of blood relations." At the same time, the (vanishing) twin rekindles in us the belief in magic powers such as telepathy and miracle making in an age shot through with mechanical power.[17] Or perhaps both kinds of powers reinforce each other rather than cancel out each other, just as cinema, for example, has also served as the premier medium for modern magic by possessing a power for enchantment, healing, and spiritual contact between nature and culture.[18] It is thus not surprising that modern commercial aids are replete with twin images; they are not paraded as counterfeits but

Wang Quan'an (center), writer and director of *Lunar Eclipse*, with the author and Jia Zhijie (right), co-organizers of the Urban Generation film series.

Poster for *Lunar Eclipse*: "Two stories, One woman / Two woman, One story" (English original). The image is that of Jia Niang, the bar girl adrift among the denizens of Beijing. (Courtesy of Wang Quan'an) as proofs of authenticity and scientific efficacy (when used as a control group) and of the doubling of "exponential powers" of modern technology and commodity, along with their sex appeal.[19]

On the fundamental level of epistemology and subjectivity, twins or multiples induce our fascination as well as uneasiness with the boundaries of perception, knowledge, and identity. They challenge our ability of discernment while giving us the comforting image of likeness or familiarity. They provide us with metaphors of self-reflection and intersubjectivity, while also haunting us with the very idea of an unreasonable facsimile and its spectral embodiment. On the one hand, the ubiquitous trope of the vanishing twin and dubious double is symptomatic of uprootedness and fragmentation, and occasionally split personality or multiple personality disorders that often beset the modern individual.[20] On the other hand, the same trope invokes in us a longing for sorority, fraternity, and companionship. On these multiple, ambivalent registers, doubleness or double consciousness has become the hallmark of modernity, if not its very definition.

Modernity, however, is also profoundly historical. Films like *La double vie de Veronique, Lunar Eclipse,* and *Suzhou River* were conceived in the post–cold war period and thus offer a cinematic update of modernity's genealogy of the mass-mediated production of artificial life and the destruction of real life. If they share the broad post–cold war representational space, especially as in some way or other they concern the former socialist bloc that included both Poland and China, they differ in the particular location and articulation of the diverse postsocialist experience after the fall of the Berlin Wall and the suppression of the student demonstrations at Tiananmen Square in Beijing.

Veronique and Veronika   Although Kieslowski's film is not my chief concern here, a quick summary of its plot may help us achieve a more nuanced understanding of the two Chinese films given the basic narrative device that they share. Veronika (played by Irene Jacob) lives in Poland with her widowed father. A talented young singer, she participates in a competition singing a haunting piece by Van Den Budenmayer. During her song, however, she suffers from a sudden heart attack and dies. Veronique, her uncanny French double (also played by Irene Jacob), lives in a small town. Also a singer, she too suffers from a heart problem. Drawn by a call from an unknown man and mystified by a package containing a cassette of Van Den Budenmayer's music, among other things, she goes to Paris to find the caller and source of the package. The man she finds, who is a marionette artist, becomes her lover. At one point he tells her of his new play in progress, about the parallel life of two women born in 1966.[21] Among their many shared traits and physical resemblance, Veronika and Veronique are connected above all by a sort of telepathy and two common "gifts": the congenital heart problem and music (each girl's heart beats to the same "rhythm"). While Veronika dies from singing, Veronique gives up singing and carries on her life as a music teacher. Yet Kieslowski's artfully arranged audiovisual cues (especially in the beginning and ending) indicate that they are not exactly twins living in two different countries, they are more like phantom sisters in largely parallel, vaguely successive, universes that intersect only at fatal or redemptive moments.

While Kieslowski's "metaphysical" parable meditates obliquely on the fate of a "unified" Europe after the fall of the Berlin Wall, *Lunar Eclipse* and *Suzhou River* are primarily concerned with the fragmentation of the social fabric of post-1989 Chinese society—or the emergence in it of separate, disjointed spheres, particularly in the cities. Their phantom sister tales are clearly staged against the background of the accelerated transformation of a socialist state to a market-driven capitalist economy, which has created vast social unevenness, sensory and psychological overload, and above all a shift in cultural paradigms. However, neither Wang nor Lou is in a strict sense a documentarist.[22] Even less are they inclined to contain what they see and want to express in reified realist conventions—that is, transparent representation in a concealed illusionary world, which is largely the domain of the leitmotif and mainstream commercial cinema. Instead, their sharp observation and subtle social critique are conveyed through an evocative and provocative visual style that pushes into disarray the divide between form and content, the material and the immaterial, surface and depth. The phantom sisters and the parallel or intersecting worlds in which they inhabit indicate on one hand the suspension of a normative or taken-for-granted perception of time and space, experience and identity, and the exploration of other possible worlds in life and film art, on the other.

As is the case in *La double vie*, despite being the semblance of twins the two women, played by the same actress in both Wang's film and in Lou's, are not biological twins but are at best "virtual" twins as they operate on crisscrossing planes of reality. However, in what is different from *La double vie*, the Chinese doubles do not appear as same-aged twins but more like older and younger sisters (if in real time), or each one's ghostly other (seen supernaturally), or even mutual incarnations (in a religious sense). They hardly meet in a strictly diegetic space (except for one moment in *Suzhou River* when one sees the dead body of the other on a sidewalk by the river). This departs from the "metaphysical" ending of *La double vie*, where in an extraordinary long shot we see, through two juxtaposing window frames (and worlds), two pairs of different daughters and fathers embracing each other. Both of the Chinese films are about urban youth's difficulty in knowing who they are and what they want. Other than the figure of the double and some other similar elements, such as the issue of a heart problem in *Lunar Eclipse*, Wang's and Lou's meditations on transpersonal selfhood and virtual sisterhood are more earthbound than metaphysical; indeed, they are directly aimed at the relentless social world and a moral universe not governed by celestial bodies or divine grace but by worldly desire and disenchantment.

Ya Nan and Jia Niang　In *Lunar Eclipse* two girls with a striking resemblance, Ya Nan and Jia Niang (both played by Yu Nan), have mysterious interactions even though each lives a separate life in Beijing. Their disparate stories but shared destiny unfold in a complex spatial and temporal web. In a manner reminiscent of *Knife in the Water* by Roman Polanski, *Lunar Eclipse* (which even has a knife as a love token) opens with the newlywed Ya Nan and her husband out for a drive in their bright-red sports car, an incongruous sight in the rural landscape outside Beijing with its topography characteristic of a poor developing country. They meet Hu Xiaobin, an unkempt young photographer who says he knew a girl who looked exactly like Ya Nan. Ya Nan is drawn to the photographer, whose real job turns out to be a cab driver, and through him she enters the story of Jia Niang, her younger look-alike. Meanwhile, her marriage begins to show signs of trouble.

If *La double vie*'s metaphysical power pivots around the likeness of the two women in a (formerly) divided Europe, *Lunar Eclipse* quickly departs from the realm of sameness in order to reveal the radical difference in "one woman, two stories." The comforting metaphysical horizon is ironed out to pave way for a fable of social hierarchy and division. Ya Nan, who has given up acting due to her heart ailment, is a sophisticated urban woman living with her well-to-do (or nouveau riche) husband in an elegant apartment, whereas the younger Jia Niang drifts in the lower strata of the city, dreaming of a career as a film actress. Both suffer from a congenital disease: Ya Nan's heart problem is from her father's side, while Jia Niang is plagued by latent schizophrenia inherited from her institutionalized mother. Both have trouble with their right eye—one of the many references to the problem of vision in the film. The two do not meet until a moment at the end of the film, when Ya Nan rushes away from her unfaithful husband only to "witness" a violent car accident. In a nightmarish scene at a key intersection in downtown Beijing (the street sign says "Xisi," a major intersection in the old city west), Ya Nan comes face to face with the blood-drenched Jia Niang who has just been hit by a truck.

The ending consists not as a climax but rather a recurrence, thereby underscoring the circuitous or spiraling structure of the narrative. The film began with an accident in which Ya Nan is seen lying unconscious in a street with heavy traffic. She has been hit by a car, "as if in a dream." After the accident she is taken to the hospital, where her heart condition is detected. As a result, Ya Nan decides to give up her acting career to prepare for marriage. The mystery surrounding the identity of the double seems to come to a full circle at the final moment of recognition when the shocked Ya Nan and the dying Jia Niang see the (approximate) mirror image of each other. Instead of using superimposition or other techniques to place the two in the same frame, the uncanniness of their encounter is rendered in a shot and reverse shot structure, which then is followed by a pan that reveals that they do not actually occupy the same life space. At the crossroads of their lives as well as the film narrative, the hitherto diverse planes of existence have collided or wedged into each other momentarily, but the film as a whole does not try to achieve a "reunion" with this coincidence.

The power of the last scene in *Lunar Eclipse* comes not so much from the impact of the accident and the fateful encounter as it does from the intersecting (hence the crossroad) of disparate dimensions of experience and consciousness. The mirror image is only approximate because the cues from the women's dress, hairstyle, and manners indicate that they cannot be more different. One is a stylish, educated woman in her late twenties or early thirties—she is a "new human being" (*xin renlei*) who chooses to be a housewife (a class index for the nouveau riche).[23] The other, somewhat younger and with a head of intractable dreadlocks and navel-exposing pants, stands for the

Lunar Eclipse: Ya Nan, the actress, as an alienated middle-class woman.
(Courtesy of Wang Quan'an)

Lunar Eclipse: The problem of vision and telepathic pain.
(Courtesy of Wang Quan'an)

so-called "new-new human being" (*xinxin renlei*), whose favorite pastime is dancing into a trance at discos.[24] They embody visibly different social standings and lifestyles, and thus divergent destinies, yet both seem to have arrived at the same crossroads in their life after fleeing from the abuse, physical or emotional, of men. The crossroads where their final, purportedly "accidental," encounter takes place underscores the contemporaneous nonsynchronicity of the women's lives. Jia Niang's violent death paradoxically reveals the vacuity and artificiality in the life of Ya Nan, who, however, through her "telepathic" witness gains a new understanding of her own life. In this "transfinite universe," the endings and beginnings of both of their lives and stories converge and diverge, rupture and resume.[25]

A fleeting allusion to twinhood early in the film foretells the women's shared fate as phantom sisters. As an avid amateur videographer, Ya Nan enjoys shooting randomly on the street. One of her takes includes a pair of twin sisters; but at that early point neither Ya Nan nor the viewer heeds their significance. If her initial attraction to the amateur photographer and her curiosity about a girl who resembles herself stems from her desire for finding her true self, a self repressed by the boredom of her middle-class life, then her search for the other girl increasingly takes on the urgency of finding a vanished kin, a phantom sister.[26] This "virtual" sisterhood is reinforced by the fact that each woman seems to be rootless and left on her own. Ya Nan has a sick father we never see; Jia Niang has a mother locked up in a faraway mental hospital. That sense of compounded alterity and affinity leads Ya Nan to enter the world in which Jia Niang lives or once lived, while the compression of the temporal distance between them propels each toward the final scene of the fatal accident, one that encapsulates the series of "accidents" that structure an erratic narrative of chance encounters and impossible rescues. Such a deliberately convoluted temporal arc is distinctly noir-influenced, as it is more inclined to show "how" rather than "what" in a social world beyond the control of the characters themselves.[27]

The figure of the phantom sister and the underlying "surreality" of social relations affords a poignant exposure of the pain of countless separated siblings, humiliated women, and torn families in a society undergoing drastic and often violent transformations. Indeed, references in the films to physical and emotional pain are legion. This cruel story of youth, as the Chinese film critic Dai Jinghua concludes, is thus also about the "cruelty of existence and society."[28] There is nothing more compelling than for the unstable physical and psychological identity of a young woman on the edge of the society, exposed to visible or invisible dangers, to stand for the shifting form of a relentlessly changing society and the urgency of intervention on the brink of catastrophe.

Meimei and Mudan   How does Lou Ye's *Suzhou River* assemble its version of a cruel story of two look-alike young women? Released only a few months after *Lunar Eclipse* (though initial footage was shot in 1996), at the outset Lou Ye's film seems an uncanny double of *Lunar Eclipse*, a resemblance that underscores the contemporaneity and historical valence of their shared narrative motif and noir style. As the film's title indicates (Suzhou River is the city's "maternal river," or *muqinhe*), the film is conspicuously set in Shanghai. Mudan (which means peony) and Meimei (both played by Zhou Xun), like their counterparts in *Lunar Eclipse*, are not real twins but virtual incarnates, or phantom sisters. Mudan, a teen daughter of a businessman involved in smuggling an Eastern European brand of Vodka,[29] is the love interest of a young drifter, Mada, one of numerous motorbike messengers seen in the busy streets of Shanghai. Mada is hired to escort Mudan out of the house when her father takes prostitutes home. After Mada takes part in kidnapping her for ransom, Mudan runs away and, in a slow-motion shot, jumps from the picturesque Waibaidu ("Garden") Bridge into the mouth of the Suzhou River near the Bund, where she vanishes without a trace. The attentive viewer will, however, notice her clutching a blond mermaid doll—a birthday gift to her from Mada. After this point, boat passengers and passersby occasionally spot a beautiful mermaid on the banks of the river, her shining image and supernatural presence highly incongruous with the notoriously smelly and polluted river.

This tale of affection, betrayal, and loss crisscrosses with, or rather is framed by, another tale of attraction and distance between a videographer and the character Meimei. Meimei works as a performer in a huge fish tank, swimming in a blond wig and mermaid costume to entertain the customers of a seafood restaurant located on the riverbank. The vanished Mudan seems to have returned, as if the mermaid doll in her hand becomes animated and incarnated into Meimei. The "maternal river" has perhaps given a new life to her. When after an unspecified amount of time has passed Mada returns from a prison term to the city, he finds in Meimei his lost Mudan.[30] The latter in turn comes to identify herself with Mudan through Mada's storytelling (in a manner similar to what happens in *Lunar Eclipse* between Ya Nan and the photographer). Mada finally locates the real Mudan as a cashier in a convenience store, only to die with her in a violent motorcycle accident soon thereafter. When the videographer returns to Meimei's boathouse, she is nowhere to be found. Throughout the film, the trope of the double is enshrouded in the ambience of a ghost story, which is evidenced by the fake peony tattoo on the left thigh of both Mudan and Meimei. A Chinese viewer is likely to associate this motif with Tang Xianzu's classical play from the sixteenth century, *The Peony Pavilion* (*Mudan ting*)—perhaps the most famous ghost romance in Chinese literary and theatrical canons.[31] And the image of the mermaid as a hybrid figure, as the art historian Jerome Silbergeld keenly observes, can also be projected back into Chinese cultural tradition, wherein the lore of beautiful women committing suicide by drowning and returning as spirits is legion.[32] Yet here these classical allusions serve as a reminder of the "spectral" nature of the present. As Harry Harootunian suggests, the figure of the revenant arrives, constantly, in the form of the "ghosts of what had been past and the premodern culture of reference that had not yet died, returning from a place out of time to haunt and disturb the historical present."[33]

Ultimately, it matters little whether or not Mudan and Meimei are the same girl—either one could be among the countless young women in Shanghai today who experience the loss of innocence more rapidly than in any previous generation but who also are more adept at performing multiple identities and quick changes. Lou Ye has confessed that because the film was derived from two made-for-TV projects, and as such resolving the mistaken identity was not his chief concern, it took him some time to decide whether to have one actress playing two parts or two actresses playing the same part. Meimei's job performing as an enticing half-human half-fish creature is hardly shocking to customers who are used to seeing young women eating their "rice-bowl of youth" in various capacities or disguises, mostly in the service and entertainment industry.[34] In an age when eating expensive fresh seafood is a status symbol for the nouveau riche, who themselves have often "plunged into the ocean" (meaning into the risky business world as opposed to the low-paying, stagnant state sectors), there is little difference between a live exotic fish and a body to be bought and consumed.[35] A large number of Shanghai's seafood restaurants are concentrated on two famous food streets, Huanghe Road on

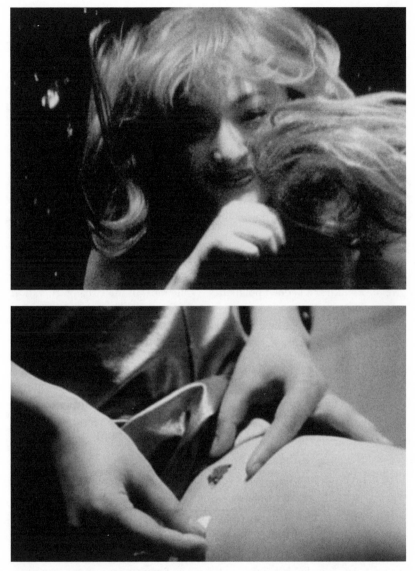

Suzhou River: After Mudan's disappearance, a "mermaid" surfaces at a seafood joint by the river.

Suzhou River: The peony tattoo—marker of authentic identity?

the south side of Suzhou River and Zhapu Road on the north side. A mermaid in a fish tank also invokes the prevalent image of the "caged golden sparrow," which refers to the young female gold diggers who trade youth and sex for luxury, often in the confines of a modern apartment or villa. Within this context the aquatic reference is hardly arbitrary. In this regard, Mudan's plunging into the river mouth—which not only is the most photogenic spot in Shanghai's iconography but also an emblem of a backward China connecting with the global trends at the end of the twentieth century—captures the troubled spirit of China's globalization. As the daughter of a businessman engaged in illegal transnational trade, and as the barter for a ransom in an underworld rivalry, Mudan falls prey to the multiple forces of globalization that have been eroding the metropolis in the 1990s. This globalizing ambition, while contributing to a large-scale facelift for cities like Beijing and Shanghai, is also shattering countless ordinary lives and youthful dreams.

These social subtexts, sedimented under a vertiginous narrative surface, give *Suzhou River* an added poignancy. While most of the Urban Generation films are set in China's political and cultural capital of Beijing, Lou Ye's film offers a rare and penetrating look at Shanghai's urban geography and social ecology that has seen the rise, decline, and revival of a Chinese metropolis. Instead of Huangpu River, which boasts the window-dressing Bund lined with its colonial bank buildings on one side and the soaring skyscrapers in Pudong on the other, Lou Ye chose to portray the smelly waterway that has served as a vital link between the city and the surrounding rural areas and thus has been the central artery of the expanding metropolis since the beginning of the twentieth century. For most of the past century, the Suzhou River, which used to be called Wusongjiang,[36] has been the transient home of countless boatmen who carried in migrants as well as vegetables, soy sauces, rice wines, and silks and cottons, and then freighted out the city's sewage and trash. The river, with its winding course and multiple heavily used bridges, is also a vital connection between the northern and southern part of the city. Historically, the river has served as a major divide separating the foreign concessions on the southwest side and the Chinese domains in large parts of the northeast, and thus also is a divide between different social classes and cultural communities. On multiple levels, the Suzhou River, far more than the Huangpu, is the artery of the city and the reservoir of its memories.

Suzhou River's quality as a "dreamy documentary" of Shanghai is displayed

Suzhou River as the "maternal river" and reservoir of urban memory.

in the opening of the film before the title appears. In fact, Lou began working on the film as a "documentary" before the story took salient shape. For a month he wandered along the river and shot footage with a super-8 video camera; in so doing he gradually entered the space of the narrative in which the border between reality and fiction is never clearly demarcated.[37] The invisible narrator holds his camera and drifts down the river on a boat, from which he surveys the people and the surrounding urban landscape. In the film we see the turbid water, then the embankments lined with decrepit buildings —many in the process of being demolished. We wonder what happened to the people who used to live or work there. Shots of buildings are intercut jaggedly with boats, boatmen loading or unloading cargos, people cooking or eating, and city people standing on the bridges—many of them looking straight into the camera. The swish pans and the erratic editing are characteristic of amateur videography yet are also lyrical and candid. The videographer's voice-over glides into this urban dreamscape of ruins and memory: "I often go out to shoot the Suzhou River with my camera, floating down the river from West to East and cutting across all of Shanghai. The river is a century's worth of legends, stories, memories and all that rubbish, all of which makes it the filthiest river. But there are still many people here, making a living on the river.

If you look long and hard, the river will let you see everything . . . people, lonely people . . . I have seen the birth of a baby, a girl jumping into the river, the corpses of a pair of lovers being lifted out of the water by the police . . . As for romance, I have seen a mermaid who was combing her blond hair . . . But don't believe me, I'm making all this up."

Lou Ye's urban legend of the mermaid is in fact a disguised city symphony of which the river—and by extension, Shanghai—is its true protagonist. As the film critic J. Hoberman aptly notes: "Lou has transformed Shanghai into a personal phantom zone. Named for an urban stream of consciousness, *Suzhou River* is a ghost story that's shot as though it were a documentary— and a documentary that feels like a dream."[38] Lou's dreamy documentary has quickly become a part of the city's archive. By the time of the film's release, the river had been cleaned up through a large infusion of money from the World Bank. Expensive condominiums and office complexes are rapidly taking root along the riverbanks, where the half-torn buildings seen in the film once stood. The boathouses have been forced out, and the sewage pits on the embankments, at least those near the river mouth and the Bund, have been replaced by strips of green promenades. The urban lore today has it that even edible fish have begun to return to the river after decades of absence.

Suzhou River might be seen as an unwitting sequel to *Lunar Eclipse* in the itinerary of their phantom sisters in the national urban geography. In fact, the two films make up one tale of two cities. Jia Niang repeatedly states her desire to "go south" (*nanfang*, referring to the coastal cities like Shenzhen or Shanghai, areas known for their Special Economic Zones and hence opportunities) to both flee from her misery in Beijing and seek her luck in the milder and more prosperous south.[39] Before her disappearance from the story, Jia Niang is seen spending a good deal of time losing herself in a place called the Beijing Oriental Imperial City of Entertainment, which features, among other things, a tawdry karaoke bar with plush patterned sofas and a neon-colored cocktail called "Pink Lady." In Lou Ye's Shanghai, Mudan's look-alike resurfaces in the sleazy, neon-decorated "Happy Tavern" bar-cum-seafood restaurant, a place where Jia Niang could have landed if she indeed had fled the harsh north. If the "south" in *Lunar Eclipse* still carried an aura, a destination for worldly success and self-realization, then *Suzhou River*, with its unflinchingly gritty portrayal of a rusting metropolis as an industrial wasteland (the river has also been the primary site of heavy industry) and its unhappy souls, shatters the

Suzhou River: "Happy Tavern" (Shiji kaixin Bar, literally Century Happy Bar).

myth of the "south" to its core. Jia Niang and Meimei are thus the transient inhabitants of Beijing and Shanghai. Like those tender-aged female migrant workers (*dagongmei*) swarming into the cities, these women are relegated to the margins but also proliferate as their adopted cities grow and decay, and grow again. Their fast-changing shapes and fluid identities render them the very flesh and blood, figuratively and literally, of the tantalizing urban dream.

Dabao and Erbao (an Interlude from the Past)   *Suzhou River*'s meditation on the city's unconscious and woman's fate in modernity's labyrinth takes us back to where Chinese cinema's early "golden age" began in the 1930s. While a contemporary art film lover would instantly draw a synchronic parallel between Lou's and Wang's films with those of Kieslowski or Wong Kar-wai, a historian of Chinese cinema would not resist the temptation to make a diachronic connection between Lou's and Wang's tales of phantom sisters with Zheng Zhengqiu's classic *Sister Flowers* (Zimeihua, 1933), so as to ponder the relevance of the trope of female twins for both urban memory and film history. In both its narrative and cinematic registers *Sister Flowers* exemplifies the problem of the vanishing kin, of difference and affinity, and of heredity versus sociality. The apparent class allegory embodied by the twin sisters, made vis-

Sister Flowers: A tale of twin sisters and contrasting fates in 1930s Shanghai.
(Courtesy of the China Film Archive)

ible and visceral by double exposure and other cinematic devices, forges a
powerful commentary on the experience of modernity and its representability.

A culminating success in Zheng's career before his death in 1935, *Sister
Flowers* portrays the divergent fates of a pair of twin sisters. Unlike Lou's and
Wang's films, *Sister Flowers* is ostensibly a family melodrama, a genre that
served as a chief winning formula for the Mingxing Company, which was
founded in 1922. Based on a three-act "Civilized Play" by Zheng,[40] the film
features the popular Hu Die, who plays both sisters, or, as the title suggests,
"two flowers of the same stem." The twins, Dabao and Erbao, were born to a
poor family in the country. The good-for-nothing father, a gun smuggler by

trade, deserts the family for the city, taking with him the better-looking Erbao who subsequently becomes a high official's concubine. Years later, Dabao is married and gives birth to a son. The distressful conditions in the country during the warlord period force the rest of the family to move to the city, where Dabao becomes, unwittingly, a wet nurse for Erbao's newborn baby. She is chosen for the reason that she has the same blood type as Erbao and produces good milk. Desperate to save her husband who has been injured in a factory, Dabao attempts to steal the baby's silver charm necklace but is caught in the act. The mother of the sisters finds their father, who is now a high official, and begs him to help release Dabao. The family is finally reunited at the end of the film when the twins' identity is revealed to each of them.

Sister Flowers premiered at the first-run Xinguang Grand Theater in Shanghai in summer 1933 and ran consecutively for two months to enormous popular and critical acclaim—a record for a Chinese production in a time when Hollywood imports dominated the market. In a fashion not entirely different from *Lunar Eclipse*'s and *Suzhou River*'s forays into international art houses where the work is transported by the filmmakers or actors themselves, *Sister Flowers* was taken by Hu Die to the Moscow International Film Festival in 1935 (a previous incarnation of that attended by Wang Quan'an), where it was one of only a few Chinese films from that period exhibited in Europe.[41] The film appealed to the Chinese audiences, especially members of the lower and lower-middle classes. Its melodramatic mode served as an efficient vehicle for processing and understanding the social contradictions and alienation that beset a modernizing society.[42]

Another reason for the success of *Sister Flowers* is that the film served as a star vehicle for Hu Die, yet this time with an added dimension.[43] Her star power is literally doubled by the plot (as was the movie ticket cost), which in her roles as two diametrically different sisters provided a showcase for her acting skill. For the audience, however, that power was not just about seeing two Hu Die films in one. Because the film was one of the first in China to have sound, for the audience it was a way to experience once more the magic power of film technology and its impact on the modern perception of corporeality and selfhood. It is important to stress that the attraction of the film owes much to the (more or less) successful "union" between image and sound; the previously popular melodrama of the silent period is now injected with the "life" of human voice and other sounds.

While Wang's and Lou's contemporary noirish art house tales of phantom sisters are obviously not modeled on Zheng's socio-biological drama of twin-hood, the affinity of the films may be located in the way each generation discerns the connection between women's fate and the lure of the metropolis in periods of accelerated modernization. Wang Quan'an told a Boston audience that his writing of the script was motivated by his sympathy for Chinese women's hardship today, "because, regardless of who they are and what they do, many of them are sad and unhappy."[44] On another occasion he confessed, in a possible allusion to melodrama, "Actually the basic structure of the film is very simple and traditional."[45] However, it is family, the hallmark of Zheng's melodrama, that is conspicuously missing or broken beyond repair in *Lunar Eclipse* and *Suzhou River*. The sultry, precocious "new-new human being" generation of girls in dreadlocks, tattoos, and blond wigs are perhaps Dabao's grandchildren in age, but they do bear resemblance to Erbao in that they share with her the desire for material comfort, on one hand, and a compassionate heart on the other. The migrant young female workers in the 1990s may not work as wet nurses, but there is an army of maids who clean and cook for the urban middle or upper class as well as care for their old and young. Erbao's role as a concubine is thus familiar again, filled in by all-too-many willing "golden sparrows." It would be hardly surprising today to find one of the daughters from a rural family working as a maid while a prettier and more ambitious one becomes a rich man's extramarital love object (or *xiaomi*, "little mistress," like the secretary of Ya Nan's husband).[46]

The end of the twentieth century was also the age when the making of twins and multiples became no longer the exclusive domain of nature but part of the enterprise of biogenetic engineering. In *Lunar Eclipse*, for example, there are passing references to plastic surgery and sex change or identity change.[47] In China, after long periods of relative social stasis imposed from above, the post–cold war period has witnessed tremendous upheavals in family structure and in ethics, with the rigid enforcement of the one-child policy on the one hand and the rising rate of "illegal" births by migrant and rural populations on the other. At the same time, those in the emerging urban white-collar class, especially the young and ambitious, are less inclined to have children. With the dissolution of the extended family, the rising divorce rates in the cities, and the massive migration and dislocation in the society as a whole, there is an increased anxiety about the breakdown of generational continuity, loss of innocence, and lack of human connection. I think it is the simultaneous apprehension of this identity crisis and the desire to connect with real or imagined kin and stranger alike that informs the moral and social concerns of these recent films about missing bodies and phantom sisters.

If during the transition to sound *Sister Flowers* harnessed the technology of sight and sound to realize a hyperbolic melodrama about social inequity, Wang's and Lou's innovative, albeit at times jarring, narration and visual style foreground the insufficiency or instability of either the homegrown melodrama or the imported noir form in giving expression to the complex social experience and psychological baggage of the new generations. In watching *Lunar Eclipse* and *Suzhou River* the viewer hesitates to determine which story in the "either/or" structure is more reliable, because beneath the surface symmetry there is structural asymmetry and inequity. And the closure of a happy ending is out of the question in either film—each is possessed by a deep sense of fatefulness, a distinctive noir feature that strangely dovetails with the Chinese Buddhist–influenced perspective on desire, life, and death. A faint sense of consolation comes from elsewhere, where it is conveyed, as Rey Chow states, by "an alternative temporality of community," however "mythic" it may be.[48] These films are not about two equally divided selves but about forms of succession and extension; not about reunion but about an open, almost superstitious belief in afterlife; and not about reconciliation but about transmigration and transformation. In the absence of a happy ending, both films suggest something more—in the form of eternal returns, discontinuous continuity, and life after death—while accomplishing a cinematic anatomic operation of the fin-de-siècle Chinese urban life.

PHOTOGRAPHY, VIDEOGRAPHY, AND A TACTILE CINEMA

Despite their social and historical resonance, *Lunar Eclipse* and *Suzhou River* are not copies of *Sister Flowers* for the chief reason that the two contemporary filmmakers consciously engage the act of cinematic narration by inserting the figure of the photographer/videographer in tandem with the figure of the phantom sister.[49] Considering the extent to which the end of the twentieth century was an age in which new information and audiovisual technologies, after several decades of near stagnation, began to inundate and penetrate everyday life in China on an unprecedented scale, the reemergence of twins and doubles on the screen is all the more thought provoking. Unlike the use of double exposures and mise-en-scène elements such as makeup and props to conceal the double identity of Hu Die in *Sister Flowers*, the presence of cameras in both *Lunar Eclipse* and *Suzhou River* does not simply serve diegetic functions. Rather, on a metanarrative level such presence *mediates* or triggers the magical transformation of virtual twinhood. This metanarrative quality illustrates Deleuze's notion of "fabulation" (*récits*; a form of storytelling that is "performative in the philosophical as well as the theatrical sense"), which is central to a "minor cinema." It is "an act of telling inseparable from the time of enunciation," which "gravitates" between the documentary and the fictional.[50]

The self-reflexive impulse in these two films distinguishes itself from the kind of "documentary impulse" detected by Yomi Braester in several mainstream commercial films about the demolition of cities, the destruction of communities, and the "real-time nostalgia" produced by the diegetic cameras, such as is found in *Stand Up, Don't Stoop* and *Shower*.[51] While the "documentary impulse" in these commercial urban films is by and large contained within the realist conventions and melodramatic formula (albeit sometimes with a touch of parody for constructing a more or less illusory world) and couched in ideological security, Wang's and Lou's experimental films are part of an effort to create an alternative cinema with an avant-garde spirit. Their visual style, liberally blending art cinema and pop idioms (from MTV, karaoke, and computer games), is made up largely by a synergic use of noirish lighting (particularly emphasizing shadows and neon-lit night streets), jostling camera movement, jump-cuts, close-ups and extreme-close framing, long takes, direct address to the camera (and audience), discontinuous editing, shifting color schemes, and a contrapuntal and pastiche soundtrack. All of these elements create a plasmatic and tactile surface and a roller coaster–like viewing experience. Such a film form exemplifies what Deleuze sees as the "direct time-image" that seeks to restore time, and thought, to cinema. Because thought here is no longer the domain of abstraction but rather a philosophical sensorium, a machine or body "without organs," it is capable of affectivity and transformation. In this regard the visual style of these films can be understood as a transposition of the sense of loss and doubt permeating the society onto "mannerism and style" through noir-inflected idioms,[52] thereby exposing and commenting on the prevalent epistemological and moral uncertainty that has overwhelmed a postsocialist consumerist China.

There is a perceivable skepticism toward the truth value of the technologically reproduced image that informs and structures both films, yet each is permeated with a paradoxical scopophila and delight in capturing, photographically or videographically, the strange beauty of the "flow of life,"[53] be it the smelly Suzhou River or a container of developing agent (in a bathtub full of floating pictures in the photo studio in *Lunar Eclipse*). *Lunar Eclipse* is in particular a story about light and shadow, the essential material of photography and cinematography. In addition to the amateur photographer Hu Xiaobin, Ya Nan is also an avid picture taker whose video camera functions as her prosthetic arm and eye, whether in public or private realms. Walking on the streets she tapes couples dancing the tango (a form of mass self-enjoyment and the quotidianization of Western culture). At home, she documents her husband's sleepwalking and obsessive shoe polishing (a sign of domestic neurosis). After finding the photographer snapping her image during their excursion to the country, she captures him and returns her gaze through her video camera. Throughout the film, there is a sustained competition between multiple photographers and their different technologies.

Photography serves as the crucial medium of communication or miscommunication across the perceived class divide in *Lunar Eclipse*. Ya Nan visits the photo shop, called The Origin of Beauty Creative Studio, where Hu Xiaobin works directing and shooting wedding albums—a trendy and profitable business in urban China today (which the film parodies on several occasions, including Ya Nan's own wedding). Hu shows her the darkroom—and the magic of photochemistry—where she later will encounter Jia Niang's blownup image, her phantom other. The photographer serves as the medium in bringing Ya Nan face to face with her look-alike but then vanishes from Beijing altogether. But is Jia Niang's larger-than-life image believable? In the same room Hu and his boss have doctored the funeral picture of Hu's father who died the moment his only picture has been taken by his son (as if photography triggered the death). In the remainder of the film Ya Nan is stalked by a stranger, who follows her in sinister dark alleys and takes her photograph. The flashes from this unidentified photographer's camera become a kind of optical rape, parallel to or echoing the violence done to Jia

Niang. The title of the film, *Lunar Eclipse*, intimates a state of mind as well as a cosmic phenomenon, a process of change that resembles the photochemical procedure and creates a penumbra zone between light and darkness, the visible and the invisible, the material and the immaterial. It is also an allegory for women's fate; the feminine (*ying*) radiance and "negative" energy symbolized by the moon in Chinese cosmology are here transmitted to the cinematic universe, illuminating the "eclipse" of women's place in the social world.

As a whole, the photographical images in the film, mobilized for either proleptical or retroactive narration, carry a certain ambiguity and a sense of the uncanny, never telling their entire stories and at times simply reversing our expectations of their meaning (as with the father's deadly photographic session and the gallant images of Hu's wretched coworkers). As capable of "betrayal" as much as "fidelity" the photo images lay bare the gray zone between reality and its representation, the image and its absent referent. They seem to be hovering in the borderland of stasis and movement (the film is full of sudden freeze-up images), truth and lie, and life and mortality, exposing the ontological ambiguity of photography as a medium of mechanically reproducible images and artificial memory. In its direct association with Jia Niang and the father's death, photography here accentuates the medium's nature as a form of "farewell" to the living and a "mode of bereavement," and as such it "acknowledges what takes place in any photograph—the return of the departed."[54] These photographs of one's beloved on the threshold of life and death, unlike staged wedding pictures, create a kind of time capsule and memory bank.

What does videography, the postmodern hybridization of photography and cinema, stand for in these two films? In *Lunar Eclipse* we find video footage on Ya Nan's home video equipment as well as on the multiple screens in public space, including the disco where Ya Nan finds the stimuli lacking in her married life. (The images on the screen there show the explosion or demolition of city buildings.) The photographs in the film capture many auratic or memorable moments (Ya Nan's joyful dancing on a sheet of ice; the father's serene dying in a decaying hutong courthouse; and even the past romance of Ya Nan's unfaithful husband) in a life of boredom or disappointment. The video footage, however, shows either the atrophy of the everyday or violence or disaster as sensation. The class inflection attached to each medium—Hu Xiaobin with photography (especially his old camera) and Ya Nan with video—seems further to underscore the "decline of photography" (or loss of aura) in the face of ever "perfected" representational technologies.[55] Yet Ya Nan's penchant for videography seems also connected to her extraordinary sensory capacities, which not only aligns her with Hu Xiaobin but also makes her a competing narrator in the film.

The deployment of video in *Suzhou River* is more integrated into the narrative and at the service of a gender orientation that invokes classical film noir. The disjointed story is told through a male videographer ("I") who remains invisible (except for his hands) throughout the film. Despite the combination of footage shot for two TV-films, the edited feature, in using a consistent male voice-over, implicated yet detached, gives the film a more salient noir inflection. The copresence of a messenger's and a videoman's love for the "same" woman molds together while also deconstructs two kinds of American male noir protagonists in the postwar period: the "cool" criminal in the "criminal-adventure thriller" and the "tough" investigator in the "investigative thriller," respectively. Frank Krutnik, in his study on noir and masculinity, defines the "criminal" hero as "a male overachiever who seeks through his defiance of the law to set him above it, and to set himself in its place, as omnipotent." "His daring gamble against the delimitations of his place within culture, under the law, represents a transgressive fantasy which is marked, in multiple ways, by the inevitability of its failure."[56] The investigative hero, on the other hand, is embodied as the "private eye" who "occupies a mediating point between the worlds of crime and legitimate society. He proves himself by his ability to withstand any challenges to his integrity—and to his very status as the active hero (i.e., to his masculine professionalism, or his professional masculinity)."[57] *Suzhou River* departs, however, from either of these classical noir subgenres precisely in selectively scrambling two strands together while injecting a free dose of the ghost story genre ingrained in Chinese narrative and dramatic tradition.

The videographer is not only an illegitimate investigator (due to his amateur status—that is, he was hired to make a promotion, not an investigation), he is also an absent hero. Despite his disembodied voice-over, elements such as the unsteady, intrusive video filming and the visibility of his hands foreground him as en embodiment of the video camera. His obsessive (paid or unpaid) filming wherever he is present creates an impression that the world itself has taken on a "videographic face" (to play on Kracauer's famous comment on photography).[58] Video services such as his are in urban China today as common as *Lunar Eclipse*'s The Origin of Beauty Creative Studio; amateur videographers are routinely hired to shoot weddings, funerals, and birthday parties, and to make advertisements. But here, the videographer's matter-of-fact business assignment quickly turns into a subjective exploration of the enigma surrounding Meimei, the mermaid girl. As the line between her identity and that of Mudan begins to blur, the distinction between the videographer and Mada (which literally means a motor or engine) begins to dissolve as well. If Meimei is a ghost from the past, and her only purchase on the present is the fake peony tattoo on her left thigh (as on Mudan's—a tactile yet disposable inscription on the body), how real and alive then is the videographer who intermittently slips in and out of Mada's body and mind? As many point-of-view shots are taken from the camera mounted on Mada's motorcycle, the two "machines" do share one body, or a "body without organs," as it were. We cannot help but wonder if Mada has reinvented himself as the videographer just as Mudan seems incarnated in the mermaid girl. The identities of the two pairs of doubles, female or male, do not refer to literal persons with fixed social profiles, but rather are immanent bodies in the process of becoming-other or transformation. Each is the simulation, not copy, of the other, and whose identity as a "body without organs" consists of a "bundle of virtual affects" and constant "flights" or movement between I and the Other.[59]

Lou Ye is not interested in solving the enigma about the two women as would a typical noir investigative hero. Ultimately his intent is to compose a love poem, a Baudelairesque "fleur du mal," about a river, a city, and the impossible task of giving both a total representation. If Wang Quan'an allows the cab driver to dream of becoming a cinematographer and even to act heroically on behalf of Jia Niang, Lou Ye's darker urban vision makes Mada a betrayer and the videographer an unreliable witness and lackadaisical lover who even lacks Mada's intensity. Lou, however, makes a point by framing the voyeuristic film as a whole through a videographer's viewfinder in order to show a trace of sympathy if not intervention. This absent hero unwittingly helps Mada to find Mudan, although he himself lacks the commitment to search for Meimei when she vanishes in the end. Yet his business assignment has turned into an epistemological adventure all the same. "Voyeurism and hiding behind a camera are not the same thing," emphasizes Lou. "When you're making a movie, you're impacting the world that you're filming, which in turn impacts you. It can be a dangerous position." Yet this danger is not entirely futile because it is invested with a possibility for creating connection, as manifested in the fleeting romances in the film. Lou concedes that using romantic elements in a film can "evoke real emotion." "In real life there is little romance of any real quality—you need to evoke it, just like when you're watching or making a film."[60]

Obviously, despite their noirish vision and a touch of nihilism, both Wang and Lou share a conviction in cinema's capacity to create a new order of reality—a dimension of evoked memory and felt affect and connectivity. Photography and videography in the films may at times carry with them a sense of reification as surveillance apparatus or instruments of alienation. However, the ubiquity of photographers and videographers is not so much a cynical record of the rampant industry of mass images that has changed China beyond recognition as it is a meditation on the pervasive impact, destructive as well as transformative, of these imaging technologies on the human mimetic faculty. The films are hardly suggestive of a nostalgic return to some pre-reform era, technologically impoverished state, but rather are hard at work to mobilize these old and new media, through their encounter with the lives of phantom sisters, for the revivification of cinema and its power to restore sensory affect and mimetic faculty. In the films the men and women with a camera move in various (narrative or literal) vehicles on the "two-way street" of a mimetic race,[61] alternately being the subject or object of photography and videography—that is, as passive witnesses or intervening agents in "accidents" that seem beyond their control yet always are fatefully rewarding in the form of doubles and returns. This explains in part both films' genre-bending qualities that blur the boundaries between the representational and the reflexive, as well as the qualities of intermittent humor and warmth, especially when the diegetic photographers and videographers try to get closer to their object of love or observation (often literally through zoom-in and extreme close-ups).

More important, a cinema that holds the potential to not just provide solace but also to restore affect to a bruised humanity is a sensuous cinema that touches and moves the spectator, teaching people to "cry again."[62] It is a cinema of the body instead of abstraction or illusion.[63] The tactile quality is often literalized through the films' emphasis on touching and embracing.

While the problem with Ya Nan's marriage can be glimpsed through her husband's shoe polishing (an alienated, or fetishist, form of touch or being out of touch), the amateur photographer connects with Ya Nan during their first encounter by touching her shoulder in the car while asking, "Are you cold?" As revealed later, a similar gesture has also been made toward Ya Niang. When vision alone cannot prove the materiality and certitude of life, touching is believing.

Tactility is the conduit of affect in *Suzhou River* as well. The videographer, as mentioned above, is perceived as a body without organs—a machine with a pair of hands. The hands are inseparable from his work (and by extension the work of the filmmaker behind him); their omnipresence evidences the film-maker's insistence on exposing the materiality and labor of cinema. These hands do the work of posting a video services sign, receiving a paged call, and by shooting a job at the "Happy Tavern," but they quickly move on to engage in the courting of Meimei. They clap her hands, a popular game among children; they stroke her hair while lovingly watching/shooting her sensuous face. The images are so close and vivid that they seem on the verge of spilling out of the screen. We as viewers feel pulled toward her and the screen by these bodyless hands as though they have become our own prosthetics. The MTV-style footage of the "hair stroking" scene evolves into a visual, acoustic, and tactile refrain throughout the film and endows an otherwise disenchanting urban legend with a measure of warmth and affect.

The redemptive power of a tactile cinema is encapsulated in a key scene in *Lunar Eclipse*, when the line between cinema and reality is dissolved. After Jia Niang and Hu Xiaobin exit a movie theater—the site where they had met the first time and where they have now just seen *Titanic*—they enter a conversation about cinema that solidifies their connection. Earlier in the theater the flood of *Titanic*'s melodramatic images has pushed the young couple together; in the midst of the bombarding sound of the broken iceberg and the sinking of the ship, Hu extends his arm to hold the crying Jia Niang. The two under-dogs thus find each other on the brink of a Hollywood manufactured virtual catastrophe as well as on another real one in store for them in the streets of Beijing.[64] Sitting inside his cab parked outside the theater, Hu Xiaobin affirms Jia Niang's ambition of becoming a movie actress and Jia Niang reciprocates with encouraging him to be a cinematographer. While they are excited by their ten-year plan to realize this dream, a flickering flame slowly rises on the

Suzhou River: Tactile contact.

front car window caressing the dreamy faces of the young couple. The flame turns out to be the reflection of the neon lights from the theater and street.[65] In this heartwarming moment, the artificial flame fueled by the city and the celluloid world not only rekindles hope and love in the wounded and numbed, it also seems to melt the glass and the car. Conversely, it could also be the intensification of the emotion and the warmth of two bodies in touch with each other that reconnect them with the elements of the phenomenal world. Indeed, Hu Xiaobin's cab, the China-made yellow *miandi* (now obsolete), which used to be driven by his father, magically turns into a furnace of love, in obvious contrast to the luxurious but ever so cold red sports car owned by Ya Nan's husband. (Its convertible cover has been stuck when the three meet on that freezing cold day.)

The "flow of life" is in this moment given back its concrete form of ceaseless motion and metamorphosis. The commingling of the couple's cinephilia and the "process of materialization," figuratively rendered in this scene, would exemplify for Kracauer (and in the words of Miriam Hansen) the "aesthetic possibilities of film to stage, in a sensory and imaginative form, a fundamental experience of the twentieth century—an experience that has been variously described in terms of reification and alienation, fragmentation and loss, but

Lunar Eclipse: Hu Xiaobin inside his *miandi* cab. (Courtesy of Wang Quan'an)

that . . . no less held a significant share of exhilarating and liberatory impulses."[66] The artificial flame exteriorizes the psychic states of the lovers, linking their private reverie with the larger social and material world that surrounds and transforms them. We watch these cinephiles, through the car window, as if watching a budding but doomed romance of this young couple in a film. "If the world has become a bad movie," like the circumstances that have been preying on them, "a true cinema can contribute to giving us back reasons to believe in the world and in vanished bodies."[67]

This "reflexive" scene, despite the absence of a diegetic camera, crystallizes the emergence of a hyperreal dimension in these recent art films. The disappointment in the here and now is swept by a passion for a reimagined or transformed reality (as embodied in the glow that turns a shabby cab into a love boat) that defeats the atrophy of the present. It is a utopian moment lodged within yet revising the present. Cinema serves as a crucial mediating agent in creating a new plane of perception on which the limitations of the lived social reality, as well as the distance between it and the world of narrating and overcoming that reality, is exposed and challenged simultaneously. This re-enchanted dimension is enabled by an attempt to both reveal the alienated form of the social present and find its antidote, hence the conscious, almost frantic, formal experimentation for achieving a new (or renewed) level of sensory experience. On this heightened perceptual and experiential plane, the phantom sister is at once a real social actor and a poignant allegory for the era of "transformation."

CONCLUSION

The arsenal of filmic vocabularies and narrative vehicles mobilized by these recent experimental films to restore the body and senses to the inchoate experiences of the underdogs or victims of the era of reform and globalization distinguishes itself from the kind deployed in some of the innovative Fifth Generation films set in an illusory narrative world, be it a remote mountain village or a mythical past. If stasis and contemplation constitute the keynote in the Fifth Generation's canon, the experimental cinema of the Urban Genera-tion is marked by motion and a heightened awareness of the ephemeral temporality of contemporary urban life. The radical contemporaneity of both *Lunar Eclipse* and *Suzhou River* lies in their insistence on introducing a dif-ferent politics and poetics of phenomenology. In choosing the phantom sister as a compounded figure of the present and the past, both incomplete and overlapping, they are registering the unevenness of development and the casualties inflicted by the ideology of progress while reaffirming the tenacity of social memory, aided and processed by various sensory prostheses. From a broader perspective in world film history, these films contribute to what Deleuze called the "direct time-image." The phantom sister is thus a kindred spirit to and embodiment of such an alternative film image: "The phantom which has always haunted the cinema, but it took modern cinema to give a body to this phantom."[68] Undoubtedly, their visual style and narrative tech-nique (including the figure of the double) are by no means original home-grown recipes. Their originality comes rather from their identification, emu-lation, and, more important, transformation of contemporary art cinema within a global spectrum, heralded by people with different cultural origins and personal styles, particularly those such as Tarkovsky, Kieslowski, Hou Hsiao-hsien, Wong Kar-wai, and Kiarostami who come from the former Socialist bloc or non-Western countries.

The cosmopolitan outlook of these and other Urban Generation films, however, should not obscure our recognition of their local conditions of conception, production, and reception. These filmmakers may now be traveling more freely and have almost unlimited exposure to world cinema—notably through the inexpensive but legally dubious VCD technology (hinted by Mada's obsessive watching of pirated VCDS in *Suzhou River*). It remains, however, their primary preoccupation to portray contemporary Chinese society. Their cosmopolitan film language is intimately bound to the social experience that has modeled them and shaped their cinematic vision. Wang Quan'an, for instance, cites in his autobiographic sketch a turning point in his life that has made him the filmmaker he is today. In the early 1980s, after a visit to France where he fell in love with cinema, he applied to the Lyon Film Institute and was accepted there. But upon departure he realized that although he might learn how to make a film at the institute, he would never be able to make a "real French film," and later would probably not be able to make a Chinese film, either. As a result, he opted not to go. While studying at the Beijing Film Academy, he also came to the realization that many of the so-called great Chinese films were replete with "dead and false emotions": "These films are neither about my life nor about those around me. They have very little to do with us and our perception of contemporary life, even less with our need for the pleasure of the cinematic aesthetic [experience]." He thus decided to make his own films—ones that would give expression to a kind of "truth" about China yet also about humanity at large and about film as art.[69] In the Chinese critic Chen Xiaoming's view, *Lunar Eclipse*'s subjective lens and firm grasp of the "material sense" (*zhigan*) accomplishes a higher degree of "contemporaneity" (*dangdaixing*) and "nativeness" (*bentuxing*) than those Fifth Generation films heavily coded with literal idioms of "tradition" and "nativism." "The true nativeness is really contemporaneity, revealing the living present in a changing, complex discursive environment."[70]

The creatively recycled international art film language and postmodern pop idioms provide the occasion or a filter to reactivate, albeit unconsciously, melodramatic elements that can be traced to films such as *Sister Flowers* or classical canons of tales of the strange. While these Urban Generation filmmakers are writing a new chapter in Chinese film history, the cultural legacy of the past also finds them and asks to be reprocessed and renewed. On the other hand, as suggested by the scene in *Lunar Eclipse* after the lovers watch *Titanic*, these innovative filmmakers do not necessarily reject in total the imported mass images and storytelling formulas represented by Hollywood, but rather actively engage and transform them in order to tell stories about their generation in their own language. Along these parallel and at times intersecting trajectories, *Lunar Eclipse* and *Suzhou River* stand as a pair of remarkable signposts in the transformation of Chinese cinema at the turn of a new century.

NOTES

Many people contributed to the conception and development of this essay. Above all I thank Wang Quan'an and Lou Ye for our conversations, which first spurred my interest in writing this piece. I benefited greatly from my engaging discussions with Miriam Hansen, Tom Gunning, Josh Yumibe, and others at the Mass Culture Workshop at the University of Chicago on February 16, 2002. I also thank Magnus Fiskesjö and Charley Leary for their comments on an earlier version of this essay.
1. The VCD version of *Suzhou River* that I own is produced by the Hong Kong–based Winson Entertainment Distribution Ltd. VCD is notorious for its untrustworthy quality, especially the pirated versions that are routinely sold in black markets both inside and outside of China.
2. Gilles Deleuze, *Cinema 2: The Time-Image*, trans. Hugh Tomlinson and Robert Galeta (Minneapolis: University of Minnesota Press, 1986), 206.
3. Ibid., 195–96.
4. A number of retrospectives or selections of European, Japanese, and other international art films took place in Beijing and Shanghai in the 1980s. The Beijing Film Academy and other film-related cultural institutions have more regular access to classical or contemporary world cinema as a whole. In the 1990s, cheap VCD technology further popularized (or "copied") the archives of international art cinema as well as the Hollywood blockbusters.
5. Interview with Wang Guan'an, June 13, 2000, Beijing.
6. Siegfried Kracauer, *From Dr. Caligari to Hitler: A Psychological History of the German Film* (Princeton: Princeton University Press, 1947). See especially the section (pp. 28–31) concerning the doppelganger figure in films such as *A Student of Prague* (1913).
7. The term used above is borrowed from Harold Bloom, *The Anxiety of Influence: A Theory of Poetry* (New York: Oxford University Press, 1997 [1975]). The anxiety is caused by a simultaneous desire to emulate predecessors and to surpass them.
8. It has been a common practice to assign graduates jobs in their hometowns or native provinces. Since Lou is from Shanghai and Wang is originally from Yan'an in Shanxi Province, it was only "natural" for them to go back to where they came from.
9. Filmed-for-TV is a new trend in contemporary Chinese "film" culture that gives

young filmmakers a chance to work in a medium with less political and financial pressure. Guan Hu's unreleased *Yexingren* (A walker by night), also a noirish tale of a deranged young man set in Shanghai, is part of the aborted *Super City* series.

10. Dennis Lim, "Voyeur Eyes Only: Lou Ye's Generation Next," *Village Voice*, November 4, 2000, 140. At the question and answer session after the screening of *Suzhou River* at MoMA, Lou Ye mentioned that on-location shooting was also in part constrained by the difficulty of obtaining permissions from local authorities; the use of a handheld 16mm camera and video camera considerably eased the shooting in the always-bustling area of central Shanghai.

11. For example, Chen Kaige's father is the famous director Chen Huaikai, and Tian Zhuangzhuang's mother, Yu Lan, is a well-known actress and the head of the Children's Film Studio.

12. In December 1997, the Film Bureau promulgated the document on regulations on "granting permission for single feature film production," making it possible for provincial and municipal TV stations as well as film studios or related entities with equivalent statue and capacity to submit scripts to the bureau for production permissions.

13. Wang Quan'an's brief acting career includes a leading role in Zhang Nuanxin's *Good Morning, Beijing* (1990), presumably during his student years at the Beijing Film Academy where Zhang Nuanxin also taught until her death in 1995.

14. Conversation with Wang Quan'an, June 2001.

15. See Kai Yan, "Zhengjin yu ruili de 'Yueshi' " [The shocking and uncompromising *Lunar Eclipse*], posted in November 2001 in the "movie" section at http://www.movie.newyouth.Beida-Online.com.

16. The film's producer, Leonardo de la Fuente, is allegedly the author of this "genre" label. See Annette Insdorf's *Double Lives, Second Chances: The Cinema of Krzysztof Kieslowski* (New York: Hyperion, 1999), 123. For a detailed, compelling reading of *Suzhou River* in light of Hitchcock's influence, see Jerome Silbergeld, *Hitchcock with a Chinese Face: Cinematic Doubles, Oedipal Triangles, and China's Moral Voice* (Seattle: University of Washington Press, 2004), chapter 1.

17. Hillel Schwartz, *The Culture of the Copy: Striking Likeness, Unreasonable Facsimiles* (New York: Zone Books, 1996), 24.

18. Walter Benjamin, "The Work of Art in the Age of Mechanical Reproduction," in *Illuminations: Essays and Reflections*, ed. Hannah Arendt, trans. Harry Zohn (New York: Schocken, 1969), 217–52; especially parts 2 and 3. For a brilliant reading of Benjamin's idea of the cinematic "innervation" of senses in modernity, see Miriam Hansen, "Benjamin and Cinema: Not a One-Way Street," *Critical Inquiry* 25, no. 2 (winter 1999): 306–43. For an insightful investigation into the early conceptualization of cinema as modern magic, see Rachel Moore, *Savage Theory: Cinema as Modern Magic* (Durham, N.C.: Duke University Press, 2000).

19. Schwartz, *The Culture of the Copy*, 38.

20. This resonates with the identification of the schizoid, in particular, and the

somatic modality of the body in Gilles Deleuze and Félix Guattari, *Anti-Oedipus: Capitalism and Schizophrenia* (Minneapolis: University of Minnesota Press, 1983).

21. This synopsis is partly adopted from Annette Insdorf's *Double Lives, Second Chances*, 126–28.

22. For an overview and assessment of the documentary movement, which also emerged in the 1990s, see my introduction to this volume as well as Chris Berry's essay.

23. Under the aegis of state feminism, all Chinese women were supposed to work. Over time, the freedom to work was eclipsed by the imperative to work for subsistence, and women had to work both outside and inside the home. It thus became fashionable in the 1990s for certain women to choose to stay at home if their husbands made more than enough to maintain a comfortable standard of living. For a sociological study of the social and ethical characteristics of the emerging middle class in urban China of 1990s, see Duan Yiping, *Gaojihui: Zhongguo chengshi zhongchan jieceng xiezhen* [High-grade grey: A portrayal of the Chinese urban middle class] (Beijing: Zhongguo qingnian chubanshe, 1999).

24. The head-shaking dancing seen at the discos could be a covert reference to the young drug users called *yaotouzu*, or the "tribe of head-shakers."

25. The term is from J. Baudrillard, *Fatal Strategies* (London: Pluto Press, 1990), 70.

26. Her need for sisterhood is also expressed through her numerous visits to a girlfriend trapped in domestic woes. Over the course of the film, we witness how Ya Nan drifts away from the friend who has become bitter and nonchalant after her own divorce.

27. Paul Schrader, "Notes on Film Noir," in *Film Genre Reader II*, ed. Barry Keith Grant (Austin: University of Texas Press, 1995), 221.

28. Huang Shixian et al., " 'Yueshi': Chufa Zhongguo dianying jianrui huatide xinrui zhi zuo" [*Lunar Eclipse*: A dashing work of a young director which has sparked a new topic of Chinese cinema] *Beijing Dianying xuebao* [Journal of the Beijing Film Academy], no. 2 (2000): 32.

29. After the fall of the Berlin Wall, the turn to capitalism in the former Eastern bloc attracted a large number of illegal migrants and traders from China who took advantage of the trans-Siberian railroad.

30. Or, to use Linda Lai's term from her essay in this volume, Mada returns from "drifting."

31. The basic story in Tang Xianzu's play *Mudanting huanhunji* [The peony pavilion, or the souls's return] from 1589 surrounds the romance between a maiden and a scholar she meets in a dream; eventually, she dies out of unrequited love for him. The scholar later learns about her love for him and falls in love with the image of her in a self-portrait. He visits her grave and confesses his love for her. Moved, she returns from the nether world and reunites with him. Peony Pavilion is the site where this human-ghost love takes place. See Cyril Birch, trans., *The*

Peony Pavilion (Bloomington: Indiana University Press, 1980). Judith Zeitlin treats the female revenants, or the returned spirit of the dead, as a particular type of amorous ghosts. See her "Embodying the Disembodied: Representations of Ghosts and the Feminine," in *Writing Women in Late Imperial China*, ed. Ellen Widmer and Kang-I Sun Chang (Stanford, Calif.: Stanford University Press, 1997), 242–63. The "virtual" incarnation of a vanished woman in both *Lunar Eclipse* and *Suzhou River* adds to and renews, in my view, the repertoire of female revenants in Chinese cultural and women's history. The fascination with this tale seems ageless and boundless. The play was staged, in a fusion of Chinese Kunqu opera and postmodern scenography, at Lincoln Center in New York in 1997.

32. Silbergeld, *Hitchcock with a Chinese Face*, 25–29.

33. Harry Harootunian, *History's Disquiet: Modernity, Cultural Practice, and the Question of Everyday Life* (New York: Columbia University Press, 2000), 17.

34. On this widespread phenomenon and its social and gender implications, see my "Mediating Time: The 'Rice Bowl of Youth' in fin de siècle Urban China," *Public Culture* 12, no. 1 (2000): 93–113.

35. This metaphor is exploited to its fullest in Zhu Wen's DV feature *Seafood* (2001).

36. The colonial administration in the concessions changed this name to Soo Chou Creek because it connects the ports in Shanghai to the Suzhou region, which is rich with silk, tea, porcelain, and other popular export goods. According to urban geographical studies, Wusongjiang used to be larger than today's Huangpu and was directly channeled into the ocean. See Li Tiangang, *Wenhua Shanghai* [Cultural Shanghai] (Shanghai: Shanghai jiaoyu chubanshe, 1998), 252–59.

37. See, "Lou Ye: Zai yingxiang de heliu shang" [Lou Ye: On the river of filmic images], in *Wo de sheyingji bu sahuang* [My camera doesn't lie], ed. Cheng Qing-song and Huang Ou (Beijing: Zhongguo youyi chuban gongsi, 2002), 258.

38. J. Hoberman, "Vertigo-a-go-go and More Déjà Viewing: Eternal Return," *Village Voice*, November 14, 2000, 131.

39. For a brief yet pointed analysis of the cultural meaning of "south" in Chinese literary and cultural production of the 1990s, see Dai Jinghua, "Imagined Nostalgia," in *Postmodernism and China*, ed. Arif Dirlik and Xudong Zhang (Durham, N.C.: Duke University Press, 2000), 205–21, especially the section "Emergence of the South."

40. On the "Civilized Play" and its influence on early Chinese cinema, see Zhong Dafeng, Zhang Zhen, and Yingjin Zhang. "From *Wenmingxi* (Civilized Play) to *Yingxi* (Shadow Play): The Foundation of Shanghai Film Industry in the 1920s," *Asian Cinema* 9, no. 1 (fall 1997): 46–64.

41. In all, eight films representing different companies from China participated in the festival. Among them, Cai Chusheng's *Boatmen's Song* (1934) became the first Chinese film to get an international award. See Hu Die, *Yinghou shengya: Hu Die huiyi lu* [The career of the queen of cinema: Hu Die's memoir] (Hangzhou: Zhejiang renmin chubanshe, 1986), 142–45; 163–69. Other parts of the memoir describe also the occasional exhibitions of *Sister Flowers* and another Mingxing film in several European cities.

42. In the early 1930s, while Zheng Zhengqiu and many other veteran filmmakers began to make films with progressive and patriotic messages, there also emerged a left-wing cinema that more explicitly tackled the social and political issues of the day. Class and gender inequality are the primary ingredients in this radical cinema, which relied heavily on the representational techniques of contrast and conflict derived from a combination of Soviet, European, and Hollywood cinema. See, among other writings, Paul Pickowicz, "Melodramatic Representation and the 'May Fourth' Tradition of Chinese Cinema," in *From May Fourth to June Fourth: Fiction and Film in Twentieth-Century China*, ed. Ellen Widmer and David Der-wei Wang (Cambridge, Mass.: Harvard University Press, 1993), 295–326; and Ma Ning, "The Textual and Critical Difference of Being Radical: Reconstructing Chinese Leftist Films of the 1930s," *Wide Angle* 11, no. 2 (1989): 22–31. Notably, a recurring motif in this urban cinema is the arrival of rural migrants at the docks along the Suzhou River.

43. On the interplay between star power and the fate of tragic female characters in Chinese silent cinema of the 1930s, see Miriam Hansen, "Fallen Women, Rising Stars, New Horizons: Shanghai Silent Film as Vernacular Modernism," *Film Quarterly* 54, no. 1 (2000): 10–22.

44. The screening was part of "The Urban Generation: Chinese Cinema in Transformation," a program organized by Jia Zhijie and myself. Wang's remarks were reported in Wei Xin's essay, "Zhongguo dianying xunhuizhan zai Hafuo" [A touring exhibition of Chinese cinema at Harvard]," *Dajiyuan shibao* [The epoch times], March 5–11, 2001, 2.

45. Stated in a presentation at the Walter Reade Theater, Lincoln Center of Performing Arts, New York, March 1, 2001.

46. See the essay in this volume by Xueping Zhong on the phenomenon of extramarital affairs in contemporary Chinese society and its representation in cinema and literature.

47. Wang's *Story of Er Mei* (Jing Zhe, 2003) revolves around a girl's attempt to regain her virginity through plastic surgery.

48. Indeed, Rey Chow's nuanced reading of Stanley Kwan's *Rouge*, also a postmodern film about a female revenant or "amorous ghost," is germane to my interpretation here. See Rey Chow, "A Souvenir of Love," *Modern Chinese Literature* 7 (1993): 74–75.

49. In a roundtable discussion about the film organized by *Popular Cinema*, *Film Art*, and the Beijing Film Studio, Hao Jian makes a similar observation on the emphasis on the act of narration. See Huang Shixian et al., " 'Yueshi,' " 30.

50. D. N. Rodowick, *Gilles Deleuze's Time Machine* (Durham, N.C.: Duke University Press, 1997), 156–57.

51. See Braester's essay in this volume.

52. Schrader, "Notes on Film Noir," 221.

53. Siegfried Kracauer, *Theory of Film: The Redemption of Physical Reality* (Princeton University Press, 1997 [1960]), 71–72.

54. Eduardo Cadava, *Words of Light: Theses on the Photography of History* (Princeton, N.J.: Princeton University Press, 1997), 11, 13. On the "make-believe" use of photography by the "spiritualists" in late-nineteenth-century America, see Tom Gunning, "Phantom Images and Modern Manifestations: Spirit Photography, Magic Theater, Trick Films, and Photography's Uncanny," in *Fugitive Images: From Photography to Video*, ed. Patrice Petro (Bloomington: Indiana University Press, 1995), 42–71.

55. Walter Benjamin, "A Short History of Photography" (1931), *Screen* 13 (spring 1993): 5–26.

56. Frank Krutnik, *In a Lonely Street: Film Noir, Genre, Masculinity* (London: Routledge, 1991), 138.

57. Ibid., 93.

58. Siegfried Kracauer, "Photography" (1927), trans. Thomas Levin, *Critical Inquiry* 19 (spring 1993), 433.

59. Rodowick, *Gilles Deleuze's Time Machine*, 154–55.

60. Lim, "Voyeur Eyes Only," 140.

61. The term "two-way street" is derived from Miriam Hansen, "Benjamin and Cinema," 306–43.

62. Walter Benjamin, "One Way Street," in *Walter Benjamin: Selected Writings*, vol. 1, 1913–1926, ed. Marcus Bullock and Michael W. Jennings (Cambridge, Mass.: Harvard University Press, 1996), 476. On tactility as a recipe for innovation, see also Benjamin's art work essay, especially where he discusses Dada.

63. On a general discussion on the tactile "body" of cinema, see Steve Shaviro, *The Cinematic Body* (Minneapolis: University of Minnesota Press, 1993).

64. *Titanic*'s phenomenal box office record in China in 1998 spelled disaster for Chinese cinema the year that Wang made *Lunar Eclipse*. *Titanic* took in 0.3 billion yuan out of the total Chinese market of 1.44 billion yuan (which is lower than any previous year in the decade). The rest was shared by more than eighty domestic films and several dozens of other imported films. As quoted in Ying Hong, "Shiji zhijiao: 90 niandai Zhongguo dianying beiwanglu" [At the turn of the century: A memorandum for Chinese cinema of the 90s], *Dangdai dianying*, no. 1 (2000): 32.

65. This scene is reminiscent of Martin Scorsese's *Taxi Driver* in which Robert de Niro's character, who has an ambivalent relationship to both the child prostitute and the well-to-do woman, is framed in his cab whose windshield reflects the lights of the streets. My thanks to Charley Leary for pointing out this connection to me.

66. Miriam Hansen, introduction to Kracauer, *Theory of Film*, xvii.

67. Deleuze, *Cinema* 2, 201.

68. Ibid., 40.

69. Wang Quan'an, "Wo de dianying youguande lüli" [My film-related resume], typescript.

70. Chen Xiaoming, "Fenglie de liliang: Cong 'Yueshi' kan xindianying de biaoyi celue" [The Power of fission: A look at the ideographic tactics of new films from *Lunar Eclipse*], *Beijing dianying xuebao* [Journal of Beijing Film Academy], no. 37 (April 2000): 40.

Appendix:

The Urban Generation Filmmakers

COMPILED BY CHARLES LEARY

Ah Nian, director
A graduate of the Beijing Broadcasting Institute in 1987, Ah Nian began his professional career in television. After working for six years in the Zhejiang Film Studio, he returned to Beijing to make his first feature film, which squarely placed him in the Sixth Generation movement.

Age of Sensitivity [Ganguang shidai]
1994. Produced by Zhejiang Film Studio and Pearl River Studio. Harbin Film Festival, First Prize.

A Chinese Moon [Zhongguo yueliang]
1995. Produced by Fujiang Film Studio.

Love in the Winter [Dongri aiqing]
1997. Produced by Zhejiang Film Studio. Turin Film Festival.

Call Me [Hu wo]
2000. Produced by Beijing Film Studio. "The Urban Generation: Chinese Cinema and Society in Transformation" film series.

Cui Zi'en, director and screenwriter
An accomplished novelist and a professor at the Beijing Film Academy, Cui has been one of the most prominent figures in the promotion of a new queer Chinese cinema.

Kind Enmity Fire [Liehuo enyuan]
* Screenplay by Cui Zi'en.
1991. Produced by Beijing Youth Studio.

Hurry Up Train [Huoche huoche ni kuai kai]
* Screenplay by Cui Zi'en.
1992. Produced by XH Film Workshop.

Men Men Women Women [Nannan nunu]
* Directed by Liu Bingjian, Screenplay by Cui Zi'en.
1999. Locarno International Film Festival, FIPRESCI Prize.

Enter the Clowns [Chou jue deng chang]
2001. Produced and distributed by Cuizi Film Studio. Asian American Film
Festival (New York); International Film Festival Rotterdam; Jeonju International
Film Festival; San Francisco International Lesbian and Gay Film Festival
Vancouver International Film Festival.

The Old Testament [Jiu yue]
2002. Produced and distributed by Cuizi DV Studio. Berlin International Film
Festival; The First China Gay and Lesbian Film Festival; Philadelphia
International Gay and Lesbian Film Festival.

Feeding Boys, Ayaya [Ayaya, Qu buru]
2003. Produced and distributed by Cuizi DV Studio. Asian American
International Film Festival; Hong Kong International Film Festival; Pusan
International Film Festival; Taipei International Film Festival; Vancouver
International Film Festival; Vienna International Film Festival.

Keep Cool and Don't Blush [Lian bu bianshi xin bu tiao]
2003. Produced and distributed by Cuizi DV Studio. Hong Kong International
Film Festival.

Night Scene [Ye jing]
2004. Cuizi DV Studio, Iron Rod Motion Pictures. International Film Festival
Rotterdam; Split Film Festival; Vienna International Film Festival.

Pirated Copy [Manyan]
* Directed by He Jianjun. Cowritten by Cui Zi'en and He Jianjun
2004.

Diao Yinan, director and screenwriter
Diao has written many well-known Sixth Generation films such as *Spicy Love
Soup* and *Shower*. Having made documentaries for Taiwanese television, *Uniform*
was his critically well-received directorial feature film debut. He also works as an
actor (appearing in *All Tomorrow's Parties*, directed by Yu Lik-wai), a Hong Kong
filmmaker, and a frequent cinematographer for Jia Zhangke (also an executive
producer for *Uniform*).

Spicy Love Soup [Aiqing mala tang]
* Directed by Zhang Yang. Cowritten with Cai Jun, Liu Fendou, and Zhang Yang.
1997.

Shower [Xizao]
* Directed by Zhang Yang. Cowritten with Cai Jun, Liu Fendou, and Zhang Yang.
1999.

All the Way [Zou daodi]
* Directed by Shi Runjiu.
2000.

Uniform [Zhifu]
2003. Produced by Hu Tong Communication. Distributed by Ying e Chi.
International Film Festival Rotterdam (Hubert Bals); Melbourne International
Film Festival; Pusan International Film Festival; Taipei International Film
Festival; Vancouver International Film Festival, Dragons and Tigers Award for
Young Cinema.

Night Train
In production. Global Film Initiative, grant recipient.

Guan Hu, director
Born in 1967, Hu received a BA in directing from the Beijing Film Academy in
1991. He heads the Film and Television Artistic Creation Centre at the Beijing
Film Studio. Like *Beijing Bastards*, Guan Hu's acclaimed *Dirt* focuses on the
Chinese rock scene, while his latest and better-known *Eyes of a Beauty* explores
the lives of women in modern China via a legendary opera.

Cello in a Cab [Shangche, zou ba]
1993. Changchun International Film Festival; Hong Kong International Film
Festival; Montpellier Asia Film Festival; Shanghai International Film Festival;
Tokyo International Film Festival; Vienna International Film Festival.

Dirt [Toufa luanle]
1994. Produced by Inner Mongolia Film Studio. Copenhagen Film Festival; Hong
Kong International Film Festival.

The Street Rhapsody [Langman jietou]
1996. Produced by Beijing Film Studio.

Farewell Our 1948 [Zaijian womende 1948]
1996. Produced by Liaoning North Film Studio.

Midnight Walker [Yexing ren]
1998. Produced by Dream Factory for the City Project series. Jeonju International Film Festival.

Eyes of a Beauty [Xishi Yan]
2002. Produced by Beijing Jiatong Century Movie and TV Cultural Communication Co. Distributed by Beijing Link and Chain Advertising. Hawaii International Film Festival, NETPAC Award.

He Jianjun (aka He Yi), director
Before embarking on his own directorial career, He Jianjun assisted Chen Kaige, Zhang Yimou, and Tian Zhuangzhuang—all renowned figures of the Fifth Generation school of Chinese filmmaking.

Self-Portrait [Zihua xiang]
1993. International Film Festival Rotterdam, FIPRESCI Prize.

Red Beads, aka *Suspended Love* [Xuanlian]
1993. Produced by Shu Kei Creative Workshop. Distributed by Fortissimo Film Sales. Berlin International Film Festival; International Film Festival Rotterdam, FIPRESCI Prize.

Postman [Youchai]
1995. Produced by United Frontline and Shu Kei Creative Workshop. Distributed by Fortissimo Film Sales. International Film Festival Rotterdam, FIPRESCI Prize and VPRO Tiger Award; New Directors/New Films Festival (New York); Singapore Film Festival, Special Jury Prize; Thessaloniki Film Festival, Golden Alexander; "The Urban Generation: Chinese Cinema and Society in Transformation" film series.

Scenery [Fengjing]
1999. Produced by Yan Chen. International Film Festival Rotterdam.

Butterfly Smile [Hudie de weixiao]
2001. Produced by Beijing Film Studio, CCTV Movie Channel, China Film Group Co. Distributed by Butterfly Films. International Film Festival Rotterdam; San Sebastian Film Festival; Seattle International Film Festival.

Pirated Copy [Man yan]
2004. Produced by Fanhall Studio. International Film Festival Rotterdam, Hubert Bals Fund; Jeonju International Film Festival; Vienna International Film Festival.

Jia Zhangke, director
Jia is a native of Shanxi Province, the setting for many of his films. His films address the changing social landscape of China, and his recent *Unknown*

Pleasures shows the possibilities of cinematic pleasures in the DV format. His films have garnered numerous international awards, while his latest film, *The World*, will be his first to receive a theatrical release in China.

One Day, in Beijing [You yitian, zai Beijing]
1994. Produced by the Youth Experimental Film Group.

Xiao Shan Going Home [Xiao Shan huijia]
1995. Produced by the Youth Experimental Film Group. Hong Kong Short Film and Video Awards, Gold Prize.

Du Du
1995. Produced by the Youth Experimental Film Group.

Xiao Wu
1998. Produced by Hu Tong Communication. Berlin International Film Festival, Prix Wolfgang Staudt; Brussels International Film Festival, Prix de l'Age d'Or; International Film Festival Rotterdam; Korea Film Festival, Top Prize; New Directors/New Films Festival; Pusan International Film Festival, Best Asian Film and New Current Prize; Rimini Film Festival, Grand Prize; San Francisco International Film Festival, Skyy Prize; Trois Continents, Montgolfiere d'Or; "The Urban Generation: Chinese Cinema and Society in Transformation" film series; Vancouver International Film Festival, Dragons and Tigers Award for Young Cinema.

Platform [Zhantai]
2000. Produced by Hu Tong Communication (Hong Kong), T-Mark, and Office Kitano. Distributed by Ad Vitam. Fribourg International Film Festival, Don Quixote Award and FIPRESCI Prize; Hawaii International Film Festival; New York Film Festival, Venice Film Festival.

In Public [Gonggong changsuo]
2001. Produced by the SIDUS Corporation for the Jeonju International Film Festival. Festival International de Documentaire de Marseilla, Grand Prix; New York Film Festival; Yamagata International Documentary Film Festival.

Unknown Pleasures [Ren xiaoyao]
2002. Produced by T-Mark, Hutong Communication, Office Kitano, Lumen Films, and E-Pictures. Distributed by New Yorker Films. Cannes Film Festival, Official Competition; Hong Kong International Film Festival; New York Film Festival; Vancouver International Film Festival.

The World [Shi jie]
2004. Produced by Office Kitano. Distributed by Celluloid Dreams. New York Film Festival; Hong Kong International Film Festival; Toronto International Film Festival; Venice International Film Festival; Vienna International Film Festival.

Li Yu, director
Li is a former television host who worked on documentaries before embarking on her first feature fiction film, *Fish and Elephant*. This film is also one of the few to openly depict the lives of lesbians in urban China.

Sisters [Jiejie]
1999. Documentary.

Fish and Elephant [Jinnian xiatian]
2001. Produced by Cheng Yong Productions. Distributed by China Film Assist. Berlin International Film Festival, NETPAC Prize, Special Mention; International Film Festival Rotterdam; New Festival; Seattle Lesbian and Gay Film Festival; Vancouver International Film Festival; Venice Film Festival.

Liu Fendou, director and screenwriter
Spicy Love Soup [Aiqing mala tang]
* Directed by Zhang Yang. Cowritten with Cai Jun and Zhang Yang.
1997.

Shower [Xizao]
* Directed by Zhang Yang. Cowritten with Cai Jun, Diao Yinan, Huo Xin, and Zhang Yang.
1999.

A Beautiful New World [Meili xin shijie]
* Directed by Shi Runjiu. Cowritten with Wang Yao.
1998.

Spring Subway [Kaiwang chuntian de ditie]
* Directed by Zhang Yibai. Written and produced by Liu Fendou.
2002. Produced by Electric Orange Entertainment. Udine Far East Film Festival.

The Green Hat [Lu maozi]
2003. Produced by Almost Entertainment Pictures. Distributed by Arc Light Films. Edinburgh International Film Festival; Hong Kong International Film Festival; Tribeca Film Festival, Best New Director and Best Narrative Feature; Vienna International Film Festival.

Lou Ye, director
Born in Shanghai to a family of theater performers, Lou studied painting at the Beijing Film Academy. He formed one of the first independent film companies in China, Dream Factory. Hoping to create more opportunities for his fellow struggling independent filmmakers, Dream Factory produced the well-received Super City Project television series, composed of digital video work made

in Shanghai. His *Suzhou River* is one of the most acclaimed of the Urban Generation films, while his latest film, *Purple Butterfly*, enjoyed theatrical releases worldwide.

Weekend Lovers [Zhoumo qingren]
1994. Mannheim-Heidelberg Film Festival, Rainer Werner Fassbinder Prize for Best Director.

Suzhou River [Suzhou he]
2000. Produced by Dream Factory. Distributed by The Coproduction Office. International Film Festival Rotterdam, VRPO Tiger Award, 2000; New Directors/New Films Festival; Vienna International Film Festival, FIPRESCI Prize.

In Shanghai
2001. Produced and distributed by International Film Festival Rotterdam. International Film Festival Rotterdam; Rencontres internationals du documentaire de Montréal; Vienna International Film Festival.

Purple Butterfly [Zi hudie]
2003. Produced by Shanghai Film Studios. Distributed by Palm Pictures. Cannes Film Festival, Official Competition; Hong Kong International Film Festival; Taipei Golden Horse Film Festival; Toronto International Film Festival.

Lu Xuechang, director
After graduating from the Beijing Film Academy in 1987, Lu Xuechang joined the Beijing Film Studio as a director. With his debut *The Making of Steel*—about a teenage boy coming of age during the Cultural Revolution—Lu was hailed as an outstanding member of the Sixth Generation directors. The film was also one of Beijing's ten biggest box office hits in 1997.

The Making of Steel, aka *How Steel Is Forged* [Gangtie shi zheyang lian cheng de]
1998. Produced by Beijing Film Studio. Distributed by Beijing Pesage Cultural Communication Centre, Beijing Film Studio/Golden Network Ltd. Cannes Film Festival; Pacific Rim Film Festival; "The Urban Generation: Chinese Cinema and Society in Transformation" film series.

A Lingering Face [Feichang xiari]
1999. Produced by Beijing Film Studio, China Film Corp., and the Center for Satellite Broadcasting. Distributed by China Film Group. Golden Rooster (Jinji) award, Best Director; Locarno International Film Festival.

Cala, My Dog [Kala shi tiao gou]
2003. Produced by Huayi Brothers and Taihe Film Investment Co. Distributed by Celestial Pictures. Berlin International Film Festival; Hong Kong International Film Festival, Closing Film; Melbourne International Film Festival.

Lu Yue, director and cinematographer
Lu has had an extensive working relationship with Fifth Generation filmmaker
Zhang Yimou, and he earned an Academy Award nomination for cinematography
for his camerawork on *Shanghai Triad*.

To Live [Huozhe]
*Directed by Zhang Yimou.
1994.

Shanghai Triad [Yao a yao, yaodao waipo qiao]
*Directed by Zhang Yimou.
1995.

Keep Cool [Youhua haohao shuo]
*Directed by Zhang Yimou.
1997.

Xiu-xiu: The Sent-Down Girl [Tian yu]
*Directed by Joan Chen.
1998.

A Beautiful New World [Meili xinshijie]
*Directed by Shi Runjiu.
1998.

Mr. Zhao [Zhao xiansheng]
1998. Locarno Film Festival, Golden Leopard; "The Urban Generation: Chinese
Cinema and Society in Transformation" film series.

The Foliage [Meiren cao]
2005. Produced by Wenzhou TV Drama Production Center, Beijing 21st Century
Bona Film and TV Co., Dongfang Shenlong Film Co., Xi'an Meiya Cultural
Communication Co., Ltd. Distributed by Mei Ah. Vancouver International Film
Festival.

Meng Jinghui, director
Chicken Poet [Xiang jimao yiyang fei]
2002. Hong Kong International Film Festival, FIPRESCI Prize; Jeonju
International Film Festival; Locarno International Film Festival; Toronto
International Film Festival.

Ning Ying, director
Ning is a graduate of the 1982 class of the Beijing Film Academy, where she
majored in recording. She then studied editing and directing at the Rome Film
Laboratory Center, and was Bernardo Bertolucci's assistant director on *The*

Last Emperor. Since returning to Beijing in 1987, Ning has successfully pursued a career as a director and screenwriter. Her first film, *Someone Happened to Fall in Love with Me*, is a comedy. Her following work, *For Fun*, marked the first collaboration with her sister, the screenwriter Ning Dai, and the film's documentary style captured the attention of critics. Ning financed her next project, *On the Beat*, largely with prize money earned from international festivals. Recently she has returned to filmmaking in Italy and has made short films for UNICEF in collaboration with the Renshou Women's Federation.

Someone Happened to Fall in Love with Me [Youren pianpian aishang wo] 1990. Produced by CCTV.

For Fun [Zhaole]
1992. Produced by Beijing Film Studio. Distributed by Eurasia Communications. Jeonju International Film Festival; Nantes International Film Festival, Golden Baloon Prize; New Directors/New Films Festival; San Sebastian Film Festival, Euskal Media Prize; Thessaloniki Film Festival, Best Director; Tokyo Film Festival, Young Cinema Gold Prize.

On the Beat [Minjing gushi]
1995. Produced by Eurasia Communications, Euskal Media, and the Beijing Film Studio. Distributed by Eurasia Communications and Filmmuseum Distributie. Fribourg International Film Festival, International Film Societies' Award Special Mention; International Film Festival Rotterdam; Jeonju International Film Festival; Nantes International Film Festival, Silver Baloon; New Delhi Film Festival, Silver Peacocks Award for Most Promising Director; New Directors/New Films Festival; San Sebastian International Film Festival, FIPRESCI Award; Singapore International Film Festival, Special Jury Prize; Turin International Film Festival, First Prize; "The Urban Generation: Chinese Cinema and Society in Transformation" film series.

Du Ling—Torino
1996. Produced by Group Cooper Srl. International Festival for Architecture in Video (Florence); Valladolid International Film Festival.

Railway of Hope [Xi wang zhi lu]
2001. Produced for Asia Now TV Documentary Proposals Competition. Fribourg International Film Festival; London International Film Festival; Vancouver International Film Festival.

I Love Beijing [Xiari nuan yangyang]
2001. Produced by Eurasia Communications Ltd. and Happy Village Ltd. Distributed by Celluloid Dreams. Hawaii International Film Festival; Hong Kong International Film Festival; Jeonju International Film Festival; International Film Festival Rotterdam.

In Our Own Words [Rang women ziji shuo]
2001. Produced for UNICEF.

Looking for a Job in the City [Jin cheng dagong]
2003. Produced for UNICEF.

Perpetual Motion [Wu qiong dong]
2005. Produced by Beijing Happy Village Ltd. Hong Kong International Film Festival; San Francisco International Film Festival; Toronto International Film Festival.

Shi Runjiu, director
A 1992 graduate of the Central Drama Academy in Beijing, Shi first became well known as a director of underground music videos. In addition to feature filmmaking, he has worked on documentaries and award-winning Japanese television programming.

A Beautiful New World [Meili xinshijie]
1998. Produced by Xi'an Film Studio and Imar Film Company. Distributed by Fortissimo Film Sales. Berlin International Film Festival; Far East Film Festival d'Udine; Fribourg International Film Festival; Hawaii International Film Festival, Special Jury Award for Actor (Jiang Wu); Melbourne International Film Festival; Seattle International Film Festival; "The Urban Generation: Chinese Cinema and Society in Transformation" film series.

All the Way [Zou daodi]
2000. Produced by Imar Film Company in association with Xi'an Film Studio. Distributed by Fortissimo Film Sales. Far East Film Festival d'Udine; Festival du Film Asiatique de Deauville; International Film Festival Rotterdam. Tang Danian, director and screenwriter.

Tang Danian, director and screenwriter
Crazy Guy
1996. International Scriptwriting Award, Sundance Film Festival.

Beijing Bastards [Beijing zazhong]
* Directed by Zhang Yuan. Co-written by Tang.
1992. Produced by the Beijing Bastards Group, made with aid from the Hubert Bals Fund. Distributed by Fortissimo Film Sales. International Film Festival Rotterdam; Locarno International Film Festival, Special Mention; Singapore International Film Festival, Special Jury Prize.

Beijing Bicycle
* Directed by Wang Xiaoshuai. Written by Tang.
2000.

Good Morning, Beijing [Zaoan, Beijing]
* Directed by Pan Jianlin. Written by Tang.
2003.

City Paradise [Du shi tian tang]
1999.

Wang Guangli, director
I Graduated! [Wo biye le]
* Codirected with Shi Jian. Produced by Structure, Wave, Youth and Cinema
Experimental Group. Documentary.
1992.

Maiden Work [Chunu zuo]
1998. International Film Festival Rotterdam; San Francisco International Film
Festival; Vancouver International Film Festival.

Go for Broke [Heng shu heng]
2000. Produced by Shanghai Film Studio. Distributed by East Line
Entertainment and Media.

Wang Quan'an, director
After graduating from the Acting Department of the Beijing Film Academy in
1991, Wang worked as a scriptwriter for the Xi'an Film Studio. In 1999, he made
his directorial debut with *Lunar Eclipse*, a story about love, desire, and betrayal
mixed with a touch of mystery told in a cinematic language rarely seen in
Chinese films. Dai Jinhua, one of China's leading film critics, describes *Lunar
Eclipse* as one of the most uncompromising Chinese films ever made and a
landmark work in Chinese cinema.

Lunar Eclipse [Yueshi]
1999. Produced by Beijing Film Studio. Distributed by Far Light Motion Picture
Corp. Jeonju International Film Festival; Moscow International Film Festival,
FIPRESCI Prize; "The Urban Generation: Chinese Cinema and Society in
Transformation" film series.

The Story of Guan Ermei [Jingzhe]
2003. Produced by Beijing Silk-Road Productions. Distributed by The Film
Library. Berlin International Film Festival.

Wang Xiaoshuai, director
For film festival audiences Wang is one of the better-known Sixth Generation
filmmakers, due in part to financing from European sponsors for his recent
films. His film *Frozen* played in festivals with the director's credit listed as

"anonymous" at the behest of Chinese authorities—neither his first nor last clash with censors. Originally from Guizhou, Wang graduated from the Beijing Film Academy in 1989.

The Days [Dongchun de rizi]
1993. Produced by Shu Kei Creative Workshop. Distributed by Fortissimo Film Sales. Berlin International Film Festival; International Film Festival Rotterdam; New Directors/New Films Festival; Taeormina Film Festival, Best Director; Thessaloniki Film Festival, Golden Alexander; Toronto International Film Festival.

Frozen [Jidu hanleng]
1995. Produced by Another Film Company and Shu Kei Creative Workshop. Distributed by Winstar Cinema. International Film Festival Rotterdam, FIPRESCI Award; Rimini Film Festival, Silver R.

So Close to Paradise [Biandan guniang]
1998. Produced by the Beijing Film Studio, Beijing Jin Die Yingshi Yishu and Han Sanping. Distributed by First Run Features. Cannes Film Festival, Un Certain Regard; International Film Festival Rotterdam, Best Film; Singapore International Film Festival, FIPRESCI Prize; Toronto International Film Festival; "The Urban Generation: Chinese Cinema and Society in Transformation" film series.

The House [Menghuan tianyuan]
1999. Produced by Beijing Film Studio, Movie Channel, China Film Company.

Beijing Bicycle [Shiqisui de danche]
2000. Produced by Arc Light Films, Pyramide Productions, Fonds du Cinema (Ministry of Foreign Affairs, France), Public Television Service Foundation and Eastern Television (Taiwan), Asiatic Films, and the Beijing Film Studio. Distributed by FPI-FLACH Pyramide International. Berlin International Film Festival, Silver Bear Grand Prix and Piper Heidsieck New Talent Award; Singapore International Film Festival, Best Asian Feature Film Silver Screen Award; Toronto International Film Festival; Vancouver International Film Festival.

Drifters [Er di]
2003. Produced and distributed by Arc Light Films. AFI Film Festival; Cannes Film Festival, Un Certain Regard; Hawaii International Film Festival; International Film Festival Rotterdam; Jeonju International Film Festival; Seattle International Film Festival; Singapore International Film Festival; Thessaloniki Film Festival; Toronto International Film Festival; Vancouver International Film Festival.

Shanghai Dreams [Qing hong]
2005. Produced by Debo Films. Distributed by Fortissimo. Cannes Film Festival, Prix du Jury.

Wang Yu, cinematographer
A Lingering Face [Feichang xiari]
*Directed by Lu Xuechang.
1999.

Suzhou River [Suzhou he]
*Directed by Lou Ye.
2000.

Quitting [Zuotian]
*Directed by Zhang Yang. Co-cinematographer with Cheng Shouqi.
2001.

Purple Butterfly [Zi hudie]
*Directed by Lou Ye.
2003.

Wu Di, cinematographer and director
The Days [Dongchun de rizi]
* Directed by Wang Xiaoshuai.
1993.

Postman [Youchai]
* Directed by He Jianjun.
1995.

Goldfish [Huang jinyu]
1995. Vancouver International Film Festival, Dragons and Tigers Award for Young Cinema.

Butterfly Smile [Hudie de weixiao]
* Directed by He Jianjun (He Yi).
2001.

Eyes of a Beauty [Xishi Yan]
* Directed by Guan Hu.
2002.

Xu Jinglei, director and actor
Xu Jinglei is a celebrated actress and the star of a number of Sixth Generation films such as Zhang Yang's *Spicy Love Soup* and Zhang Yuan's *I Love You,* as well as various big-budget Hong Kong films. The documentary *Father and I* is her first film, and her first fiction film, *A Letter from an Unknown Woman* is an adaptation of a Stefan Zweig novel, also adapted in a famous version by Max Ophuls.

Spicy Love Soup [Aiqing mala tang]
* Directed by Zhang Yang.
1997.

I Love You [Wo ai ni]
* Directed by Zhang Yuan.
2002.

Spring Subway [Kaiwang chuntian de ditie]
* Directed by Zhang Yibai.
2002.

Father and I [Wo he baba]
2002. Produced by Asian Union Film and the Beijing Yinian Cultural Development Co. Toronto International Film Festival.

A Letter from an Unknown Woman [Yige mosheng nuren de laixin]
2004. Produced and distributed by Poly-Asian Union Film and Media. San Sebastian International Film Festival, Best Director; Vienna International Film Festival.

Yang Fudong, director
Well known in the contemporary arts world, Yang is a visual artist who has recently embarked on feature-length filmmaking. His work, which usually takes the form of photography or video installation, has been exhibited extensively worldwide, including at the Centre Pompidou in Paris and at the Venezie and Shanghai Biennales.

Backyard: Hey! Sun Is Rising [Houfang tian liang]
2001.

Liu Lan [Liu Lan]
2003.

An Estranged Paradise [Mosheng tiantang]
1997–2003. Produced for Documenta 11.

Seven Intellectuals in a Bamboo Forest [Zhulin qixian]
Part I. 2003.
Part II. 2004.

Zhang Ming, director
Born in 1961 in Sichuan Province, Zhang studied as a youth in Wushan, the
city by the Three Gorges Dam that provides the somber setting for his first
film. He studied in the Fine Arts Department at Xi'nan Teachers College in
Chongqing and then at the Beijing Film Academy. Before directing feature films,
he worked on various dramatic television series and taught at the Beijing Film
Academy.

Rainclouds over Wushan [Wushan yunyu]
1995. Produced by Beijing Film Studio and Beijing East Earth Cultural
Development. Distributed by Filmmuseum Distributie and Beijing East Earth
Cultural Development. Fribourg International Film Festival, Granx Prix, FICC,
and Prix Don Quixote; International Film Festival Rotterdam; New Directors/
New Films Festival; Pusan International Film Festival, Best Asian Film; Turin
Film Festival, top Prize and FIPRESCI Award; "The Urban Generation: Chinese
Cinema and Society in Transformation" film series; Vancouver International
Film Festival, Dragons and Tigers Award for Young Cinema.

Weekend Plot [Miyu shiqi xiaoshi]
2001. Produced by Nitu Film, Beijing Film Academy, and Beijing East Earth
Cultural Development. Distributed by Nitu Film. Hong Kong International Film
Festival; International Film Festival Rotterdam; Vancouver International Film
Festival.

Zhang Yang, director
Zhang received a BA in Chinese Literature from Zhongshan University before
studying in the Directing Department at Beijing's Central Drama Academy.
Upon graduation, he began work at the Beijing Film Studio. His first film,
Spicy Love Soup, was one of the few independent films to achieve domestic box
office success, and it was followed by the international success of *Shower*. His
father, Zhang Huaxun, was a director specializing in martial arts films in the
1970s.

Spicy Love Soup [Aiqing mala tang]
1997. Produced by Imar Film Company. San Francisco International Asian
American Film Festival.

Shower [Xizao]
1999. Produced by Imar Film Company. Distributed by Sony Pictures Classics.
International Film Festival Rotterdam, Audience Award; New Directors/New

Films Festival; San Sebastian International Film Festival, Silver Shell for Best Director and ocic Award; Sundance Film Festival; Thessaloniki Film Festival; Toronto Film Festival, fipresci Award.

Quitting [Zuotian]
2001. Produced by Imar Film Company and Xi'an Film Studio. Distributed by Fortissimo Film Sales. International Film Festival Rotterdam; Venice Film Festival; Stockholm Film Festival, fipresci Award.

Sunflower [Xiangrikui]
2005. Produced by China Film Group Corp. and Fortissimo Films and Ming Productions. Distributed by Fortissimo Film Sales. Berlin International Film Festival, Hong Kong International Film Festival; San Sebastian International Film Festival, Silver Shell for Best Director and Jury Award for Best Photography.

Zhang Yuan, director
An accomplished documentarian, award-winning music video director, and feature filmmaker, Zhang received a degree in cinematography from the Beijing Film Academy in 1989. Zhang's work highlights the vibrant underground cultural scene around China's urban centers, ranging from queer culture in *East Palace, West Palace* to the political rock scene in *Beijing Bastards*. A number of his films have been banned and officially boycotted in China, yet he also was the first filmmaker to be allowed to film inside a Chinese prison ward (for *Seventeen Years*). He is generally regarded as one of the primary figures of the Sixth Generation.

Mama [Mama]; aka *The Tree of the Sun*
1990. Produced by Shu Kei Creative Workshop/Xi'an Studio. Distributed by Fortissimo Film Sales. Asian American Film Festival (Washington, D.C.); Berlin International Film Festival; Fribourg International Film Festival, Grand Prix of the City of Fribourg; Human Rights Film Festival (New York); International Film Festival Rotterdam; Nantes International Film Festival, Prize of the City of Nantes and Special Mention.

Beijing Bastards [Beijing zazhong]
1992. Produced by the Beijing Bastards Group, made with aid from the Hubert Bals Fund. Distributed by Fortissimo Film Sales. International Film Festival Rotterdam; Locarno International Film Festival, Special Mention; Singapore International Film Festival, Special Jury Prize.

Flying [Feile]
1994. Music video. Produced and distributed by the Beijing Film Company. International Film Festival Rotterdam.

The Square [Guangchang]
* Codirected with Duan Jinchuan.
1994. Hawaii International Film Festival, Jury Prize; International Film Festival Rotterdam.

Sons [Erzi]
1996. Distributed by Face Cultural Communication Center of Beijing.
International Film Festival Rotterdam, FIPRESCI Award and VPRO Tiger Award; "The Urban Generation: Chinese Cinema and Society in Transformation" film series.

East Palace, West Palace [Donggong xigong]
1996. Produced by Ocean Film Co. and Quelqu'un d'Autre. Distributed by Cinemien, Homescreen. Cannes Film Fesitval, Un Certain Regard; International Film Festival Rotterdam.

Seventeen Years [Guonian huijia]
1999. Produced by Keetman Lts., Xian Film Studio, and Ocean Film Co. (Hong Kong). Distributed by Celluloid Dreams. International Film Festival Rotterdam; Venice International Film Festival, Special Prize for Directing.

Crazy English [Fengkuang yingyu]
1999.

Miss Jing Xing [Jing Xing xiaojie]
2000. Short produced for Tom.com. Jeonju International Film Festival.

I Love You [Wo ai ni]
2002. Produced by Xi'an Film Studio and Diamond Film Investment Co. Distributed by Asian Union Film and Entertainment. Far East Film Festival Udine; International Film Festival Rotterdam.

Sister Jiang [Jiang jie]
2003.

Green Tea [Lu cha]
2003. Produced and distributed by Asian Union. International Film Festival Rotterdam; Far East Film Festival Udine.

Zhu Wen, director and screenwriter
Rainclouds over Wushan [Wushan yunyu]
*Directed by Zhang Ming. Screenplay by Zhu Wen.
1995.

Seventeen Years [Guonian huijia]
*Directed by Zhang Yuan. Screenplay by Zhu Wen, Yu Hua, and Ning Dai.
1999.

Seafood [Hai xian]
2001. Produced by Thought Dance Entertainment and Zhu Wen Workshop.
Distributed by Golden Network Asia. Hong Kong International Film Festival.

South of the Clouds [Yun de nanfang]
2004. Produced and distributed by China Film Assist. Berlin International Film
Festival; Hong Kong International Film Festival. FIPRESCI Award; Vienna
International Film Festival.

DOCUMENTARY FILMMAKERS

Du Haibin, director
The Lunch [Wucan]1998.

Dou tou [Dou tou]
1999.

Along the Railway [Tie lu yan xian]
2000. Berlin International Film Festival; Hong Kong International Film Festival;
Jeonju International Film Festival; Yamagata International Documentary
Festival.

Under the Skyscraper [Gaolou xiamian]
2002.

Duan Jinchuan, director
One of the most accomplished independent documentary filmmakers working in
China, Duan's films have focused on Tibetan and countryside communities. He
co-directs China Memo Films with Jiang Yue.

Highland Barley [Qingke]
1986.

The Blue Mask Consecrations [Qingmian fengna]
1988.

Tibet [Xizang]
1991.

The Sacred Site of Asceticism [Qingpu, xiuxing zhe de shengdi]
* Directed with Wen Punlin.
1992. Yamagata International Documentary Festival.

The Square [Guangchang]
* Codirected with Zhang Yuan.
1994. Hawaii International Film Festival, Jury Prize; International Film Festival Rotterdam; Yamagata International Documentary Film Festival.

No. 16 Barkhor Street South [Bakuonanjie shiliuhao]
1996. Hawaii International Film Festival.

The End of the Earth [Tianbian]
1996.

Sunken National Treasure—97 [Chen chuan—97 nian de gushi]
1999. Produced by Chuan Linyue Films. Yamagata International Documentary Festival.

The Secret of My Success [Lingqi da shetou]
2002. Produced by China Memo Films. Taipei International Film Festival; Vancouver International Film Festival.

Jiang Yue, director
Jiang has been instrumental in bringing the new Chinese documentary movement (sometimes referred to as the DV movement for its use of the easily maneuverable digital video camera) to television screens across China. His film *The Other Bank* exemplifies the recent independent documentaries' concomitant interest with, on the one hand, the disenfranchised rural poor migrating to urban centers and, on the other, recent experimental performance art. He heads a documentary film studio with Duan Jinchuan.

Tibetan Theater Troupe of Lhama [Lama zangxi tuan]
1991.

The Residents of Lhasa's Potala Square [Lasa xue jumin]
1992.

Catholics in Tibet [Tianzhu zai xizang]
1992. Yamagata International Documentary Film Festival.

The Other Bank, aka *The Other Shore* [Bi'an]
1995. Yamagata International Documentary Film Festival.

A River Is Stilled [Jingzhi de Heliu]
1998. Produced by CCTV. Distributed by Chuan Linyue Films. Yamagata International Documentary Film Festival.

This Happy Life [Xingfu shenghuo]
2002. Produced by China Memo Films. Hong Kong International Film Festival, Special Mention; Taipei International Film Festival.

Li Hong, director
Back to Phoenix Bridge [Huidao fenghuang qiao]
1997. Distributed by Women Make Movies. Yamagata International Documentary Film Festival, Ogawa Shinsuke Prize; Munich Film Festival, Special Mention, Media Net Awards; New York International Documentary Festival; San Francisco International Asian American Film Festival.

Dancing with Myself [He Ziji Tiao Wu]
2002.

Ma Yingli, director
Ma studied film at the German Film and Television School in Berlin. She has made short films and documentaries for television in both Germany and China.

A Case Study of Transference
1994. Codirected with Ai Weiwei.

Days of Miandi [Miandi shijian]
1996. Produced by Wanhai Co.

Bye Bye, Hello
1997. Produced and distributed by Jahn Filmprodutkion.

Night Girl
2001. Distributed by Women Make Movies.

Wang Bing, director
Tiexi District: West of the Tracks [Tiexi qu]
2002. Produced by Zhoa Yinou. International Film Festival Rotterdam; Vancouver International Film Festival; Toronto International Film Festival; Yamagata International Documentary Film Festival.

Wu Wenguang, director
Wu is not only the most accomplished filmmaker of the new documentary movement in China, he is also one of its most prolific critics. His work spearheaded the departure from the "talking head" format that dominated Chinese television until the early 1990s, and his ethnographic approach obliges him to live for long periods of time with his subjects—often the displaced poor outside urban centers. Much of his work also documents the vibrant experimental

art scene in China, and he is the cofounder of China's first independent dance company, the Living Dance Studio.

Bumming in Beijing—The Last Dreamers [Liulang Beijing—Zuihou de mengxiangzhe]
1990. Hong Kong International Film Festival.

1966—My Red Guard Year [1966—Wode hong weibing shidai]
1993. Produced and distributed by WALK Co., Ltd. Berlin International Film Festival; International Film Festival Rotterdam; Yamagata International Documentary Film Festival, Ogawa Shinzuke Award.

At Home in the World [Sihai weijia]
1995. Yamagata International Documentary Film Festival.

Jiang Hu: On the Road [Jianghu]
1999. Produced and distributed by Wu Documentary Studio. Berlin International Film Festival; Yamagata International Documentary Film Festival.

Diary: Snow, November 21, 1998.
1998. "Cancelled: Exhibiting Experimental Art in China," Smart Museum of Chicago; World Wide Video Festival.

Dance with Farm Workers [Yu mingong yiqi wudao]
2001. Produced and distributed by Wu Documentary Studio. London International Film Festival; Vancouver International Film Festival.

Bibliography

Abbas, Ackbar. *Hong Kong: Culture and the Politics of Disappearance.* Minneapolis: University of Minnesota Press, 1997.

Affron, Charles, and Mirella Jona Affron. *Sets in Motion: Art Direction and Film Narrative.* New Brunswick, N.J.: Rutgers University Press, 1995.

Ahlbäck, Pia Maria. "The Road to Industrial Heterotopia." In *Technologies of Landscape: From Reaping to Recycling,* ed. David E. Nye. Amherst: University of Massachusetts Press, 1999.

Ames, Walter L. *Police and Community in Japan.* Berkeley: University of California Press, 1981.

Anderson, Marsten. *The Limits of Realism: Chinese Fiction in the Revolutionary Period.* Berkeley: University of California Press, 1990.

Apel, Dora. *Memory Effects: The Holocaust and the Art of Secondary Witnessing.* New Brunswick, N.J.: Rutgers University Press, 2002.

Appadurai, Arjun. "Grassroots Globalization and the Research Imagination." *Public Culture* 12, no. 1 (winter 2000): 3.

——. *Modernity at Large: Cultural Dimensions of Globalization.* Minneapolis: University of Minnesota Press, 1996.

Armes, Roy. *On Video.* London: Routledge, 1995 [1985].

Ashplant, T. G., and Smyth, Gerry, eds. *Explorations in Cultural History.* London: Pluto Press, 2001.

Barmé, Geremie R. *In the Red: On Contemporary Chinese Culture.* New York: Columbia University Press, 1999.

Baudrillard, J. *Fatal Strategies* London: Pluto Press, 1990.

Bazin, André. *What Is Cinema?* Vol. 1. Berkeley: University of California Press, 1967.

——. *What Is Cinema?* Vol. II. Berkeley: University of California Press, 1971.

Benjamin, Walter. *The Arcades Project,* trans. Howard Eiland and Kevin McLaughlin. Cambridge, Mass.: Belknap Press of Harvard University Press, 1999.

——. "A Short History of Photography" [1931]. *Screen* 13 (spring 1993): 5–26.

——. *Walter Benjamin: Selected Writings.* Vol. 1: 1913–1926, ed. Marcus Bullock and Michael W. Jennings. Cambridge, Mass.: Harvard University Press.

——. "The Work of Art in the Age of Mechanic Reproduction." In *Illuminations: Essays and Reflections,* ed. Hannah Arendt, trans. Harry Zohn. New York: Schocken, 1969.

Berry, Chris. "Chinese Urban Cinema: Hyper-realism versus Absurdism." *East-West Film Journal* 3, no. 1 (1988): 76–87.

——. "Crossing the Wall." *Dox,* no. 13 (1997): 14–15.

——. "*East Palace, West Palace:* Staging Gay Life in China." *Jump Cut,* no. 42 (1998): 84–89.

——. "A Haunting Presence: Let's Love *Let's Love Hong Kong.*" In *Hok Yuk: Let's Love Hong Kong—Script and Critical Essays,* ed. Yau Ching. Hong Kong: Youth Literary Press, 2003. 33–37.

——. "Interview with Duan Jinchuan." *Metro,* no. 113/114 (1998): 88–89.

——. "Race (*Minzu*): Chinese Film and the Politics of Nationalism." *Cinema Journal* 31, no. 2 (1992): 45–58.

——. "Seeking Truth from Fiction: Feature Films as Historiography in Deng's China." *Film History* 7, no. 1 (1995): 87–99.

——. "Sexual DisOrientations: Homosexual Rights, East Asian Films, and Post-Modern Post-Nationalism." *In Pursuit of Contemporary East Asian Culture,* ed. X. Tang and S. Snyder. Boulder: Westview Press, 1996. 157–82.

——. "Watching Time Go By: Narrative Distension, Realism, and Postsocialism in Jia Zhangke's *Xiao Wu.*" *South Atlantic Quarterly.* Forthcoming.

——. "Zhang Yuan: Thriving in the Face of Adversity." *Cinemaya* 32 (1996): 41.

Berry, Chris, and Farquhar, Mary Ann. "Post-Socialist Strategies: An Analysis of *Yellow Earth* and *Black Cannon Incident.*" In *Cinematic Landscapes: Observations on the Visual Arts and Cinema of China and Japan,* ed. Linda Ehrlich and David Desser. Austin: University of Texas Press, 1994. 81–116.

Bloom, Harold. *The Anxiety of Influence: A Theory of Poetry.* New York: Oxford University Press, 1997 [1975].

Blunt, Alison, and Gillian Rose, eds. *Writing Women and Space: Colonial and Postcolonial Geographies.* New York: Guilford Press, 1994.

Boym, Svetlana. *Common Places: Mythologies of Everyday Life in Russia.* Cambridge, Mass.: Harvard University Press, 1994.

——. *The Future of Nostalgia.* New York: Basic Books, 2001.

Braester, Yomi. "*Farewell, My Concubine:* National Myth and City Memories." In *Chinese Films in Focus: Twenty-five New Takes,* ed. Chris Berry. London: British Film Institute, forthcoming.

——. " 'If We Could Remember Everything, We Would Be Able to Fly': Taipei's Cinematic Poetics of Demolition." *Modern Chinese Literature and Culture* 15, no. 1 (spring 2003).

Braester, Yomi, and Zhang Enhua. "The Future of China's Memories: An Interview with Feng Jicai." *Journal of Modern Literature in Chinese* 5, no. 2 (January 2002): 131–48.

Brewer, John D. et al. "People's Republic of China." In *The Police, Public Order and the State*. New York: St. Martin's Press, 1988. 189–213.

Bruno, Giuliana. *Streetwalking on a Ruined Map: Cultural Theory and the City Films of Elvira Notari*. Princeton, N.J.: Princeton University Press, 1993.

Buck-Morss, Susan. "The Flaneur, the Sandwichman and the Whore: The Politics of Loitering." *New German Critique* 39 (fall 1986): 99–140.

Cadava, Eduardo. *Words of Light: Theses on the Photography of History*. Princeton, N.J.: Princeton University Press, 1997.

Caygill, Howard. *Walter Benjamin: The Colour of Experience*. London: Routledge, 1998.

Certeau, Michel de. *The Practice of Everyday Life*. Berkeley: University of California Press, 1984.

Chai Xiaofeng. *Xiaowen ye fengkuang* [Xiaowen too is mad]. Changsha: Hunan wenyi chubanshe, 1997.

Chen Lai. "Sixiang chulu de san dongxiang" [The three directions of solution in thoughts]. In *Zhongguo dangdai wenhua yishi* [Cultural consciousness in contemporary China], ed. Gan Yang. Hong Kong: Joint Publishing, 1988.

Chen, Nancy N. et al., eds., *China Urban: Ethnographies of Contemporary Culture*. Durham, N.C.: Duke University Press, 2001.

Chen Xiaoming. "Fenglie de liliang: Cong 'Yueshi' kan xindianying de biaoyi celue" [The Power of fission: A look at the ideographic tactics of new films from *Lunar Eclipse*]. *Beijing dianying xuebao* [Journal of Beijing Film Academy], no. 37 (April 2000): 40.

Cheng Jihua, Li Shaohong, and Xin Zhuwen. *Zhongguo dianying fazhan shi* [History of the development of Chinese film]. 2 vols. Beijing: Zhongguo dianying chubanshe, 1998.

Cheng Qingsong and Huang He, *Wode sheyingji bu sahuang* [My camera doesn't lie]. Beijing: Zhongguo youyi chuban gongsi, 2002.

Chow, Rey. "A Souvenir of Love." *Modern Chinese Literature* 7 (1993): 74–75.

Chute, David. "Beyond the Law." *Film Comment* 30, no. 1 (1994): 60–62.

Clark, Paul. *Chinese Cinema: Culture and Politics since 1949*. Cambridge, U.K.: Cambridge University Press, 1987.

Cobley, Paul, ed. *The Communication Theory Reader*. London: Routledge, 1996.

Cui Shuqin. "Working from the Margins: Urban Cinema and Independent Directors in Contemporary China," *Post Script* 20, nos. 2–3 (2001): 77–93.

Dai Jinghua. "Imagined Nostalgia." In *Postmodernism and China*, ed. Arif Dirlik and Xudong Zhang. Durham, N.C.: Duke University Press, 2000. 205–21.

——. "A Scene in the Fog: Reading the Sixth Generation Films." In *Cinema and Desire: Feminist Marxism and Cultural Politics in the Work of Dai Jinhua*, ed. Jing Wang and Tani E. Barlow. London: Verso, 2002.

——.*Wu zhong fengjing: Zhongguo dianying wenhua, 1978–1998* [Spectacles in a fog: Chinese film culture, 1978–1998]. Beijing: Beijing daxue chubanshe, 2000.

——. *Xie ta liaowang: Zhongguo dianying wenhua, 1978–1998* [A broad watch from the slanted tower: Chinese film culture, 1978–1998]. Taibei: Yuanliou, 1999.

——. *Yingxing shuxie: Jiushi niandai Zhongguo wenhua yanjiu* [Invisible writing: Cultural studies of the China of the 90's]. Nanjing: Jiangsu renmin chubanshe, 1999.

Davis, Deborah et al., eds., *Urban Spaces in Contemporary China: The Potential for Autonomy and Community in Post-Mao China.* New York: Cambridge University Press, 1995.

Davis, Fred. *Yearning for Yesterday: A Sociology of Nostalgia.* New York: Free Press, 1979.

Dazhong dianying [Popular cinema], ed., "Xinren xinzuo *Yueshi*" [A new work from a newcomer: *Lunar Eclipse*], *Dazhong dianying* [Popular cinema], no. 4 (2000): 12–13.

Debord, Guy. *La société du spectacle.* Paris: Buchet-Chastel, 1967.

De Kloet, Jeroen. "'Let Him Fucking See the Green Smoke beneath My Groin': The Mythology of Chinese Rock." In *Postmodernism and China*, ed. Arif Dirlik and Xudong Zhang. Durham, N.C.: Duke University Press, 2000. 239–74.

De Lauretis, Teresa. "Rethinking Women's Cinema: Aesthetics and Feminist Theory." In *Multiple Voices in Feminist Film Criticism*, ed. Diane Carson, Linda Dittmar, and Janice R. Welsch. Minneapolis: University of Minnesota Press, 1994.

Deleuze, Gilles. *Cinema I: The Movement-Image*, trans. Hugh Tomlinson. Minneapolis: University of Minnesota Press, 1986.

——. *Cinema 2: The Time-Image*, trans. Hugh Tomlinson and Robert Galeta. Minneapolis: University of Minnesota Press, 1989.

Deleuze, Gilles, and Félix Guattari. *Anti-Oedipus: Capitalism and Schizophrenia.* Minneapolis: University of Minnesota Press, 1983.

——. *Kafka: Toward a Minor Literature*, trans. Dana Polan. Minneapolis: University of Minnesota Press, 1986.

Deng Guanghui. "Lun 90 niandai Zhongguo dianying de yiyi shengchan" [The production of meaning in 1990s Chinese cinema]. *Dangdai dianying*, no. 1 (2001): 33–39.

Ding Renren, "1993 Zhongguo dianying 'mozhe shitou guohe'" [Chinese cinema in 1993: "Crossing the river by feeling the stones"]. *Beijing ribao* [Beijing Daily], January 26 and 31, 1994.

Dirlik, Arif, and Xudong Zhang. "Introduction: Postmodernism and China." *boundary 2* 24, no. 3 (1997): 1–18.

Donald, Stephanie Hemelrik. *Public Secret, Public Spaces: Cinema and Civility in China*, Lanham, Md.: Rowman and Littlefield, 2000.

——. "Women Reading Chinese Films: Between Orientalism and Silence." *Screen* 36, no. 4 (1995): 325–40.

Duan Yiping, *Gaojihui: Zhongguo chengshi zhongchan jieceng xiezhen* [High-grade grey: A portrayal of the Chinese urban middle class]. Beijing: Zhongguo qingnian chubanshe, 1999.

Dutton, Michael. "The End of the Mass Line? Chinese Policing in the Era of the Contract." *Social Justice* 27, no. 2 (2000): 61–106.

Eckholm, Eric. "Feted Abroad, and No Longer Banned in Beijing." *New York Times*. December 16, 1999.

Ehrlich, Linda C. "Courtyards of Shadows and Light." *Cinemaya* 37 (1997): 8–16.

Fang Ke. *Dangdai Beijing jiucheng gengxin: Diaocha, yanjiu, tansuo* [Contemporary redevelopment in the inner city of Beijing: Survey, analysis, and investigation]. Beijing: Zhongguo jianzhu gongye chubanshe, 2000.

Feng Jicai. *Feng Jicai hua Tianjin* [Feng Jicai depicts Tianjin]. Shanghai: Shanghai wenyi chubanshe, 2000.

——. *Jiucheng yiyun: Tianjin lao fangzi* [Rhymes left by an old city: Old houses in Tianjin]. Tianjin: Tianjin Yangliuqing huashe, 1995.

——. *Qiangjiu laojie* [Rushing to save an old street]. Beijing: Xiyuan chubanshe, 2000.

——. *Shouxia liuqing: Xiandai dushi wenhua de youhuan* [Show leniency: The predicament of modern urban culture]. Shanghai: Xuelin chubanshe, 2000.

Foucault, Michel. *The History of Sexuality*, trans. Robert Hurley. New York: Vintage, 1990.

——. *The Order of Things*. London: Routledge, 1989.

——. *Politics, Philosophy, Culture: Interviews and Other Writings, 1977–1984*, trans. Alan Sheridan. New York: Routledge, 1988.

Friedberg, Anne. *Window Shopping: Cinema and the Postmodern*. Berkeley: University of California Press, 1993.

Fu Cheng, "Bei Ying 2000" [Beijing Film Studio in 2000]. *Dianying tongxun*, no. 6 (2000).

Gateward, Frances, ed. *Zhang Yimou: Interviews*. Jackson: University Press of Mississippi, 2001.

Gladney, Dru C. "Representing Nationality in China: Refiguring Majority/Minority Identities." *Journal of Asian Studies* 53, no. 1 (1994): 92–123.

Gleber, Anke. *The Art of Taking a Walk: Flânerie, Literature, and Film in Weimar Culture*. Princeton, N.J.: Princeton University Press, 1999.

Granet, Marcel. *La Pensée chinoise*. Paris: Albin Michel, 1981.

Grossman, Andrew. "The Wind Will Carry Us." *Scope: An On-Line Journal of Film Studies* (May 2001), http://www.nottingham.ac.uk/film/journal/filmrev/the-wind-will-carry-us.htm.

Gu Zheng. "Women yiqi lai pai dianying ba: Hui wang 'qingnian shiyan dianying xiaozu'" [Let's make a movie together: A look back at the "Youth Experimental Film Group"]. *Xianchang* [Document], vol. 1, edited by Wu Wenguang. Tianjin: Tianjin shehui kexueyuan chubanshe, 2000.

Gunning, Tom. "Tracing the Individual Body: Photography, Detectives, and Early Cinema." In *Cinema and the Invention of Modern Life*, ed. Leo Charney and Vanessa R. Schwartz. Berkeley: University of California Press, 1995. 15–45.

Guo Changmao, "Dianying tizhi gaige yinian deshi tan" [On the gains and losses during a year of reform in the film system]. *Dianying yishu* [Film art], no. 5 (1994): 66–68.

Guo Xiaolu. "Zhongguo xuyao shenmeyang de dianying? Yi ci youguan dianying de diaocha baogao" [What kinds of films does China want? A report on a survey on film]. *Film Art*, no. 278 (May 5, 2001): 16–23, 70.

Han Xiaolei. "Dui diwudai de wenhua tuwei: Houwudai de geren dianying xianxiang" [A cultural breakaway from the Fifth Generation: The phenomenon of individualist film in the post-Fifth Generation]. *Dianying yishu* [Film art], no. 2 (1995): 58–63.

——. "Tuwei hou de wenhua piaoyi" [Cultural drifting after the breakaway]. *Dianying yishu* [Film art], no. 5 (1999): 58–65.

Hansen, Miriam. "Benjamin and Cinema: Not a One-Way Street." *Critical Inquiry* 25, no. 2 (winter 1999): 306–43.

——. "Fallen Women, Rising Stars, New Horizons: Shanghai Silent Film as Vernacular Modernism." *Film Quarterly* 54, no. 1 (2000): 10–22.

Harootunian, Harry. *History's Disquiet: Modernity, Cultural Practice, and the Question of Everyday Life.* New York: Columbia University Press, 2000.

Henderson, Brian. "Toward a Non-Bourgeois Camera Style." *Film Quarterly* 24, no. 2 (winter 1970–71): 2–14.

Hetherington, Kevin. *The Badlands of Modernity: Heterotopia and Social Ordering.* London: Routledge, 1997.

Hinsch, Bret. *Passion of the Cut Sleeve: The Male Homosexual Tradition in China.* Berkeley: University of California Press, 1990.

Hoberman, J. "Conflict Management." *Village Voice*, March 2, 2001. *http://www .villagevoice.com/issues/0110/hoberman.php.*

——. "Cults of Personality." *Village Voice*, March 12–18, 2003. http://www.village voice.com/issues/0311/hoberman.php.

——. "Vertigo-a-go-go and More Déjà Viewing: Eternal Return." *Village Voice*, November 14, 2000.

Hong, Jianshe. "Shi!" [Gone!]. *Xiaofei zhe* [Consumer], no. 12 (2000): 48–49.

Hu Die, *Yinghou shengya: Hu Die huiyi lu* [The career of the queen of cinema: Hu Die's memoir]. Hangzhou: Zhejiang renmin chubanshe, 1986.

Hu Ke. "Jingqiao de xushu yishu" [An ingenious art of narration]. In *Zhongghuo dianying meixue: 1999* [Chinese film aesthetics: 1999], ed. Hu Ke et al. Beijing: Beijing guangbo xueyuan chubanshe, 2000. 275–84.

——. "The Relationship between the Minority Nationalities and the Han in the Cinema." In *Chinese National Minorities Films* [Lun Zhongguo Shaoshu Minzu Dianying], ed. Gao Honghu et al., Beijing: China Film Press, 1997. 205–11.

Hu Ke, Zhang Wei, and Hu Zhifeng, eds. *Dangdai dianying lilun wenxuan* [An anthology of contemporary film theory]. Beijing: Beijing guangbo xueyuan chubanshe, 2000.

Huang Du, ed. *Post-Material: Interpretations of Everyday Life by Contemporary Chinese Artists.* Beijing: World Chinese Arts Publication Company, 2000.

Huang Du, and Bingyi Huang. *Hou wuzhi* [The post-material]. Beijing: Shijie huaren yishu chubanshe, 2000.

Huang Jianxin. "Bu ke tidai de yishu dianying" [The irreplaceable art film]. *Film Art*, no. 278 (May 5, 2001): 9–11.

——. "Shenghuo jueding le wo de dianying" [Life decided my films]. *Dangdai dianying* [Contemporary cinema], no. 4 (July 1997): 81–83.

Huang Shixian, "Wenhua zhuanxing: Quanqiuhua qushi yu dianying tizhi gaige (1996–1999)" [Cultural transformation: Globalization and the reform of the film institution (1996–1999)]. *Spectrums of the Century: Chinese Cinemas 1896–1999.* Taipei: Council for Cultural Affairs and the Chinese Taipei Film Archive, 2000.

Huang Shixian et al., " 'Yueshi': Chufa Zhongguo dianying jianrui huatide xinrui zhi zuo" [*Lunar Eclipse:* A dashing work of a young director which has sparked a new topic of Chinese cinema]. *Beijing Dianying xuebao* [Journal of the Beijing Film Academy], no. 2 (2000): 32.

Insdorf, Annette. *Double Lives, Second Chances: The Cinema of Krzysztof Kieslowski.* New York: Hyperion, 1999.

Jaffee, Valerie. "Bringing the World to the Nation: Jia Zhangke and the Legitimation of Chinese Underground Film." *Senses of Cinema*, no. 32 (July-September 2004), http://www.sensesofcinema.com/contents/04/32/chinese_underground_film.html.

Jameson, Fredric. "Globalization as a Philosophical Issue." In *Cultures of Globalization*, ed. Fredric Jameson and Masao Miyoshi. Durham, N.C.: Duke University Press, 1998.

——. *A Singular Modernity: Essay on the Ontology of the Present.* London: Verso, 2002.

Jia Zhangke. "Cinema with an Accent: Interview with Jia Zhangke, Director of *Platform.*" By Stephen Teo. *Senses of Cinema*, no. 15 (July/August 2001), http://www.sensesofcinema.com/contents/01/15/zhangke_interview.html.

——. "Fangwen 'Xiao Wu' daoyan Jia Zhangke" [Interview with *Xiao Wu* director Jia Zhangke]. By Wu Wenguang. *Xianchang* [Document], vol. 1, ed. Wu Wenguang. Tianjin: Tianjin shehui kexueyuan chubanshe, 2000. 184–212.

——. "Jia Zhangke fangtan: You yigu qi zhengzai ningju" [Jia Zhangke interview: There's a puff of vapor that's now condensing]. *Nanfang dushi bao* [Nanfang metropolitan news], March 4, 2003.

——. "Jia Zhangke: Keyi shuo shi yi zhong tuoxie" [Jia Zhangke: You can say it's a kind of compromise]. *Qingnian bao* [Youth daily], April 15, 2003.

——. "Jia Zhangke: Zai 'zhantai' shang dengdai" [Jia Zhangke: Waiting on the "Platform"]. By Cheng Qingsong and Huang Ou. In *Wo de sheyingji bu sahuang: Liushi niandai Zhongguo dianying daoyan dang'an* [My camera doesn't lie: Files on the '60s generation of Chinese film directors], ed. Cheng Qingsong and Huang Ou. Beijing: Zhongguo youyi chuban gongsi, 2002. 341–64.

——. "Jingyan shijiezhong de yingxiang xuanze: Jia Zhangke fangtan lu" [Selecting images in the experiential world: an interview with Jia Zhangke]. By Sun Jianmin. *Jinri xianfeng* [Avant-garde today] 12 (March 2002): 18–39.

——. "Zhongguo de duli dianying ren" [China's independent filmmaker]. In *Dianying chufang: Dianying zai Zhongguo* [Film kitchen: Film in China], ed. Wang Shuo. Shanghai: Shanghai wenyi chubanshe, 2001. 146–63.

Johnstone, William Crane Jr. *The Shanghai Problem.* Westport, Conn.: Hyperion Press, 1973.

Jones, Andrew F. *Like a Knife: Ideology and Genre in Contemporary Chinese Popular Music.* Ithaca, N.Y.: East Asia Program, Cornell University, 1992.

King, Anthony D. and Abidin Kusno, "On Be(j)ing in the World: 'Postmodernism,' 'Globalization,' and the Making of Transnational Space in China." In *Postmodernism and China,* ed. Arif Dirlik and Xudong Zhang. Durham: Duke University Press, 2000.

Knabb, Ken, ed. and trans. *Situationist International Anthology.* Berkeley: Bureau of Public Secrets, 1981.

Kracauer, Siegfried. *From Dr. Caligari to Hitler: A Psychological History of the German Film.* Princeton, N.J.: Princeton University Press, 1947.

——. "Photography" [1927], trans. Thomas Levin. *Critical Inquiry* 19 (spring 1993): 433.

——. *Theory of Film: The Redemption of Physical Reality* [1960]. Princeton, N.J.: Princeton University Press, 1997.

Krutnik, Frank. *In a Lonely Street: Film Noir, Genre, Masculinity.* London: Routledge, 1991.

La Capra, Dominick. *Representing the Holocaust: History, Theory, Trauma.* Ithaca, N.Y.: Cornell University Press, 1996.

Lau, Jenny Kwok Wah. "Globalization and Youthful Subculture: The Chinese Sixth Generation Films at the Dawn of the New Century." In *Multiple Modernities: Cinemas and Popular Media in Transcultural East Asia,* ed. Jenny Kwok Wah Lau. Philadelphia: Temple University Press, 2003. 13–27.

Lee, Leo Ou-fan. *Shanghai Modern: The Flowering of a New Urban Culture, 1930–1945.* Cambridge, Mass.: Harvard University Press, 1999.

———. "The Urban Milieu of Shanghai Cinema, 1930–1940: Some Explorations of Film Audience, Film Culture, and Narrative Conventions." In *Cinema and Urban Culture in Shanghai, 1922–1943*, ed. Yinjing Zhang. Stanford, Calif.: Stanford University Press, 1999. 74–96.

Lefebvre, Henri. *The Production of Space*, trans. Donald Nicholson-Smith. Oxford: Blackwell, 1991.

Leyda, Jay. *Dianying*. Cambridge, Mass: MIT Press, 1972.

Li Xianting. "Dangdai yishu zhong de sheying meijie re" [The photography craze in contemporary art]. *Jinri xianfeng* [Avant-garde today], no. 10 (January 2001): 136–47.

Li Xingfa, "Ruhe kan Zhongguopian zai guowai huojiang?" [How to view the winning of international awards of Chinese films?]. *Dangdai dianying*, no. 4 (1997): 33–37.

Lin Xudong, interview with Jia Zhangke, "Yige laizi Zhongguo jicengde minjian daoyan" [A people's director who comes from the grassroots level of China]. *Today*, no. 3 (1999).

Li Yan. "WTO laile women zenme ban?" [What should we do when WTO comes?]. *Dazhong dianying* [Popular Cinema], no. 6 (2000): 50–55.

Li Yiming. "Cong di wu dai dao di liu dai: Jiushi niandai qianqi Zhongguo dalu dianying de yanbian" [From the fifth generation to the sixth generation: Evolutionary changes in Mainland Chinese cinema in the first half of the 1990s]. *Film Art* 1 (1998): 15–22.

———. "Shenme shi dianying?" [What is cinema?]. In *Jiushi niandai de "Diwudai"* [The "Fifth-Generation" of the nineties], ed. Yang Yuanying, Pan Hua, and Zhang Zhuan. Beijing: Beijing guangbo xueyuan chubanshe, 2000. 408–46.

Liao Yan, and Huang Dongjiang. "Duo jian jingji shiyong fang, ladong fangjia wang xia jiang" [Build more economic practical houses, bring down the price of houses]. *Chen bao* [Beijing morning post], February 7, 2001, 1.

Lim, Dennis. "Lou Ye: Generation Next." *Village Voice*, November 8–14, 2000. http://www.villagevoice.com/issues/0045/lim.php.

Lin Baocheng. "Dalu diliudai daoyan de chuangzuo tiaozhan yu meixue fangxiang" [Artistic challenges and aesthetic orientations of the sixth-generation film directors from the mainland]. *Dianying xinshang* [Film appreciation journal] (Taiwan), no. 105 (fall 2000): 67–75.

Lin Xiaoping. "Discourse and Displacement: Contemplating Beijing's Urban Landscape." *Art AsiaPacific*, no. 25 (2000): 76–81.

———. "New Chinese Cinema of the 'Sixth Generation': A Distant Cry of Forsaken Children." *Third Text* 16, no. 3 (September 2002): 261–84.

Liu, Lydia H. "*Beijing Sojourners in New York*: Postsocialism and the Question of Ideology in Global Media Culture." *positions* 7, no. 3 (1999): 763–97.

———. "Translingual Practice: The Discourse of Individualism between China and the West." *positions* 1, no. 1 (1993): 160–93.

Lo Kwai-cheng (Lo Guixiang). "Hou xiandai zhuyi yu Liang Bingjun 'you shi' (jielu)" [Leung Ping-kwan's *Wandering Poems* and postmodernism (extract)]. *Liang Bingjun juan* [Leung Ping-kwan collection], ed. Ji Si. Hong Kong: Joint Publishing, 1989.

Lou Ye. "Popular Documentary Films." *Beijing Review* 41, no. 26 (1998): 28–29.

Lu, Sheldon H. *China, Transnational Visuality, Global Postmodernity.* Stanford, Calif.: Stanford University Press, 2001.

Lu Wei. "Shuoshuo Zhou Xiaowen" [On Zhou Xiaowen in brief]. In *90 niandai de "diwudai"* ["The fifth generation" in the 1990s], ed. Yang Yuanying et al. Beijing: Beijing guangbo xueyuan chubanshe, 2000. 347–58.

Lü Xiaoming. "90 niandai Zhongguo dianying jingguan zhiyi 'diliu dai' jiqi zhiyi" [An inquiry into 'the sixth generation' as a Chinese film spectacle in the 1990s]. *Dianying yishu* [Film art], no. 3 (1999): 23–28.

Lu Xiaopeng (Sheldon H. Lu). "Gouzao 'Zhongguo' de celüe: Xianfeng yishu yu hou dongfang zhuyi" [Strategies of constructing 'China': avant-garde art and post-orientalism]. *Jinri xianfeng* [Avant-garde today], no. 10 (January 2001): 148–61.

Lu Xinyu. *Zhongguo xin jilupian yundong* [The new documentary film movement in China]. Shanghai: Shanghai Wenyi Chubanshe, 2003.

Lu Xun. *A Brief History of Chinese Fiction*, trans. Yang Hsien-yi and Gladys Yang. Beijing: Foreign Languages Press, 1959.

Ma Delin. "Meishi touzhe le sheying suibi" [Notes on the cinematography of *A Tree in House*]. *Dianying yishu* [Film art], no. 3 (1999): 21.

Ma Ning, "Satisfied or Not: Desire and Discourse in the Chinese Comedy of the 1960s." *East-West Film Journal* 2, no. 1 (1987): 32–49.

——. "The Textual and Critical Difference of Being Radical: Reconstructing Chinese Leftist Films of the 1930s." *Wide Angle* 11, no. 2 (1989): 22–31.

MacKinnon, Stephen. "A Late Qing-GMD-PRC Connection: Police as an Arm of the Modern Chinese State." *Selected Papers in Asian Studies, New Series* (Western Conference of the Association for Asian Studies), no. 14 (1983).

——. *Power and Politics in Late Imperial China: Yuan Shikai in Beijing and Tianjin, 1901–1908.* Berkeley: University of California Press, 1980.

Maggio, Meg, ed. *Gao Brothers* (exhibition catalogue). Beijing: Courtyard, 2001.

——. "Introduction." *Hong Hao: Scenes from the Metropolis (Jing xiang)* (exhibition catalogue). Beijing: Courtyard, 2000.

McCormick, Elsie. *Audacious Angles on China.* New York: D. Appleton and Company, 1923.

Meng Xianli, "Lun houxiandai yujingxia Zhongguo dianyingde xiezuo" [On Chinese cinematic inscription in the postmodern discursive context]. In *Dangdai dianying lilun wenxuan* [An anthology of contemporary film theory], ed. Hu Ke, Zhang Wei, and Hu Zhifeng. Beijing: Beijing guangbo xueyuan chubanshe, 2000.

Minh-ha, Trinh T. *When the Moon Waxes Red: Representation, Gender and Cultural Politics.* New York: Routledge, 1991.

Mittler, Barbara. "Cultural Revolution Model Works and the Politics of Modernization in China: An Analysis of *Taking Tiger Mountain by Strategy.*" *World of Music* (2003): 2.

Moore, Rachel. *Savage Theory: Cinema as Modern Magic.* Durham, N.C.: Duke University Press, 2000.

Morales, Alejandro. "Essay: Dynamic Identities in Heterotopia." In *Alejandro Morales: Fiction Past, Present, Future Perfect,* ed. Jose Antonio Gurpegui. Tempe, Ariz.: Bilingual Review Press, 1996.

Murphey, Rhoads. *Shanghai: Key to Modern China.* Cambridge, Mass.: Harvard University Press, 1953.

Ni Zhen. "Chengshi dianying de wenhua maodun" [Cultural Contradiction in City Films]. In *Dangdai huayu dianying lunshu* [Discussion of contemporary Chinese-language cinema], ed. Li Tianduo. Taipei: China Times Press, 1996. 227–47.

———. "Jishixing dianying he geren fengge de wanshan: ping *Minjing gushi*" [The perfection of docu-dramatic film and personal style: A critique of Minjing gushi]. In *Jiushi nidai de "diwudai"* [The "Fifth-Generation" of the Nineties], ed. Yang Yuanying, Pan Hua, and Zhang Zhuan. Beijing: Beijing guangbo xueyuan chubanshe, 2000. 427–33.

———. "Shouwang xinsheng dai" [Expectations for the Newborn Generation]. *Dianying yishu* [Film art] , no. 4 (1999): 70–73.

Nichols, Bill. "Frederick Wiseman's Documentaries: Theory and Structure." In *Ideology and the Image.* Bloomington: University of Indiana Press, 1981. 208–36.

Oura Kanetake, "The Police of Japan." In *Fifty Years of New Japan,* vol. 1, ed. Okuma Shigenobu. New York: Kraus, 1970. 281–95.

Palmer, Augusta. "Crossroads: Nostalgia and the Documentary Impulse in Chinese Cinemas of the 1990s." Ph.D. diss., New York University, 2004.

Pang Laikwan. *Building a New China in Cinema: The Chinese Left-wing Cinema Movement, 1932–1937.* Lanham, Md.: Rowman and Littlefield, 2002.

Petro, Patrice ed., *Fugitive Images: From Photography to Video.* Bloomington: Indiana University Press, 1995.

Pickowicz, Paul G. "Huang Jianxin and the Notion of Postsocialism." In *New Chinese Cinemas: Forms, Identities, Politics,* ed. Nick Browne, Paul G. Pickowicz, Vivian Sobchack, and Esther Yau. New York: Cambridge University Press, 1994. 57–87.

———. "Melodramatic Representation and the 'May Fourth' Tradition of Chinese Cinema." In *From May Fourth to June Fourth: Fiction and Film in Twentieth-Century China,* ed. Ellen Widmer and David Der-wei Wang. Cambridge, Mass.: Harvard University Press, 1993.

———. "Velvet Prisons and the Political Economy of Chinese Filmmaking." In *Ur-*

ban Spaces in Contemporary China: The Potential for Autonomy and Community in Post-Mao China, ed. Deborah Davis, Richard Kraus, Barry Naughton, and Elizabeth Perry. New York: Cambridge University Press, 1995. 193–220.

Pomfret, John. "From China's Feng Xiaogang, a 'Sigh' of the Times: Filmmaker Skirts the Censors—and Western Expectations." Washington Post, October 15, 2000.

Price, Mary. The Photograph: A Strange Confined Space. Stanford, Calif.: Stanford University Press, 1994.

Quiquemelle, Marie-Claire, and Jean-Loup Passek, eds. Le Cinéma chinois. Paris: Centre Georges Pompidou, 1985.

Rao Shuoguang, "Shehui/wenhua zhuanxing yu dianyingde fenghua jiqi zhenghe" [Socio-cultural transformation and the fragmentation and reintegration of cinema]. Dangdai dianying, no. 1 (2000).

Rayns, Tony. "Chinese Vocabulary: An Introduction to King of the Children and the New Chinese Cinema." In King of the Children and the New Chinese Cinema, ed. Chen Kaige and Tony Rayns. London: Faber and Faber, 1989. 1–58.

——. "Provoking Desire." Sight and Sound (July 1988): 47–48.

Reynaud, Bérénice. "Gay Overtures: Zhang Yuan's East Palace, West Palace." Cinemaya 36 (1997): 31–33.

——. "New Visions/New Chinas: Video—Art, Documentation, and the Chinese Modernity in Question." In Resolutions: Contemporary Video Practices, ed. Michael Renov and Erika Suderburg. Minneapolis: University of Minnesota Press, 1996. 229–57.

——. Nouvelles chines, nouveaux cinémas. Paris: Cahiers du cinéma, 1999.

Rodowick, D. N. Gilles Deleuze's Time Machine. Durham, N.C.: Duke University Press, 1997.

Rosen, Stanley. " 'The Wolf at the Door': Hollywood and the Film Market in China from 1994–2000." In Southern California in the World and the World in Southern California, ed. Eric J. Heikkila and Rafael Pizarro. Westport, Conn.: Greenwood, forthcoming.

Rosenbaum, Jonathan. "Critic's Choice: Platform." Chicago Reader, May 17, 2002.

Rothberg, Michael. Traumatic Realism: The Demands of Holocaust Representation. Minneapolis: University of Minnesota Press, 2000.

Ruiz, Raul. Poetics of Cinema: Miscellanies, trans. Brian Holmes. Paris: Dis Voir, 1995.

Sassen, Saskia. The Global City: New York, London, Tokyo. Princeton, N.J.: Princeton University Press, 1996.

——. Globalization and Its Discontents. New York: Free Press, 1998.

Schrader, Paul. "Notes on Film Noir." In Film Genre Reader II, ed. Barry Keith Grant. Austin: University of Texas Press, 1995.

Schwartz, Hillel. The Culture of the Copy: Striking Likeness, Unreasonable Facsimiles. New York: Zone Books, 1996.

Shaviro, Steve. *The Cinematic Body.* Minneapolis: University of Minnesota Press, 1993.

Shen Yun. "Guan yu 'Zhao le' he '"Minjing gushi'"' [About *For Fun* and *On the Beat*]. In *Jiushi niandai de "Diwudai"* [The "Fifth-Generation" of the nineties], ed. Yang Yuanying, Pan Hua, and Zhang Zhuan. Beijing: Beijing guangbo xueyuan chubanshe, 2000. 395–407.

——. "Guanyu *Zhaole* he *Minjing gushi*—Yu Ning Ying de Fangtan" [On *For Fun* and *On the Beat*—An interview with Ning Ying]. *Dangdai dianying*, no. 3 (1996): 33–38.

Shield, Rob. "Fancy Footwork: Walter Benjamin's Notes on *Flânerie.*" In *The Flâneur*, ed. Keith Tester. London: Routledge, 1994.

Silbergeld, Jerome. *Hitchcock with a Chinese Face: Cinematic Doubles, Oedipal Triangles, and China's Moral Voice.* Seattle: University of Washington Press, 2004.

Spaas, Lieve. "Center, Periphery and Marginality in the Films of Alain Tanner." In *Spaces in European Cinema*, ed. Myrto Konstantarakos. Exeter, U.K.: Intellect, 2000. 152–65.

Stam, Robert. *Film Theory: An Introduction.* Malden, Mass.: Blackwell, 2000.

Su Xiaokang. *A History of Misfortune*, trans. Zhu Hong. New York: Knopf, 2001.

Su Xiaokang, and Wang Luxiang. *Deathsong of the River: A Reader's Guide to the Chinese TV Series Heshang*, trans. Richard W. Bodman and P. Wan. Ithaca, N.Y.: East Asia Program, Cornell University, 1991.

Sullivan, Gerard, and Peter A. Jackson, eds. *Gay and Lesbian Asia: Culture, Identity, Community.* New York: Haworth Press: 2001.

Tang Xianzu. *The Peony Pavilion, trans.* Cyril Birch. Bloomington: Indiana University Press, 1980.

Tang Xiaobing. *Chinese Modern: The Heroic and the Quotidian.* Durham, N.C.: Duke University Press, 2000.

Tang Ye, "From the Fifth to the Sixth Generation: An Interview with Zhang Yimou," *Film Quarterly* 53, no. 2 (winter 1999): 12.

Wakeman, Frederic Jr. *Policing Shanghai, 1927–1937.* Berkeley: University of California Press, 1995.

Wang Anyi. *Chang hen ge.* Hong Kong: Cosmos, 1996.

Wang Jing. "*Heshang* and the Paradoxes of the Chinese Enlightenment." In *High Culture Fever: Politics, Aesthetics, and Ideology in Deng's China.* Berkeley: University of California Press, 1996. 118–36.

Wang Jing, and Tani Barlow, eds. *Cinema and Desire: Feminist Marxism and Cultural Politics in the Work of Dai Jinhua.* London: Verso, 2002.

Wang Shuo. *Feu et glace.* Arles: Editions Philippe Picquier, 1995.

——. *Je suis ton papa.* Paris: Flammarion, 1997.

——. *Playing for Thrills.* New York: Penguin Book, 1998.

——. *Please Don't Call Me Human.* New York: Hyperion, 2000.

Wang Xiaobo. *L'âge d'or*. Versailles: Éd. du Sorgho, 2001.

Wang Xiaoming. *Banzhanglian de shenhua* [Myth of the half-faced portrait]. Guangdong: Nanfang ribao chubanshe, 2000.

Wei Hui. *Shanghai Baby*, trans. Bruce Hume. New York: Pocket Books, 2001.

White, Jerry. "The Films of Ning Ying: China Unfolding in Miniature." *Cineaction* 42 (1997): 2–9.

Wilson, Elizabeth. "The Invisible Flaneur." *New Left Review* 191 (1992): 90–110.

Wu Guanping. "Fang qingnian daoyan Lu Xuechang" [An interview with young director Lu Xuechang]. *Dianying yishu* [Film art] no. 4 (2000): 61–65.

Wu Hung. "The Hong Kong Clock: Public Time-Telling and Political Time/Space." *Public Culture* 9, no. 3 (spring 1997): 329–54.

——. *Transience: Chinese Experimental Art at the End of the Twentieth Century*. Chicago: University of Chicago Press, 1999.

Wu Wenguang. "Bumming in Beijing—The Last Dreamers." In *The Twentieth Hong Kong International Film Festival*, ed. Urban Council. Hong Kong: Urban Council, 1996. 130.

——. "Fangwen *Xiao Wu* daoyan Jia Zhangke" [An interview with Jia Zhangke, director of *Xiao Wu*]. In *Xianchang* [Document], ed. Wu Wenguang (Tianjing: Tianjing shehui kexueyuan chubanshe, 2000).

——. "Just on the Road: A Description of the Individual Way of Recording Images in the 1990s." In *Reinterpretation: A Decade of Experimental Chinese Art 1900–2000*, ed. Wu Hung et al. Guangzhou: Guangdong Museum of Art, 2002.

Wu Zuguang, Huang Zuolin, and Mei Shaowu. *Peking Opera and Mei Lanfang*. Beijing: New World Press, 1984.

Xie Fei. "Dui nianqing daoyan men de san dian kanfa" [Three views on the young directors]. *Film Art*, no. 270 (January 5, 2000): 12–14.

Yang Mayfair Mei-hui. "Mass Media and Transnational Subjectivity in Shanghai: Notes on (Re)Cosmopolitanism in a Chinese Metropolis." In *Ungrounded Empires: The Cultural Politics of Modern Chinese Transnationalism*, ed. Donald M. Nonini and Aihwa Ong. New York: Routledge, 1997. 287–319.

Yang Yuanying. "Conversations with Ning Ying." In *Their Voices: Autobiographies of Chinese Women Directors*. Beijing: Zhongguo shehui chuban, 1996.

Yangzi, "Fengge yizhong, huo qita" [A style, or something else]. *Shijian shouce*, no. 4 (2001).

Yau Ching, ed. *Hok Yuk: Let's Love Hong Kong—Script and Critical Essays*. Hong Kong: Youth Literary Press, 2003.

Yau, Esther C. M. "Is China the End of Hermeneutics? Or, Political and Cultural Usage of Non-Han Women in Mainland Chinese Films." *Discourse* 11, no. 2 (1989): 115–38.

Yee, Frank Ki Chun. "Police in Modern China." Ph.D. diss., University of California, Berkeley, 1942.

Yin Hong. "Chengren yishi: Quanwei yizhi yu dongfang zhuyi de shutu tonggui"

[A rite of passage: The convergence of authoritarianism and Orientalism]. In *Zhongghuo dianying meixue: 1999* [Chinese film aesthetics: 1999], ed. Hu Ke et al. Beijing: Beijing guangbo xueyuan chubanshe, 2000. 302–10.

——. "Shiji zhi jiao: Jiushi niandai zhongguo dianying beiwang" [The turn of the century: Memo on Chinese cinema in the nineties]. In *Bainian Zhongguo dianying lilun wenxuan* [Selected works of one-hundred years of Chinese film theory], ed. Ding Yaping. Beijing: Wenhua yishu chubanshe, 2002. 2: 658–89.

——. "Zai jiafeng zhong zhangda: Zhongguo dalu xinsheng dai de dianying shijie" [Growing up between the fissures: The film world of the Newborn generation]. *Ershiyi shiji* 49 (October 1998): 88–93.

Yu, Aiyuan. "Tuwei, taoli, luowang" [Breakthrough, escape, ensnarement]. *Jinri xianfeng* [Avant-garde today] 12 (March 2002): 39.

Yu, Meiying. "Qunian Beijing shangpin fang mai le 230 yi" [Last year commodity houses worth 23 billion yuan were sold in Beijing]. *Beijing qingnian bao* [Beijing youth daily], February 13, 2001, 34.

Yu Yunke. "Toufa luanle? Mei luan!" [Disheveled hair? No!]. *Dazhong dianying* [Popular cinema] no. 1 (1995): 32–33.

Zeitlin, Judith. "Embodying the Disembodied: Representation of Ghosts and the Feminine." In *Writing Women in Late Imperial China*, ed. Ellen Widmer and Kang-I Sun Chang. Stanford: Stanford University Press, 1997.

Zhang Jianqun, "Jia Zhangke kewang zhuliu: Haishi xian pai heibang pian" [Jia Zhangke seeks the mainstream: Will shoot a gangster film first]. *Qingnian bao* (Youth daily), April 15, 2003.

Zhang Jinggan. *Beijing guihua jianshe zongheng tan* [On Beijing's urban planning and construction]. Beijing: Beijing Yanshan chubanshe, 1997.

——. *Beijing guihua jianshe wushi nian* [Fifty years of urban planning and development in Beijing]. Beijing: Zhongguo shudian, 2001.

Zhang Nuanxin, and Li Tuo. "Tan dianying yuyan de xiandaihua" [On the modernization of cinematic language]. In *Bainian Zhongguo dianying lilun wenxuan* [Selected works of one hundred years of Chinese film theory], ed. Ding Yaping. Beijing: Wenhua yishu chubanshe, 2002. 2:10–36.

Zhang Xudong. *Chinese Modernism in the Era of Reforms: Cultural Fever, Avant-garde Fiction, and the New Chinese Cinema*. Durham, N.C.: Duke University Press, 1997.

——. "Epilogue: Postmodernism and Post-Socialist Society—Historicizing the Present." In *Postmodernism and China*, ed. Arif Dirlik and Xudong Zhang. Durham, N.C.: Duke University Press, 2000. 399–442.

——, ed. *Whither China? Intellectual Politics in Contemporary China*. Durham, N.C.: Duke University Press, 2001.

Zhang Yibai. "Tongwang chuntian de wuge zhantai" [Five platforms in the subway to spring]. In *Dianying yishu* [Film art], no. 6 (2002): 76–78.

Zhang Yingjin. *Chinese National Cinema*. London: Routledge, 2004.

———. "From 'Minority Film' to 'Minority Discourse': Questions of Nationhood and Ethnicity in Chinese Cinema." In *Transnational Chinese Cinemas: Identity, Nationhood, Gender*, ed. Sheldon Hsiao-peng Lu. Honolulu: University of Hawaii Press, 1997. 81–104.

———. "Narrative, Ideology, Subjectivity: Defining a Subversive Discourse in Chinese Reportage." In *Politics, Ideology and Literary Discourse in Modern China: Theoretical Interventions and Cultural Studies*, ed. Liu Kang and Xiaobing Tang. Durham, N.C.: Duke University Press, 1993. 211–42.

———. *Screening China: Critical Interventions, Cinematic Reconfigurations, and the Transnational Imaginary in Contemporary Chinese Cinema*. Ann Arbor: Center for Chinese Studies, University of Michigan, 2002.

Zhang Yiwu. "Fazhan de xiangxiang: 1990–1994 Zhongguo dalu leixing dianying" [Imaginations on development: Genre films in Mainland China in 1990–1994]. *Film Art*, no. 264 (January 10, 1999), 68–72.

———. "Hou xinshiqi: Xinde wenhua kongjian" [Post–New Era: A new cultural space]. *Wenyi zhengmin*, no. 6 (1992): 9–12.

———. "Hou xinshiqi Zhongguo dianying: Fenglie de tiaozhan" [Chinese cinema of the Post–New Era: The challenge of fragmentation]. *Dangdai dianying*, no. 5 (1994): 4–11.

———. "Zaidu xiangxiang Zhongguo: Quanqiuhua de tiaozhan yu xin de 'neixianghua'" [Re-imagining China: The challenge of globalization and the new "inward turn"]. *Dianying xinshang* [Film appreciation journal] (Taiwan), no. 105 (fall 2000): 35–43.

Zhang Zhen. *An Amorous History of the Silver Screen: Shanghai Cinema, 1896–1937*. Chicago: University of Chicago Press, 2005.

———. "Mediating Time: The 'Rice Bowl of Youth' in Fin de Siècle Urban China." *Public Culture* 12, no. 1 (2000): 93–113.

———. "Teahouse, Shadowplay, Bricolage: *Laborer's Love* and the Question of Early Chinese Cinema." In *Cinema and Urban Culture in Shanghai, 1922–1943*, ed. Yingjin Zhang. Stanford: Stanford University Press, 1999.

———. "Zhang Yuan." In *Fifty Contemporary Filmmakers*, ed. Yvonne Tasker. London: Routledge, 2002.

Zheng Guoen, and Hong Qi. "Jiadingxing zhong xunqiu zhenshigan" [Seeking a sense of reality from a false assumption]. In *Zhongghuo dianying meixue: 1999* [Chinese film aesthetics: 1999], ed. Hu Ke et al. Beijing: Beijing guangbo xueyuan chubanshe, 2000. 292–96.

Zhong Dafeng, Zhang Zhen, and Yingjin Zhang. "From *Wenmingxi* (Civilized Play) to *Yingxi* (Shadow Play): The Foundation of Shanghai Film Industry in the 1920s." *Asian Cinema* 9, no. 1 (fall 1997): 46–64.

Zhong Xueping. *Masculinity Besieged? Issues of Modernity and Male Subjectivity in Chinese Literature of the Late Twentieth Century*. Durham, N.C.: Duke University Press, 2000.

Zhong Xueping, Wang Zheng, and Bai Di, eds. *Some of Us: Chinese Women Growing Up in the Mao Era*. New Brunswick, N.J.: Rutgers University Press, 2001.

Zhongguo dianying nianjian she, ed. *1997 Zhongguo dianying nianjian* [1997 China film book]. Beijing: Zhongguo dianying nianjian she, 1998.

Zhou Jiawang. "Xin diming Beijingren zhao bu zhao" [Beijingers can't find the new place names]. *Beijing wanbao* [Beijing evening news], March 22, 2001, 1.

Zhu Xiaoyi. "Zhongguo xianfeng yishu zhi huigu ji jiushi niandai Zhongguo xianfeng dianying" [A retrospective on the Chinese avant-garde art and the Chinese avant-garde films in the 1990s]. *Film Art*, no. 276 (January 5, 2001): 79–87.

Zhu Yujun, *Xiandai dianshi jishi* [Contemporary television documentaries]. Beijing: Beijing Guangbo xueyuan chubanshe, 2000.

Zou Yiren. *Jiu Shanghai renkou bianqian de yanjiu* [Research on Population Changes in Old Shanghai]. Shanghai: Shanghai renmin chubanshe, 1980.

Contributors

Chris Berry is a senior lecturer in the Department of Media and Communications at Goldsmiths College in London. He is the author of *A Bit on the Side: East-West Topographies of Desire* (1994), the coeditor of *Mobile Cultures: New Media and Queer Asia* (2003), and the translator of Ni Zhen's *Memoirs from the Beijing Film Academy: The Origins of China's Fifth Generation Filmmakers* (2002).

Yomi Braester is an associate professor of comparative literature and cinema studies at the University of Washington in Seattle. He is author of *Witness against History: Literature, Film, and Public Discourse in Twentieth-Century China* (2003) and has published widely on cinema and urban renewal in the People's Republic of China and Taiwan.

Shuqin Cui is an associate professor of Asian studies at Bowdoin College. She is the author of *Women through the Lens: Gender and Nation in a Century of Chinese Cinema* (2002).

Linda Chiu-han Lai obtained her Ph.D. from the Department of Cinema Studies at New York University. She is now an assistant professor in the School of Creative Media at the City University of Hong Kong. Her scholarly essays have appeared in *Gendering Hong Kong* (2003) and *At Full Speed* (2001), and in the journal *Screening the Past* (2000).

Charles Leary is a Ph.D. candidate in the Department of Cinema Studies at New York University. He has published on Chinese cinema in various publications including the online journal *Senses of Cinema*.

Sheldon H. Lu is a professor of comparative literature and codirector of film studies at the University of California, Davis. He is the author and editor of several books in English and Chinese, including *Transnational Chinese Cinemas* (1997) and *China, Transnational Visuality, Global Postmodernity* (2001).

Jason McGrath is an assistant professor of modern Chinese literature and film at the University of Minnesota, Twin Cities. He has published articles on modern and contemporary Chinese literature and film, and he is completing a manuscript on cinema, literature, and criticism in the culture market of the 1990s.

Augusta Palmer received her Ph.D. from New York University's Department of Cinema Studies in 2004, after completing a dissertation on cinematic convergences across greater China during the 1990s. She has taught film studies courses at Brooklyn College, New York University, and Sarah Lawrence College.

Bérénice Reynaud is the author of *Nouvelles chines, nouveaux cinémas* (1999) and *Hou Hsiao-hsien's A City of Sadness* (2002) and the curator of numerous Chinese film programs. She teaches at the California Institute of the Arts.

Yaohua Shi teaches Chinese, Chinese literature, and Chinese film at Wake Forest University. His primary research interests are premodern vernacular narrative and Republican Shanghai urban culture.

Yingjin Zhang is a professor of Chinese studies and comparative literature at the University of California, San Diego. His books include *The City in Modern Chinese Literature and Film* (1996), *Encyclopedia of Chinese Film* (1998), *China in a Polycentric World* (1998), *Cinema and Urban Culture in Shanghai, 1922–1943* (1999), *Screening China* (2002) and *Chinese National Cinema* (2004).

Zhang Zhen teaches cinema studies at New York University. She was the co-organizer of the film series "The Urban Generation: Chinese Cinema in Transformation" exhibited in New York and other venues in 2001. She is the author of *An Amorous History of Silver Screen: Shanghai Cinema, 1896–1937* (2005).

Xueping Zhong is an associate professor of Chinese literature and culture at Tufts University. She is the author of *Masculinity Besieged? Issues of Modernity and Male Subjectivity in Chinese Literature of Late Twentieth Century*, and coeditor of *Some of Us: Chinese Women Growing Up in the Mao Era* and of *Yuejie de Tiaozhan* (The challenges of border crossing), a collection of translations of Western interdisciplinary feminist scholarship.

27, 32, 34, 37, 42 n.24, 53, 61, 65, 67, 69, 73, 85, 104, 106–7, 108 n.1,118, 141, 149, 220, 227–29, 234 n.10, 241–43, 245, 250, 268. *See also* Leitmotif film

Making of Steel, The, 14, 54, 61, 77 n.37

Mama (The Tree of the Sun) , 83, 85, 128, 264–65, 267, 271, 286, 324

Mandarin, 20, 146, 310–11, 315 n.13, 330, 334, 342 n.40. *See also* Dialect

Mannerism, 226, 370

Mao Dun, 200–201

Mao Xiaorui, 14

Mao Zedong, 51–2, 56, 58–59, 64, 75, 100, 131, 158, 213, 252, 277–78, 283, 296, 304; ideology of, 83, 117, 278, 281; and the post-Mao era, 3, 50–2, 75, 97, 102, 121, 161–62, 296, 298, 310, 314 n.4. *See also* Reform

Marginality, 1, 19, 34, 51, 53, 62, 67, 70–72, 75, 93, 108, 141, 233 n.54, 268, 281, 287, 295, 330

Market economy, 3, 5, 11, 34, 51, 53–54, 67, 71–74, 121, 125, 139, 147, 150, 155, 158, 207, 248, 261, 296–69. *See also* Capitalism

Marriage Certificate, 68

Marxism, 158, 212; Sino-, 52

Masculinity, 38, 298, 303, 307, 312, 373; male desire 284–85, 287, 295–96, 298, 303–4, 306; and male perspective, 255–59, 261. *See also* Sexuality

Masculinity Besieged, 298

Masochism, 154, 327, 329

Mass Culture, 3, 7, 13, 18, 71, 156

Materialism, 121, 150, 158–9, 218. *See also* Post-Materialism

Materiality, 43 n.38, 139, 158–59, 205, 219, 225, 227, 376

Media Conglomerate, 73

Mei Lanfang, 278

Melancholy, 56, 99, 106, 223, 226, 275

Melodrama, 7, 23, 53, 68–69, 74, 138, 141, 146, 156, 163, 173, 277, 283, 346, 366–70, 376, 380

Memory, 5, 11, 56, 82, 118, 162, 165–66, 168–70, 173, 178, 184, 186, 194, 244, 247, 266, 363, 365, 372, 375, 379, and history, 55, 59–60, 140, 182, 217. *See also* Collectivity; Nostalgia

Metanarrative, 211, 370

Middle East, 106

Migration, 186, 189, 322–23, 331, 368

Mi Jiashan, 51, 166, 214, 286, 293 n.52

Millenium Mambo, 106

Mimetic Faculty, 375

Ming Dynasty, 101

Mingong (peasant or migrant workers), 3, 5–6, 16, 86, 147, 365

Mingxing Company, 366

Minh-ha, Trinh T., 19

Ministry of Broadcasting, Television, and Film, 12–13

Ministry of Culture, 12

Minor: cinema, 1–2, 25, 31–32, 39, 114 n44, 350, 370; history, 231. *See also* Independent cinema

Missing Gun, The, 69

Miss Jin Xing, 287

Mittler, Barbara, 277

Mizoguchi, Kenji, 106, 345

Modernism, 6, 37, 50, 84, 205, 219, 223–25, 228–30, 255

Modernity, 8, 16, 97–98, 124–25, 138, 144, 151, 216–17, 227, 243, 246, 250, 256, 266, 274, 281, 288, 313, 318, 353, 365–36. *See also* Postmodernity

Modernization, 2, 5–7, 36, 90, 97–100, 112 n.29, 138–40, 143–44, 147, 153, 207, 267, 283, 284, 298, 313, 368; of cinematic language, 84. *See also* Globalization; Urbanization

Modern magic, 351, 382 n.18

Mom and Dad, 148

Monologue, 63, 221

Oriental Moment, 127, 130
Orphan of Anyang, 96, 288
Ostrovsky, Nikolai, 184
Other Bank, The, 17, 131, 132 n.10, 324
Outsider (waidi ren), 17, 86, 92, 130, 228
Ozu, Yasujiro, 106

Pa-dga' Living Buddha, 121
Pang, Laikwan, 202
Pan Wenzhan, 278
Parents, 148
Parody, 51, 165, 253, 370
Part A Part B, 146
Pastiche, 51, 186, 201, 370
Patriarch, 143, 253, 263 n.19, 272
Patrol and Arrest Office, 318
Peony Pavilion, 360, 383 n.31
People's Republic of China, 49–50, 83, 115–17, 121, 130, 161, 183, 190, 213, 267, 281, 319, 321–22
Performance Art, 165, 200, 207, 249, 270, 278, 288
Performativity, 10, 211, 215–16, 219, 223, 225–26, 230–31, 370. See also Speech act
Personal filmmaking (geren dianying), 346
Phantom, 39, 344, 346, 351, 354, 358–59, 364–65, 368–69, 371, 375, 379. See also Twin
Photography, 8, 35, 39, 140, 162–65, 170, 174, 201, 211, 221–22, 237 n.34, 254, 347, 360, 369, 371–76; avant-garde, 138, 140, 148–49, 151–53, 155, 164–65, 170 ; and cinema's photographic realism, 18, 101, 209; and nostalgia, 174, 177
Physiognomy, 6, 346
Pickowicz, Paul, 50–52, 54
Pickpocket, 16
Pingyao, 101, 104

Pirated copy, 26–27, 81–82, 108 n.1, 114 n.39, 317, 380
Platform, 15–17, 20, 72, 81–82, 96–106, 111 n.18, 112 n.29, 124, 231
Pluralism (duoyuanhua), 122
Poetics of Discovery, 224–26, 231
Poetics of Signification, 224–25
Polanski, Roman, 355
Police, 241, 243–45, 251–54, 262, 316–37
Police Story, 317
Political economy, 34, 50–53, 72–73
Politics: of urban cinema, 20, 34–35, 116, 147, 163, 182, 209, 218, 224, 228, 297, 328, 379; and leitmotif film, 50, 71–73, 75; and postsocialism, 258, 271; and sexuality, 38, 235, 253, 302–3
Popular Cinema, 74
Popular cinema, 35–36, 138, 140–41, 149, 155, 350. See also Mainstream cinema
Popular culture, 7, 17, 104–5, 181, 201, 311, 319, 348
Pornography, 298, 327, 331, 337
Postcoloniality, 246, 266. See also Colonialism
Postman, 11, 63, 67, 72, 109 n. 4, 214
Post-materialism, 138–39, 150, 158–59. See also Materialism
Postmen in the Mountains, 65
Postmodernity, 8, 18, 27, 37, 50–52, 116, 124, 151, 224–26, 230, 256, 283, 372, 380. See also Modernity
Post–New Era (hou xinshiqi), 2, 52, 296
Postsocialism, 23, 34, 39, 49–54, 65, 68, 70, 115–16, 118, 121, 128, 130–31. See also Socialism
Power: relation, 248, 250, 323; of state and bureaucracy, 51, 249–50, 327
Practice Society, 28–31
Pressure Points, 57
Price, Mary, 221
Price of Frenzy, The, 51, 340 n.21

LIBRARY OF CONGRESS CATALOGING-IN-PUBLICATION DATA

The urban generation : Chinese cinema and society
at the turn of the twenty-first century / edited by Zhang Zhen.
p. cm.   Includes bibliographical references and index.
ISBN-13: 978-0-8223-4053-9 (cloth : alk. paper)
ISBN-13: 978-0-8223-4074-4 (pbk. : alk. paper)
1. Motion pictures—China. 2. Cities and towns in motion pictures.
3. City and town life in motion pictures.
I. Zhang Zhen, 1962 July 8–
PN1993.5.C4U73 2007
791.430951′09049—dc22   2006032812